Isolation and Involvement
An Interpretive
History of
American Diplomacy

W. Patrick Strauss / Oakland University

Xerox College Publishing

Waltham,Massachusetts / Toronto

For Laura and Jane

Contents

Prologue   1

Part I. The Struggle for Independence, 1775-1825

1. The Beginning of a National Foreign Policy   9
2. Land, Maritime Policy, and the Federalists   24
3. The Jeffersonians and Their Foreign Policy   39
4. The Jeffersonians and the Rise of American Nationality   56

Part II. The Continent Within: Manifest Destiny and Imperialism, 1825-1900

5. Andrew Jackson and the Continental Spirit   69
6. The Diplomacy of Manifest Destiny   81
7. Young America and the Coming of the Civil War   94
8. Civil War Diplomacy and the Clash of Empires   106
9. American Foreign Affairs in the Gilded Age   121
10. The End of Continentalism, 1890-1900   136

Part III. The World Without: America as a World Power, 1900-1945

11. The United States and Latin America: The Protector
    and the Unprotected   153
12. Worldwide Interests and International Rivalries, 1900-1914   166
13. World War I: The Scars of Victory   180
14. The Diplomacy of a Creditor Nation, 1920-1933   198
15. American Foreign Policy in the New Deal Era   214
16. World War II and the Shaping of Global Diplomacy   233

Part IV. The Nuclear Age: America as a World Leader Since 1945

17. The Revolution in American Foreign Policy: Cause and Effect, 1945-1947   257

18. World Challenge and American Response, 1947-1955   273

19. The Resurgence of Europe and the Problem of the Middle East   292

20. The United States and Latin America: Old Fears and New Concerns   305

21. American Policy in Africa and Asia: The Problems of Leadership   318

Epilogue: Today and Tomorrow   333

Index   335

Picture Sources   343

Prologue

The origins of diplomacy and international relations are older than recorded history, and the majority of ancient civilizations have left tangible evidence of concern for their relations with other peoples and states. Though the Greeks and the Romans systematized certain diplomatic procedures, they contributed relatively little that was new to the practice of diplomacy. During the millennium after the fall of Rome, diplomacy and diplomatists receded in importance as the Roman Catholic church increasingly assumed the role of international diplomatist.

Modern relations among nation-states derive from three major influences, the oldest of which is Machiavelli and other Italian diplomatists of the sixteenth century. They were followed by Hugo Grotius, the father of international law, in the seventeenth century and by the French school of diplomacy in the eighteenth. All these influences must be considered in the larger context of the rise of the European nation-state and the corresponding loss of political influence suffered by the Catholic church and its ally, the Holy Roman Empire, in the same period. Beginning in Machiavelli's time, and for a century thereafter, the focus of Europe centered on the struggle between the Bourbons in France and the Hapsburgs in Austria and Spain for possession of Italy. Cynical awareness of this often unscrupulous tug of war led Machiavelli to write in *The Prince* (1513) that a ruler was measured only by his success, and that although it was laudable for him to keep faith with his subjects, "he who has known best how to employ the fox has succeeded the best." Machiavelli influenced diplomatists for centuries, and is still worth studying, but his patent expediency and complete disregard for ethical considerations encouraged the unhealthy international atmosphere that prevailed during most of the sixteenth and early seventeenth centuries. Diplomacy often succumbed to intrigue, assassination, bribery, and deception.

More than a century later, the great humanitarian scholar Hugo Grotius reacted to the unspeakable cruelty demonstrated by both sides in the Thirty Years' War. There were at that time no uniform provisions for the treatment of sick and wounded, for noncombatants, or for the victims of rape and pillage. Grotius' views in *On the Law of War and Peace* (1625), the first

1

important treatise on international relations, while not always observed, became increasingly influential as more European nation-states stabilized their internal politics.

The French school of diplomacy dated from the time of Richelieu and Louis XIV and was best expressed by François de Callières in *De la Manière de négocier avec des souverains* (1716). Callières professionalized the art of diplomacy by insisting that diplomatists be specially chosen and trained. The purpose of diplomacy, he wrote, was not to deceive but rather to create a sense of confidence. A good diplomatist should be "quick, resourceful, a good listener, courteous and agreeable," and should know "the German, Italian and Spanish languages as well as the Latin. . . . He should also have some knowledge of literature, science, mathematics and law." Callières' influence was paramount in having a special school for diplomatists established in France in 1712. England followed by offering comparable courses at both Oxford and Cambridge. The success of the French school of diplomacy was so pronounced that from the advent of Richelieu in 1616 until the French Revolution in 1789 it served as the European model, and French gradually replaced Latin as the language of diplomacy.

From the fifteenth through the first part of the eighteenth century, England's aim was to maintain a major influence in Continental European affairs by a judicious use of the balance of power. This straightforward policy was complicated in 1714 when the first of the Hanoverian kings ascended the British throne. Since the first two Georges retained major financial and property interests in the German state of Hanover, there ensued a continuing eighteenth-century debate as to whether England should engage in dynastic struggles on the Continent or, rather, assume the role of a spectator primarily concerned with the building of her own empire. In any case, England became involved in the four European wars that began in 1688 and culminated in 1763, known collectively as the Second Hundred Years' War because they ultimately developed into a world conflict for empire between the British and the French. Each of the four wars had its American counterpart, as shown below:

SECOND HUNDRED YEARS' WAR

American War	European War	Duration	Peace Treaty
King William's War	War of the League of Augsburg	1688-1697	Treaty of Ryswick
Queen Anne's War	War of the Spanish Succession	1702-1713	Treaty of Utrecht
King George's War	War of the Austrian Succession	1740-1748 (1739 in America)	Treaty of Aix-la-Chapelle
French and Indian War	Seven Years' War	1756-1763 (1753 in America)	Treaty of Paris

The American colonists, who participated with varying degrees of reluctance and ability, not only made little appreciable difference in the final outcome of the struggle but were scarcely considered even in the diplomacy that most directly affected them. Colonial wishes were often ignored. For example, in 1745, colonial forces succeeded in capturing Louisburg, the most important French fort guarding the entrance to the St. Lawrence; yet in 1748 it was restored to France in exchange for Madras in India. A subsequent parliamentary grant to the colonies, especially Massachusetts, did little to mollify them. Only in 1763, at the conclusion of the Seven Years' War, which ended France's North American empire, did British foreign policy coincide with colonial desires.

More often during the eighteenth century, Britain fought wars and made peace on a global scale strictly in her own interests. Only incidentally did the American colonies gain privileges or new territory. Thus the Treaty of Utrecht in 1713, which ended the War of the Spanish Succession, successfully thwarted French designs on the Spanish throne. But equally important to Britain was the wresting from Spain of the *asiento;* this allowed an English company a thirty-year monopoly over the slave trade to the Spanish American colonies. Likewise, England acquired both Newfoundland and Nova Scotia from the French; this gave her strategic control over the St. Lawrence waterway, a control that would later take on more significance in colonial eyes.

For the century following 1651, Britain's commercial empire was capably buttressed by a series of Navigation Acts that protected the English and colonial carrying trade. Developing comparably was a strong maritime policy that culminated in the Rule of 1756. Issued during the Seven Years' War, it became the cornerstone of Britain's concept of maritime rights in wartime. The Rule of 1756 modified a practice dating back a century; it insisted that trade and ports closed in time of peace could not be opened to neutrals in time of war. Accordingly, neutral Dutch ships trading with French colonies during the Seven Years' War were captured and their cargoes confiscated because such trade had not existed before the war. When various neutral states attempted to evade the Rule of 1756 by transshipping goods or engaging in trade with legal ports (though carrying contraband), the British retaliated with the "doctrine of continuous voyage." This maintained that the cargo carried was the determining factor in granting a ship a neutral, friendly, or enemy status; and if a cargo was contraband, then the ship as well as the cargo was confiscable. Neutral countries, and other states too, objected vainly to these stringent maritime rules, but so long as Britain's navy was superior, she was able to invoke and uphold them. Though these policies protected American carriers, they also restricted the illicit but highly profitable trade with the French West Indies and the Spanish American colonies.

By the end of the Seven Years' War some leaders in each of the thirteen colonies had developed attitudes that anticipated many of the views on foreign policy later adopted by the young nation. Chief among these was recognition of North America's importance to the European balance of power. Certain prominent colonists argued from the early eighteenth century on that the colonies needed to unite and to pursue policies designed to bolster and promote trade and defense and at the same time to thwart the colonial ambitions of France and Spain. Benjamin Franklin's Albany Plan of Union in 1754, although premature, was but one attempt to do this.

There is little question that America's earliest diplomatists, especially Benjamin Franklin and John Adams, worked and thought in terms of continental expansion at the expense of the French, the Spanish, and the Indians. Franklin, for example, devoted thirty pages of an influential pamphlet published in London in 1760 to this topic. The reasons given by Franklin and others were, in the final analysis, almost entirely economic, usually related to land speculation west of the Appalachians or to the fear of losing first rights to the natural resources of the West. Colonial spokesmen often mentioned their fears of a French or Spanish "encirclement" that would confine the American colonies east of the Appalachians and thus end their access to the West.

On the other hand, the same balance of power consideration led Thomas Paine, a recently arrived Englishman, to come to the opposite conclusion in his famous and influential pamphlet *Common Sense* (1776). "It is the true interest of America," he wrote, "to steer clear of European contentions, which she never can do while, by her dependence on Britain, she is made the makeweight in the scale of British Politics." He further insisted that America's trade suffered when she was drawn like a pawn into European affairs by a continent that was "too thickly planted with Kingdoms to be long at peace. . . ."

While there may have been differing opinions as to America's role in the balance of power system, there were few concerning her maritime rights, another major concern of future foreign policy. The colonists entered the Revolutionary War with a complete set of maritime demands for maximum freedom for their ships and cargoes. Along with the Dutch and others, they early indicated their belief that "free ships make free goods." Such a view practically ensured continuing difficulties with Great Britain.

In addition to anticipating many features of America's future foreign policy, the new practitioners of American diplomacy entered the world scene during a most propitious time. Foreign affairs and the art of diplomacy, though remaining the preserves of the nobility and the few, had been influenced markedly by the Enlightenment. Rationalism and cosmopolitanism became the hallmarks of diplomats, succeeding custom based upon hereditary or other prerogatives. This atmosphere freed diplomatists from many of the provincial national restraints of an earlier day and paved the way for the reception of such American ministers as Benjamin Franklin, John Adams, and John Jay. The era from the end of the Seven Years' War in 1763 to the outbreak of the French Revolution in 1789, which also witnessed the conception and birth of the new republic in North America, was the high-water mark of enlightened balance of power diplomacy among European countries.

Further Reading

At the end of each chapter the student will find mentioned several books, paperbound if possible, that treat specific aspects of diplomatic history in more detail. The stress on readability reflects the author's conviction that most bibliographies are written with the instructor in mind, not the student. More extensive bibliographies may be found in any of the excellent larger one-volume diplomatic texts by Thomas A. Bailey, Alexander De Conde, Robert Ferrell or Richard W. Leopold. Paperbound books are marked with an asterisk and bibliographic information for that edition is shown.

Sir Harold Nicolson has written an interesting general survey on diplomacy entitled *The Evolution of Diplomacy* (New York, 1962). The classic work about diplomats by François de Callières has been translated and edited by Stephen D. Kertesz, a distinguished diplomat in his own right, as *On the Manner of Negotiating with Princes* (Notre Dame, Ind., 1963).

For a complete background of the history of American diplomacy through the French and Indian War, see Max Savelle, *Origins of American Diplomacy: The International History of Angloamerica, 1492-1763* (New York, 1967).

Part I • The Struggle for Independence, 1775-1825

1

The Beginning of a
National Foreign Policy

Six months after the "shot heard 'round the world" was fired at Lexington, the Second Continental Congress, in late November 1775, made plans for a united foreign policy by appointing five men to a Committee of Secret Correspondence. The committee, which at first included such luminaries as Benjamin Franklin, John Dickinson, and John Jay, and its successor in 1777, the Committee for Foreign Affairs, conducted American diplomacy throughout most of the Revolution. It was succeeded in 1781 by a single secretary of foreign affairs. Congress also appointed many ad hoc committees during this period, which often led to overlapping authority and a confusion of aims.

ON TO CANADA

Some of the cross-purposes were illustrated in the first major American military campaign of the Revolutionary War, which was directed against Canada. American continentalists believed that Canada, although French and Catholic, was a ripe plum to be picked by as few as 1,200 men; according to George Washington, a small force would be ample because Quebec was "an easy prey." Some months earlier Congress had issued a proclamation inviting Canada to join with the thirteen American colonies against Britain. By the time the American expeditionary force left in September 1775, however, there had been ominously little response from the Canadians. The following March, after the capture of Montreal by British forces and the loss at Quebec, Congress sent a delegation of three commissioners — Benjamin Franklin, Samuel Chase, and Charles Carroll — to help win over the Canadians to the American view. Franklin, the most prestigious member of the delegation, did little because he was ill and also because Chase and Carroll were both French-speaking Catholics. In addition, Carroll was accompanied by his brother, a Jesuit priest. Their efforts were as unrewarding as those of the army, and the acquisition of Canada remained throughout the war a frustrating priority for the United States. Several expeditions were planned, including one to be led by Lafayette, but all were canceled before the scheduled dates arrived.

THE MILITIA DIPLOMATS

The work of the Committee of Secret Correspondence, especially after the Americans had declared their independence, was relatively uncomplicated in that its one overriding task was to ensure that independence. As the means to this end, its principal object was to secure military and financial aid, formal recognition, and commercial alliances from various European countries. At the same time, Congress waged a persistent struggle for liberal maritime rights. To implement these policies, the committee appointed a number of men, most of whom were then in Europe or had been colonial agents in London or had commercial interests there. The deciding factor in these appointments was not ability so much as social and political prestige. Called "militia diplomats" because of their instant readiness for duty, they were often more enthusiastic than diplomatic, with results to match. Arthur Lee was appointed the first agent in December 1775 and sent to France. His failure typified the difficulties faced by the new nation in depending on untrained diplomats. From a notable Virginia family, Lee had studied law in England, and was an early supporter of independence. Unfortunately, he was also of unstable temperament and more than a little paranoid, so that at a crucial juncture he spent more time composing letters to relatives in Congress attacking Franklin and Silas Deane than in trying to solve the problem with which he was charged.

THE FRENCH AND THEIR AID

To assuage the humiliation of defeat in the Seven Years' War, the French turned to intrigue and espionage against the British. They sought not only revenge but restoration of their rightful place as the dominant European land power. Led by two capable foreign ministers, the Duc de Choiseul (1764-1770) and the Comte de Vergennes (1774-1787), they sent a succession of secret agents to America to report on colonial affairs and to attempt to influence local opinion. (One of the best agents, Baron Johann de Kalb, later became a general in the Continental Army.) Although most of the reports were filed until Vergennes' time, they were then studied and used as one strand in the tangled skein of French-American relations.

It should be no surprise that one of Franklin's first acts as the most powerful member of the Committee of Secret Correspondence was to write to a friend in Paris, Dr. Barbeu Dubourg, and to another in Holland inquiring about the possibility of securing commerical treaties with France and the Netherlands. But long before his letter reached Paris, Vergennes had already decided to aid the colonists in the hope that they would break free of Britain. A key figure behind the decision was Caron de Beaumarchais, one of the great intriguers of the day. A well-known dramatist, author of two popular comedies, *The Barber of Seville* and *The Marriage of Figaro*, Beaumarchais was a favorite courtier of Louis XVI. He had been a secret agent in Britain, where he met Arthur Lee and became a warm supporter of the colonies. Beumarchais' memoranda to the king aided Vergennes in convincing Louis that France should give the colonists large-scale secret assistance. Thereafter, Vergennes sent an astute agent, Achard de Bonvouloir, posing as an Antwerp merchant, to confer with Franklin and his committee. Bonvouloir assured them not only of France's interest in the thirteen colonies but of her disinterest in regaining any part of Canada.

The problem of securing guns, ammunition, and other war supplies had become acute by the time Lee was ready to leave for France. Some munitions had been purchased in the West Indies, but most had come from the Netherlands via St. Eustatius, which is actually part of the Lesser Antilles but was grouped with the Dutch Virgin Islands, or via French and Spanish ports in the Caribbean. Two months before the Committee of Secret Correspondence was established, Congress had appointed an ad hoc committee of nine members to contract for importing war material. Including Franklin, who served on this committee too, and Robert Morris, another illustrious member, all were merchants and most were speculators. One recent authority has stated that the entire committee (excepting Franklin and possibly two others) used their positions "for the enrichment of themselves, their relatives, and their friends." However, at that time a conflict of interests was not viewed in the same light as it is today; Robert Morris, in fact, once remarked to a business associate: "I shall continue to discharge my duty faithfully to the public and pursue my private means as the times will admit of, and I dare say you will do the same."

Though profits were handsome and certain international business arrangements were set up, it quickly became apparent that more massive aid would be required immediately. At this point, and with the concurrence of Bonvouloir, Franklin's committee decided to send Silas Deane, member of the ad hoc committee of nine and an influential Connecticut merchant and patriot, to France to arrange for larger shipments of supplies. Unknown both to Deane and the Committee of Secret Correspondence, Vergennes had persuaded both Louis XVI and Charles III of Spain to guarantee a subsidy of one million livres (about $200,000), in the form of munitions from the royal arsenals, that would be channeled through a dummy commercial firm expressly organized for that purpose. Vergennes' creation, Rodrigues Hortalez et Compagnie, had Beaumarchais, who was anything but a businessman, as its operating head. Deane arrived in Paris from Bordeaux, where he had been arranging for munitions on credit against a future tobacco crop. He had hoped to arrange for large-scale aid through French merchants, to the profit of all; his instructions called for him to obtain "clothing and arms for twenty-five thousand men, with a suitable quantity of ammunition, and one hundred field pieces." He was most chagrined to find Beaumarchais in charge of the munitions he had been sent to procure. Deane agreed to pay for the material that Beaumarchais had received from the royal arsenals, thereby provoking a bitter argument that led to years of factional dispute over the matter. In any event, munitions began flowing in large amounts, and their arrival in America was of such importance that without them the United States would have been unable to win the Battle of Saratoga in 1777.

THE DECLARATION OF INDEPENDENCE

A group of radical leaders in Congress, including Benjamin Franklin, John Adams, and Thomas Jefferson, to name three, had in the meantime pressed for and finally won a declaration of independence. While a variety of motives lay behind this move, Franklin, for his part, felt that control of the colonies' own foreign affairs would prevent Englishmen from entangling them in "all the plundering wars, which their desperate circumstances, injustices, and rapacity, may prompt them to undertake." The Declaration of Independence also served as strong propaganda for the colonies in foreign affairs. Besides indicting George III, it irrevocably announced to the states of Europe the freedom of the thirteen American colonies.

THE FRENCH AND AMERICAN MARITIME RIGHTS

Silas Deane had accomplished the major goal of his mission, that of securing arms; he next turned to the second and third goals, the signing of commercial and military alliances with France.

The two types of alliances must be clearly differentiated because they explain many of America's later policies and attitudes. For Deane and most contemporary Americans the term "alliance" meant a commercial pact between nations that contained a most-favored-nation clause giving the signatory equal rights with those granted other nations by other pacts. The Committee of Secret Correspondence had paved the way for such a treaty by asking Congress to open American ports to other countries; until then,

American ports had been open only to American and British shipping. On April 6, 1776, Congress finally acceded to Franklin's request, opening American ports for trade with all countries except Britain. From this time on, the colonies aggressively asserted their maritime rights. In September 1776, just three months after declaring independence, Congress published an ad hoc committee report (John Adams had made the major contribution) delineating the terms of an ideal American commercial treaty. The Plan of 1776, as the report was called, incorporated American sentiments on maritime law and neutral rights and became the model for treaties of friendship and commerce negotiated thereafter. It reiterated the colonial idea that "free ships make free goods," sharply restricted the list of articles classified as contraband, and, in general, stated principles of neutrality that favored small-navy countries having large commercial interests.

THE FRENCH ALLIANCE

The Plan of 1776 accurately reflected American maritime concerns while at the same time supporting the views of men like John Adams and Thomas Paine who rejected political alliances with unregenerate European nations. Thus, when Congress in the fall of 1776 sent Franklin and Lee to join Deane in France, it offered the trio nothing new to bargain with except the statement in their instructions that "It is highly probable that France means not to let the United States sink in the present contest."

The witty, seventy-year-old Dr. Franklin at once became the favorite of Paris. Lionized by French society as the greatest American, living or dead, Franklin shrewdly played his part as sage and patriot, wearing simple homespun and discarding his wig for a fur cap. French intellectuals in the throes of the Enlightenment vied with each other to pay him homage.

Vergennes also greatly admired Franklin, but although he was eager to aid the United States, he preferred to do so secretly out of deference to the qualms of his Spanish ally. Franklin spent more than a year attempting to convince Vergennes of the value of a commercial alliance and recognition of the colonies. Lee, now in Spain, had equally frustrating results. During this same period in Paris, Franklin was the recipient of various feelers from the British, who had not yet relinquished all hope of reconciliation short of independence.

One interesting aspect of the work of Franklin and the other commissioners was that secret agents from France, England, and Spain (and occasionally from Russia, Prussia, and Austria) had ready access to whatever the Americans were discussing, so that the major European countries were kept well informed. For example, Dr. Edward Bancroft, a peripatetic Massachusetts physician and long-time friend of Franklin who served as secretary to the American commissioners throughout the war, was also a most competent British agent who faithfully copied all documents for the British.

REMINISCENCES OF A DOUBLE AGENT, 1784

I went to Paris, and during the first year resided in the same house with Dr. Franklin, Mr. Deane, etc., and regularly informed this [British] Government of every transaction of the American Commissioners; of every step and vessel taken to supply the revolted Colonies with artillery, arms, etc.; of every part of their intercourse with the French and other European courts; of the powers and instructions given by Congress to the Commissioners, and their correspondence with the Secret Committees, etc.; and when the Government of France at length determined openly to support the revolted Colonies, I gave notice of this determination, and of the progress made in forming the two Treaties of Alliance and Commerce, and when these were signed, on the evening of the 6th of Feb'y [1778] I at my own expence, by a special messenger and with unexampled dispatch conveyed this intelligence to this city, and to the King's Ministers, within 42 hours from the instant of their signature, a piece of information for which many individuals here would, for purposes of speculation, have given me more than all that I have received from Government.

After the signal American victory at Saratoga on October 17, 1777, the French moved more rapidly, although Vergennes had decided on a treaty even before the battle. Additionally, he felt that the imminence of war with Britain necessitated a military alliance with the Americans as well as the formal recognition and commercial treaty they so ardently desired. On February 6, 1776, Vergennes and Franklin signed a treaty of friendship and commerce that closely followed the Plan of 1776. Shortly after, they signed a second pact for a "conditional and defensive alliance"; this guaranteed the independence of the United States and provided that neither nation should make peace without the other's consent. No time limit was specified for the duration of the military alliance. This was an unusual feature, especially when the prevailing American attitude toward Europe is considered. A little later, Vergennes dispatched Count Conrad Alexandre Gérard, Under-Secretary of State for Foreign Affairs, to the United States as the first minister plenipotentiary. Gérard was received by Congress with elaborate ceremony; his charm and tact were so effective that the usual colonial suspicion of all Europeans actually began to give way to enthusiasm for the French.

BENJAMIN FRANKLIN AT THE SIGNING OF THE TREATY OF FRIENDSHIP AND
COMMERCE BETWEEN FRANCE AND THE UNITED STATES

FRANCE AND CONGRESSIONAL POLITICS

Almost immediately, however, Gérard became embroiled in the controversy between Arthur Lee and Silas Deane and their respective supporters in Congress. At Lee's demand, Deane had been recalled in 1778 for his alleged improper commercial activities, and his reputation was attacked so vigorously by Thomas Paine and other radicals that it never recovered. Gérard retaliated by twice denouncing Lee publicly, but before permanent damage was done to the future of the alliance, he retired because of ill health. His successor, the Chevalier de la Luzerne, proved a far more able diplomat. He reconciled members of the Lee faction, although politically this feud and its aftermath divided Congress throughout the war. Luzerne worked tirelessly to aid American independence, and because of his popularity he successfully completed the work of gaining popular American support for the alliance.

SPAIN AND OTHER EUROPEAN COUNTRIES

Both France and the United States continued to woo Spain, but the Spanish king distrusted any nation born out of rebellion against a constituted ruler. This sentiment was widely held throughout Europe and is one reason why the "militia diplomats" were so woefully unsuccessful. Examples would include Ralph Izard in the Grand Duchy of Tuscany, Arthur Lee in Spain and Prussia, his brother William Lee in Austria, and

Francis Dana in Russia. Izard cooled his heels for two years in Paris and never did get to Florence. In any case, he had his family with him and was considerably better off than was Francis Dana, a Massachusetts lawyer who had been serving as John Adams' secretary. Dana was sent to the court of Catherine the Great at St. Petersburg in December 1780; there, for the next two years, he was refused admittance at court and also suffered great hardships because of inadequate housing and his inability to speak either Russian or French — though his secretary, fourteen-year-old John Quincy Adams, did have a schoolboy's knowledge of French.

For Spain, the overriding consideration in her relations with the Americans had little to do with the United States. Having lost Gibraltar to England by the terms of the Treaty of Utrecht, from 1713 onward she ceaselessly plotted and struggled to regain it. In April 1779, Spain's new foreign minister, the Conde de Floridablanca, signed a treaty of alliance with France providing, among other things, that France would continue the war against England until Spain recovered Gibraltar. This indirectly involved the United States. Hoping to turn the provision to American benefit, Congress thereupon sent John Jay to Spain as minister plenipotentiary to seek a formal alliance, recognition of the United States, and perhaps substantial loans. However, Floridablanca's suspicion of Americans, especially their claims to the left bank of the Mississippi as a boundary, would not permit him to recognize the new nation, though he did grant Jay a small loan.

THE LEAGUE OF ARMED NEUTRALITY

One of the by-products of British domination of the seas was a collective attempt by smaller maritime nations in Europe to uphold their versions of maritime rights in wartime. In 1780 Catherine suggested joint action; shortly thereafter, Russia, Denmark, and Sweden signed a defensive treaty incorporating the League for Armed Neutrality. The treaty closed the Baltic Sea to warships and embodied most of the principles of the Plan of 1776, emphasizing that "free ships make free goods." The belligerents were invited to subscribe to the League's provisions, and the other European states were encouraged to join. By the end of the war the League included the Netherlands (1781), Prussia (1782), the Holy Roman Empire (1781), and Portugal (1782). Spain and France agreed to abide by the principles of the League, but Britain demurred. The United States sought to join, partly to ensure recognition, but was rejected as a belligerent. More pertinent was the unfortunate fate of the Netherlands, which had hoped by this means to escape England's long sea arm.

Dutch commerce had been waxing fat on the profits of the French and

American trade. As a deterrent, Britain declared war, not because the Netherlands had joined the League but ostensibly over an incident involving another "militia diplomat," Henry Laurens of South Carolina. A friend of the Lees, Laurens had been appointed minister plenipotentiary to the Netherlands in 1780. En route, he carried with him the unofficial draft of a treaty based on the Plan of 1776 that had been negotiated privately by William Lee two years earlier. Laurens' ship was captured at sea; endeavoring to destroy his private papers, Laurens put them in an insufficiently weighted trunk which he then threw overboard. The British officers easily retrieved the trunk and its contents intact. Laurens was taken to England and imprisoned in the Tower of London until just before the end of the war. This draft of a "secret treaty" was England's pretext for declaring war on the Dutch. As a result, Dutch commerce suffered severely and the Netherlands turned to the League for armed help, but was refused. Serious as was the loss of Dutch shipping to the United States, even more serious was the capture of St. Eustatius by a British fleet, which thus cut off a major entrepôt from the colonies.

JOHN ADAMS IN THE NETHERLANDS

In spite of the troubled situation in the Netherlands, Congress decided to send another envoy, this time John Adams, to attempt to secure recognition, alliance, and a loan. The triumvirate of Franklin, Jay, and Adams were responsible for American diplomatic success during the war, though Adams served in the Netherlands nearly two years before he convinced the war-weary but canny Dutch to make common cause with the United States. Considering his deserved reputation for testiness, Adams did a remarkable job, patiently negotiating with Dutch officials and bankers. In April 1782 the Dutch at last officially recognized the United States, being the second nation to do so. A treaty of friendship and commerce according to the Plan of 1776 was signed the following October. Of pressing importance were the two loans that Adams secured, one for $2 million, which the French government guaranteed, and the other for slightly over $1 million. These proved to be only the first of several loans the Dutch were to advance during the 1780's.

THE WAY TO PEACE

Franklin summoned both Adams and Jay to Paris in June 1782 (though Adams did not arrive until late October) to discuss another peace feeler from the British. As early as September 1776, Congress had sent Franklin,

Adams, and Edward Rutledge, a South Carolina lawyer, to Staten Island, where they and Admiral Lord Howe were unable to arrive at a peaceful settlement because Howe could not grant the colonies independence. Two years later, Lord North's government sent the Carlisle Commission to America on the same errand. The Earl of Carlisle offered the colonies a truce on the basis of *uti possedetis*, that is, on the basis of the boundaries occupied by each army at the time of the truce. Carlisle's timing was unfortunate because news arrived that the French treaty had been signed. The commission fared poorly both with Congress and several state legislatures, and when one of its members attempted to bribe certain American leaders, the entire group was discredited and accomplished nothing.

Besides direct efforts between the belligerents, offers to mediate were made by Spain, Russia, and Austria from 1780 until peace actually came. Each of these countries hoped to gain something at Britain's expense and none was prepared to grant the United States more than *uti possedetis*. As a matter of fact, Vergennes himself had decided to accept Austrian mediation, in violation of the French-American alliance, when the victory at Yorktown intervened.

LORD HOWE AND THE AMERICAN COMMITTEE

Franklin, Adams, and Rutledge at the interview in the Billopps House on Staten Island, 1776.

The efforts of foreign mediators, added to division among the colonists themselves, soon led Congress to consider peace terms. In 1779 Adams was appointed sole peace negotiator for the colonies and was sent to France. He disapproved of Vergennes, saying that the French minister meant "to keep his hand under our chin to prevent us from drowning, but not lift our heads out of the water." Vergennes, for his part, considered Adams an impossible diplomat and would deal only with Franklin.

THE PRELIMINARY PEACE TREATY

Cornwallis' surrender at Yorktown in October 1781 determined the British government against continuing the war. Another influence, often overlooked, was the growing demand of the English merchants to end the conflict. American privateers had successfully preyed on their shipping throughout the war. As a result of these depredations, English insurance rates for shipping had risen to unprecedented levels.

England's primary diplomatic goal was to drive a wedge in the French-American alliance and at the same time to end the costly American war. With the advent of a new ministry in March 1782, another attempt to make peace began. Robert Oswald, an elderly Scottish merchant and old friend of Franklin who had made a fortune in the slave trade, was sent to Paris. Franklin reiterated to Oswald approximately the same terms that Congress had been insisting on since 1779, labeling these as "necessary" and adding others that he called "desirable." The "necessary" terms included recognition of American independence, fishing rights and drying privileges on the Newfoundland banks, and restoration of the Canadian boundaries to those existing before the Quebec Act of 1774. (The Quebec Act had put Canada's southern boundary at the Ohio River.) Franklin's "advisable" suggestions called for the cession of Canada, indemnification of Americans who had suffered losses as a result of the war, trade on an equal footing between Britain and the United States, and a statement to be made by Parliament of "our error in distressing those countries as much as we had done." Then began a period of intensive diplomatic negotiation, punctuated by Oswald's frequent trips to London for advice and another change in the British cabinet. The war situation suddenly favored England when Admiral Rodney won a resounding victory over DeGrasse's fleet in the West Indies. In addition, though Spain had blockaded Gibraltar, she was still unable to recapture it.

It was at this time, late June 1782, that Jay arrived in Paris to help Franklin with the negotiations. In addition to Adams, Congress had appointed four more peace commissioners: Jay, Franklin, Henry Laurens (then still in the Tower of London), and Thomas Jefferson (who did not reach Europe until after the final treaty was signed). Jay served to complement Franklin because the two men differed sharply over the French alliance; like Adams, Jay personally disliked and distrusted Vergennes. Adams usually supported Jay's position and the two managed to persuade Franklin to concur, although it is difficult to understand how the "greatest American" could have been swayed against his own inclinations. Laurens was paroled and came to Paris but had little to do with the negotiations, though he signed the preliminary treaty.

All through the summer of 1782 negotiations proceeded slowly, with Oswald deferring to London at almost every turn. In October he was joined by a second and much younger British representative, David Hartley, and together they accepted, for the most part, Franklin's "necessary" terms. At first it appeared that the British would even cede Canada to the United States, but then the British attitude stiffened and the point was not mentioned in the preliminary treaty that was signed on November 30, 1782.

FRANCE AND THE TREATY OF PARIS (1783)

Contrary to specific instructions from Congress, the American peace commissioners signed the preliminary treaty without notifying France of their intentions. Though Vergennes, kept informed of the negotiations by agents, was piqued at the favorable terms secured by the Americans, he was also relieved to know that now France could likewise negotiate for peace. Spain followed suit, and the final treaties between Great Britain, the United States, France, and Spain were signed on September 3, 1783. Except for the loss of the thirteen colonies, Britain had ceded no territory to France and only the Floridas and Minorca to Spain.

Notwithstanding Congress' wrath at their cavalier treatment of France, the American diplomatists had won a stunning victory over Britain. In addition to independence, they had achieved liberal fishing rights, a northern boundary that passed through the center of the Great Lakes, a western boundary at the Mississippi River, and free navigation of the Mississippi. Many years later, John Adams was able to write truthfully that "Undisciplined marines as we were, we were better tacticians than was imagined."

TREATY OF PARIS, 1783

Article I.—His Britannic Majesty acknowledges the said United States, viz. New Hampshire, Massachusetts Bay, Rhode Island, and Providence Plantations, Connecticut, New York, New Jersey,

Pennsylvania, Delaware, Maryland, Virginia, North Carolina, South Carolina, and Georgia, to be free, sovereign and independent States. . . .

Article II.—And that all disputes which might arise in future, on the subject of the boundaries of the said United States may be prevented, it is hereby agreed and declared, that the following are, and shall be their boundaries. . . . [See Map 1, p. 22]

Article III.—It is agreed that the people of the United States shall continue to enjoy unmolested the right to take fish of every kind on the Grand Bank, and on all the other banks of Newfoundland; also in the Gulph of Saint Lawrence, and at all other places in the sea where the inhabitants of both countries used at any time heretofore to fish. . . .

Article IV.—It is agreed that creditors on either side shall meet with no lawful impediment to the recovery of the full value in sterling money, of all bona fide debts heretofore contracted.

Article V.—And that persons of any other description shall have free liberty to go to any part or parts of any of the thirteen United States, and therein to remain twelve months, unmolested in their endeavours to obtain the restitution of such of their estates, rights and properties as may have been confiscated; and that Congress shall also earnestly recommend to the several States a reconsideration and revision of all acts or laws regarding the premises, so as to render the said laws or acts perfectly consistent. . . .

Article VI.—That there shall be no future confiscations made, nor any prosecutions commenced against any person or persons for, or by reason of the part which he or they may have taken in the present war. . . .

Article VII.—There shall be a firm and perpetual peace between His Britannic Majesty and the said States, and between the subjects of the one and the citizens of the other, wherefore all hostilities, both by sea and land, shall from henceforth cease; All prisoners on both sides shall be set at liberty. . . .

Article VIII.—The navigation of the river Mississippi, from its source to the ocean, shall forever remain free and open to the subjects of Great Britain, and the citizens of the United States. . . .

Article IX.—In case it should so happen that any place or territory belonging to Great Britain or to the United States, should have been conquer'd by the arms of either from the other, before the arrival of the said provisional articles in America, it is agreed, that the same shall be restored without difficulty, and without requiring any compensation.

THE LEGACY OF PEACE

Successful as her diplomats had been, the new nation, burdened with domestic and foreign debts, faced a hostile Europe. To France she owed her very existence for aid rendered before Saratoga, and later for cooperation

Lake of the Woods

Northwest "Boundary Gap"

C A N A D A

L. Superior

St. Lawrence R.

45°

Ft. Michilimackinac

L. Huron

L. Michigan

Ft. Oswegatchie

Pointe au Fer
Dutchman's Point

L. Champlain

45°

L. Ontario

Ft. Oswego

Ft. Niagara

L O U I S I A N A

Ft. Detroit

L. Erie

U N I T E D

Ft. Miami
(built 1794)

Ohio R.

S T A T E S

A T L A N T I C   O C E A N

Mississippi R.

Chattahoochee R.

31°

St. Mary's R.

31°

F L O R I D A

■ Principal British forts held after 1783
── Boundaries of 1783
········ First U.S. northern boundary proposal
── ── Second U.S. northern boundary proposal
▨ Claimed by U.S. until 1842
▨ To be held by Great Britain if she retained Florida

Map 1.   The United States after the Treaty of Paris, 1783

and aid that made Yorktown possible. To Spain and the Netherlands, too, America owed large sums of money as well as gratitude. By 1783, according to Samuel F. Bemis, the leading historian of Revolutionary War diplomacy, the United States' foreign debts, exclusive of subsidies, were as follows: $6,352,500 to France, $248,000 to Spain, and $1,600,000 to the Netherlands.

When Franklin, Adams, and Jay bested English diplomats at the peace table, they began America's official diplomatic existence on a note that represented to many Americans the triumph of the New World over the Old as well as the triumph of a new diplomacy. The victory also reflected the origins of the United States in a revolution based, at least in theory, upon democratic ideas, some realized already and some never to be. Her diplomats would shortly discover the abyss between their expectations at the end of the war and the bitter reality of their impotence in the following two decades.

Further Reading

There are many good general histories of the American Revolution. One that projects an especially useful global view is Piers Mackesy, *The War for America, 1775-1783* (Cambridge, Mass., 1964). The best single volume on diplomacy is *Samuel F. Bemis, *The Diplomacy of the American Revolution,* 3rd ed. (Bloomington, Ind., 1957). Another fascinating history is *Richard W. Van Alstyne, *Empire and Independence: The International History of the American Revolution* (New York, 1965). Professor Van Alstyne has written two other useful books which cover a longer time span, *The Rising American Empire* (Chicago, 1965) and *Genesis of American Nationalism* (Waltham, Mass., 1970).

A recent book explaining the all-important French Alliance is William Stinchcombe, *The American Revolution and the French Alliance* (Syracuse, N.Y., 1969). A different aspect of the war and its diplomacy is treated in Helen Augur, *The Secret War of Independence* (New York, 1955) and in *Carl Van Doren, *Secret History of the American Revolution* (New York, 1968).

Richard B. Morris, *The Peacemakers: Great Powers and American Independence* (New York, 1965) is an excellent work describing the machinations leading to the peace treaties. Individual biographies are suggested for details about the men responsible for the treaty, and Gerald Stourzh, *Benjamin Franklin and American Foreign Policy,* 2nd ed. (Chicago, 1969) is especially recommended.

Asterisk denotes paperback edition.

2

Land, Maritime Policy, and the Federalists

During its first three decades of existence the new nation was buffeted not only by the force of hostile international winds but also by the ambiguities of its own foreign policies. Maintaining independence was, of course, the foremost American foreign policy goal and one about which there was virtually complete agreement. However, closely following in importance were two aims which often conflicted with such a policy: the continuation of maritime practices according to the Plan of 1776, and the acquisition of land and expansion to the Mississippi River. The pursuit of these goals again deeply involved the United States with England as well as with Spain and France.

Throughout the 1780's America's external problems were complicated by the relative lack of coordination within the government. For example, after approval of the peace treaty, each side was to exchange ratification within six months; but such was the disorganization within Congress that it was unable to do so, although Great Britain overlooked the technicality.

TRADE WITH OTHER NATIONS

During the period of Confederation, and in the succeeding decades as well, the United States sought to implement its liberal maritime practices by means of treaties with other nations; but in this it had indifferent success. By 1787 only three treaties had been concluded: with Sweden in 1783, with Prussia in 1785, and with Morocco in 1787. Despite the best efforts of John Jay, the results were unsatisfactory.

John Jay was a New York lawyer and an experienced diplomat whom Congress had appointed Secretary of Foreign Affairs in 1784. Although he was an early American patriot and generally able, he was pro-British and, like Alexander Hamilton, closely allied with New York commercial interests. Because Jay's long tenure in American foreign policy making continued in part through the Federalist era, he became a leading influence in shaping policy toward the commercial ends espoused by the Federalists after 1789.

TRADE WITH GREAT BRITAIN

Unfortunately, American maritime hopes received a rude jolt almost at once from Great Britain. At the end of the war the United States' emissaries had been slightly encouraged to hope for an early commercial treaty. But British shipowners, other commercial interests, and Canadian merchants combined to force their governments to shut the door on the Americans. Subsequent orders in council supplemented a parliamentary act, which ended for all practical purposes the lucrative West Indies trade. Individual New England sea captains did resort to smuggling, some successfully, but the total amount of goods shipped was only a fraction of prewar amounts.

The United States then began a search for new trading partners; but France and Spain, the two most logical possibilities, proved illusory. In spite of a commercial treaty with France, trade never reached the anticipated level, while Spain proved intransigent because of southwest border difficulties and the sharp increase in American Mississippi River trade.

In 1784 the *Empress of China* succeeded in opening a China trade that soon became centered in Salem, Massachusetts. The United States provided the Chinese with sea otter skins, which were hunted off the Pacific northwest coast, and, later, with even more esoteric cargoes such as *bêche-de-mer* and edible birds' nests. But even though this and other new areas of trade were opened, by the close of the Confederation period about 75 percent of the total still went to Great Britain, discriminatory tariffs notwithstanding. In turn, the infant American republic remained the most important overseas customer for England's manufactured goods.

FIRST AMERICAN DIPLOMATIC RELATIONS WITH ENGLAND

The government of the Confederation continued to lack the central authority that would have permitted it to threaten retaliatory tariffs and other reprisals best calculated to induce the British government to listen to American commercial overtures. When John Adams was appointed the first American minister to Great Britain, he had expected to negotiate some of the problems between the two countries. But he was doomed to three frustrating years of failure; the British government simply ignored him. After a year he wrote to John Jay: "I am likely to be as insignificant here as you can imagine." England did not reciprocate by appointing a minister to the United States until 1791, although consuls were sent to take care of British commercial dealings.

AMERICAN LAND POLICIES DURING CONFEDERATION

The British reluctance to treat diplomatically with the United States was based in part on problems and disputes relating to land in the West and Northwest. Indeed, little had changed since Franklin published his pamphlet in 1760. Land continued to be the single most important commodity in which Americans bought, sold, and speculated. While many of the founding fathers engaged in land dealings, among the most active dealers were planter aristocrats grouped geographically in the southeast — for instance, George Washington, George Mason, Richard Henry Lee, Edmund Randolph, and Patrick Henry — though the last was anything but an aristocrat.

During the Revolution there had been much bickering among several of the states over the future of their western land claims. In Virginia, Pennsylvania, and Maryland, some of the most influential politicians had dealt in large tracts. They demanded that their titles be validated even if the states ceded the land to the national government. By the war's end the inability of the states to pay for policing their western territories, together with Congress' urgent need for a source of revenue, resulted in fundamental changes in land policies. Thomas Jefferson's historic Ordnance of 1784, followed by those of 1785 and 1787, not only ceded the disputed lands to the national government but provided for their orderly settlement and eventual statehood as well. By the 1830's, according to one authority, the United States had sold nearly $45 million worth of land comprising over 21,000,000 acres. At the same time, the adoption of the three ordnances amply warned the world powers that American interest in North American land was to be a major factor in United States foreign policy for the foreseeable future, a period which lasted for three quarters of a century.

BRITISH FORTS AND AMERICAN SOVEREIGNTY

The British did not make it easy for the American government to implement its sovereignty over the western lands. They refused to give up eight key forts in the Northwest Territory, though this had been provided for in the peace treaty. (See Map 1, p. 22.) Ostensibly, British actions were based upon the failure of the Confederation to force repayment of debts contracted before the war and the refusal of the states to compensate

Loyalists for the persecution and loss of property they had suffered during hostilities. The American government was powerless in the face of the states' refusal to act, but John Adams attempted, unsuccessfully, to counter these claims by demanding recompense for the unknown number of slaves — probably several thousand — carried off by the British forces in Virginia and South Carolina. The forts remained occupied during the Confederation era because, in fact, the British had several reasons for doing so. In the first place, the Canadian merchants of Montreal demanded that the principal fur trade routes via the Great Lakes through Fort Michilimackinac not be cut off so precipitously. Then, too, the British had carefully nurtured Indian friendship in the West, to the continued peril of American settlers there, and persisted in supplying the Indians with guns and ammunition. Finally, Guy Carleton, Lord Dorchester, the able Governor-General of Canada, astutely practiced diplomacy on the nearby Vermonters, who had been rebuffed in their first bid for statehood. Under the famous Allen brothers — Ethan, Ira, and Levi — the Vermonters showed little reluctance to discuss the possibility of rejoining the empire. The result of all these factors was that the British did not abandon the last fort until well into the Federalist period.

THE CONTINUATION OF THE FRENCH ALLIANCE

The failure of France to replace England as America's foremost trading partner did not weaken the alliance between the two countries. When Thomas Jefferson succeeded Franklin as minister to France in 1785, he was welcomed as a worthy successor. However, during the next year when Jefferson turned to France under the terms of the alliance for support in ousting the British from the frontier, Vergennes replied noncommittally and did nothing to help. On the contrary, he asked the United States to repay its debt after America had defaulted on an interest payment. It was not forthcoming, but Vergennes and his successor in 1787 both felt that a weak American confederation was preferable to a stronger central government that would perhaps repay the loan. In spite of this problem, during the entire Confederation period and early into the Federalist era France was considered by the United States government and the American people to be their staunchest friend. When news of the French Revolution in 1789 reached America, the bonds between the two countries seemed to be confirmed and strengthened.

Not to be overlooked as valuable allies during this period were the Dutch bankers who three times between 1782 and 1788 made loans to the central government. Their goal was manifestly profit, and after the Constitution was adopted and the new central government organized, they succeeded in their aim.

TROUBLE WITH SPAIN

If the Netherlands at least professed friendship, regardless of its motives, then Spain made no secret of its hostility. The basic conflict was again land. Spain had learned of a secret clause inserted into the preliminary peace treaty that would have given the United States a southwestern boundary more than a hundred miles north of the 31° latitude stipulated in the final treaty. The secret clause would have gone into effect only if Britain had retained its hold on West Florida at the end of the war; but since she did not, Spanish troops successfully occupied the area. This disputed territory together with Spain's other territories gave the Spaniards almost all of Alabama and Mississippi and claims to parts of Georgia, Tennessee, and Kentucky — all east of their vast Texas and western holdings. As a result, the southwestern area seethed with intrigue, warlike Indians, and divided loyalties during the next two decades.

As the American population in the West grew, so too did the threat to Spanish sovereignty, which was weak and exerted only sporadically during the Confederation period. In 1785 Spain reacted to the western onrush by closing the lower Mississippi to navigation. This effectively ended a practical means by which western farmers could transport their produce to market. They had floated it down the Mississippi in barges for transshipment at New Orleans to foreign or American markets.

Unlike Britain, however, Spain appeared willing to negotiate these difficulties with the United States. In 1785 Spain's foreign minister sent a veteran diplomat, Don Diego de Gardoqui, to treat with Jay, who had been asked to secure the demands of the western farmers. Jay was more interested in obtaining a commercial treaty, even though trade with Spain was small, than in acceding to the farmers' vociferous demands. A treaty reflecting this bias was arranged, but when Jay asked Congress for permission to depart from his instructions by giving up questionable Mississippi navigation rights in order to complete negotiations, all five Southern states voted against him. This nullified the treaty's chances of ratification, which would have required affirmation by nine of the thirteen states.

Jay's failure to open the Mississippi spurred new intrigues and schemes comparable to those in which the Allens were involved in Vermont. Gardoqui stayed on in New York until 1788, plotting and attempting to implement conspiracy. The best-known conspirator was General James Wilkinson, who had been a youthful Revolutionary War hero. He plotted with several congressmen to create an independent state. The details, as with those of the later Burr conspiracy, are obscure, but it is known that Wilkinson was being paid simultaneously by both the United States and Spain (and later Great Britain) for his intrigues. He succeeded in enriching himself by winning a temporary monopoly over the use of the Mississippi. Such a licensing system partially opened the river to those who could afford to pay. However, the problem was not really solved until the mid-1790's, and Spanish-American relations remained strained.

THE CONSTITUTION AND AMERICAN FOREIGN POLICY

The making and adopting of the Constitution in the latter part of the 1780's clarified many of the difficulties that had plagued the Confederation in the conduct of foreign policy. The new Constitution's Article II, Section 2, made foreign affairs solely the responsibility of the executive. At the same time, Congress, through the Senate, retained an important check by obtaining the right to approve by a majority vote the appointment of ambassadors and ministers. Further, the Senate received the important right to advise on all treaties negotiated by the executive; moreover, consent by a two-thirds majority was required. This provision was insisted upon by Southerners as a result of the abortive Jay-Gardoqui negotiations.

During the battle over the adoption of the Constitution in New York, John Jay, James Madison, and Alexander Hamilton published *The Federalist,* a series of essays supporting the Constitution. Several numbers by Hamilton and Jay reiterated the basic foreign affairs arguments concerning the best way of maintaining America's independence.

THE FOREIGN POLICY OF THE FEDERALISTS

John Jay acted as Secretary of State in Washington's cabinet until the new appointee, Thomas Jefferson, could arrive from France to take over the position. Of the four cabinet posts established — Secretary of the Treasury, of State, of War, and Attorney-General — contemporaries considered the Treasury the most important and State the least. In foreign affairs the Federalist emphasis on commercial relations continued, but the new government, much against its will, found itself caught up in European politics. In fact, the pressures of the world situation, combined with Federalist predilections, resulted in foreign and domestic policies with which James Madison in Congress and Thomas Jefferson in the cabinet could not agree. Eventually, their opposition gave birth to political parties, in spite of Madison's earlier strictures in *The Federalist* No. 10 and Washington's desires at the time.

STATE DEPARTMENT BUDGET, 1790

	dollars
The Secretary of State, his salary	3500
1st The Home Office	
One Clerk a 800 doll ^{rs} and one d° a 500 doll ^{rs}	1300
Office Keeper and Messenger	200
Stationary	110
Firewood	50
Newspapers from the different States, suppose 15 a 4 dollars	60
A collection of the Laws of the States to be begun, suppose	200
Drenan's account of 1789, August 19th going express.......... 6 dol ^{rs}	
Maxwell's D° 10	16
	1836

2 ^{d} The Foreign Office	
One Clerk a 800 doll ^{rs} two d° a 500 doll ^{rs} each	1800
The french interpreter	250
Officer-Keeper and Messenger	200
Rent of the Office	200
Stationary &c	75
Firewood	50
Gazettes from abroad, and d° to be sent abroad	25
Contingencies	25
	2625
	7961

NEW YORK, June 16th 1790

"NUMBER 7" AND THE NOOTKA SOUND INCIDENT

The government was barely launched when it faced a crucial foreign policy decision concerning Britain and Spain. Spain had attempted to close to British traders territory in far off Nootka Sound, located on the west coast of Vancouver Island. The British reacted to Spanish claims of sovereignty over the area by a policy of coercion, and war appeared imminent. Washington then asked his cabinet members for their written opinions, a form he thereafter adhered to, as to what American policy should be in the event war broke out and the British demanded military transit through the United States in order to strike at Spanish territory. The necessity of making a decision was in any event obviated when the Spanish withdrew their claim to exclusive sovereignty in the area and war was averted.

However, this incident was of great importance to the history of American foreign policy for another reason. The British had been kept informed not only of the cabinet's decision but of the substance of individual members' briefs. The informant was Alexander Hamilton. Believing that a pro-British policy was vital to the success of his domestic policies, he acted as a British agent from the time of his appointment in 1789 until 1794. Hamilton used the designation "Number 7," and his contact was Major George Beckwith, a recognized, long-time British agent. Beckwith forwarded the information he received from Hamilton directly to the Governor-General of Canada, Lord Dorchester, who speeded it on to England. Thus the British government knew within several months of the cabinet's division over the question of the British army's transit.

Alexander Hamilton's effectiveness as a British agent is illustrated by what happened to the able financier Gouverneur Morris. Washington had sent Morris to England as his executive agent to improve relations between the two countries and to obtain concessions. Beginning with Morris' appointment, executive agents have proved an efficient means whereby presidents could send personal representatives on ambassadorial missions without the necessity of first obtaining Congressional approval. The ability to name his own man has historically contributed to the authority of the President to speak for the nation in foreign affairs. In this instance, however, Morris accomplished nothing because Hamilton had secretly sent libelous information about him that completely discredited him. Hamilton, who was trying to force any Anglo-American negotiations to take place in New York under his scrutiny, achieved his goal.

WASHINGTON'S FIRST TERM AND RELATIONS WITH ENGLAND

In 1791 Great Britain finally appointed a minister to the United States. The decision was made because of the need to maintain a strong pro-British faction in the United States to counteract the growing Jeffersonian opposition. Jefferson had proposed retaliatory legislation against British goods that had only narrowly been defeated. Also, Hamilton's financial and commercial policies were anchored to the British Empire, so that normal diplomatic representation became a necessity. In exchange for the unknown twenty-seven-year-old George Hammond, whom the British sent, the United States sent to England the venerable and august signer of the Constitution, Oxford-educated Thomas Pinckney, a South Carolina

Federalist. Hammond succeeded Beckwith as Hamilton's contact, and during his sojourn was in fact little more than a messenger.

Jefferson's talks with Hammond were inconclusive, partly because of Hammond's prior knowledge of American demands. Finally, in reaction to Hamilton's interference and Washington's strong Federalist stance, Jefferson resigned at the close of 1793. Thereafter, he joined with Madison to oppose the Federalists and worked to build a political party that would support his presidential ambitions in the election of 1796.

AMERICAN NEUTRALITY AND JAY'S TREATY

In 1794 the United States approached a crisis with Great Britain. Since the previous year, England and revolutionary France had been at war, as the result of which American maritime trade flourished briefly. But England soon invoked both the Rule of 1756 and the doctrine of continuous voyage and proceeded to confiscate a number of American ships and cargoes, mostly in the West Indies. Although the French probably confiscated a like number of vessels, American public opinion became especially enraged at Great Britain. In the West, Lord Dorchester's intemperate remarks to his Indian allies inflamed that area even more. Congress reacted by imposing a month's embargo against foreign shipping and by passing various defense measures. Mobs in several Eastern cities attacked British sailors and suspected sympathizers.

To head off an unwanted, and what could only have been a disastrous, war, Washington decided to send a special emissary to Britain. He chose John Jay, then Chief Justice of the Supreme Court, who was to try to settle maritime problems, debts, and the continued occupation of western forts. But as Hamilton had already informed the British of exactly the lengths to which the United States would go to avert war, Jay's position was effectively undercut. As a matter of fact, the treaty for which Jay ultimately settled became the most unpopular in American history and contributed measurably to the unpopularity of the Federalists.

Jay's Treaty, or the Treaty of London — its official but little used name — gave but one rather weak concession to the United States: the guarantee that the western forts would be evacuated by June 1, 1796. Actually, this had been a foregone conclusion since General "Mad Anthony" Wayne's victory over the British-supported Indians at the Battle of Fallen Timbers on August 20, 1794. All other problems between the two countries were either ignored or passed on to one of four mixed commissions set up to discuss Caribbean spoliations, debts of various kinds, and disputed boundaries. The commissions were not binding, had no disinterested arbitrators, and were only able to settle the spoliation claims. Britain continued to apply its strict maritime rules and the United States was forced to accept these at the expense of its own Plan of 1776.

George Washington was so keenly disappointed in the treaty that he considered not submitting it to the Senate for approval. Eventually, he did submit it only because he was deeply committed to keeping peace between the two countries. Also, some of the provisions had already been published in pro-Jefferson newspapers. The public outcry over the treaty reached new heights: John Jay was burned in effigy, and other Federalist leaders, including even Washington, were reviled in the growing opposition press. Nevertheless, the Senate approved the treaty by a vote of 20 to 10, and the threat of another war with England was temporarily averted.

JOHN JAY BURNED IN EFFIGY

BURNING JAY'S EFFIGY.

MAKING A TREATY

1. The President or his representative negotiates and signs a preliminary agreement.

2. The Senate gives its "advice and consent," making amendments or reservations as it chooses. The former require approval of the other

party, the latter do not. The Senate then approves the treaty by a two-thirds vote of those present.

3. The President ratifies the treaty by signing at least two copies of it. The official seal of the United States is attached to the documents.

4. The United States exchanges ratification by delivering an official copy to the other government. A similarly ratified document is received, and the treaty becomes binding upon the exchange of ratification.

5. The President officially proclaims the treaty, and at that time it becomes a law of the land.

SPAIN AND AMERICAN DIPLOMACY

Jay's Treaty affected relations with Spain because of that country's apprehension of a possible Anglo-American attack on Spanish possessions in America. Spain, though formerly Britain's ally, was now allied with France and hence anticipated war with England. In 1794 Spain requested new American representation in Madrid, which was tantamount to asking for negotiations. Thomas Pinckney was sent from London and speedily concluded the Treaty of San Lorenzo in 1795, known ever since as Pinckney's Treaty. Pinckney took advantage of Spain's weak bargaining position, due to her fear of the British, to score a stunning diplomatic victory. At last the United States received unrestricted navigation rights to the Mississippi, deposit privileges at New Orleans for a period of three years, which were renewable, and a southern boundary settlement at 31° latitude. Both sides agreed to restrain the Indians within their territories. Finally, Spain recognized American maritime rights according to the Plan of 1776. Pinckney's Treaty was as popular as Jay's had been unpopular, and the Senate, in a rare show of enthusiasm, approved it unanimously.

Pinckney's Treaty, together with the British evacuation of the northwest forts, stabilized the West. It put an end to Wilkinson's schemes and pointed to new frontiers for restless Americans.

FRANCE AND THE AGE OF REVOLUTION

The Federalists encountered their greatest difficulties in foreign policy not with Spain or England but with France. Less than three months after Washington's inauguration, France entered an era of revolution. Because it seemed comparable to their own recent struggle, most Americans enthusiastically supported it. The Declaration of the Rights of Man and

Citizen had a most familiar ring and pro-French clubs sprang up throughout America. Washington himself was at first sympathetic to the ideas of the revolution, but as each regime became ever more radical than the one before, his attitude changed. His administration was eventually faced with a difficult and vital decision when France declared war on England early in 1793. Should the United States support France and help protect French possessions in the West Indies? The principles adopted were embodied in an executive statement and then passed by Congress as the Neutrality Act of 1794. Ignoring the Alliance of 1778, which the French chose not to invoke, this legislation provided for impartial neutrality and forbade any military or naval belligerent activity in America and its coastal waters.

CITIZEN GENÊT

Much of the Neutrality Act of 1794 was directed at the activities of the young French Minister to the United States, Edmond Genêt, who represented the revolutionary Girondist government. Jefferson had insisted on recognizing the French government, holding that the Girondists were in power with the consent of the nation. This rule, which became the American criterion for recognizing new governments, posed few difficulties in the next century but many thereafter.

Genêt was instructed to raise an American army to attack the British in Canada. He began by enlisting the services of the Revolutionary War hero George Rogers Clark. Genêt was to outfit and send out privateers from American ports and at the same time to propagandize for the French cause. Flamboyant and popular with the crowds who greeted him on his arrival, Genêt was less successful in tempering Washington's pro-British leanings. Even Jefferson, still the Secretary of State, condemned Genêt after he had outfitted at Philadelphia and sent to sea a captured British ship, *The Little Sarah,* in violation of the neutrality law and in breach of a personal promise to Jefferson. Supporting Jefferson, the cabinet unanimously requested Genêt's recall, which came quickly, the Girondists having been ousted by a new faction. The French in turn demanded the recall of the United States Minister, Gouverneur Morris, who had publicly expressed anti-Republican sentiments and engaged in repeated royalist intrigues.

Morris was succeeded by a Jeffersonian appointee, James Monroe, who erred in the opposite direction by openly repudiating Jay's Treaty. This angered Britain as well as the Federalists, causing Washington to recall him in 1796. But while in Paris, Monroe was able to aid the American Revolutionary propagandist Thomas Paine, who, now a French citizen, had been imprisoned by the Jacobins. Monroe's popularity in France also blunted much of the official anger over Jay's Treaty. With the departure of Monroe, the French government terminated diplomatic relations with the United States, intending to wait until it could further Jefferson's cause in the election of 1796.

WASHINGTON'S FAREWELL ADDRESS

When George Washington retired at the end of his second term, his popularity was diminished and many of his hopes unfulfilled. His valedictory speech, written by Hamilton and published in September 1796, reiterated Federalist beliefs. More political than statesmanlike, the address included a sharp attack on both the French and the Jeffersonians. Unfortunately, the twentieth century has lifted those portions dealing with European relations out of context and made claims for the address that would be incomprehensible even to the Federalists.

JOHN ADAMS AND THE FRENCH

Carrying the Federalist banner in the election of 1796, John Adams narrowly bested Jefferson by two electoral votes. Although Adams was one of the most experienced Americans in foreign affairs, he faced increasing difficulty in dealing with the French. They claimed, with a certain amount of accuracy, that Jay's Treaty was incompatible with the Alliance of 1778. Therefore, after Monroe's departure, the Directory — the new French executive — authorized French privateers to capture American merchant ships. Before he retired, Washington had sent C. C. Pinckney, Thomas' brother, to France to try to reverse the French position. The Directory refused to receive him. Adams, with Senate approval, thereupon appointed John Marshall and Elbridge Gerry to join Pinckney as members of a commission charged with alleviating the worsening situation. The French, who had no intention of negotiating with the commission, demanded a bribe before announcing their position. They assigned the letters X, Y, and Z to the representatives who were to receive the bribe to meet with the commission; hence the episode has been called the XYZ Affair. While such procedure was not unusual at the time, the Adams administration was so infuriated that it urged war preparations.

THE UNDECLARED WAR OF 1798

Adams balked at formally declaring war against France. This split the Federalist party because Alexander Hamilton, Washington's second in command of the army, demanded an all-out declaration of war. The internal political clash was heightened by strong Jeffersonian opposition, although Congress was narrowly Federalist after the election of 1798. The result was a quasi-war, entirely naval, which proved inconclusive. One positive result was the creation of a permanent American navy in 1798. Less positive were those actions to which Adams highhandedly resorted in order to silence his persistent critics. These included the infamous Alien and Sedition Acts. One of the three Alien Acts demanded the deportation of foreign-born citizens who wrote seditious articles or were suspected of being dangerous or treasonable. The Sedition Act provided for punishment for "false, scandalous, and malicious" statements against the government. Though the acts were only sporadically enforced, they represented a patent threat to Jeffersonian dissent and were extremely unpopular.

Another act passed in 1799 came about because of the efforts of a Quaker leader, George Logan, to effect a peace by visiting France. The provisions of the Logan Act stated that, unless officially empowered, no individual American had authority to speak for the United States under penalty of criminal liability. This act is still in force.

The quasi-war ended abruptly; after Napoleon Bonaparte came to power, France had new goals. Napoleon, desiring to reestablish France's colonial empire in the lower Mississippi valley — an area controlled by Spain — needed peace with the United States. John Adams accepted Napoleon's overtures and courageously sent a commission to Paris, despite the opposition of Hamilton and his followers. The commission negotiated the Treaty of Mortefontaine, usually called the Convention of 1800. It called for the abrogation of the Alliance of 1778, thus giving the United States surcease from its "entangling alliance," but did not mention the considerable American spoliation claims. The Federalist Senate approved the treaty, albeit reluctantly.

THE FEDERALIST ERA

The election of Thomas Jefferson in 1800 ended the Federalist era, yet the Jeffersonians pursued markedly similar policies for the next dozen years. Perhaps the most ironic feature of Federalist foreign policy was that it was least successful in promoting its own maritime ambitions and most successful in furthering typical Jeffersonian goals such as the settlement and stability of the West.

Further Reading

Two excellent general surveys which together span the period from 1781 to 1801 are
*Merrill Jensen, *The New Nation: A History of the United States during the Confederation,*

1781-1789 (New York, 1956) and *John C. Miller, *The Federalist Era, 1789-1801* (New York, 1960). The origin of specific foreign policy ideas, several still influential, is discussed in *Joseph Charles, *The Origins of the American Party System* (New York, 1961) and in *Felix Gilbert, *Beginnings of American Foreign Policy: To the Farewell Address* (New York, 1965).

Alexander Hamilton's controversial relations with the British are explored and documented by Julian P. Boyd in *Number 7: Alexander Hamilton's Secret Attempts to Control American Foreign Policy* (Princeton, N.J., 1964).

Samuel F. Bemis deals with two treaties, the first of which is more important, in *Jay's Treaty: A Study in Commerce and Diplomacy,* rev. ed. (New Haven, Conn., 1962) and *Pinckney's Treaty: America's Advantage from Europe's Distress, 1783-1800,* rev. ed. (New Haven, Conn., 1960).

The domestic political situation in the Adams administration is part of Marshall Smelser's study, *The Congress Founds the Navy: 1787-1798* (Notre Dame, Ind., 1959). The diplomatic and war aspects of this period are admirably covered in *Alexander De Conde, *The Quasi-War: The Politics and Diplomacy of the Undeclared War with France, 1798-1801* (New York, 1966).

Several books extend far beyond this period. Two classic works, obtainable in most university libraries, are Henry M. Wriston, *Executive Agents in American Foreign Relations* (Baltimore, 1929) and Charles O. Paullin, *Diplomatic Negotiations of American Naval Officers: 1778-1833* (Baltimore, 1912). Books dealing with the relationship of the armed services to American foreign policies are Marcus Cunliffe, *Soldiers and Civilians: The Martial Spirit in America, 1775-1865* (Boston, 1968), *Walter Millis, *Arms and Men: A Study in Military History* (New York, 1967), and *Harold and Margaret Sprout, *The Rise of American Naval Power: 1776-1918,* rev. ed. (Princeton, N.J., 1946).

Asterisk denotes paperback edition.

3

The Jeffersonians and Their Foreign Policy

The election in 1800 of Thomas Jefferson and his followers so firmly entrenched their party that it completely dominated American politics at the national level for the next quarter of a century. In spite of Jefferson's conciliatory inaugural address, the Federalists expected many changes in foreign policy because of the new President's preoccupation with the West.

WAR WITH TRIPOLI

First, however, Jefferson was forced to deal with the increased harassment of American shipping in the Mediterranean. The United States, as well as every other maritime nation, had found it expedient to pay an annual tribute to the rulers of the Barbary States — Morocco, Algiers, Tunis, and Tripoli — and Jefferson had every intention of continuing this policy. Bribes notwithstanding, the North African countries were notoriously undependable and during the 1790's had captured and enslaved more than a hundred American seamen. Soon after Jefferson took office, the Pasha of Tripoli, dissatisfied with his annual payment, declared war against the United States. This led to a dilemma that Jefferson was never able to resolve. He had, on the one hand, committed his administration to saving money while simultaneously reducing taxes. He and his able and enthusiastic Swiss-born Secretary of the Treasury, Albert Gallatin, had begun to accomplish this by wholesale reductions in the size of both the army and the navy. The new plans for the navy called for building small, inexpensive, lightly armed gunboats for defensive use in American coastal bays and waters. On the other hand, when the Pasha declared war, Jefferson had to retain more large ships than he had intended, which thereby obliged him to temper his austerity plan for the navy.

Although Jefferson did not ask Congress to declare war, he dispatched a small naval squadron to blockade Tripoli harbor. There was little action

WAR WITH TRIPOLI

"The burning of the American Fregate the Philadelphia in the Harbour
of Tripoli happily executed by the valiant Cap: Decatur to whom this
Plate is respectfully dedicated by his Obedient Servant,
John B. Guerrazzi."

until 1803, when the *Philadelphia*, the largest and finest warship in the American navy, ran aground and was captured with her crew of 307 officers and men. Soon after, in a daring exploit, Lieutenant Stephen Decatur and a small band of volunteers succeeded in burning and destroying the *Philadelphia* as it lay at anchor in the harbor.

The ragtag army recruited by the American consul at Tunis, William Eaton, had only limited success. In 1805 the Pasha concluded a treaty with the blockading naval commander which ended the war but ignominiously forced the United States to pay $60,000 ransom for the captured men. From the American standpoint there were only two positive gains from the war: the forced retention of larger naval vessels; and Lieutenant Decatur's exploit, which gave Americans their first naval hero since John Paul Jones. Otherwise, the situation in the Mediterranean remained about the same until the War of 1812, when American shipping in that area all but ceased.

THOMAS JEFFERSON AND THE WEST

Jefferson demonstrated a lifelong interest in the American West. His motives may have been a mixture of altruism and national self-interest, but in any event they resulted in the most spectacular land bargain in American history. As far back as his sojourn in France in the 1780's, Jefferson had planned with an American adventurer, John Ledyard, that the latter should explore the western part of the North American continent, starting from the Pacific Northwest. But Ledyard went to the Asian portion of Russia, where he was arrested and deported by the Russians before he could sail for the Northwest. Later, Jefferson tried unsuccessfully to interest Congress in an overland expedition — long before the Lewis and Clark Expedition of 1804-1806 became a reality.

THE AMERICAN STANDARD OF LIVING, 1800

The standard of comfort [in 1800] had much to do with the standard of character; and in the United States, except among the slaves, the laboring class enjoyed an ample supply of the necessaries of life. In this respect, as in some others, they claimed superiority over the laboring class in Europe, and the claim would have been still stronger had they shown more skill in using the abundance that surrounded them.

By day or by night, privacy was out of the question. Not only must all men travel in the same coach, dine at the same table, at the same time, on the same fare, but even their beds were in common, without distinction of persons. Innkeepers would not understand that a different arrangement was possible. When the English traveler Weld reached Elkton, on the main road from Philadelphia to Baltimore, he asked the landlord what accommodation he had. 'Don't trouble yourself about that,' was the reply; 'I have no less than eleven beds in one room alone.' This primitive habit extended over the whole country from Massachusetts to Georgia, and no American seemed to revolt against the tyranny of innkeepers.

NAPOLEON, FRANCE, AND THE DREAM OF EMPIRE

Napoleon Bonaparte too had plans for the West. At the time the United States and France were signing the Convention of 1800, another of Napoleon's ministers was wresting the Treaty of San Ildefonso from Spain. By its provisions, Spain retroceded to France the Louisiana territory but not Spanish Florida. At nearly the same time, but quite coincidentally, Spain revoked the Americans' right of deposit at New Orleans in violation of Pinckney's Treaty. This action infuriated and agitated Westerners, who mistakenly blamed France for the act.

Napoleon's grand scheme — originally conceived in the 1780's — was to use the Louisiana territory as a great granary and supply base for the sugar-rich French islands of Guadeloupe, Martinique, and especially Santo Domingo. But the slaves on Santo Domingo revolted and took over the island. Their success was due in part to the presence of a large British fleet anchored off Jamaica which was poised to attack should the French attempt to land an army. However, this threat was removed when the Peace of Amiens was confirmed in March 1802, thus temporarily ending the long war between France and England. Napoleon then sent an army commanded by his brother-in-law, General Charles Leclerc, to reconquer Santo Domingo. A larger contingent commanded by one of Napoleon's most successful generals, Claude Victor, was fatefully delayed in the Netherlands through the winter of 1803 and never did sail.

General Leclerc reached Santo Domingo and there defeated the rebel army several times, though not decisively. The enemy, commanded by the gifted ex-slave Toussaint L'Ouverture, turned to guerrilla warfare and effectively harassed the French. Toussaint was treacherously captured and imprisoned in France, where he died from tuberculosis contracted in a damp prison cell. But the revolt did not end with Toussaint's capture, and soon Leclerc was fighting not only the rebels but yellow fever as well. In September 1802 alone, 4,000 French soldiers died of fever. By the time the general himself succumbed, over 50,000 troops had perished in less than a year.

THOMAS JEFFERSON AND LOUISIANA

When Jefferson became President he had not yet heard of the retrocession of Louisiana, but when he did he reacted swiftly. First he began to arm the western militia, which somewhat appeased their fury against France. More importantly, and owing more to Secretary of State James Madison's astuteness than to his own predilections, Jefferson threatened to become an ally of England in order to block French ambitions. He coupled the threat with an offer to purchase both Spanish Florida and New Orleans from Napoleon, mistakenly believing that Florida had been included in the Treaty of San Ildefonso. Congress appropriated $2 million and approved the appointment of James Monroe as Minister Extraordinary to assist Robert R. Livingston, the United States Minister to France. Because of Monroe's popularity in the West, his appointment did much to calm bellicosity in that region. He sailed for France in March 1803, but by the time he arrived in April the situation had changed dramatically.

Napoleon suddenly renounced his dream of an American empire in favor of a renewed attack on England. Since in that event Louisiana would become an easy prey for the British fleet, he directed Foreign Minister

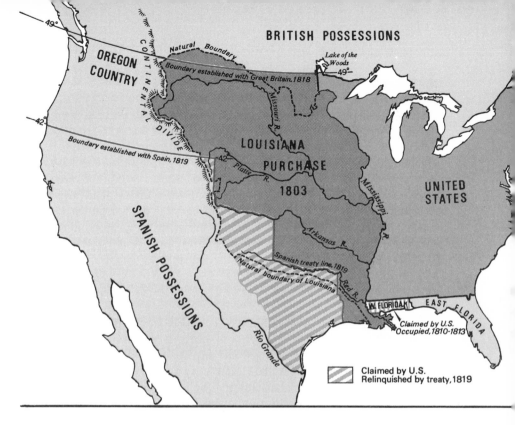

Map 2. The Louisiana Purchase, 1803

Charles Maurice de Talleyrand to sell the entire holding immediately. The day before Monroe reached Paris, Talleyrand stunned Livingston by asking for an offer from the United States for the entire Louisiana territory instead of for New Orleans alone. Thereafter, Monroe and Livingston bargained not so much with Talleyrand as with the French Minister of Finance, who was determined to get the highest possible amount to provide funds for Napoleon's war machine.

Monroe and Livingston had been authorized to pay up to $10 million for New Orleans and part of Spanish Florida *east* of the Mississippi River. Instead, after a week's negotiations, they purchased for approximately $15 million New Orleans and over 800,000 square miles of territory north and *west* of the Mississippi. The price included claims owed to Americans by France. On April 30, 1803, fifteen days before the renewal of war between France and England, treaties were signed consummating the transaction. The actual boundaries of the purchase were so unclear that in spite of repeated attempts at clarification, the United States had difficulties with both England and Spain over them—just as the astute Napoleon had predicted. Robert Livingston struck the right note when he concluded, "We have lived long but this is the noblest work of our whole lives."

JEFFERSON AND THE CONSTITUTION

Thomas Jefferson did not hesitate to submit the treaty to the Senate for approval, but privately he questioned the legality of adding territory to the national domain without a constitutional amendment. The Federalists too raised this point but were overruled. Thus the Louisiana Purchase was swiftly confirmed by the Senate, with the House voting the necessary appropriations. Since Napoleon demanded cash rather than American securities, Gallatin was forced to apply to English and a few Dutch sources. One source, Baring Brothers of London, subscribed over $10 million, and Alexander Baring—later Lord Ashburton—came to America to deal with Gallatin personally, notwithstanding the fact that his country and France were at war.

THE LOUISIANA PURCHASE AND AMERICAN OCCUPATION

When ratification was exchanged and the United States took possession of Louisiana on December 20, 1803, there were about 900,000 inhabitants of the region between the Appalachians and the Mississippi but very few living west of the river. The acquisition opened this vital water artery, now

THE TRANSFER OF LOUISIANA FROM FRANCE TO THE UNITED STATES

The Place D'Armes at New Orleans, December 20, 1803.

completely within the nation's boundaries, to new markets. In addition, the size of the United States had been doubled, while a seemingly inexhaustible amount of rich farmlands west of the Mississippi offered limitless possibilities. To size up the dimensions of the vast area, Jefferson reconstituted his old plan for exploration and sent a party under Lewis and Clark overland to the northwest. This expedition not only succeeded in charting the new territory and in identifying and describing its flora and fauna but also provided a solid basis for later American claims to the northwest region.

The imprecise boundaries of the Louisiana Purchase eventually aided the United States at the expense of both Spain and England. Jefferson, for example, attempted to force Spain to relinquish West Florida, an area along the Gulf of Mexico extending east of New Orleans to the Perdido River. The Spanish withstood Jefferson's pressure in 1803, only to lose much of the territory in 1810 under much less advantageous circumstances.

THE BURR CONSPIRACY

One of the most sensational episodes in the history of the West occurred in the fall of 1806. For reasons that are still unclear, it is thought that Aaron Burr, who had been Vice-President of the United States in Jefferson's first term, conspired to raise an army in the West to overthrow the government. Perhaps he planned to create a personal empire by annexing part of Texas, which was owned but ineffectually governed by Spain. One of his fellow plotters and an old hand at conspiracy was General James Wilkinson, commander of the American military forces in the Louisiana department. At the last minute, instead of joining Burr, Wilkinson warned Washington, and the conspiracy was easily crushed. In a memorable trial presided over by John Marshall, Chief Justice of the Supreme Court, Burr was found not guilty. Although he disappeared from public notice, Burr was by no means the last American to attempt to separate western lands from their legal owners.

EUROPEAN WAR AND AMERICAN MARITIME RIGHTS

The resumption of the war between France and England in May 1803 served American maritime interests. The American merchant marine became the largest neutral trader in the world, with expanding profits. The most lucrative trade was with Spanish and French colonies in the Caribbean and with continental France. To circumvent England's Rule of 1756 and the doctrine of continuous voyage, American traders first brought goods from the Caribbean to the United States, paying low import duties, usually refunded, thus making them free goods. They then exported these goods, often to France, at a large profit. The British attempted to thwart this process, but in a decision involving the ship *Polly,* engaged in such a voyage, the High Admiralty Court declared the "broken voyage" legal. The decision remained in force until 1805, when, in the *Essex* case, pressure from the British navy forced a reversal. After this, British warships stopped, searched, and confiscated cargoes on American merchantmen coming from the Caribbean.

As the war intensified, neutral rights were more and more ignored, especially after the devastating British sea victory at Trafalgar and the equally signal French land triumph at Austerlitz. But though neither side showed consideration for neutrals on the high seas, each was negotiating with neutral governments to prevent aid going to the other belligerent.

Napoleon countered the British orders in council of 1806 by setting up his own blockade in Europe. By the terms of his Berlin and Milan decrees, the British Isles were said to be blockaded and all trade with them forbidden. The British, possessing control of the seas, retaliated by instituting a licensing system for neutral trade, which for all practical purposes limited trade to their own domains.

THE GROWTH OF THE IMPRESSMENT ISSUE

The difficulty between the United States and Great Britain concerning maritime rights was compounded by the growth of the impressment issue. Forced to recruit men by press-gang methods, the British navy was usually shorthanded. Desertion rates were high, and many deserters made their way into the American merchant marine where citizenship and nationality were of little consequence. The British navy contravened American rights by stopping and searching merchant ships, often forcibly removing seamen for their own service. The United States contended that its immigrant population acquired citizenship by naturalization; Britain, in common with other European countries, recognized citizenship as based solely on the country of one's birth. This proved to be an insoluble problem. In spite of Jefferson's diplomacy and a war in 1812, England refused to accept the American point of view until later in the century.

THE *CHESAPEAKE* AFFAIR

The first retaliatory law the Jefferson administration passed was the Non-Importation Act of 1806, which answered British orders in council banning

American re-exports. At the same time, an American mission sought to replace Jay's Treaty, due to expire in the fall of 1807, with one more favorable to United States maritime rights. The new treaty, however, was so little changed from the old and so devoid of concessions that Jefferson chose not to submit it to the Senate for approval. Although the Non-Importation Act was supposed to be in force from November 1, 1806, Jefferson delayed putting it into effect for over a year, until negotiations with England had failed.

During the interim American hostility toward England reached a new high. In June 1807 the frigate *Chesapeake,* largest warship in the American navy, sailed from Norfolk with three, possibly four, deserters from the British navy who had enlisted for a cruise on the ship. Just outside the three-mile limit the *Chesapeake* was stopped by a slightly larger British frigate, the *Leopard,* whose captain demanded the deserters. When the *Chesapeake*'s commander, Commodore James Barron, refused, the *Leopard,* guns and deck cleared for action, fired several broadsides into the totally unprepared American ship. Barron struck his colors after firing a token shot; three of his men were killed and eighteen wounded. The four men were then forcibly removed by the British, although three were American-born citizens who had been impressed originally, and the *Chesapeake* limped back to port.

The public outcry was such that President Jefferson ostensibly began to prepare for war. Actually, he delayed calling Congress into special session until the following October, thus allowing time for the public clamor to subside and for Britain to admit having erred in this case; however, the British still refused to abandon impressment.

THE EMBARGO

The special session of Congress called by Jefferson passed the Embargo Act, which was signed on December 22, 1807. This law represented the high-water mark of Jeffersonian attempts to coerce England by peaceful economic means. The Embargo Act restricted American commerce to coastal waters and required heavy bonds to be posted to ensure compliance. Jefferson believed that this extreme economic sanction would injure England, also France to a lesser extent, and would force both nations to stop violating American maritime rights. His reasoning proved correct, but the cost was a sharp depression in the nation's seaports, which soon became a forest of masts from the dismantled and laid-up ships anchored in them. Jefferson clung to the embargo until nearly the end of his second term before yielding to the mounting pressures from both his own party and from the Federalists. The Embargo Act was replaced by the Non-Intercourse Act of March 1809, which in effect repealed the embargo for all countries except

France and England. While the Embargo Act failed in the short run, its long-range consequences were more successful, as Jefferson had foreseen. He wrote a friend that "It [the embargo] has set us all on domestic manufacture, & will I verily believe reduce our future demands on England fully one half."

JAMES MADISON AND THE ROAD TO WAR

Thomas Jefferson picked his Secretary of State, James Madison, to succeed to the presidency. Although a brilliant theorizer and a lifetime scholar, Madison proved a poor choice. During times of crisis he tended to vacillate or to allow himself to be carried along by the tide of Congressional and public opinion. Nevertheless, his first term began auspiciously when the British government allowed its young minister, David Erskine—who had an American wife—to attempt to negotiate a settlement of the constricting non-importation embargo. In April 1809 the Erskine Agreement, by which Britain agreed to withdraw its restrictive orders in council, was completed. However, the agreement was moot as to whether the United States would accept the British Rule of 1756, a point which had been a sine qua non of Erskine's instructions. When the British Foreign Minister George Canning learned of the contents of the agreement, he promptly repudiated it and recalled Erskine.

Madison had meanwhile lifted the ban against trading with England, but the humiliating outcome of the agreement forced him to reinstitute the Non-Intercourse Act in August 1809. The breach between the two countries widened after Erskine's departure, although Napoleon too had begun to capture ships and impress crews. Erskine's successor, Francis J. "Copenhagen" Jackson, proved to be arrogant and anti-American. After strongly implying that Madison was a liar, Jackson was ignored by the government and soon left Washington. Eventually summoned home, he was not replaced for two fateful years during which diplomatic relations between the countries were practically suspended. The United States Minister to England, William Pinckney, had also returned during this period, leaving American affairs in the hands of a lower-ranking chargé d'affaires.

In May 1810 Madison signed Macon's Bill No. 2, his final effort at economic coercion. This allowed trade with all countries except France and England, but provided that should either of these countries cancel its restricting maritime decrees, trade would be resumed with the one but not the other. Napoleon responded with an ambiguous letter in which he stated that certain conditions would have to be met before he could lift his Berlin and Milan decrees. Madison understood this, but nevertheless took the remarkable step of declaring that France had met the terms of Macon's Bill No. 2 but that England had not!

THE *PRESIDENT* AND THE *LITTLE BELT*

A devastating blow to hopes of reconciliation between England and the United States occurred in May 1811. An American 44-gun frigate, the *President,* attacked a much smaller 20-gun British sloop, the *Little Belt,* in the process almost destroying her and killing nine and wounding two of her crew. American public opinion illogically greeted the news with tumultuous demonstrations, looking upon the affair as revenge for the *Chesapeake.* Almost unnoticed was the arrival the next month of a new British minister, Augustus John Foster, who, although a moderate, could do little to restore normal relations between the two nations.

THE RISE OF THE WAR HAWKS

Shortly after the repeal of the Embargo Act, a group of Southerners and Westerners formed a strong prowar faction within the Jeffersonian party. Notably successful in the Congressional elections of 1810, this group elected many who were pledged to work for a declaration of war against Britain. Called the War Hawks, the faction included such notables as Henry Clay of Kentucky, John C. Calhoun of South Carolina, Langdon Cheves of North Carolina, Richard M. Johnson of Kentucky, Felix Grundy of Tennessee, William Crawford of Georgia, and Peter B. Porter of New York. Although they had individual grievances against the British, they were unanimously agreed that Indian depredations on the frontier must be halted and that a policy of territorial expansion, which would include Upper Canada, ought to be pursued. Just after the War Hawks had succeeded in electing thirty-four-year-old Henry Clay as Speaker of the House, they received news of the battle fought at Tippecanoe Creek in Indiana on November 7, 1811. An American army, commanded by the bumbling governor of the territory, William Henry Harrison, had inconclusively driven off Indians representing a short-lived confederacy of Ohio Valley tribes. Led by the gifted Shawnee chief, Tecumseh—who was not present at Tippecanoe—and his powerful brother, the Prophet, the Indians had British support. The large number of American casualties were blamed on the British-made guns the Indians used rather than on Harrison's ineptness. The episode measurably strengthened Clay's position in Congress.

THE WAR HAWKS AND FLORIDA

While some War Hawks decried the continuing impressment of American sailors, others welcomed the onrush of war as an opportunity to occupy part

JOHN C. CALHOUN

FELIX GRUNDY

WILLIAM H. CRAWFORD

RICHARD M. JOHNSON

of West Florida. In 1810 the area from just east of New Orleans to the Pearl River had been hurriedly annexed after a contrived revolution freed the territory from the almost nonexistent authority of Spain. As the Latin American revolutions had begun, Spain could little more than hold the more important land, which included Mobile Bay east to the Perdido River and East Florida. Madison spent much of his time in the months preceding the War of 1812 attempting to wrest East Florida from Spain. Aside from his long-standing expansionist views, Madison felt that in the event of war with England, Spain would be vulnerable to British coercion and might therefore allow a British army to be based in that area. To forestall such a possibility, Congress passed a secret resolution on January 15, 1811, forbidding Spain to transfer East Florida to any other power. Later, this resolution was to become an integral part of the Monroe Doctrine.

Madison attempted to foment the same sort of revolution in East Florida that had been successful in West Florida. To that end, he sent as an agent the seventy-three-year-old George Mathews, a Revolutionary War veteran and, later, Governor of Georgia. In March 1812 Mathews and a motley army launched an offensive, but even with the support of American gunboats they failed to capture any strategic Spanish installations. A short time later, war with England being imminent, Madison repudiated the insurrection. The Americans withdrew, but retained a small part of Florida near Mobile. As Madison had predicted, the British effectively used Pensacola in East Florida as a base until late in the war.

THE WAR OF 1812

By the spring of 1812 the War Hawks were clamoring for war against Britain. In early June, Congress passed a war resolution, 79 to 49 in the House of Representatives and 19 to 13 in the Senate. The large House majority was due to the work of the War Hawks, but in the Senate there were Federalist members as well as several Easterners who were more anti-French than anti-British. Ironically, a week later, the British government announced the suspension of the orders in council that had prompted American attempts at economic coercion. Was there a primary cause of the war? Impressment? Western expansion? Commercial regulation? Most historians cite these reasons, but to contemporary Americans — even those in the West — the impressment issue was the single topic that kept public passions at fever pitch against England.

THE AMERICAN EFFORT IN WARTIME

America's unreadiness to fight such a war soon became woefully apparent. The government, overwhelmed by the task of undertaking the conflict, failed not only to constitute itself for the job but even to find leaders for the army. The army depended largely on poorly trained militia for the bulk of its fighting strength, and the results were often disastrous. For example, the campaign the Westerners had demanded to invade and take Upper Canada proved an utter fiasco. Other American armies lost a series of battles; the British even captured and burned Washington after routing the Maryland militia in its first encounter with British regulars. The situation worsened after the British defeated Napoleon, for then these battle-trained veterans became available for American duty. Only General James Wilkinson's occupation of Mobile in 1814 and Andrew Jackson's decisive victory at New Orleans on January 8, 1815, gave hope to the American people.

At sea the story was outwardly different because American frigates gave a good account of themselves in individual duels, thus helping morale and providing Americans with new war heroes. However, these victories had no effect whatsoever on the outcome of the war. British naval superiority was demonstrated by their total of 230 ships of the line; in contrast, the United States had none. American naval victories on Lake Erie and Lake Champlain were more important than any of the land battles fought. As in the Revolutionary War, the privateers, of which there were about 1,500, played an important role; all told, they captured and destroyed enough British commerce to cause London merchants to complain vociferously.

In addition to difficulties with the armed services, the country was weakened by dissidence in New England, which remained vocal throughout the war. In 1812 Madison was reelected by the combined votes of the South and the West; New England had been solidly against him, and this hostility continued. It culminated in the Hartford Convention of 1814, to which five New England states sent representatives. The convention discussed secession but settled for considerably less. By the time its leaders submitted their demands to Congress the war was nearly over, and they were unsuccessful. While the sum of the many problems the United States faced explains why the government did not perform effectively, it does not account for England's failure to crush America. The answer is that for the second time in the brief history of the United States, French aid proved decisive. For much of the war period, Great Britain was primarily concerned with defeating Napoleon; it therefore relegated the American operation to second place.

THE ROAD TO PEACE

Because of the importance of the European theater, England had considered a peaceful settlement quite early in the War of 1812. In fact, both sides put out feelers, but since the Americans insisted that the impressment issue was a sine qua non for settlement, the talks failed. The Czar of Russia then proposed mediation, which Madison accepted in March 1813. The President appointed Albert Gallatin, Secretary of the Treasury and the ablest man in the cabinet, and Senator James A. Bayard, a Delaware Federalist, as special envoys to assist John Quincy Adams, United States Minister to Russia. The British refused the Czar's offer but suggested instead direct negotiations with the Americans. Madison quickly accepted, sending the same three men, with the addition of Henry Clay and Jonathan Russell, a former chargé d'affaires in London, to Ghent. In early August 1814 began one of the strangest negotiations in United States history. The five Americans were able, prominent, and decisive; in fact, two of them — Clay and Adams — proved to be of presidential caliber. Against them were arrayed three thoroughly undistinguished English diplomats. All eight tried to negotiate for the best possible terms while simultaneously keeping their ears cocked toward Vienna, where the Congress of Vienna was remaking the map of Europe, and their eyes on the distant battlefields of America.

The members of the United States delegation differed so widely in temperament and personality that, while personal clashes were frequent, their varying traits complemented each other in the bargaining process. Of the three notable members, Henry Clay personified the Westerner; a riotous liver, even in Ghent, he brought to the conference table an easy give-and-take and a mastery of bluff, sharpened by long bouts of card playing. His opposite was the stiff, puritanical, and vain John Quincy Adams, who often arose in the morning — so he noted in his diary — at the same hour that Clay was boisterously returning from a night's carousing. The counterweight was Albert Gallatin, who was cosmopolitan in outlook and possessed many of Benjamin Franklin's diplomatic skills. He was the unofficial but begrudgingly acknowledged leader of the American delegation.

At the outset, the major stumbling block was the American demand that the British give up impressment. This issue resulted in a deadlock, but as soon as Madison reluctantly changed his instructions to the negotiators, the bargaining moved forward. The outcome of five months of negotiating was the second decisive American diplomatic victory in thirty years. The question had become not whether the United States would gain its demands but rather how much it would have to pay for peace. The answer from Ghent was, "Remarkably little"!

The Treaty of Ghent, signed on Christmas Eve 1814, provided that the boundaries of the United States would remain in the status quo ante bellum; four joint commissions, comparable to those established by Jay's Treaty, were provided to settle boundary disputes. Left completely unmentioned were the issues of impressment, Britain's Rule of 1756, or American maritime rights according to the Plan of 1776.

THE SIGNING OF THE TREATY OF GHENT, CHRISTMAS EVE, 1814

Left to right: Anthony St. John Baker, Henry Goulburn, William Adams, Lord Gambier, John Quincy Adams, Albert Gallatin, Christopher Hughes, James Bayard, Henry Clay, Jonathan Russell, unidentified.

As news of the treaty reached America shortly after Jackson's triumph at New Orleans, most Americans enthusiastically equated it with the liberal treaty terms won and concluded that the war had ended as an American victory. The Senate unanimously approved the Treaty of Ghent and thus formally ended the War of 1812. However, although American independence remained intact, there seemed little gained; worse, the same schisms and problems that had divided the country during the war remained unsolved — a portent of difficulties to come.

Further Reading

A good survey of this period is *Marshall Smelser, *Democratic Republic: 1801-1815* (New York, 1969). The best diplomatic background to the War of 1812 is found in the two volumes by Bradford Perkins, *The First Rapprochement: England and the United States, 1795-1805* (Berkeley, Calif., 1967) and *Prologue to War: England and the United States, 1805-1812* (Berkeley, Calif., 1961). The war itself is competently explained in *Harry L. Coles, *The War of 1812* (Chicago, 1965), while a more diplomatically oriented book on the same subject is *Patrick C. T. White, *A Nation on Trial: America and the War of 1812* (New York, 1965). For a fascinating account of the making of the Treaty of Ghent, read Fred L. Englemann, *The Peace of Christmas Eve* (New York, 1962).

The best materials dealing with the accomplishments of Thomas Jefferson and James Madison are found in multi-volume biographies by Dumas Malone and Irving Brant, respectively. Other good biographies of the leading men of the age abound and one, Samuel F. Bemis, *John Quincy Adams and the Foundations of American Foreign Policy* (New York, 1949), is indispensable for an understanding of the period.

In addition John A. Logan, Jr., *No Transfer* (New Haven, Conn., 1961), which extends beyond any one period, is particularly useful.

Asterisk denotes paperback edition.

4

The Jeffersonians and the Rise of American Nationality

The War of 1812 proved to be a quickly forgotten military failure. The inadequacies of the government and the divisiveness within the nation seemed to fade under the firm leadership of the newly elected President James Monroe. As a matter of fact, when he visited New England in 1816, he was greeted tumultuously, prompting a Boston newspaper to describe the ensuing period as the "era of good feelings." However, this may have reflected more the euphoria of a country that had courted disaster and recovered than it did actual conditions.

All the same, a warm glow of nationalism seemed to suffuse Congress, led by Henry Clay. Congressmen not only continued financial support for the armed services, based upon wartime expenditures; they also rechartered a national bank, took halting steps toward a system of protective tariffs, and made the first appropriation for federal support of internal improvements. Albert Gallatin, a lifelong Jeffersonian, summed up the change:

> The war has renewed and reinstated national feelings and character which the Revolution had given, and were daily lessened [afterwards]. . . . [Now there] are more Americans; they feel and act more as a nation.

THE UNITED STATES AND THE BARBARY STATES

One example of the new nationalism was America's altered relationship with Algiers, one of the Barbary States. Toward the end of Madison's second term, after confirmation of the Treaty of Ghent, he had recommended and Congress had passed a declaration of war against Algiers for piracy. The President dispatched a well-armed naval squadron under Commodore Stephen Decatur, the hero of the earlier *Philadelphia* exploit. The Algerians quickly withdrew their demands for tribute; in fact, they paid the United States a small reparation. A year later, a British fleet destroyed the corsair navy, which permanently ended the payment of bribes to the

Barbary States. Henceforth, American relations with the North African countries were harmonious and at times commercially significant.

JOHN QUINCY ADAMS AND AMERICAN FOREIGN POLICY

James Monroe was the last of the Revolutionary generation to be President, and his able cabinet reflected the newly emerging America rather than the country of an earlier day. His most notable cabinet appointee was John Quincy Adams, whose formidable diplomatic and political career led to his appointment as Secretary of State, a post he held during Monroe's two terms. In 1824 Adams succeeded to the presidency for one term. In habits and personality Adams was nearer his father's generation than the generation of his own day, which included such full-living politicians as Henry Clay and Richard M. Johnson. Nevertheless, Adams understood the art and practice of diplomacy as well as Jefferson. He was the first secretary of state to combine astute global strategic insights with effective diplomacy. Ranking with Jefferson and, later, William Seward, Adams was one of the three giants of nineteenth-century American foreign policy. Unfortunately, history has been less than kind to him; Monroe's name was given to his most fervent expression of expansion, while his importance in the cabinet was subsequently downgraded because of his inept performance as President.

JOHN QUINCY ADAMS

AMERICAN DIPLOMACY AND THE PAX BRITANNICA

At the conclusion of the Napoleonic wars and the War of 1812, Great Britain was indisputably the most powerful nation in the world. As such, she exerted a powerful influence over other countries to keep the peace and to localize their wars. During the nineteenth century, England was interested in creating and expanding markets to ensure the prosperity of her highly industrialized homeland. As a result, Great Britain's interests often coincided with those of her best customer, the United States, to the benefit of the latter. One expression of the Pax Britannica policy with the United States concerned the mixed commissions provided for by the Treaty of Ghent. One commission, whose agreement was later named the Convention of 1818, fixed the boundary between Canada and the United States west of the Lake of the Woods at the 49° parallel all the way to the Rockies. The land west of the Rockies was to be opened jointly, and individual claims of the respective countries were to be suspended for a ten-year period. This was usually referred to as "joint occupation." From the American point of view, this served as an effective block on Canadian access to the Mississippi and ended long-standing British demands for navigation rights on that river. On the other hand, the United States was forced to compromise on its demands for free and unlimited fishing rights off Newfoundland and Labrador and to settle for a mere grant of privileges to American fishermen; this, though it could be revoked, actually proved to be highly profitable for New Englanders.

Another Anglo-American agreement had its genesis in 1817 when Richard Rush, acting as Secretary of State at the end of Madison's second term, agreed with the British Minister, Charles Bagot, to reduce naval armaments on the Great Lakes. This became the Rush-Bagot Agreement of 1818; although it did not affect land fortifications, the impetus from it resulted in an unfortified border between the United States and Canada.

THE CONVENTION OF 1818 AND SLAVERY

The Convention of 1818 also extended a previous commercial treaty for another ten years. This was of limited value because, as was true of an earlier treaty, it prohibited American trade with the British West Indies.

Another clause of the Convention of 1818 provided for arbitration in settling American slaveowners' claims to restitution for slaves carried away by the British during the War of 1812. Eventually, an arbitrator did award over $1 million for the claims.

The convention's concern with slavery was one indication of the growing international importance attached to the institution of slavery. In the United

States, Congress had implemented the constitutional provision for ending the slave trade in 1808 by providing stringent penalties for infractions, and most of the states had followed suit. In 1820 Congress further declared that the slave trade was equivalent to piracy, and it decreed the death penalty for convicted offenders. At the same time, Great Britain urged the United States to negotiate a treaty that would allow the British navy to stop and search American vessels on the high seas as a deterrent to the illicit trade. Britain had similar treaties with Spain, the Netherlands, France, and other countries. The United States, represented by John Quincy Adams, refused on principle because the British, although no longer practicing impressment, still would not agree to give up the theory.

One alternative to the right of search suggested by the British called for the United States to station naval units off the West African coast to cooperate with the Royal Navy in stopping the slave trade at its source. In 1820 four small warships were sent to the area, but their crews found the task almost impossible because, even though slavers abounded, almost every vessel had its papers in order and was not flying an American flag. As one officer reported: "The slave trade is carried on to a very great extent. There are probably not less than 300 vessels on the Coast engaged in the trade, each having two or three sets of papers." Furthermore, and as the British learned subsequently, it was one thing to apprehend an alleged slaver but quite another to prosecute him successfully. These problems, as well as the proslavery sympathies of many Washington officials, caused the United States to withdraw its squadron after three years; thus, the illicit slave trade flourished throughout the remainder of the decade, usually flying an American flag.

Once the slave traders escaped patrolling naval units, if there were any, it was not difficult to bring the slaves into the South. The human cargo was often landed in Spanish Florida or, later, in Mexican Texas and was easily smuggled into the lower South for sale.

THE ACQUISITION OF FLORIDA

Smuggling based on Florida together with the bands of marauding Indians and runaway slaves who lived there and made raids into Georgia were but two reasons for the American acquisition of East Florida. When the War of 1812 ended, the United States controlled West Florida, Mobile being still occupied by Wilkinson. Realizing the peril to its East Florida territory, Spain had asked for support from the European powers at the Congress of Vienna. Aid was refused, and John Quincy Adams recognized that the time was at hand to pursue Madison's continentalism. In late 1817 he therefore began a protracted negotiation with Don Luis de Onís, the

Spanish Minister to the United States, who was at once placed in a most difficult situation. Don Luis had been instructed, on the one hand, to keep the United States from recognizing the rebellious Spanish colonies in Latin America; on the other, he was to insist on a clear title and definite boundaries for Spanish possessions west of the Mississippi that bordered on the original Louisiana Purchase territory.

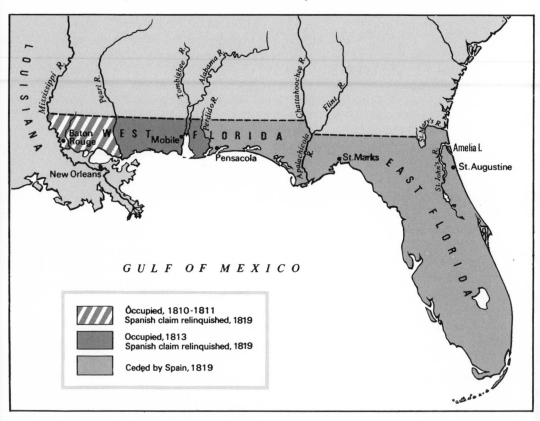

Map 3.   Acquiring Florida, 1810-1819

During the Onís-Adams negotiations, President Monroe ordered General Andrew Jackson, the most popular military hero of the War of 1812, to punish a band of Creek and Seminole Indians who had raided along the frontier. Jackson pursued the band over the border into East Florida, where he not only defeated the Indians but went on to capture Pensacola as well. Earlier he had taken a fort at St. Marks, where he found two British subjects whom he accused of furnishing arms to the Indians. Jackson tried, convicted, and hanged the pair and went on his way. Spain vigorously objected to Jackson's invasion of Spanish territory, while England added strong protests over the execution of British nationals who were not even on American soil. The Monroe administration, with the exception of Adams, wanted to chastise Jackson publicly in spite of the popularity of his move. Adams strongly defended Jackson, insisting that the government back his foray as a necessary measure of self-defense. Monroe agreed, but then Adams—to Jackson's disgust—returned East Florida to Spain and continued negotiations with Onís. As the revolutions in Latin America became more successful, Onís' position became weaker; he was forced to choose between giving up East Florida or losing it anyway, with the added risk that the United States might recognize the rebellious Latin Americans. On February 22, 1819, Onís signed the Transcontinental Treaty, which gave the United States East Florida for the sum of $5 million. In addition, the boundaries dividing Spanish possessions from the Louisiana Purchase territory were settled. The United States relinquished its weak claim to Texas, which in 1819 was occupied by very few Americans, and received a satisfactory northern boundary at the 42° north latitude. In turn, Spain abandoned its equally weak claims to Oregon, leaving only the United States and England to contend for that region, which in any case was covered by the joint occupation pact.

With the Senate's unanimous approval of the treaty, the Americans' long struggle to add the Spanish southeast to their domain appeared to be over, but events in Latin America delayed the exchange of ratification. Spain procrastinated out of fear that the United States would not only recognize the Latin American countries but would assist them militarily as soon as the treaty was confirmed. To forestall this, the Spanish government attempted to make non-recognition a prior condition to ratification. Adams, with the support of Monroe, countered with a threat of hostilities; the Spanish king, having more wars than he could cope with at one time, therefore ratified the treaty. It went into effect in February 1821, exactly two years after it had been signed.

LATIN AMERICA AND THE UNITED STATES

Spain's reluctance to make concessions to the United States without a binding agreement was based upon solid evidence. The rebelling countries worked hard for both recognition and military aid. The United States refused the latter, but as early as January 1819 Adams told the British government that American recognition was imminent for at least one of the former Spanish colonies. He was motivated largely by the need to protect and encourage the growing American trade; but an American commission sent to survey the situation presented a negative report, emphasizing the instability of the new regimes. The American public, led by Henry Clay in Congress, clamored for recognition, but it was to be three years before the act came about.

THE MONROE DOCTRINE

By the early 1820's, Adams had still another world power—Russia—to contend with in his attempts to expand American territory and influence. Beginning in the 1780's, American traders and fur trappers had hunted seals and sea otters in the waters off the northwest coast of America and Alaska. In the fall of 1821 the Czar of Russia issued an edict banning foreign vessels from coming within 100 miles of Russian America, an area extending from 51° north latitude to Alaska. Adams protested vigorously against "the right of Russia to *any* territorial establishment on this continent." This statement was somewhat surprising in view of the fact that Russia had long maintained settlements in Alaska and down the Pacific coast as far south as Fort Ross in northern California.

Most of Adams' belligerence toward Russia had nothing to do with Alaska. In reality, he was concerned about the Czar's participation in the Quadruple Alliance, a pact signed in 1815 by Russia, Austria, Prussia, and England for the purpose of maintaining the status quo in Europe by restraining the formidable French army, which France was not likely to use while she was waiting to enter the pact. France was permitted to join the alliance in 1818, but British interest soon waned and then died altogether. The Czar had also attempted to cement the alliance by a mystical union of the heads of state, but England declined the proposal.

As a matter of fact, Great Britain was wary of the Czar's influence in the alliance and had decided on a course of diplomatic action involving Latin America. When the revolts began, British merchants moved in quickly, bested the weak American competition, and soon monopolized a lucrative market that depended upon Latin American independence. The British Foreign Minister, George Canning, thereupon suggested to the United States Minister to England, Richard Rush, that America join Great Britain in forestalling Russian and Austrian attempts to use the Quadruple Alliance to aid Spain in subduing its colonies. Canning also wanted to preclude the possibility that any other European power might establish an economic hegemony in Latin America.

The Canning-Rush negotiations soon broke down, but when Adams learned of the possibility of a joint statement, he submitted the proposal to Monroe, who laid it before the cabinet for discussion. Monroe consulted Jefferson and Madison, who both agreed that it would be a propitious move for the United States. The cabinet, with the exception of Adams, concurred with their opinion. Adams, however, insisted that the United States issue a statement unilaterally, preferring, as he said, not to "come in as a cock-boat in the wake of the British man-of-war." Monroe reluctantly agreed, and Adams drafted the foreign policy part of the President's annual message to Congress, which was presented on December 2, 1823.

The Monroe Doctrine consisted of two passages within a speech that made three negative foreign policy statements and implied a fourth. The doctrine as a whole rehashed principles that had been stated before, some of them several times. In sum, the provisions were:

1. Non-colonization. No foreign power would be allowed to establish colonies in the Americas.
2. Non-intervention. No foreign power would be allowed to intervene in the internal affairs of American countries.
3. Non-interference. The United States pledged itself to stay out of the internal affairs of European countries.

Implied was the no-transfer principle, which prohibited European nations from transferring holdings in the New World to each other. This principle had been stated by Madison in 1811 with regard to East Florida.

THE MONROE DOCTRINE

From President James Monroe's Annual Message to Congress, December 2, 1823

... the occasion has been judged proper for asserting, as a principle in which the rights and interests of the United States are involved, that the American continents, by the free and independent condition which they have assumed and maintain, are henceforth not to be considered as subjects for future colonization by any European powers. ...

We owe it, therefore, to candor and to the amicable relations existing between the United States and those powers to declare that we should consider any attempt on their part to extend their system to any portion of this hemisphere as dangerous to our peace and safety. ...

Our policy in regard to Europe, which was adopted at an early stage of the wars which have so long agitated that quarter of the globe, nevertheless remains the same, which is, not to interfere in the internal concerns of any of its powers; to consider the government *de facto* as the legitimate government for us; to cultivate friendly relations with it, and to preserve those relations by a frank, firm, and manly policy, meeting in all instances the just claims of every power, submitting to injuries from none. But in regard to those continents [North and South America] circumstances are eminently and conspicuously different. It is impossible that the allied powers should extend their political system to any portion of either continent without endangering our peace and happiness; nor can anyone believe that our southern brethren, if left to themselves, would adopt it of their own accord. It is equally impossible, therefore, that we should behold such interposition in any form with indifference.

The non-intervention and non-colonization statements applied directly to the Quadruple Alliance. However, unknown to Adams and Monroe, Canning had already removed the threat of the French army's being sent to Latin America. In early October 1823, he had concluded a pact with the French representative in London, Prince Jules de Polignac, in which France gave up any intention of armed intervention.

America's assurance to the European nations that she would not meddle in their affairs was not entirely gratuitous. Monroe's immediate reference was to the numerous unofficial American activities that had been undertaken in behalf of the Greeks, who in 1821 were fighting for their independence from Turkey. The problem was complicated by Russian aims in the Balkans, where it appeared that the Turks might prove to be the strongest buffer against them.

LATIN AMERICAN HOPES AND THE MONROE DOCTRINE

More than a year earlier, Monroe and Adams had recognized five of the new Latin American states. Recognition owed as much to the pressure exerted by Henry Clay and other vocal congressmen as it did to the completion of the Transcontinental Treaty. In recognizing the existence of Argentina, Chile, Colombia, Mexico, and Peru, the United States became the first nation to do so, thereby storing up a reserve of good will. When the Monroe Doctrine was first promulgated, several of the new states were mildly enthusiastic about its possibilities. Colombia, Mexico, and Brazil—the latter recognized in 1824—asked for either a treaty of alliance or one of economic and military assistance, or both. The United States responded so evasively, however, that the Monroe Doctrine was interpreted by the Latin Americans as just another expression of American expansionist ambitions. This appeared to be borne out by two unrelated episodes. First, the American ministers appointed to the new republics included such well-known expansionists and proslavery men as Joel Poinsett. Even more damaging, Canning circulated throughout Latin America copies of the Polignac Memorandum, which demonstrated that the British and not the Americans were the real protectors of the infant republics. The result was a suspicion and hostility on the part of the Latin American republics toward the United States that would continue throughout the nineteenth century.

THE CONGRESS OF PANAMA

Late in 1824 the hero of the Andes, Simón Bolívar, called a hemispheric conference to discuss questions of mutual assistance and defense. John Quincy Adams, who had been elected President in 1824, accepted the invitation. His Secretary of State, Henry Clay, supported most of Adams' foreign policies. Clay, being even more commercially minded, envisioned using the conference as a means of encouraging commercial agreements with the new countries that would uphold American maritime traditions and expand American trade. He also spoke vaguely about a "good neighbor" policy.

Adams appointed two delegates, but a minority of Andrew Jackson's supporters in Congress, who objected to the possibility of entangling alliances with the South and Central American republics, effectively delayed making the appropriations for the trip. The result was that both delegates missed the conference, one of them dying on the way. In any case, the conference proved to be a fiasco and was a foretaste of the reluctance of the Latin Americans to cooperate with each other for their mutual benefit.

THE MONROE DOCTRINE AND AMERICAN FOREIGN POLICY

At the time of Monroe's message, and even extending beyond the close of the Civil War, European powers paid little attention to the strictures embodied in the document. Both England and France on several occasions violated the non-colonization principle, and at other times the non-intervention aspect was endangered. Nevertheless, the very fact that the United States had unilaterally issued the Monroe Doctrine represented a diplomatic warning to Europe. It suggested to Europeans that America's ideas of expansion within the Western Hemisphere were unlimited and constituted a force to be reckoned with.

AMERICA'S FIRST HALF-CENTURY

In 1776 the United States had tumultuously ushered in the age of revolutions by identifying its revolutionary spirit with the Declaration of Independence. But half a century later, although the young nation still indulged in the rhetoric of revolution—especially in dealing with the states of Europe—its actions were far different. No longer was the maintenance of independence an issue, as the United States had an assured place among the nations of the world. The more than 10,000,000 Americans were primarily concerned with settling and expanding their own continent, content to allow England to dominate the remainder of the world.

The period after the Louisiana Purchase also coincided with the hesitant beginnings of a native industry, for which the War of 1812 served as a catalyst in spurring the development of textiles and the manufacture of small arms. In addition, the war forced the United States to seek a solution to some of its horrendous transportation and communication problems. Finally, by 1825, the American nationality was firmly established, and the rampant nationalism was to find new outlets for its exuberance in the coming decades. Alexis de Tocqueville, the most perceptive observer to visit America during this period, best summed up the era when he wrote: "The Americans arrived but as yesterday on the territory which they inhabit, and they have already changed the whole order of nature for their own advantage."

Further Reading

A good general survey of the period is *George Dangerfield, *The Awakening of American Nationalism, 1815-1828* (New York, 1965). An earlier work, which is both useful and readable, is his *The Era of Good Feelings* (New York, 1964). For a greater emphasis on diplomacy see Bradford Perkins, *Castlereagh and Adams: England and the United States, 1812-1823* (Berkeley, Calif., 1964).

The acknowledged authority on the Monroe Doctrine, Dexter Perkins, has written four books about it. The most instructive general treatment is *A History of the Monroe Doctrine, rev. ed. (New York, 1955). *Arthur P. Whitaker, *The United States and the Independence of Latin America: 1800-1830* (New York, 1964) traces early United States-Latin American relations.

Two treatments of the African slave trade are the 1896 classic by W. E. B. DuBois, recently reprinted, *The Suppression of the African Slave Trade* (New York, 1969) and Peter Duignan and Clarence Clendenen, *The United States and the African Slave Trade: 1619-1862* (Stanford, Calif., 1963). Also appropriate is W. E. F. Ward, *The Royal Navy and the Slavers* (New York, 1969).

Biographies are helpful for this period. Bemis' volume on Adams, cited at the end of the last chapter, is especially pertinent.

Asterisk denotes paperback edition.

Part II • The Continent Within: Manifest Destiny and Imperialism, 1825-1900

5

Andrew Jackson and the Continental Spirit

On close inspection, Andrew Jackson seems an unlikely candidate to symbolize the aspirations of most Americans of his day. A rags-to-riches lawyer, he owned a large plantation and more than a hundred slaves. Before he became a nationally known hero as the result of his victory at the Battle of New Orleans, Jackson had been a somewhat conservative local judge and a congressman. He effectively used his popularity to build a political party which elected him to the presidency in 1828 and 1832. As President, Jackson engaged in several notable political feuds while hewing to a Southern states' rights position. Paradoxically, he also became the first President since Washington to strengthen the prerogatives of that office by effective use of the veto and the expansion of patronage.

Andrew Jackson also used his considerable influence and popularity in formulating foreign policy. A strong moralist, he told Congress in 1829 that he advocated a foreign policy based upon this premise: "to ask nothing that is not clearly right and to submit to nothing that is wrong." This attitude toward what was "clearly right" justified his attempts to aggrandize land suitable for slavery to the south, to the west, and in the Caribbean. In fact, from the beginning of his administration until well into the 1850's the most severe crises in foreign relations were those brought about by American continentalism.

Jackson had little respect for Europeans or their attitudes, and he especially disliked the British because of his own boyhood experiences during the Revolutionary War. He chose as his secretaries of state men of far less ability than Clay, Adams, or Monroe; most were selected more in the interests of the new Democratic party than for either ability or experience.

THE WEST INDIAN SETTLEMENT

Jackson's first administration had its initial foreign policy success in opening trade with the British West Indies, an unlikely victory considering

Jackson's antipathy to the British. Although John Quincy Adams had earlier seemed close to agreement on reopening the trade, he failed ultimately because he attempted to force British acquiescence by resorting to discriminatory legislation, in much the same way as had Jefferson and Madison before the War of 1812. The British response was to suspend the trade altogether. Although the British West Indies had lost their economic importance for the United States, owing to two generations of restricted trade, they still represented a lucrative attraction for New Englanders.

During the presidential election of 1828 Jackson's supporters made much of the issue; after the election he moved rapidly to settle the long-standing problem. The Reciprocity Treaty of 1830 provided for trade on an equal basis for all countries. It represented a compromise between what maritime interests hoped for — free trade — and what England was ready to concede at the time.

ANDREW JACKSON, DANIEL WEBSTER, AND HENRY CLAY

ANDREW JACKSON AND THE FRENCH

Jackson displayed more prejudice than diplomacy toward France in his efforts to collect the spoliation claims dating from the Napoleonic era. He was more successful in handling the claims on other countries — for example, the Two Sicilies, Russia, Denmark, and Portugal. When collection became difficult, the President appointed executive agents as negotiators and judiciously used the navy to back them. In this way, all claims were settled except those owed by France. The French king had approved payment of the bill for $9 million, but the National Assembly refused to appropriate the money. In a belligerent speech to Congress in 1834, Jackson threatened retaliation, and both sides broke off diplomatic relations. Despite lively public interest in the matter, Congress was unwilling to take further action. In any case, the French assembly voted the money in its next session and diplomatic relations were quickly resumed.

ANDREW JACKSON AND AMERICAN EXPANSION

Andrew Jackson aggressively pursued American continental expansion, particularly the acquisition of Texas. Failing to establish American claims to Texas in the Transcontinental Treaty, Adams had already tried unsuccessfully to obtain the territory by negotiation and purchase. Jackson now reopened the matter by appointing a friend, Colonel Anthony Butler, as United States Minister to Mexico. During his incumbency from 1829 to 1836, Butler did not hesitate to use bribery, deception, threats, and attempts to foment revolution in a vain effort to acquire Texas. He was authorized to offer up to $5 million for the territory, but his only success was in stirring up the hostility of successive Mexican governments.

Meanwhile, American settlers had begun to pour into the sparsely settled province. Mexico had made Texas a district of the state of Coahuila after winning independence from Spain in 1821. Mexican immigration laws were liberal and land was but a few cents an acre, as compared to $1.25 an acre in the United States. In the late 1820's the surge to the Mexican territory was so great that so-called "Texas fever" swept the lower South. Ironically, American settlers were required to become Catholics and Mexican citizens — at a time when the United States was anti-Catholic and nativistic. In 1830, when Mexico slammed the door on immigration, there were about 8,000 Americans in Texas. During the next four years the American settlers organized secret committees to fight for self-government. They were able to exert enough pressure on the Mexican government to get the ban on immigration lifted. Thereafter, Americans poured in by the thousands; by 1835, when the Texas revolt began, there were about 30,000 Americans in Texas as compared with only 3,000 Mexicans.

The war for Texan independence was replete with massacres of the Texans at Goliad and the Alamo. But the smashing victory over the Mexicans at San Jacinto gained for Texas a *de facto* independence, which, however, could not have been won without massive unofficial American aid. Men, arms, money, and other necessities were enthusiastically supplied to the fledgling republic, mostly from the South, although some aid came from as far away as New York and Pennsylvania. The Texan leader Sam Houston had been Jackson's protégé in Tennessee, where he had risen to the governorship; he resigned abruptly to build a new career in Texas. Mexico protested the unneutral actions of the United States, but to no avail. By the winter of 1836 Andrew Jackson appeared near his goal of acquiring Texas.

However, 1836 was also an election year, and Jackson had determined to hand over the presidency to Vice-President Martin Van Buren of New York. Fearful lest Northern antislavery sentiment should militate against Van Buren, Jackson refused to make any overt move to annex Texas or even to recognize its independence. After Van Buren was elected, the United States recognized Texas on March 3, 1837, but the President declined to ask Congress for annexation because of the political opposition. When the Panic of 1837 burst, the Texas question was shelved; Texas withdrew its request for annexation and for the next five years took the perilous course of nationhood.

Jackson did not confine his continentalism solely to the acquisition of Texas. In 1835 Butler was instructed to offer the Mexican government $0.5 million for the region including San Francisco Bay and northern California. When the Mexican government refused, Jackson raised the offer to $3.5 million. At the same time, he was secretly urging independent Texas to extend its borders westward to include California! The matter was officially dropped until 1842, but Americans were cognizant of the possibilities of the area because Lieutenant Charles Wilkes, on his voyage around the world, had described San Francisco Bay as "the best harbor in the world."

PROBLEMS WITH ENGLAND

Martin Van Buren, Jackson's hand-picked successor, fell heir to the problems of another popular revolution. In Canada, in 1837, an insurrection erupted against the ruling interests in Upper Canada — the Family Compact. Simultaneously, though not coordinated with it, another insurrection broke out against the governing body in Lower Canada — the Château Clique. The rebels fared badly. Van Buren proclaimed neutrality, but did little to enforce it; men and war materials were gathered at Buffalo, New York, destined to aid the Canadian rebels. The strong anti-British sentiments of the Irish immigrants, who were arriving in the United States in large numbers, exacerbated the situation. One group hired the steamboat *Caroline* to ferry supplies to Canada. The Canadian army in a daring raid captured and burned the *Caroline* while it was docked on the New York side of the border, killing one American in the process. This inflamed the already hostile feelings along the border, especially when the British government declined to act on the complaint. Even before hearing from Britain, Van Buren issued a strongly worded statement of neutrality and sent General Winfield Scott to take charge of the troubled area, where he acted with firmness and authority to restore order.

THE BURNING OF THE *CAROLINE* IN THE NIAGARA RIVER, 1837

One of the greatest difficulties facing General Scott was the precipitous rise in extremist societies, which kept the border inflamed for the next three years. The largest of these groups was the Hunters and Chasers of the Eastern Frontier, called Hunters' Lodges, whose membership of avowedly anti-British partisans reached over 100,000. It was a secret paramilitary society that undertook hit-and-run guerrilla raids across the border, most of which were unsuccessful. After a major defeat at the Battle of the Windmill, its importance declined. Many of the Americans captured in this battle were deported by the British to a penal colony in Tasmania, halfway around the world. The repatriation of these errant Americans spanned more than a decade, remaining a footnote in American diplomacy for some time to come.

ALEXANDER McLEOD AND THE AROOSTOOK WAR

Though the frontier had become relatively quiet, an incident soon occurred which threatened to become the most explosive yet. In November 1840, New York authorities arrested a Canadian, Alexander McLeod, a locally known and highly unpopular deputy sheriff, on the charge of arson and murder in connection with the *Caroline* incident. The British minister in Washington protested strongly, but Van Buren was helpless, the episode having occurred within the jurisdiction of the state of New York. The case dragged through the courts for two years, during which time John Tyler became President and Daniel Webster Secretary of State. Although public opinion on both sides of the Atlantic was aroused, Governor William

Seward of New York privately assured Tyler and Webster that if McLeod were convicted, he would be pardoned. McLeod was acquitted, but the ramifications of the case caused Congress to pass legislation that gave jurisdiction in similar cases in the future to Federal courts. The matter of blame and reparations in the *Caroline* incident now moved to the bargaining table to be treated in the Webster-Ashburton negotiations in 1842.

While Van Buren was occupied with the McLeod affair, he was faced with still another border explosion hundreds of miles from New York. The boundaries of a fertile timber and farming area between Maine and New Brunswick had been in dispute ever since the Treaty of 1783, which had failed to clarify the question. Both Maine and New Brunswick wanted the valuable timber stands and the farmlands. In addition, the Canadian province needed a clear title to the region in order to build an all-weather road and, later, a railroad linking Halifax with Quebec via St. John. In 1827 the king of the Netherlands had been appointed arbitrator; four years later, he awarded each contestant half of the nearly 1,200 squares miles. But Maine balked and persuaded the Senate to reject the decision. Matters dragged on until 1838, when the Canadians wanted to build the road. Late that year, Canadian lumberjacks began cutting timber along the Aroostook River in the heart of the disputed area. A band of Maine lumberjacks tried and failed to drive out the Canadians. Each side threatened war and called up the militia. At this point, Van Buren dispatched General Winfield Scott to the disaffected region, and Scott speedily negotiated a truce in the Aroostook — or Lumberjack — War, the war that never was.

DANIEL WEBSTER, LORD ASHBURTON, AND AMERICAN DIPLOMACY

Both Daniel Webster, a business- and maritime-oriented New England Whig, and the British foreign minister had much more to gain from negotiating outstanding differences than from resorting to war. Judging from contemporary newspaper and journal evidence, war seemed possible. The British government appointed a special emissary to deal with the wide range of Anglo-American problems. Alexander Baring, now Lord Ashburton, who had banking interests in the United States and whose wife was American, could expect a sympathetic reception from the American government. Baring had served in the House of Commons, where for three decades he was an indefatigable spokesman for commercial and banking interests. His wife's father, a prominent Federalist, had paved the way for Baring's banking association with prominent American mercantile companies. The mutual admiration for each other shared by Webster and

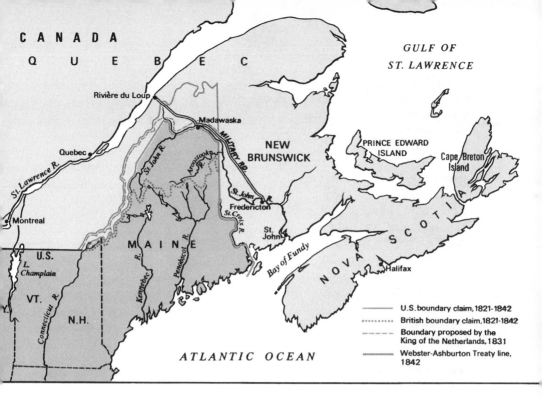

Map 4. The Maine Boundary Settlement, 1842

Legend:
- ———— U.S. boundary claim, 1821-1842
- ·········· British boundary claim, 1821-1842
- — — — Boundary proposed by the King of the Netherlands, 1831
- ═══════ Webster-Ashburton Treaty line, 1842

Baring boded well for an amicable settlement of some of the problems between their countries.

The Webster-Ashburton negotiations covered a broad range of topics and did indeed settle several of the outstanding difficulties. Agreement was generally arrived at by compromise. The most pressing problem was the Maine boundary dispute. To clear the way for a settlement, Webster coerced both Maine and Massachusetts into accepting whatever accord might be reached. Then, in an *opéra bouffe* episode, Webster turned to doctored maps that seemed to prove that the boundary included far less of Maine than had been supposed. On this basis he made a great show of settling for five twelfths of the disputed territory. Canada thereby got its road and the unremitting enmity of Maine. Long afterward, a historian found in the Spanish Archives in Madrid a copy of Benjamin Franklin's original map, with the boundaries drawn in red. It showed, as Lord Ashburton suspected, that the United States should have had *all* the disputed territory.

In the course of the negotiations, Ashburton made what he considered to be two slight concessions. One gave the United States a small bit of disputed land at the northern end of Lake Champlain; the other defined the boundary running west from Lake Superior to the Lake of the Woods. This gave the United States the immensely rich iron-ore fields of northern Minnesota, which were only later discovered.

A second treaty, signed on the same day as the one incorporating the boundary agreements, provided in one part for an extradition treaty with Canada. It called for the mutual surrender of fugitive criminals between the two countries; never again would the expression "gone to Canada" be applicable to escaped felons.

The other part of the treaty concerned the suppression of the African slave trade. Under its terms the United States agreed to keep a naval force in African waters to cooperate with the British navy in suppressing the rising slave trade. The agreement stated that a "sufficient and adequate squadron of naval forces" was to be maintained, but from the outset the United States either evaded the issue or only minimally met its requirements. In 1843 two thirty-gun ships were sent; the average over a fourteen-year period was a squadron of less than five, with a maximum of seven ships employed at any one time. The British, on the other hand, averaged twenty ships on patrol and never maintained less than twelve during the same period.

Ashburton pressed for the right of search, but Webster, as had Adams, refused. The issue was complicated by Webster's efforts to obtain compensation for the owners in the *Creole* case. The *Creole*, a slave ship, had loaded a cargo of 135 slaves in Virginia for the New Orleans slave market. At sea the slaves seized the ship, killing one man and forcing the crew to sail the vessel to the British port of Nassau in the Bahamas. In 1833 the British had emancipated all slaves in the empire and thereafter continued to wage an aggressive, if unsuccessful, battle against illicit slave traders. Thus, when the *Creole* touched British soil, the slaves were automatically declared free, with the exception of those responsible for killing the crew member. Webster did not receive any compensation for the value of the human cargo of the *Creole,* but Ashburton, for his part, was forced to yield to the liberal American maritime principles which had seemed so important to the United States since 1776. However, the nefarious slave trade not only continued but increased during the 1840's, due to the slave traders' use of the American flag as a shield and to the United States' lack of enforcement of the provisions of the Webster-Ashburton treaty. In his old age, John Quincy Adams wrote bitterly of his "shame for the honour and good name of my country whose government [has made] a false and treacherous pretense of cooperating with Great Britain for the suppression of one of the forms of this execrable system of slavery."

MARITIME EXPANSION AND THE JACKSONIANS

American maritime rights together with the search for new markets were vigorously prosecuted by Andrew Jackson and his contemporaries.

American traders were to be found throughout the world, and Americans possessed the largest whaling fleet in existence. To protect these interests the United States sometimes resorted to gunboat diplomacy, especially in the Pacific. When in 1831, for instance, a Sumatran village captured an American merchant ship, Jackson quickly sent a naval vessel to exact retribution from the guilty village. The presence of American warships often exerted a powerful influence over native chiefs, and naval officers found themselves acting as diplomatic agents in protecting and enlarging United States commercial interests in the Pacific area.

In the 1830's a major surveying and exploring expedition was mounted. The United States Exploring Expedition — or the Wilkes Expedition — (1838-1842) had avowedly commercial goals. Its commander, Charles Wilkes, in common with most ranking naval officers of the period, was not only alert to commercial expansion and possible territorial gain but was actively engaged in diplomacy. He conducted commercial negotiations with the rulers of various Pacific countries; he also appointed acting consular officials, all of whom were later approved.

Andrew Jackson, during his first term, appointed Edmund Roberts as special agent to conclude favorable commercial treaties with Asian countries. Roberts, a New Hampshire merchant experienced in trading in the Far East, only succeeded in signing most-favored-nation treaties with Siam and Muscat. Jackson sent him back in 1835 to negotiate similar treaties with Japan, but Roberts died en route and Japan remained isolated from Western civilization for another two decades.

China, the most important Asian market, all but eluded Americans during the 1830's. Roberts had failed to negotiate a treaty with China because the Chinese government refused to recognize American consuls as representing American merchants. Thus, Yankee trading in China remained an individual and risky, though profitable, business. By the end of the decade Americans were obtaining cargoes of silk, porcelain, and tea in exchange for more and more of the illegal opium. Continued American mercantile pressure caused President John Tyler in 1843 to appoint Caleb Cushing, a New England Whig lawyer and congressman, as a special commissioner to China. Cushing, who spoke Chinese and appreciated Chinese culture, arrived near Macao in time to reap full advantage of the Opium War (1839-1842). The victorious British had gained from the Chinese full diplomatic recognition, acceptance of the importation of opium, and a most-favored-nation status. Cushing, using diplomacy laced with the threat of his four-vessel flotilla, speedily concluded a comparable pact, the Treaty of Wanghia, in 1844. In addition to the privileges obtained by the British, the treaty allowed a considerably broader extraterritoriality in civil as well as in criminal cases. The Treaty of Wanghia, unanimously approved by the Senate, marked the entrance of the United States government into Asian affairs.

THE REORGANIZATION OF THE STATE DEPARTMENT

The importance of the burgeoning Pacific trade, coupled with American continental aspirations, necessitated the first thorough reorganization of the State Department since its inception in 1789. Seven bureaus were set up, the two most pertinent being the Diplomatic Bureau and the Consular Bureau. The former handled all correspondence and records for the nineteen American diplomats abroad. The Consular Bureau, in addition to taking charge of the consular service and being responsible for handling the day-to-day business of Americans and American interests abroad, received salaries based upon fees collected from Americans transacting business in foreign countries. The result was that although the size of the service had increased from 16 consular agents in Washington's time to 152 by 1833, its representation of American interests was only poor to mediocre. The record is replete with instances of knavery and skulduggery as well as of dishonesty and indifference.

To cite just one example, when Great Britain annexed New Zealand in 1840, the British government immediately issued discriminatory laws aimed at freezing out extensive American interests there. The American consul, an Englishman, did not bother to notify the State Department of the changes for a full eighteen months, and for much of that time he was off speculating successfully in New Zealand land! It was not until 1855 that Congress limited consular service to American citizens.

THE REFORM SPIRIT AND AMERICAN FOREIGN POLICY

Coincident with Jackson's presidency and the expansion of universal white manhood suffrage, a spirit of reform, reflecting the strong American individualism of the era, began to manifest itself. Ralph Waldo Emerson, Henry David Thoreau, and others gave literary and ideological substance to the perfection of the individual. Nowhere was this spirit better shown than in the crusade for world peace. Such an ephemeral goal did not seem out of keeping with the ebullient, optimistic spirit of the age. Indeed, in 1840 William Ladd appeared to point a way to lasting peace with the publication of his *Essay on the Congress of Nations,* though it was to have greater influence three quarters of a century later. Nevertheless, he and the Reverend Elihu Burritt were the driving force behind the American Peace Society, which had wide backing even among government leaders. The Mexican War considerably dampened the peace advocates, but reformers were vocal enough to engage in a bitter and fruitless public debate as to its necessity.

AMERICAN INDIVIDUALISM, 1841

From Ralph Waldo Emerson, "Self-Reliance"

Whoso would be a man, must be a nonconformist. He who would gather immortal palms must not be hindered by the name of goodness, but must explore if it be goodness. Nothing is at last sacred but the integrity of your own mind. Absolve you to yourself, and you shall have the suffrage of the world. . . .

What I must do is all that concerns me, not what the people think. This rule, equally arduous in actual and in intellectual life, may serve for the whole distinction between greatness and meanness. It is the harder, because you will always find those who think they know what is your duty better than you know it. It is easy in the world to live after the world's opinion; it is easy in solitude to live after our own; but the great man is he who in the midst of the crowd keeps with perfect sweetness the independence of solitude.

A second reform attempt with consequences for American foreign policy was the antislavery crusade. Literally hundreds of organizations devoted to ending slavery became effective lobbyists at the state level. But though they were led by such eloquent spokesmen in Congress as John Quincy Adams and Joshua R. Giddings, the antislavery forces were less successful at the national level because of Southern domination of the government, including the navy. Such spectacular affairs as the *Creole* and *Amistad* cases kept alive and vociferous the demand for ending the slave trade. The latter case involved a slave mutiny on the Cuban schooner *Amistad* in 1839. Spanish-owned slaves captured the *Amistad* but were eventually apprehended by an American warship off New England and brought to New London, Connecticut. There the court took custody and a long legal battle ensued, culminating in a Supreme Court decision in 1841 that all but one of the slaves were to be freed and returned to Africa. Spain continued to demand recompense for the human cargo, and until the eve of the Civil War various presidents recommended payment, but Congress refused to appropriate the money.

THE MISSIONARIES AND AMERICAN FOREIGN POLICY

Another aspect of American individualism was the attempt to propagate fundamentalist Christian teachings throughout the world. By the 1830's and

1840's. American missionaries representing several Protestant denominations were active in China, India, the Middle East, and the Pacific islands. Their need for protection and the nature of their work raised the question as to whether they retained American citizenship when they lived and worked in a foreign country. The issue was not decided until 1842, when Daniel Webster took his cue from British practice. Webster, himself a director of one of the larger missionary societies, directed an American diplomatic official abroad "to extend to them [missionaries] all proper succor and attentions, of which they may stand in need, and in the same manner that you would to other citizens of the United States." Thereafter, gunboat diplomacy had ample occasion to aid the missionary as well as the merchant.

Andrew Jackson died in 1844; he did not live to see his continentalism become a reality. But he had helped expand American commercial enterprise throughout the Pacific to Asia. He kept inviolate American maritime rights, and he vigorously began the work of American territorial expansion that was to bear fruit but a few years after his death.

Further Reading

A competent survey of the period extending through the Mexican War is *Glyndon Van Deusen, *The Jacksonian Era: 1828-1848* (New York, 1960). The diplomatic aspects are stressed in *William H. Goetzmann, *When the Eagle Screamed: The Romantic Horizon in American Diplomacy, 1800-1860* (New York, 1966).

Men of this age — with the exception of Andrew Jackson — have generally fared well at the hands of biographers. Robert V. Remini's biography of Jackson is the most satisfactory. James K. Polk has been well treated in the excellent two-volume biography by Charles Sellers. The life of John Quincy Adams has been completed magnificently by Samuel F. Bemis in *John Quincy Adams and the Union* (New York, 1949). There are also good paperbound biographies available of Henry Clay, Daniel Webster and John C. Calhoun.

The diplomacy of the period as it relates to China is found in *Maurice Collis, *Foreign Mud* (New York, 1968) and *John K. Fairbank, *Trade and Diplomacy on the China Coast: The Opening of the Treaty Ports, 1842-1854* (Stanford, Calif., 1969). For American diplomacy in Hawaii and the south Pacific, see W. Patrick Strauss, *Americans in Polynesia, 1784-1842* (East Lansing, Mich., 1963).

Asterisk denotes paperback edition.

6

The Diplomacy of Manifest Destiny

The period following Martin Van Buren's presidency was marked by a rapidly accelerating change in the number of Americans and in their way of life. Immigrants from Ireland and northern Europe poured into the United States; between 1840 and 1850 alone, over 370,000 arrived. The total population increased by nearly half during the decade, by 1850 reaching 23,000,000 people. At the same time, the nation made giant industrial strides because for the first time the domestic market was profitably enlarged. Basic problems in transportation and communication were overcome, which in turn helped to produce new markets. The cost of transporting goods by both water and rail dropped precipitously in the early 1850's. The communication revolution resulted from Samuel F. B. Morse's invention of the telegraph in 1844, which began the age of instantaneous communication. Other fundamental inventions — the sewing machine, the mechanical harvester, and the Hoe rotary press — paved the way for the large-scale business and farming enterprises beginning in the 1850's.

Essentially, however, the United States was still very much a rural country, depending upon farming and maritime activity for its prosperity. Three quarters of its total exports were farm products, and of all exports, half went to Great Britain. In the 1840's and 1850's cotton was by far the single most important item of export. This helps explain why Southern hegemony over the national government continued long after the population disparity between the North and South had increased markedly.

THE LAST JACKSONIAN

The presidential election of 1844 firmly committed Jackson's Democratic party to the pursuit of continentalism. The Democratic candidate was James K. Polk, Governor of Tennessee, former Speaker of the House of Representatives, and a long-time protégé of Andrew Jackson. The old general lived long enough to see Polk narrowly defeat the Whig candidate, Henry Clay. Clay had taken an equivocal stand regarding expansion, but the limitation of slavery was also an important factor. Polk's campaign featured such ringing slogans as "Reannexation of Texas and the reoccupation of Oregon" and, with reference to Oregon, "fifty-four forty or fight." Polk also unabashedly pledged himself to acquire California.

THE ANNEXATION OF TEXAS

Prior to the election of 1844, President John Tyler had hoped to revive his own popularity and at the same time help the Whig party by annexing Texas. A treaty was again submitted to the Senate, although by this time Sam Houston was reluctant, Texas having too often been a bride left waiting at the altar. Once again the effort proved abortive, but after the election Tyler determined to have his way. He resubmitted the annexation treaty for approval by a joint resolution of the lame duck Congress, because it would then need only a majority to pass. Congress narrowly approved the resolution, voting by party rather than by section. The Democrats unanimously supported the measure, while Tyler's own Whig party voted almost solidly against it. Tyler signed the resolution shortly before leaving office. Mexico vigorously protested the action and, supported by Britain and France, offered to recognize an independent Texan republic.

A specially elected Texan convention met to consider the alternatives. The convention voted to join the United States, ratified the decision, and adopted a constitution allowing slavery. President Polk signed the final papers in December 1845, admitting Texas, its border problems unresolved, as the twenty-eighth state.

MANIFEST DESTINY, 1845

Texas is now ours. Already, before these words are written, her Convention has undoubtedly ratified the acceptance, by her Congress, of our proffered invitation into the Union; and made the requisite changes in her already republican form of constitution to adopt it to its future federal relations. Her star and her stripe may already be said to have taken their place in the glorious blazon of our common nationality; and the sweep of our eagle's wing already includes within its circuit the wide extent of her fair and fertile land. . . .

. . . it [reason for annexing Texas] surely is to be found . . . in the manner in which other nations have undertaken to intrude themselves into it, between us and the proper parties to the case, in a spirit of hostile interference against us, for the avowed object of thwarting our policy and hampering our power, limiting our greatness and checking the fulfillment of our manifest destiny to overspread the continent allotted by Providence for the free development of our yearly multiplying millions. . . .

California will, probably, next fall away from the loose adhesion which, in such a country as Mexico, holds a remote province in a slight equivocal kind of dependence on the metropolis. . . . Its necessity [a transcontinental railroad] for this very purpose of binding and holding together in its iron clasp our fast settling Pacific region with that of the Mississippi valley — the natural facility of the route — the ease with which any amount of labor for the construction can be drawn from the overcrowded populations of Europe, to be paid in the lands made valuable by the progress of the work itself — and its immense utility to the commerce of the world with the whole eastern coast of Asia, alone almost sufficient for the support of such a road — these considerations give assurance that the day cannot be distant which shall witness the conveyance of the representatives from Oregon and California to Washington within less time than a few years ago was devoted to a similar journey by those from Ohio; while the magnetic telegraph will enable the editors of the "San Francisco Union," the "Astoria Evening Post," or the "Nootka Morning News" to set up in type the first half of the President's Inaugural, before the echoes of the latter half shall have died away beneath the lofty porch of the Capitol, as spoken from his lips.

THE ACQUISITION OF OREGON

The Webster-Ashburton negotiations had failed to reach accord regarding the Oregon territory. In 1827 the joint occupation was renewed for an indefinite period, and neither side showed an inclination to settle until the 1840's. By that time, Americans wanted a good harbor in the Northwest, but the best alternative, the Columbia River, seemed worthless after Charles Wilkes reported that there was a sandbar across its mouth. Other possibilities farther north were the entrance to Puget Sound or Vancouver Island. But the British wanted to safeguard their profitable investment in the Hudson's Bay Company, with its monopoly on the fur trade. Its headquarters, Fort Vancouver, was located on the north bank of the Columbia River. The company's territorial authority extended to the northern limit of Oregon at 54°40′ and, to the south, almost to the 42° line marking the northern boundary of Mexico's California possessions.

Until about 1840 the sovereignty of the Hudson's Bay Company went virtually unchallenged, there being but a few hundred Americans in the entire territory, most of whom had some working relation with the company. But Oregon had become the focus of nearly a decade of publicity in the East, some of which was quite lurid, and the aftereffects of the Panic of 1837 made the territory seem more attractive as an economic opportunity. Beginning in the early 1840's, "Oregon fever" caused a steady stream of Americans to trek westward along the Oregon Trail. By the time Polk was elected there were 2,000 Americans in Oregon and more were arriving daily. Almost everyone settled in the Willamette Valley along the Willamette River, south of present-day Portland.

The British government, alarmed by the growing number of American settlers, attempted to reach an agreement concerning the fate of the territory. The American government refused, playing a waiting game in the hope of obtaining more. President Polk was soon aggressively telling Congress that the United States ought to have the entire territory; to this end, he asked for authority to give the one-year notice before abrogating the joint occupation pact. Congress debated the request for four months, during which time the concept of manifest destiny was the paramount theme. To expansionists of the Democratic party, manifest destiny was interpreted as the god-given right of the United States to expand American civilization throughout the continent, the end justifying almost any means.

In his original message of December 1845, Polk told Congress that the American title to the entire Oregon territory was buttressed by "irrefragable facts and arguments." In April he received Congressional approval to end the joint occupation, and he promptly so informed the British.

"WHAT? YOU YOUNG YANKEE-NOODLE, STRIKE YOUR OWN FATHER!"

This British cartoon views a young and restive America pressing its claims to the Oregon territory.

The British Foreign Minister, Lord Aberdeen, was not averse to settling for a 49° boundary, in spite of his country's stronger claims to the territory, except that such a settlement would cut off the southern tip of Vancouver Island and deprive the British of the entrance to Puget Sound. He resolved the problem by proposing to the President that the boundary be set at the 49° line as far as Vancouver Island, then moved south around its tip, which would thus neatly bisect the entrance to Puget Sound. This solution fell far short of Polk's announced requirements, but it did give the United States the possibility of many harbors in Puget Sound. The Mexican War had begun, and Polk took the unusual step of submitting the treaty to the Senate for advice before he signed it. This step served to commit the Senate while relieving the President of his all-or-nothing commitment. The senators advised approval, Polk signed the treaty, and the Senate consented to it, 41 to 14, without changes.

An interesting diplomatic footnote to the treaty was that both sides disagreed as to the exact point in the Sound where the line swung south around Vancouver Island. At stake were the small San Juan Islands, strategically important to the protection of Vancouver Island. The problem dragged on through two international arbitration attempts to reconcile the parties. A permanent solution was not achieved until 1872, when the disputed islands were finally awarded to the United States.

MEXICO AND ITS INTERNAL PROBLEMS

While Southern expansionists like Jefferson Davis campaigned for the annexation of Oregon on the basis of manifest destiny, their focus remained on Texas and other lands and islands to the south and west. Their immediate objective, the annexation of Texas, was realized, but their victory was incomplete because Texas, instead of being divided into several slave states, entered the Union as only one.

As the result of the annexation of Texas, the Mexican government withdrew its minister and broke off diplomatic relations with the United States. This was not serious since the Mexican government suffered from chronic instability. Political fluctuation led to rapid changes of regime, and a measure of equilibrium was not restored until 1867. Short-lived governments led to bureaucratic inefficiency and a consequent dearth of dependable civil servants. A deep hatred of the United States pervaded the whole of the Mexican body politic, further contributing to the pattern of instability. For example, in 1839 one Mexican government agreed to indemnify American claims of over $2 million in twenty installments; but after the third installment was paid, a succeeding regime defaulted on the remainder.

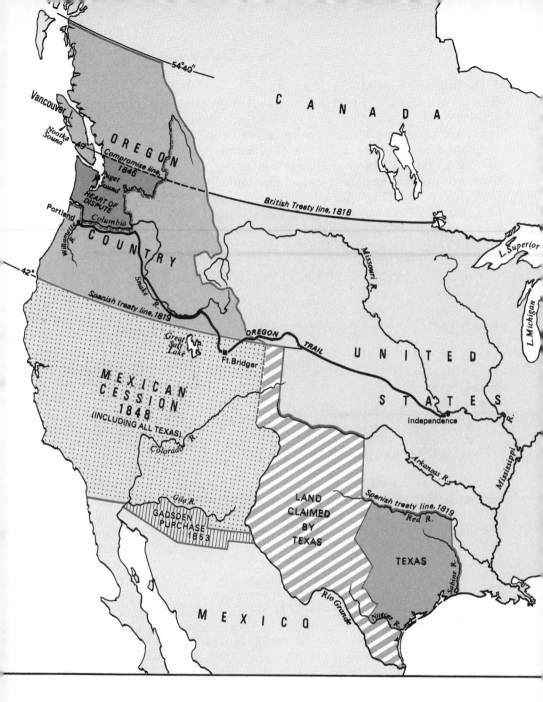

Map 5.   Acquiring Oregon and the Mexican Territory, 1846-1853

THE CALIFORNIA STORY

President Polk tried to take advantage of Mexico's governmental weaknesses by offering to cancel the debt as bait for acquiring California. In addition, Polk appointed Thomas O. Larkin, American consul and Monterey merchant, as a secret agent in California. Larkin was instructed to foment revolution among the few Americans living in the sparsely populated territory. To aid in the scheme, an American fleet cruised close to the California coastline. In fact, three years earlier, in 1842, an overanxious fleet commander, Captain Thomas Ap Catesby Jones, had captured Monterey and raised the American flag in the mistaken belief that war with Mexico had been declared! Although speedily rectified, this episode did not enhance American relations with the government or the people of Mexico.

The British also showed a lively interest in California and promoted the same type of activity as Larkin's. The United States, however, made the first overt move. Captain John C. Frémont, a colorful soldier-explorer *cum* adventurer, heading a small, well-disciplined band, conducted a topographical survey of California in 1845 over the protests of local Mexican officials. When war came the next year, the combination of the American fleet, Frémont, and an army under General Stephen W. Kearny, which had marched overland from Santa Fe to southern California, effectively crushed the feeble Mexican resistance. By early 1847, nearly a year before the end of the Mexican War, California was already an American possession.

THE BEGINNING OF THE MEXICAN WAR

James K. Polk's manifest destiny, which resolutely included California, had already resulted in the acquisition of Oregon and Texas. At first, the President contemplated the possibility of buying California rather than resorting to war with Mexico. To that end, he sent two special agents to reestablish diplomatic relations with Mexico and then to offer to purchase California for as much as $30 million, plus the assumption of the debt owed Americans. The second agent, a Louisiana expansionist named John Slidell, stayed on in Mexico through a change of regime in the winter of 1845-1846. However, the new government found it just as inexpedient to receive him, and he returned to Washington. Slidell's mission having failed, Polk ordered General Zachary Taylor to march south of the Nueces River. Historically, the Nueces had long been considered the southern boundary of Texas, but the Texans themselves claimed over a hundred miles beyond to the banks of the Rio Grande. The Mexican government regarded Taylor's act as an invasion of Mexican soil; it therefore sent a large army across the Rio

Grande toward the Nueces, where contact with Taylor was but a matter of time. On April 23, 1846, Mexico proclaimed a defensive war; two days later, a sharp clash between the two forces began the shooting phase of the conflict. President Polk had chosen the alternative of open hostilities after Slidell's return; he now asked Congress to declare war.

PRESIDENT JAMES K. POLK'S WAR MESSAGE TO CONGRESS, 1846

The cup of forbearance had been exhausted even before the recent information from the frontier of the Del Norte [Rio Grande]. But now, after reiterated menaces, Mexico has passed the boundary of the United States, has invaded our territory and shed American blood upon the American soil. She has proclaimed that hostilities have commenced, and that the two nations are now at war.

As war exists, and, notwithstanding all our efforts to avoid it, exists by the act of Mexico herself, we are called upon by every consideration of duty and patriotism to vindicate with decision the honor, the rights, and the interests of our country. . . .

In further vindication of our rights and defense of our territory, I invoke the prompt action of Congress to recognize the existence of the war, and to place at the disposition of the Executive the means of prosecuting the war with vigor, and thus hastening the restoration of peace.

"MR. POLK'S WAR"

Derisively called "Mr. Polk's War" by the Northern Whig press, the conflict was as unpopular with a sizable minority at home as it was successful on the fighting front. Antislavery forces cutting across party lines were able to mobilize a respectable segment of public opinion against the war by calling it a Southern slaveholding conspiracy. The Whigs, looking toward the election of 1848, likewise used the war as a political issue. A first-term Whig congressman from Illinois, Abraham Lincoln, repeatedly rose in the House to introduce his "spot resolution," which called upon the administration to identify the exact spot where the first shooting occurred. His purpose — to embarrass Polk's supporters — was easily thwarted. Lincoln himself was defeated for reelection in 1848.

Much of the opposition's anti-Polk ammunition could be traced to the rising American literati, who vigorously protested the war. Ralph Waldo

Emerson, James Russell Lowell, John Greenleaf Whittier, and many others effectively wielded their pens as cudgels. Henry David Thoreau was so incensed that he refused to pay a tax, on the grounds that he would not help support a corrupt government. His classic "Essay on Civil Disobedience" is a reasoned, radical statement of a citizen's moral duty to protest overtly an unrighteous act of the government.

Polk meanwhile found himself with an escalating war on his hands. He had secretly helped a former dictator, Santa Anna, who had been exiled to Cuba, to return to Mexico. In exchange, Santa Anna promised that when he regained power he would sell California to the United States. But, once having seized control again in May 1846, he vigorously prosecuted the lagging war.

THE MEXICAN WAR

The United States' military prowess in the war was little short of incredible, at least to the British and French military observers. The American army was commanded by two excellent Whig generals, Zachary Taylor and Winfield Scott. The army clearly reflected the value of West Point training in the ability shown by its junior officers. General "Rough

SCOTT'S ENTRANCE INTO MEXICO CITY

and Ready" Taylor struck across the Rio Grande, fighting his way south to Monterey. General "Old Fuss and Feathers" Scott launched an amphibious attack on Vera Cruz, landed his army, and fought his way to Mexico City. Together with General Kearny, whose army held California, the three armies had by September 1847 militarily overwhelmed the Mexican forces.

PRESIDENT POLK AND NICHOLAS P. TRIST

In early 1847 President Polk began to think of making peace with Mexico. In mid-April he appoined a chief clerk in the State Department, Nicholas P. Trist, as his executive agent with extensive authority. Trist was chosen partly because of his excellent political and social qualifications, which included having served as a secretary to Andrew Jackson and being married to Jefferson's granddaughter. In addition, he spoke fluent Spanish, having served as a consul in Cuba, where he distinguished himself by his zeal in issuing certificates of American nationality to slave traders, thus enabling them to sail with impunity under the American flag.

Trist was also known for his letter-writing proclivity, pronounced even in an age of letter writing. Having joined Scott, with instructions to conclude a favorable peace at an opportune moment, he proceeded to send the General, with whom he had quarreled, a thirty-page epistle. He followed this with a sixty-five-page missive to Polk, explaining why he had disobeyed instructions in acceding to an armistice in August. The President summarily recalled Trist, but Trist refused to obey, writing another long letter to explain why. In brief, he contended that he had established cordial relations with General Scott and was now in a position to negotiate a treaty with the more moderate government that had succeeded Santa Anna's. Trist pointed out that his treaty could always be disavowed "should it be deemed disadvantageous to our country." He then compounded his refusal to leave by negotiating with the Mexicans throughout the month of January 1848. On February 2 he signed the final draft at the little town of Guadalupe Hidalgo near Mexico City.

THE TREATY OF GUADALUPE HIDALGO

In the Treaty of Guadalupe Hidalgo Trist achieved the sine qua non of his instructions, which called for cession of the Mexican holdings west of the Rio Grande to the Pacific Ocean. This area comprised California, Nevada, Utah, most of New Mexico and Arizona, and parts of Wyoming and Colorado. The Rio Grande was to be the southern boundary of Texas. Finally, the United States was to pay $15 million for the land and to assume the debt Mexico had been unable to pay. In one stroke Mexico lost about half its domain, while the United States achieved Polk's continental ambitions. (See Map 5, p. 86.) Polk, however, was so incensed at Trist's disobedience that he would have nothing to do with him, then or ever. Trist therefore spent the next twenty-three years petitioning Congress before he finally received recompense for his services!

Polk had little choice but to submit the treaty to the Senate. He was in ill health and had stated firmly his intention to serve but one term. In addition, he wanted to end the talk of annexing all of Mexico that was rife in Washington. The Senate ratified the pact on March 10, 1848, bringing to fruition the last of Polk's major promises regarding expansion.

James K. Polk also made a few unsuccessful attempts to expand the national domain that foreshadowed the more determined efforts of the 1850's. After 1846 the expansion of slavery became the most important as well as the most divisive issue in American public life. The stage was set by the introduction of the Wilmot Proviso in 1846, which prohibited slavery in the lands acquired from Mexico. Pushed through the House by a coalition of Whigs and Northern Democrats, the proviso failed in the Senate. It was thereafter introduced in almost every session of Congress, forcing the members to choose one side or the other and offering no middle ground.

THE TRY FOR CUBA

Cuba, like Canada, seemed to many Americans of the 1840's and 1850's to possess all the requisites for annexation by the United States. Cuba had a population of over 1,000,000 inhabitants, half of whom were white, and a firmly entrenched system of slavery. Thomas Jefferson had first viewed Cuba as a likely acquisition, and every succeeding president had had similar thoughts. The island's attractiveness increased with the decline of Spanish power. Before Polk left office in 1848 he offered Spain up to $100 million for Cuba. The Spanish government adamantly refused, the foreign minister threatening that "sooner than see the island transferred to *any power,* they [the Spanish people] would sink it in the Ocean."

The Whig administration of General Zachary Taylor, which succeeded Polk's, was not interested in pursuing the matter. However, a group of expansionists backed the return to Cuba of a Venezuelan general, Narciso López, who had once held office there. López, aided by wealthy Cuban landowners, had attempted an abortive insurrection and been forced to flee, first to New York and then to New Orleans. There he began an incredible filibustering, or freebooting, career during which he unsuccessfully invaded Cuba in 1850 with 750 men recruited in New Orleans. Returning to Key West, López was arrested by Federal authorities and indicted for violating the neutrality of the United States. Still under indictment, López raised another army of 450 men, his second in command being Colonel W. L. Crittenden, nephew of the Attorney-General of the United States. Once more the filibusterers landed in Cuba, but, unable to gain Cuban support, the band was trapped and captured. Colonel Crittenden and hundreds of others were quickly executed. López himself was garroted in a great public ceremony in Havana. Americans in New Orleans reacted to news of the fate of the filibusterers by destroying Spanish property, including the consulate. The United States government indemnified Spain for the loss, but the incident prompted Britain and France jointly to ask for a declaration disavowing any intent to possess Cuba. However, other considerations, such as the possibility of an isthmian canal, caused Taylor and his successor Fillmore to temporize. The next administration, that of Franklin Pierce, was stridently expansionist and refused outright to agree to the suggested declaration.

AMERICA AND THE REVOLUTIONS OF 1848

With the exception of England, the major European powers in 1848 were primarily concerned with putting down the rampant revolutionary uprisings that had broken out all over the Continent. This no doubt deterred them from becoming involved in the United States' unrestrained continentalism. Americans, for their part, not only supported their own expansion but were equally enthusiastic in supporting European revolutionary regimes. The American attitude was demonstrated in 1851 when Louis Kossuth, the revolutionary hero of Hungary, was lionized and flattered to a degree unique in American history. Daniel Webster, again Secretary of State, together with members of Congress, extolled Kossuth at a public banquet. The representative of the Austrian government, who naturally considered Kossuth a traitor, demanded Webster's removal for having officially greeted the Hungarian. As Webster was not removed, the Austrian refused to have further intercourse with the United States government until Webster left office.

By the early 1850's, the success of the country's expansionist policies was not lost upon the nations of Europe. In European eyes, the image of America became that of a restless, loud, self-confident adolescent impatiently jostling the older members of the family of nations.

Further Reading

Most of the books cited at the end of the last chapter are pertinent here. Although manifest destiny has been the subject of many works, only two, one old and one new, are listed. The older, first published in 1935 but still helpful, is *Albert K. Weinberg, *Manifest Destiny* (Chicago, 1963); the other is *Frederick Merk, *Manifest Destiny and Mission in American History: A Reinterpretation* (New York, 1966). Two aspects of this question are treated in Norman A Graebner, *Empire on the Pacific: A Study in American Continental Expansion* (New York, 1955) and Frederick Merk, *The Oregon Question: Essays in Anglo-American Diplomacy and Politics* (Cambridge, Mass., 1967).

A readable study of the Mexican War is *Otis A. Singletary, *The Mexican War* (Chicago, 1960). This war inspired much antiwar writing, some of lasting value, including essays by Henry David Thoreau and poetry by John Greenleaf Whittier and James Russell Lowell. Also refer to those books cited at the end of Chapter 2 dealing with the relationship of the armed services to American diplomacy.

Asterisk denotes paperback edition.

7

Young America and the Coming of the Civil War

The completion of continental American expansion in 1848 resulted in acute communications and transportation problems. During the 1850's these were attacked vigorously, if not always successfully; several times the solutions directly involved United States foreign policy. An episode such as the California gold rush of 1849 and its attendant circumstances is illustrative. Gold was discovered in California in 1848, and by the time California became a state two years later, the population was over 100,000; by 1852 it had doubled again. Because of the urge to reach California more quickly than was possible in the 1840's, several projects were proposed. One longstanding plan was to construct a canal across the isthmus of Panama, which would provide a cheap, efficient, and much shorter route to the west coast.

THE ISTHMUS AND THE CLAYTON-BULWER TREATY

At the time of the Mexican War the United States unexpectedly acquired access to land that could be used for a canal through the isthmus of Panama. New Granada (later Colombia), feeling itself threatened by British moves in nearby Nicaragua, had turned to the United States as a counter. The American chargé d'affaires in Bogotá, although without instructions, signed a treaty incorporating the offer. Bidlack's Treaty was approved by the Senate in June 1848.

This gave the United States control over one of the two best canal routes — the other being through Nicaragua, part of which was controlled by Britain. Now Nicaragua, using the same ploy to block the British, offered its route to the United States too. After several incidents between the Nicaraguans and the British, the latter decided to deal with the problem diplomatically. The British minister and the Secretary of State negotiated the Clayton-Bulwer Treaty in 1850 but in doing so pleased neither constituency. The treaty provided for joint Anglo-American control of the canal routes, a statement on the neutrality and non-fortification of the canal when it should be built, and a guarantee of sovereignty for Central American countries. The treaty was approved, and although it was never popular with Americans, it did give the United States a vital legal equality with Great Britain in the event that such a canal was built.

THE COMING OF YOUNG AMERICA

The Democratic party, headed by Franklin Pierce — "the Young Hickory from the Granite Hills" — won the election of 1852. Having expansionist visions comparable to those of Polk, Pierce appointed several cabinet officers of like mind. His Secretary of State was William L. Marcy of New York. Marcy represented a proslavery group that looked upon the United States as "Young America," a country that could expand almost limitlessly. Although he had little diplomatic experience, he was a former governor of New York, a presidential hopeful, and an ardent expansionist. As Secretary of War, Pierce appointed Jefferson Davis, a former West Pointer and a successful Mississippi planter and politician.

Marcy, in turn, added others of the Young America stripe to the diplomatic corps, including the fiery French-born Louisiana planter Pierre Soulé as Minister to Spain and John Y. Mason, a Virginia judge, as Minister to France.

YOUNG AMERICA AND CUBA

The Young America group made several notable attempts to acquire new territories, though all but one failed. The best known involved Cuba. First, the Pierce administration backed another filibustering expedition, this one headed by John A. Quitman, a former Mississippi governor and a proslavery extremist. But in spite of generous support, Quitman proved such a poor leader that the expedition never sailed.

At the end of February 1854, shortly after the Quitman fiasco, Spanish authorities in Cuba confiscated a cotton-laden American steamship, the *Black Warrior*, on an alleged customs violation. Soulé used this incident not only to demand redress but, exceeding his instructions, to threaten Spain should compensation not be forthcoming within forty-eight hours. The Spanish merely ignored Soulé, settling directly with the shipowners and thereby closing the affair.

Soulé, Pierce, and Marcy may have wished to pursue the matter, but the issue of the Kansas-Nebraska Bill, which was then before Congress, forestalled any overt act likely to affect the bill's passage. Afterwards, however, they again turned their attention to Cuba. Soulé was instructed to offer up to $130 million for Cuba. If the Spanish government refused — which it did — he was to use any other means "to detach that island from the Spanish dominion." But Soulé was no more equal to the task of stirring up a revolution that his better-qualified predecessors had been.

THE OSTEND MANIFESTO

Only temporarily restrained by failure, Soulé, having loftier political ambitions, convened a meeting with Judge Mason and James Buchanan, the moderate United States Minister to England. The outcome of the meeting, the Ostend Manifesto, was surely one of the most unusual American diplomatic documents ever produced. It was a secret dispatch to Marcy justifying the acquisition of Cuba by force. The contents of the manifesto leaked out, resulting in such adverse publicity that it was partly responsible for the administration's defeat in the 1854 Congressional elections. Pierce then ordered Soulé to cease his activities in Cuba, and Soulé promptly resigned.

After a single term as President, Pierce was succeeded by James Buchanan. Although the Democrats came out with a strong statement in favor of acquiring Cuba, Buchanan was unable to implement it. Growing Northern hostility in Congress toward adding slave territory to the national domain made any move on the subject out of the question. Only after the Civil War had settled the issue of slavery, did Cuba once again become a focus of expansionist activity.

Santo Domingo was another Caribbean island sought by the Young America group. In 1854 only the intervention of England and France prevented the cession of the best harbor on the island to the United States. Both Pierce and Buchanan continued to stalk the island, but to no avail. Santo Domingo also turned up after the Civil War as a possibility for American acquisition.

YOUNG AMERICA AND THE TRANSCONTINENTAL RAILROAD

A continuing theme during the 1850's, which ultimately led to the acquisition of more territory, was the building of a transcontinental railroad. First seriously advocated during Polk's term, its supporters veered between four different routes across the United States, not to mention a combination rail and water route involving Mexico. Advocates of the

Mexican route envisioned a railroad across the isthmus of Tehuantepec, the narrowest part of Mexico, as an alternative to an isthmian canal, arguing that it would be cheaper than a transcontinental railroad, especially since the eastern terminus would be a Gulf of Mexico port. Nicholas Trist attempted to obtain transit rights when he was negotiating the Treaty of Guadalupe Hidalgo, but was unsuccessful on this score. Later American diplomats pursued the possibility, but successive Mexican governments, though usually willing because of the money offered, dared not make concessions in the face of hostile Mexican public opinion.

When members of the Young America group came to office, they combined this problem with the need to acquire more Mexican land for a New Orleans to San Diego railroad that would traverse a minimum of mountainous terrain. President Pierce appointed James Gadsden — a South Carolina slaveholder, politician, and railroad promoter — to undertake negotiations with Mexico. By a combination of coercion and diplomacy, Gadsden negotiated a pact in 1853 as the result of which the land for the New Orleans to San Diego route was acquired together with transit rights across the Tehuantepec isthmus. The Gadsden Purchase incorporated parts of southern Arizona and New Mexico, for which the United States paid $10 million. The Senate approved the treaty only after acrimonious debate. Shortly after the ratifications were exchanged in 1854, the Mexican government responsible for the agreement fell from power, even though the land parted with was a relatively worthless area of the national domain.

THE UNITED STATES AND NICARAGUA

Closely linked to Mexican transit rights in the State Department's thinking was the isthmian canal. By the mid-1850's a highly profitable American-owned railroad spanned Panama, while a comparable competing rail and steamboat combination crossed Nicaragua. Governmental instability plagued both Colombia and Nicaragua, but it was the latter that became the target of a Young America filibusterer. William Walker, an adventurer from Louisiana, and later California, landed in Nicaragua with fifty-eight men in 1854. This "grey-eyed man of destiny" allied himself with American entrepreneurial interests and with their support soon made himself dictator of the country. Almost at once he quarreled with his backers, who cut off his supplies and ousted him in 1857. In 1856 the United States had recognized Walker's government, an action which also contributed to his unpopularity in Central America. Walker tried three times to regain control of the country, which he envisaged as the center of a projected Central American proslavery federation. On Walker's last return in 1860 he was captured and executed by a Honduran firing squad. By then the United States and Britain had resolved their difficulties in the region; however, the Central American governments continued to be unstable for many years.

TWISTING THE LION'S TAIL

During the 1850's America competed with Great Britain both diplomatically and economically in several parts of the world. There was little love lost between the two nations and the Americans often said so publicly. Symptomatic of this attitude was their indifference to the English and French role in the Crimean War (1854-1856), which the American press covered lightly. When Britain suffered a manpower shortage, aggravated by heavy battle losses, she turned to other countries for volunteers. John Crampton, Brisith Minister to the United States, indiscreetly enlisted American volunteers, who were formally to join the British army in Halifax. The outcry in the American press was strongly supported by Irish-American groups. William Marcy remonstrated, but the English government refused to recall Crampton. At this juncture, the United States government dismissed Crampton, and the British were forced to send a new envoy.

CANADA, THE BRITISH, AND YOUNG AMERICA

Canada continued to be another source of friction between England and the United States. In the late 1840's a conservative business minority, located mostly in Montreal, advocated joining the United States for commercial reasons. The possibility — not only of annexing part of Canada but of admitting many more free states to the Union, and thereby upsetting the balance between free and slave states — loomed larger than it actually was.

Great Britain tried to quiet the economic discontent in Canada with a minimum of concessions. Most of the difficulties could be traced to England's free trade laws, which militated against the imperial preference formerly given Canadian goods. In 1854 Governor-General Lord Elgin, an experienced diplomat, went to Washington to negotiate a commercial agreement on behalf of Canada. Using much tact, combined with lavish entertaining, Lord Elgin won an amazing pact. Ratified in the summer of 1854, the Marcy-Elgin Treaty set up a long list of Canadian goods that would be admitted duty free into the United States in return for a similar American list to be admitted into Canada. This reciprocity was to last for a ten-year period. In return for this major concession, the United States obtained additional and more clearly stated fishing rights, which aided New England fishermen.

The Marcy-Elgin Treaty quickly alleviated Canada's economic distress. It also effectively ended talk of annexation on the part of Canadians, though Irish-Americans kept the issue alive until after the Civil War when border incidents occurred once more.

YOUNG AMERICA AND EXPANSION IN THE PACIFIC

To contemporaries, American efforts to expand economically as well as territorially in the Pacific and in Asia seemed scarcely more successful than those in Cuba and Santo Domingo. In retrospect, however, the actions of the Young America group in that part of the world appear among the most successful of the entire century.

By the early 1850's the United States had gained economic and political domination over the Hawaiian Islands. The combination of American missionaries and whaling and trading groups, although often at odds with each other, had bested similarly determined British and French attempts. In 1842, for example, a British naval officer annexed the islands, but his action was immediately repudiated. In the early 1850's the Hawaiian monarch and his advisers, former American missionaries, sought annexation by the United States. Pierce was agreeable and went so far as to sign a treaty of annexation in 1854, but he did not submit it to the Senate. The Hawaiian king died soon after and was succeeded by a pro-British sovereign, which ended the matter for the moment. Twenty years later, when American naval considerations, as well as sugar interests, caused the matter to be reopened, Hawaii had already become an economic fief of the United States.

Other Pacific islands far more remote than Hawaii became the focus of other American commercial interests. Some searched for guano, the phosphate-rich excrement of sea birds found on desolate, uninhabited Pacific islands. In 1856 Congress passed the Guano Act, which provided for American annexation of uninhabited islands where Americans were collecting guano. Two islands — Baker and Jarvis — situated some 2,000 miles southwest of Hawaii were thereby added, and dozens more were used under the terms of the act.

YOUNG AMERICA AND ASIA

In the 1850's the United States achieved notable diplomatic success in opening Japan to trade and in broadening American commercial prerogatives in China.

After early cultural contact with the West, Japan had been virtually closed to outsiders since the seventeenth century. Western sailors shipwrecked on its coast were treated as felons or worse. But by the 1850's internal events, combined with Commodore Matthew Perry's historic visit of 1853, helped to force a reversal of attitudes. A senior naval officer, Perry was an early devotee of the use of steam in the navy and enjoyed a high reputation as one of the most able officers in the service. Like most other naval personnel, he was an ardent expansionist. Looking beyond the extension of American commercial activity, Perry also considered sites for their future possibilities as coaling stations. He has been given ministerial diplomatic status and had carefully prepared himself by learning as much about Japan as he could. These preparations aided him when, in July 1853, he entered Tokyo Bay in command of a four-ship flotilla that included two steamships. Perry refused to deal with local officials; instead, he sent a letter to the emperor from the President, telling the discomfited officials that he would return for an answer the next spring with an even larger fleet.

In the eight-month interim the busy commodore annexed the Bonin Islands and, later, the Ryukyu group for their possibilities as coaling stations. When he returned to the United States, Perry urged Congress not only to approve annexation of the two groups of islands but to annex Formosa as well. However, none of his proposals was accepted because of the critical domestic situation.

COMMODORE PERRY, OFFICERS, AND MEN OF THE SQUADRON LAND AT YOKU-HAMA, JAPAN, MARCH 8, 1854

Meanwhile, some Japanese leaders had decided to westernize their country in order to escape the encroachments of Russia and the economic dismemberment that had befallen China. Thus, when Perry returned in March 1854, he was greeted warmly and was able to sign the first treaty that Japan had negotiated in several centuries. The Treaty of Kanagawa gave the United States restricted trading privileges at only two isolated Japanese ports, but it permitted an American consul to reside at Shimoda. Unexpectedly, a most-favored-nation clause was inserted, although it seemed of little importance at the time. Later, this clause became the basis for many of the United States' commercial dealings with Japan. Nevertheless, the treaty was only a small beginning. For that reason, contemporary Americans never gave Commodore Perry the attention he so well merited.

President Pierce appointed Townsend Harris to the post of American consul. Harris was a merchant experienced in Far Eastern trade who, in an age of almost frenzied entrepreneurial activity, was able to accomplish far more than men with extensive diplomatic backgrounds. On his arrival in Japan in 1856 he was subjected to numerous petty annoyances at the hands of the Japanese, many of whom disliked the Treaty of Kanagawa. With infinite patience, and aided by his Japanese mistress, he slowly won over the reluctant officials to his side. In ten months he was able to sign another convention which only slightly expanded the original treaty. After another year, however, he attained the foreign policy objective of his government by signing a treaty of friendship and commerce. This treaty set up normal diplomatic representation between the two countries, opened other ports to American trade, established a fixed tariff to be charged by the Japanese, and permitted extraterritoriality in civil and criminal cases. Harris' treaty of 1858 was widely copied in European nations and served as a cornerstone of Japan's foreign policy until the Sino-Japanese War of 1894. By the time of its ratification James Buchanan had been succeeded by Abraham Lincoln and the Republicans. Lincoln appointed Harris the first United States Minister to Japan in recognition of his services.

Townsend Harris had already left Japan when, three years later, an outbreak of antiforeign sentiment threatened to oust foreign diplomats residing there. The American minister, Robert H. Pruyn, did not hesitate to order the warship *Wyoming* to attack the dissident fleet. The *Wyoming* fought a battle in the Straits of Shimonoseki, sinking a steamer and a brig. In 1863 a combined foreign fleet, including one hastily rented armed steamer representing the United States, bombarded and reduced the enemy stronghold at Shimonoseki. Although American commercial activity was temporarily reduced by the Civil War, Pruyn strongly advanced the United States' interests until the end of the war.

AMERICA AND THE CHINA TRADE

Since 1844, when Caleb Cushing signed the Treaty of Wanghia, Americans had broadened their commercial activities in China. Part of the increase was attributable to the acquisition of western ports in North America; but an even greater part derived from the profitable opium trade, for which American traders used Hong Kong, the Philippines, and other Asian ports as bases of operation.

In 1849 a bloody revolt, the Taiping Rebellion, attempted to overthrow the emperor. Although ultimately unsuccessful, the rebels initially enjoyed wide support among Westerners because of their pro-Christian statements. Among their supporters was Dr. Peter Parker, United States Commissioner to China. Appointed by Pierce in 1855, Parker was a long-time resident medical missionary in China who occasionally performed diplomatic assignments and who had assisted Cushing in 1844. Parker also supported Commodore Perry in his desire to acquire Formosa.

By the time Parker left China in 1857 the Taiping Rebellion has been crushed, and China was at war with England and France. On Marcy's orders, Parker assumed a neutral position; however, after the victory of the Western powers, the United States benefited by sending diplomatic representatives to negotiate new and more liberal treaties with China. The Treaties of Tientsin of 1858 became the foundation of Chinese international relations for the remainder of the century. United States policy at this point was to risk little militarily but to demand the same concessions other Western countries had wrested from the Chinese as the result of their victories.

AMERICAN MISSIONARIES IN CHINA, 1858

From a dispatch of William B. Reed, U.S. Minister to China

I cannot allow this occasion to pass without an incidental tribute to the missionary cause, as I observe it promoted by my own countrymen in China. Having no enthusiasm on the subject, I am bound to say that I consider the missionary element in China a great conservative and protecting principle. It is the only barrier between the unhesitating advance of commercial adventure and the not incongruous element of Chinese imbecile corruption. The missionary, according to my observation is content to live under the treaty and the law it creates, or if, in his zeal, he chooses to go beyond it, he is content to take the risk without troubling his government to protect him in his exorbitance. But taking a lower and more practical view of the matter, I am bound to say further that the studies of the missionary and those connected with the missionary cause are essential to the interests of our country. Without them as interpreters, the public business could not be transacted. . . .

There is not an American merchant in China (and I have heard of but one English) who can write or read a single sentence of Chinese.

During the 1850's and 1860's American missionaries living in China were more numerous than those from any other country. Led by Dr. Peter Parker, founder of the Medical Missionary Society, which introduced Western medicine into China, they strongly supported American policies. Many were consuls and commercial agents too, and they served to publicize China and its people to Americans. The most notable successor to Parker, and American envoy to China, was Anson Burlingame. He was a former congressman from Massachusetts who has been appointed minister by Lincoln as a reward for his electioneering in 1860. Burlingame's personality was compelling; he soon became the acknowledged spokesman of the diplomatic corps in Peking. During the Civil War he effectively used his talents to induce the European nations to live up to their treaty obligations and to refrain from dismembering China politically. This reflected American interests at the time, but because it likewise served the Chinese government, Burlingame became popular in that quarter. When he retired in 1867, the Chinese government appointed him a roving minister so that he could continue his effective work. Although he retained his American citizenship, Burlingame nevertheless negotiated treaties guaranteeing China's sovereignty with the United States (1868), Great Britain, and France, He thus anticipated the American Open Door Policy by more than thirty years. One interesting feature of the pact with the United States was that — on Secretary of State William Seward's insistence — it provided for unrestricted Chinese immigration to America.

THE PANIC OF 1857 AND AMERICAN FOREIGN POLICY

A sharp business recession in the North from 1857 until the eve of the Civil War temporarily halted internal business expansion. Together with the election of a Republican-controlled Congress in 1858, it also ended the Young America movement. The slump resulted in the collapse of American shipbuilding. The annual tonnage of ships built in the decade before 1858 averaged 400,000; but in 1858 tonnage dropped to 244,000, and in 1859 to 156,000. Part of the difficulty was that shipyards were geared for constructing wooden ships, which were rapidly being replaced by those made of iron. At the same time, the whaling industry, once a mainstay of American commerce, was rapidly declining due to the use of other kinds of oil for lighting. While the impact of the Panic of 1857 was short-lived, it virtually ended the aggressive foreign policy of the Democrats in the areas of economic and territorial expansion.

THE AFRICAN SLAVE TRADE IN THE 1850's

The proslavery orientation of the Democratic party paved the way for a rise in the illegal African slave trade in the 1850's. The American navy continued to maintain a small flotilla off West Africa, but it relied on antiquated ships and unsympathetic officers to enforce the ban. The record spoke for itself: up to 1857 the navy captured only 19 ships, 6 of which were condemned as slavers. In the same period, the British navy seized nearly 600, with all but 38 classified as illegal slave traders. Most of the slave ships were outfitted and crewed in New York and Massachusetts ports — 85 in an eighteen-months' period covering 1859-1860! In addition, a vocal minority in the South continually pressured Congress to reopen the slave trade. But after the election of 1858, which returned a Republican Congress, Buchanan deferred to Republican sentiment by attempting to enforce the slave trade ban; thus, two fast steamships were added to the African fleet. Nevertheless, since flying the American flag was generally tantamount to immunity from search, "the African slave trade," according to one authority, "was more virulent than ever in 1860."

As we have seen, during most of James Buchanan's term, foreign affairs, together with hopes of expansion, were muted by the severity of the domestic problems facing the country. By the election of 1860 these problems had captured the attention of the American public. For the next five years, therefore, foreign policy would be entirely subordinated to winning the Civil War. In addition, United States foreign policy would be turned in new directions, altering historic assumptions and long-standing policies.

Further Reading

This period is treated generally in William H. Goetzmann's book cited at the end of Chapter 5. The works by Maurice Collis and John K. Fairbank listed there are also pertinent. Consult Foster R. Dulles, *Yankees and Samurai: America's Role in the Emergence of Modern Japan* (New York, 1965) and *William L. Neumann, *America Encounters Japan* (Baltimore, 1969) on the opening of Japan and subsequent relations with that country.

For a discussion of the slave trade during the 1850's, see the books cited at the end of Chapter 4. The role of some Americans and their diplomatic endeavors is examined in Roy F. Nichols, *Advance Agents of American Destiny* (Philadelphia, 1956). A good book on Americans in Hawaii is Harold W. Bradley, *The American Frontier in Hawaii: The Pioneers, 1789-1843* (Stanford, Calif., 1942). A useful work on United States-Canadian relations is Donald F. Warner, *The Idea of Continental Union: Agitation for the Annexation of Canada to the United States, 1849-1893* (Lexington, Ky., 1960).

Biographies of William L. Marcy, James Buchanan and Franklin Pierce may also be profitable. Finally, for a readable biography of the naval officer who opened Japan, see Samuel E. Morison, *"Old Bruin": Commodore Matthew Calbraith Perry* (Boston, 1967).

Asterisk denotes paperback edition.

8

Civil War Diplomacy and the
Clash of Empires

With the election of Abraham Lincoln and a Republican Congress, the infant Republican party suddenly came of age. Various Southern states, led by South Carolina, had threatened secession if the antislavery Republicans proved successful. Consequently, on December 20, 1860, South Carolina seceded, followed shortly by Georgia, Alabama, Florida, Mississippi, Louisiana, and Texas. Naming themselves the Confederate States of America, they immediately applied to England and France for recognition in order to make alliances and to procure money and supplies.

At the same time, the North continued under the lame duck President James Buchanan until March 4, 1861. Buchanan vacillated, and this mood of suspended decisions pervaded the entire government. When Lincoln was sworn in as President he called for moderation, but by this time it was too late for compromise and peaceful settlement with the South.

WILLIAM H. SEWARD AS SECRETARY OF STATE

Abraham Lincoln succumbed to political necessity in appointing as Secretary of State William H. Seward, former titular head and most popular leader of the Republican party. Though Seward's knowledge of diplomacy and foreign affairs was slight (he had vacationed in Europe in 1859), it was at least greater than Lincoln's, for the new President had no experience whatsoever. Seward had been successively a member of the anti-Masonic party, a Whig, and then a Republican, serving as Governor of New York (1838-1842), United States Senator from New York (1849-1861), and, finally, Secretary of State (1861-1869). As a politician Seward was noted for his lifelong abolitionism, his statements on American expansionism, and his lack of balance in dealing with crucial issues. On the subject of expansionism, he once wrote: "The nation that draws most materials and provisions from the earth, and fabricates the most, and sells the most of

WILLIAM H. SEWARD

productions and fabrics to foreign nations, must be and will be, the great power of the earth." However, most of his expansionist plans were of necessity deferred until the end of the Civil War. In any event, Seward gave little promise of becoming the most effective secretary of state in the nineteenth century and — with Adams and Jefferson — the most important in formulating and implementing American foreign policy.

THE NEW SECRETARY AND THE DEPARTMENT OF STATE

One of Seward's first tasks was to ascertain the loyalty of State Department employees and to organize their operation efficiently. Fortunately, the first career departmental executive, able William Hunter, who had begun as a clerk in Jackson's administration, was Chief Clerk. He had charge of from twenty-four to thirty clerks, sufficient for the task of transacting business even during wartime, when a temporary bureau to handle political prisoners was added.

Seward's attempt to invigorate the diplomatic corps by appointing able and efficient men was only partially successful. His most outstanding appointment was that of Charles Francis Adams as Minister to Great Britain. Lincoln had preferred another man, but when Seward persisted, he agreed to Adams. Adams, the reserved son of John Quincy Adams, went to England at a critical time. Other appointments were less fortunate: Cassius Clay, for example, was appointed Minister to Russia as a political reward and as a means of getting him out of the way, the mercurial Kentuckian having wanted to be named Secretary of War.

At the beginning of his term, Seward completely misjudged Lincoln, confiding to friends that he expected to act as a prime minister in the administration. On April 1, 1861, Seward sent Lincoln a memorandum entitled "Some Thoughts for the President's Consideration." It called for an aggressive foreign policy against Spain and France (who were interfering in Mexico); if a convincing answer was not forthcoming, war should be declared against them. Britain and Russia were also mentioned as nations the United States should "seek explanations of." Lincoln pocketed this remarkable document, never mentioned it, and soon Seward became one of his most loyal associates.

SEWARD AND GREAT BRITAIN

Seward's most pressing diplomatic problem was to prevent Britain from recognizing the Confederacy. War began on April 15; the Lincoln administration immediately labeled it an internal matter, hoping to prohibit consideration of the South as a nation. Seward emphasized this point in detailed instructions to Adams, although at the moment recognition seemed inevitable. In fact, several times early in the war England was on the verge of announcing recognition, and with reason. The Southern cotton crop had long supported the huge British textile industry centered around Manchester and Liverpool. An estimated 5,000,000 Britons directly or indirectly owed their livelihoods to this industry. Next, British politicians of the upper class were on the whole supporters of the Confederacy, which had demonstrated little of the economic competitiveness shown by the North. Seward himself had a record of anti-British statements dating back to his governorship of New York, and the sentiment was returned in kind. Finally, a permanent breakup of the United States would have confirmed those aristocratic naysayers who had long predicted just such an event.

While circumstances momentarily favored British recognition, several mitigating factors operated for the Union. The British, for one thing, had ended slavery nearly thirty years before, and most Englishmen were very much opposed to the South's slaveholding. However, Lincoln did little to encourage this sentiment because of the critical attitude toward the Union of the slaveholding border states and the necessity of retaining their loyalty. He therefore insisted that the purpose of the war was to preserve the Union, not to abolish slavery.

Also helpful was English dependence on Northern corn and wheat, due to poor crops in England in the early 1860's. Lastly, a comparatively small group of liberal British statesmen, mostly from the middle class, was always pro-Union in sentiment. Adams effectively made use of all these factors, adding to them the implied threat of war and the end of profitable munitions sales should the Confederacy be recognized.

In May 1861 Great Britain issued a statement of neutrality which, in effect, recognized a state of belligerency between the North and South rather than the existence of internal civil strife that Lincoln and Seward had sought. For the present, the British were content to go just that far, until force of arms should decide the issue one way or the other. Suffering did result from the South's withholding the 1861 cotton crop and from the North's blockade of Southern ports, but the situation in Britain was alleviated somewhat by the substitution of Indian and Egyptian cotton. The swollen war profits from munitions also helped.

THE *TRENT* AFFAIR

The Confederacy early sent Harry Hotze, an able diplomat, to plead its cause in England. But when recognition was not forthcoming, the South decided to bolster Hotze's efforts by sending a special commission to Europe. James M. Mason was to join Hotze in England and John Slidell was to go to France. In August 1861 they traveled from Charleston to Havana, easily evading the Union blockade. Together with their secretaries they took passage on the British steamer *Trent,* which was bound first for a West Indian port and then for England. On November 8, 1861, the *Trent* was overhauled by the Union sloop of war *San Jacinto,* commanded by Captain Charles Wilkes, who two decades earlier had headed an exploring expedition. On his own initiative, and with complete disregard for international law, Captain Wilkes forcibly stopped the *Trent,* firing several shots over her bow. He removed the two commissioners and carried them off to Boston. The North enthusiastically acclaimed his exploit and Congress voted him a gold medal. Lincoln, however, had sober second thoughts, telling Seward, "One war at a time." The British delivered a virtual ultimatum demanding an apology as well as the release of Mason and Slidell. The crisis was quickly resolved when the United States acceded to the demands; however, by the time the commissioners arrived in England, their presence had become comparatively useless. The North was content with Seward's note of apology to Britain, which could be variously interpreted and did not directly blame Wilkes. As for Wilkes, he eventually became a rear admiral and soon afterwards was retired.

THE AMERICAN BLOCKADE AND THE RIGHTS
OF NEUTRALS

European statesmen were quick to point out that Wilkes had resorted to impressment in the *Trent* case. In fact, Wilkes could well have confiscated both ship and cargo to be ruled on by a Northern prize court, on the grounds that the two commissioners were carrying treasonous dispatches. Such an action would have had much validity, as the future would demonstrate. In essence, the United States had abandoned its historic role as a defender of liberal maritime rights, especially in opposition to Britain's Rule of 1756. This policy began almost immediately after the fall of Fort Sumter when Lincoln proclaimed a blockade of the South, even though initially the inadequacy of the Union navy made it little more than a paper blockade.

Originally, the United States had insisted on liberal maritime rules because its navy was minuscule as compared to its merchant marine. European nations kept this factor in mind when they met in 1856 to codify international maritime rules. In the final document, the Declaration of Paris, they settled on exactly the liberal rules the United States had long demanded; in addition, they abolished the use of privateers. Secretary of State William Marcy refused to adopt the Declaration of Paris because he could foresee the use of privateers in the event of war. Now, at the beginning of the Civil War, Lincoln and Seward decided not to use them, which meant, as Seward told the British, that the United States for all practical purposes adhered to the Declaration of Paris even though it was not a signatory.

Following England's lead, the European powers recognized the South as a belligerent and at the same time accepted the North's blockade, even though it was a paper one and illegal according to the Declaration of Paris. As proof of its metamorphosis, the United States soon adopted the traditional British doctrine of continuous voyage, applying it to the confiscation of cargoes the Confederates hoped to transship on speedy blockade-runners.

The Confederate States' naval policy was almost diametrically opposed. Privateers were quickly commissioned and became an important facet of Southern strategy. As time went on and the Union blockade became more effective, the Confederacy was forced to seek other means of commissioning and outfitting raiders. One partially successful alternative was to build, commission, and outfit ships in foreign countries; but, in the main, the North was successful in containing the Confederate navy and, later, the commerce raiders also, but not before they had exacted a sizable toll. In effect, the American merchant marine was destroyed: by 1865 more than 250 merchant ships had been sunk. Insurance rates mounted, and owners transferred their remaining ships to neutral registries, often British. On the basis of all foreign commerce, the figure represented by American shipping in 1860 was 66.5 percent; by 1865 it had fallen to 27.7 percent. The demise of the once dominant American merchant marine loomed large after the war, when the North pointed accusingly at Great Britain for its part in the burial.

ENGLAND AND THE CONFEDERATE CRUISERS

The Confederacy sent to England an experienced agent, Captain James D. Bulloch, to let contracts for building warships. According to British law, a warship could be constructed in England for a belligerent provided it was armed elsewhere. Captain Bulloch was therefore able in 1862 to have built the *Florida* and the *Alabama* and to man them with English crews. Later, the *Georgiana*, the *Georgia,* the *Alexandra,* and the *Shenandoah* were also constructed.

The *Alabama* sailed even though Adams had convinced the British government that the vessel violated British neutrality despite the law under which she was built. But although bureaucratic inefficiency allowed the *Alabama* to escape, Adams was able to stay the threat of the construction of a large fleet of Confederate raiders. The *Alexandra*, for example, was detained by the British, though later released by the courts.

In the summer of 1862, before the *Alabama* sailed, Bulloch posed a more serious threat by contracting for two armored rams. To be built by Laird Brothers — hence named the Laird rams — they had the capacity to break the Union blockade by battering the wooden warships of the Union navy. For over a year Adams complained to the British government, filing affidavits and writing voluminous reports to prove that the rams were intended for the Confederate navy. On September 5, 1863, Adams threatened the British with war if the rams were released. The rams were detained and later added to the British navy. Recent scholarship has demonstrated that Foreign Minister Lord John Russell never intended to release the rams, being well aware of the danger of Union retaliation. A similar type of ship, contracted for in France, was confiscated by Emperor Napoleon III before it was finished.

THE LAST STRUGGLE FOR RECOGNITION

While the struggle over the building of Confederate ships was taking place, other Confederate officials continued to work for recognition from France and England. But officials in both countries, although still pro-Southern, hesitated until the Confederacy should win a decisive victory on the battlefield. After the second battle of Bull Run, British officials, Russell in particular, seriously considered making an offer of mediation that would have included recognition. They did nothing, however, because Seward had already stated that such an offer would not only be rejected but would be tantamount to war. Even while the British cabinet was debating Russell's proposal, General Robert E. Lee invaded Maryland, where, on September 17, 1862, he fought one of the bloodiest battles of the war at Antietam. Not only was the battle indecisive, but Lee's army sustained nearly one-third casualties, causing the Confederates to return to Virginia to regroup. The news of Antietam decided the British cabinet against the mediation proposal and recognition of the Confederacy. Since the situation remained unaltered, Charles Francis Adams, aided by good fortune, had accomplished a noteworthy diplomatic feat.

CHARLES FRANCIS ADAMS

The situation in France concerning recognition was roughly comparable. Although Napoleon III desired a Confederate victory, he took his lead from Great Britain. Seward had already strongly protested Napoleon's deep involvement in Mexico, although the United States was too concerned with the Civil War to do more than remonstrate. Like the British, Napoleon too kept a watchful eye on the battlefield, and after Antietam was much less accessible to Confederate agents.

With the exception of Russia, the role of other powers relative to the Civil War was less important. Russia, having lost the Crimean War to England in the 1850's, was engaged in quelling periodic Polish uprisings. Fearing that

England would carry out its threat to aid Poland and declare war on Russia, Czar Alexander II based his two major fleets in neutral warm-water ports when possible. Thus, in September and October 1863, Russian fleets appeared off New York and San Francisco, respectively, and remained until the following April. The American public immediately took the officers and men to their hearts as representing a friendly foreign power in a hostile world. Alexander II had seemingly provided another bond in 1861 when he freed the Russian serfs. The pro-Russian sentiment of this period was analogous to the pro-French feeling prevailing in America from the latter part of the Revolutionary War through the early days of the French Revolution.

THE QUESTION OF SLAVERY AND CIVIL WAR DIPLOMACY

In conducting American foreign policy during the Civil War both Seward and Lincoln proved themselves to be realists who dealt in the realm of the possible. For example, on the slavery question Seward had been an abolitionist and Lincoln an antislavery moderate; but the necessity of holding the border states and of pacifying the Western states with large Southern populations tended to modify their individual points of view. Abolitionist newspapers and organizations buffeted Lincoln so strongly that in July 1862 he told the cabinet he was considering freeing the slaves in the Confederacy. At this point it was Seward who counseled prudence by urging Lincoln to wait for a military victory before taking such a step. Antietam provided, if not an outright victory, at least one that could be claimed, and Lincoln issued the preliminary Emancipation Proclamation on September 25, 1862, to become effective January 1, 1863. At first public, and then world, reaction was disappointing, but American ministers abroad, including Adams, pointed out that the disenfranchised and voiceless working classes appeared to approve. The proclamation had little practical import domestically because the slaves in the border states were unaffected, but it had considerable long-range propaganda value. In fact, in late 1864, in a last bid for recognition, the Confederacy offered to free its slaves in exchange for recognition. Napoleon was amenable, but it was far too late as far as the British were concerned.

THE CIVIL WAR AND THE MONROE DOCTRINE

The four-year struggle in the United States forced a relaxation of William H. Seward's aggressive expansionism. Moreover, the war allowed European nations to encroach on countries in the Western Hemisphere and to violate the Monroe Doctrine in ways they might not have attempted otherwise. Polk had cited the Monroe Doctrine, and in the 1850's it was used against the British in Central America, but without noticeable effect. Therefore, when Seward invoked it against Spain in April 1861 at the time of Spain's annexation of the Dominican Republic on Santo Domingo, little attention was paid. By July 1865, Seward was prepared to act, but by then the Spanish had already been ousted by effective Dominican guerrilla tactics.

THE UNITED STATES, THE FRENCH, AND MEXICO

The situation in Mexico was far different. After a long period of internal instability accompanied by guerrilla warfare and rampant factionalism, Mexico seemed destined for better days. Benito Juárez, a Zapotec Indian who represented a republican and anti-clerical regime friendly to the United States, gained power in 1861. His government promised to be more stable than its predecessors had been because it enjoyed a broader base of support. Juárez suspended payment on European claims for two years owing to the financial plight of his government.

In October 1861, after an exchange of notes with Juárez, Britain, France, and Spain agreed on a joint expedition to force Mexico to pay its debts. The United States, also a creditor because of investments by individual Americans, was invited to join, but Seward refused. In January 1862 an army representing the three powers occupied Vera Cruz and seized the customs. When this did not produce the desired revenue, the French marched on to Mexico City, although the British and Spaniards withdrew. Napoleon III, a pale image of his illustrious uncle, hoped to establish an American empire. Posing as the savior of the Catholic faith in Mexico, he won the backing of the conservative and aristocratic elements in the population. At his bidding, they invited the thirty-one-year-old Hapsburg archduke, Maximilian of Austria, to become emperor of Mexico. The fuzzy-thinking but well-intentioned Maximilian accepted, on condition that the Mexican people voted their approval. Napoleon obligingly rigged an election and Maximilian and his consort Carlotta became emperor and empress of Mexico.

**HOUSE RESOLUTION ON FRENCH INTERVENTION
IN MEXICO, 1864**

Resolved. That the Congress of the United States are unwilling, by silence, to leave the nations of the world under the impression that they are indifferent spectators of the deplorable events now transpiring in the Republic of Mexico; and they therefore think fit to declare that it does not accord with the policy of the United States to acknowledge a monarchical government, erected on the ruins of any republican government in America, under the auspices of any European power.

Juárez' guerrilla army kept large sections of the country in his control despite the 30,000 French troops supplied by Napoleon. The United States continued to recognize Juárez, though the European powers recognized Maximilian. At the end of the Civil War, Seward's tone became increasingly truculent in dealing with the French. In late 1865 and early 1866 a Union army massed on the Mexican border, with the approval of the American public and most of the politicians. On February 12, 1866, Seward delivered what amounted to an ultimatum to the French, demanding to know when their army would leave Mexico. Ten days later Napoleon announced the withdrawal of his forces. When this was finally accomplished — some thirteen months later — Maximilian's government collapsed like a house of cards. Maximilian himself refused to flee; he was captured and executed by Juárez. Although the implicit use of the Monroe Doctrine in this instance was apparently effective, Napoleon's sudden change of mind may also have been due as much to the expense and growing unpopularity of the occupation in France as to the menacing gestures of the United States.

GREAT BRITAIN, CANADA, AND THE CLASH OF EMPIRES

If Seward was angered by the French to the south, he was even more provoked by the Canadians to the north. During the war Canada had become a haven for draft dodgers and deserters from both the Union and the Confederacy. Most humiliating of all, a series of Confederate raids was mounted from Canada. The culmination was an attack on St. Albans, Vermont, in October 1864, during which fires were set, two banks robbed, and one American killed. In retaliation, Congress gave Britain a year's notice, after which the United States would abrogate the Marcy-Elgin Treaty and end reciprocity.

Two other factors complicated United States-Canadian relations. First, a militant Irish-American organization called the Fenian Brotherhood was working to keep the border area in such a ferment that the United States would become embroiled in a war with Great Britain; this, in turn, it was hoped, would aid the Irish in their struggle for independence. To that end, the Fenians raised troops, organized a government in exile, and, beginning in May 1866, made forays across the border. The United States government was dilatory, to say the least, in taking positive steps to restrain the Fenians. Actually, both political parties courted their favor. One leading senator, Charles Sumner of Massachusetts, Chairman of the Senate Foreign Relations Committee since 1861, suggested publicly that the raids would stop if England withdrew from Canada, allowing the United States to annex the country! Other expansionists speaking in the same vein proved to be the second complicating factor in the deteriorating relations between the two countries.

The expansionists and the Fenians both had their reply from Canada when the movement for confederation of the Canadian provinces culminated in the British North America Act of 1867, which became effective on July 1, 1867. This established the Dominion of Canada. Fenian raids ended soon after, but American dreams of annexation were yet to be stilled.

WILLIAM SEWARD AND THE *ALABAMA* CLAIMS

Secretary of State Seward had suggested as early as 1863 that Great Britain should pay compensation for the damage inflicted by British-built Confederate raiders as the result of Britain's laxity in interpreting and enforcing neutrality laws. At the time, Lord Russell refused; when the subject was reopened in 1865, Russell — now prime minister — continued to refuse, but his government fell shortly. The new prime minister accepted the principle of arbitration for claims based on the depredations of commerce raiders, chiefly the *Alabama.* The about-face was due in part to a unanimous resolution passed by the House of Representatives calling for a modification of the neutrality laws which would enable the United States to build and sell ships to belligerents. The British envisaged the possibility of the United States providing Russia or other powers with hordes of raiders that would decimate the British merchant marine in the event of war.

Nevertheless, the negotiations collapsed; it was not until three years later that talks began again in earnest. By that time, William E. Gladstone and the Liberal party were in power and Charles Francis Adams had been succeeded by the less able former Maryland senator, Reverdy Johnson. Johnson finally worked out a settlement of individual claims in the Johnson-Clarendon Convention of 1869. Contrary to Seward's insistence, the pact contained no British apology for the *Alabama's* escape.

The day before the Senate was to vote on the convention, Sumner delivered one of the most remarkable speeches ever made in the Senate by an official actively engaged in foreign policy matters. He attacked the Convention of 1869 as representing only a fraction of Britain's debt to the United States. He first added another $10 million to cover the loss of revenue from destroyed ships and the higher insurance rates on the remaining vessels. Then came the bombshell: he demanded that Great Britain pay half the estimated cost of the Civil War — $2 billion — because, Sumner said, their recognition of a state of belligerency had doubled the length of the war. His speech was reprinted widely; later it was circulated in pamphlet form. Needless to add, the Convention of 1869 was defeated, ending Seward's attempts to settle the *Alabama* claims. More importantly, Anglo-American relations remained perilously strained during the Grant administration, which supported Sumner's views.

WILLIAM SEWARD AND THE CARIBBEAN

The Civil War prevented Seward from developing his program of expansionism, but after the war, he began to cost his eye over the Caribbean. He discussed the purchase of two Danish-owned islands of the Virgin Islands group, following it up by a trip there with his son, ostensibly for reasons of health, to look over the fine harbor at St. Thomas in terms of its potential as a naval base. When he returned, negotiations began in earnest; Denmark was to receive $7.5 million for two islands in the group, including St. Thomas. Although the Danish parliament ratified the treaty, the Senate disapproved, considering and rejecting it twice.

The terms of a pact signed with Nicaragua in 1867 had given the United States the right of transit for a canal through that country and had thus reopened the dream of an isthmian canal from which England would be excluded. To further this desirable end, Seward wanted to establish a protectorate over the willing Haiti, which would have given the United States control over Santo Domingo and a strategic hold on an approach to the isthmus of Panama. The Dominican Republic, which Seward had also visited during his famous health trip, was also willing to be annexed by the United States. Congress, however, rebuffed Seward on all counts, and territorial acquisition seemed destined to await the end of domestic preoccupation with reconstruction.

THE PURCHASE OF ALASKA AND AMERICAN INTERESTS IN THE PACIFIC

Notwithstanding his failure in the Caribbean, Seward was at least able to achieve one of the least likely aspects of his master plan; this concerned American interests in the Pacific. Recognizing the strategic importance of the Hawaiian Islands, Seward attempted to sign a reciprocity treaty with them in 1867, but again Congress balked. Then in August 1867 Seward directed the navy to occupy the Midway Islands, a series of coral atolls located about 1,100 miles northwest of the Hawaiian group.

At the time of the negotiations for Alaska, Seward was also working toward the opening of Korea. He successfully concluded the Burlingame Treaty of 1868, which allowed unrestricted Chinese immigration for use as cheap labor on the transcontinental railroads under construction.

Undoubtedly the culmination of Seward's efforts was the purchase of Alaska. Russia seemed willing to sell the territory after the Crimean War had convinced Russian leaders of Alaska's vulnerability. Serious talks began in 1860 but were suspended with the coming of the Civil War. During the war Russia defmitely decided to sell Alaska at the earliest opportunity, hoping that the United States would be the purchaser, which would be an added strength against Great Britain. At the end of the war, the Russian Minister to the United States, Baron Edouard de Stoeckl, was instructed to interest the United States in purchasing Alaska for a sum not less than $5 million. The Russian government was dimly aware of Alaska's mineral wealth as well as of its fish, fur, and lumber resources, but felt it was better to sell the territory than to risk its eventual loss to England or the United States.

Stoeckl found Seward so eager to purchase that the Secretary of State offered $2 million more than was necessary. Later in the negotiations, Seward added another $200,000 to the price to settle the claims of the Russian-American Company. By the end of March 1867 the treaty was completed, signed, and forwarded to the Senate for approval — all on one day. The Senate was caught unawares; like their fellow Americans, most Senators knew little about the area. Seward therefore began a nationwide educational program about Alaska in the press to convince the public of its great potential.

Seward stressed the demonstration of Russian friendship during the war and suggested that the Senate could do no less than approve the treaty. The Senate was amenable, but the House of Representatives, occupied by impeachment proceedings against President Andrew Johnson, at first refused to appropriate the money. Baron de Stoeckl then used the extra $200,000 promised by Seward for lobbying and outright bribery. The United States was already flying the American flag at Sitka, and the House reluctantly reversed its stand and voted the appropriation on July 23, 1868.

In this way, an area of nearly 600,000 square miles became part of the national domain, the greatest land bargain since the Louisiana Purchase. As to why the United States purchased Alaska, each official had his own reasons. For Charles Sumner the annexation was a step toward the ultimate annexation of Canada. For Seward, on the other hand, Alaska fulfilled a strategic role as an "advanced naval outpost" to aid in American domination of the north Pacific. Others, while professing to see a future for

"Seward's Icebox," held little hope of return in the near future. They were averse to making a large investment that supported the purchase, against their own inclinations, for the most ephemeral of reasons; feeling that the purchase represented an act of friendship between the two nations so different in history, mode of government, language, and national interests.

RUSSIAN AMERICA.

Canvassing the state ticket.

This 1867 American cartoon ridicules Seward's purchase of Alaska.

RUSSIAN AMERICA.
CANVASSING THE STATE TICKET.

WILLIAM H. SEWARD AND AMERICAN EXPANSIONISM

In spite of his ill success in acquiring territory — except for Alaska and the Midway Islands — Seward correctly foresaw America's need to locate and acquire new markets. He considered that an isthmian canal and strategic access to it were basic to this policy, as was the need for overseas colonies. Thus Seward never ceased his activities in the Caribbean and continued to work for the annexation of Canada and the far-off Pacific islands. Toward the same end, he fostered the importation of cheap labor, believing that completion of the transcontinental railroads would increase accessibility to Asian markets. This in turn would give the United States a broader base of agricultural and commercial development. Seward's ideas and his implementation of them were so striking that even though the succeeding period was not expressly interested in foreign affairs, his policy was easily revived a generation later when, at the turn of the century, American imperialism at last hit its full stride.

Further Reading

The diplomacy of the Civil War is colorfully outlined in *Jay Monaghan, *Diplomat in Carpet Slippers: Abraham Lincoln Deals with Foreign Affairs* (Indianapolis, 1962). An excellent discussion of Confederate diplomacy appears in Frank L. Owsley, *King Cotton Diplomacy,* ed. Harriet Owsley, rev. ed. (Chicago, 1959).

American-Canadian relations during and after the War are discussed by Donald F. Warner, cited at the end of the last chapter. Also see Robin W. Winks, *Canada and the United States: The Civil War Years* (Baltimore, 1960).

The work of William H. Seward, including his purchase of Alaska, is detailed in Glyndon G. Van Deusen, *William Henry Seward* (New York, 1967). Biographies of Charles Francis Adams, Abraham Lincoln and others are also helpful here. One of the best sources for this period and the next half century is the recently reprinted autobiography of Seward's son, himself a diplomat. See Frederick W. Seward, *Reminiscences of a War-Time Statesman and Diplomat, 1830-1915* (New York, 1969).

Asterisk denotes paperback edition.

9

American Foreign Affairs in the Gilded Age

The retirement of William H. Seward in 1869 marked the end of an epoch in American foreign policy. The men who succeeded him as secretaries of state during the next three decades were virtually prisoners of the political machinations that had delivered them to their offices. Even more, they reflected the domestic ills — social, economic, and psychological — that followed in the wake of the Civil War. The result was a marked deterioration in public-service ethics, which descended to a new low in the mid-1870's and improved slightly thereafter. Mark Twain aptly labeled the period "the Gilded Age."

THE STATE DEPARTMENT IN THE GILDED AGE

The era was accurately reflected in the weaknesses of the State Department. President Ulysses S. Grant, for example, while disapproving in theory of the spoils system, retained only three ministers and two other diplomatic representatives out of a total of thirty-five. Most of the new appointees, usually personally selected by Grant himself, were poor to incredibly bad. In the second category General Robert C. Schenk and General Daniel E. Sickles were typical. Schenk had once befriended Grant while he was in Congress; he was rewarded by being appointed Minister to England. He served without distinction until he supported and aided the sale of stock in a bogus Western mine. Today he is remembered for having taught English society how to play draw poker, a game about which he later wrote a book. Sickles, a colorful individualist who had lost a leg at Gettysburg, was made United States Minister to Spain. He soon became notorious for his lurid love affairs, the most celebrated of which was one with the former Spanish queen!

PRESIDENT GRANT CHOOSES A CONSUL, 1873

President Grant filled the consular service with especially poor and unqualified appointees. He usually sent the applicant with a signed presidential card to the State Department. In one instance the Secretary of State asked President Grant:

"Do you really wish George S. Fisher of Georgia given a place?"

"Yes," replied the President, "I want to get him out of the country."

"Well," said the Secretary, "La Guayra [Venezuela] will do."

While Grant appointees did not enjoy long tenures in office, the caliber of the diplomatic corps nevertheless continued to be only average during succeeding presidencies — all Republican — until Grover Cleveland, a Democrat, was elected in 1884. Then major changes were made, not only in diplomatic and consular representation but in the Washington bureaucracy as a whole. The State Department functioned during these years with a minimum of disorder owing to the ability of a handful of loyal and dedicated government servants. A man such as William Hunter, promoted to Assistant Secretary in 1866, served fifty-seven years, to be succeeded by Alvey A. Adee, who came to the department as a clerk in 1870. Adee served notably until his death in 1924. Another effective employee was John Bassett Moore, who arrived as a twenty-five-year-old lawyer in 1885, served until 1914, and became a world authority on international law.

In addition to weak appointments and the vagaries of the domestic political situation, the State Department during the Gilded Age was plagued by a particularly poor image. While certainly better run at its worst than most other executive departments, the State Department became a favorite whipping boy of Congress. It suffered repeatedly from less than adequate appropriations, especially after the beginning of the depression of 1873.

THE AMERICAN PEOPLE IN THE GILDED AGE

The United States during the Gilded Age was far from a static society. The population increased from 38,500,000 in 1870 to nearly 63,000,000 twenty years later, and this included 8,000,000 immigrants. Rural and farm dwellers, while still numerically in the majority, lost their political influence to the rising entrepreneurial class, represented by the Republican party. The Grand Old Party continued in office by pointing to its war record, waving the "bloody shirt" at the Democrats and blaming them for slavery, the war, and all manner of treason. When the Democrats finally won the presidency

"WELCOME TO ALL!"

When this British cartoon appeared in the April 28, 1880 edition of
Punch, *immigration was increasing at an unprecedented rate.*

in 1884, they too were captured by the same business interests that
controlled the Republicans.

This dynamic group dominated both local and state politics, as well as the
national government, in its laissez-faire scramble to the top of the economic
heap. It espoused Social Darwinism, with the means justifying the ends, one
of the means being government subsidies. For instance, railroad mileage
jumped from 54,000 miles in 1870 to 163,000 in 1890. During that period,
besides monetary subsidies, Congress awarded land to the railroads
amounting to a total of one fourth of Minnesota and Washington, one fifth
of Iowa, Kansas, Montana, North Dakota, and Wisconsin, one seventh of
Nebraska, and one eighth of California.

In spite of the comparative lack of attention paid to foreign affairs at this
time, some members of the entrepreneurial group, as well as certain
politicians, continued to press for Seward's goals. Their total influence
ranged from a little to considerable; they were more successful in keeping
expansionist ideas alive during the 1870's and 1880's than in actually gaining
new territories or new markets.

GRANT AND THE SANTO DOMINGO AFFAIR

One of President Grant's earliest forays into foreign affairs was his attempt to annex Santo Domingo. Persuaded by naval officers, as well as by several unsavory promoters, Grant sent his personal secretary as an executive agent to survey the situation. The agent returned with two alternatives: one gave the entire Dominican Republic to the United States; the other merely offered one bay for use as a naval base. Although Grant usually showed little interest in foreign affairs — an attitude encouraged by his excellent Secretary of State, Hamilton Fish — in this instance he personally attempted to lobby for the treaties in the Senate. Charles Sumner opposed both alternatives, and the treaties were soundly defeated. Grant took revenge, first removing Sumner's choice for Minister to England, John Lathrop Motley, and then Sumner himself from the chairmanship of the Senate Foreign Relations Committee. The two parts of Santo Domingo, the Dominican Republic and Haiti, continued their troubled existence until early in the next century. They were bedeviled not only by their own internal difficulties but also by several European countries, which, though willing to lend them money, threatened reprisals whenever repayment was slow or not forthcoming.

CUBA AND THE *VIRGINIUS* AFFAIR

President Grant also intervened briefly with regard to Cuba. That unhappy country was in the throes of a sporadic revolution, later dignified by the name of the Ten Years' War. Actually, the war was comprised of savage rebel guerrilla attacks and even more brutal Spanish counterattacks and suppression. Most Americans supported the Cuban rebels, who were far better organized for propaganda in the United States than they were for fighting and governing at home. Influenced by their propaganda, a group of American political and military leaders headed by General John H. Rawlins, Grant's Secretary of War, demanded immediate American intervention. Grant supported Rawlins out of friendship; thus he became temporarily interested in Cuba. However, Hamilton Fish, one of only two able cabinet members, felt that not even recognition, much less intervention, could be justified under international law.

President Grant was so enmeshed in the Santo Domingo annexation problem that Fish had little difficulty persuading him to change his mind; Grant sent a special message requesting Congress to refuse to recognize the rebels. Congress thereupon turned down a resolution calling for recognition; and, for the next three years, although the savage struggle continued, Cuba faded into the background as far as most Americans were concerned.

In 1873 Cuba again became the focus of American attention when a Spanish gunboat captured the *Virginius,* a battered tramp steamer flying the American flag, on the high seas between Jamaica and Cuba. The *Virginius* was carrying a Cuban-organized filibustering expedition on its way to Cuba. The ship and its occupants were taken to Santiago, where the crew and the filibusterers were tried, sentenced, and fifty-three summarily executed. More would have been shot had not a British warship, rushed to Santiago from Jamaica, threatened to bombard Santiago unless the executions ceased. A wave of indignation and hostility toward the Spanish swept the United States. Public meetings and the news media alike clamored for war because of the insult to the American flag. Fish, however, became less bellicose when he learned that the *Virginius* was actually Cuban-owned and had been flying the American flag illegally. Spain, realizing the senselessness of the affair, released both the ship and the prisoners and admitted the illegality of the seizure.

Two years later the Spanish government paid an indemnity to the relatives of the executed Americans. Fish followed up by attempting, along with several European nations, to mediate a peace settlement, but the plan did not materialize. The war dragged on until 1878, at which point Spain promised reforms and colonial autonomy. Peace was declared, but when the reforms proved to be negligible, guerrilla warfare erupted once more, lasting until a major conflagration broke out in the 1890's.

THE ISTHMIAN CANAL

In addition to his interest in Santo Domingo and his more fleeting attention to Cuba, President Grant became enamored of the possibility of an isthmian canal. In 1870 Hamilton Fish concluded another treaty with Colombia, which provided the United States with the sole right of way across the isthmus. However, the Colombian Senate added so many amendments that the pact was never ratified. Grant then had the navy survey possible routes, ordering it to turn over the information acquired to an Interoceanic Canal Commission he had appointed in 1872. Four years later the commission unanimously recommended a route through Nicaragua.

The commission's report gathered dust as Congress remained indifferent until 1879. In that year Ferdinand de Lesseps, builder of the Suez Canal, organized a private stock company and received a concession from the Colombian government to build a canal across Panama. De Lesseps visited the United States to arouse interest in the project, but American leaders were hostile to the plan. President Rutherford B. Hayes, disturbed by the implications of De Lesseps' visit, delivered a special message to Congress clarifying American thinking on the subject of the canal. He told Congress that the United States must control any such interoceanic canal: "The United States cannot consent to the surrender of this control to any European power." To implement this view, the Secretary of State immediately attempted to abrogate the Clayton-Bulwer Treaty of 1850, which provided for the joint building and control of an isthmian canal. The British refusal became the pattern for the next twenty years as successive secretaries of state failed to change Britain's mind on the subject.

Meanwhile, De Lesseps had begun digging in Panama, and a private, American-owned company obtained similar concessions from Nicaragua in

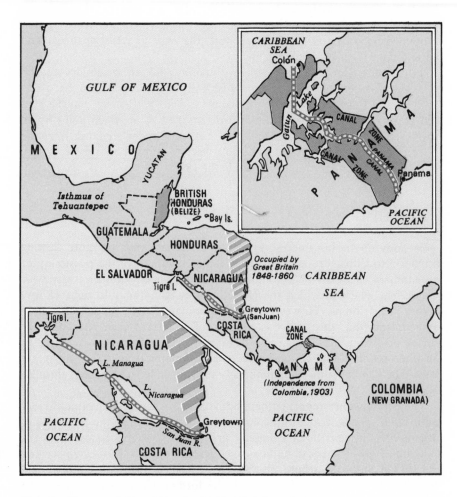

Map 6. Proposed Canal Routes in Central America

1879, but soon failed. De Lesseps' progress goaded the United States to new action. The State Department negotiated a treaty with Nicaragua in 1885, superseding that signed by Seward. This treaty for the first time incorporated the principle that the United States alone should own, construct, and operate the canal. As such, it patently violated the Clayton-Bulwer pact and infuriated the British. The Senate refused to approve the pact; and when it came up for reconsideration, the new Democratic administration withdrew it.

The United States did little more until the late 1890's, but another private American company went ahead with plans for a Nicaraguan canal. The De Lesseps company, after completing about a quarter of the excavation, went bankrupt in 1889, and much of its equipment was sold to the Nicaragua company. But the resources to sustain its effort were too limited, and in 1893 this company also declared bankruptcy. The project of an American interoceanic canal now became a temporary victim of the depression of 1893 and its aftermath. It was not until the beginning of the Spanish-American War that the question reappeared in a most dramatic fashion.

THE PACIFIC ISLANDS DURING THE GILDED AGE

Certain Pacific islands in the 1870's and 1880's reattracted the attention of American commercial interests. In Hawaii, for example, American entrepreneurs had markedly increased the production of sugar for export. They demanded reciprocity to enable them to compete with Louisiana sugar. Refining operations, using Hawaiian sugar, were set up near San Francisco; here too the operators pressed the government for reciprocity. In 1875 an initial treaty, allowing Hawaiian sugar to enter the United States duty free for seven years, was signed and ratified. During the depression of 1873, Secretary of State Hamilton Fish insisted that reciprocity was necessary to prevent the Hawaiian Islands from turning to Great Britain.

The pact climaxed the American economic hold over the islands that had been steadily increasing since the 1850's. It also stimulated the growth of the sugar industry to such an extent that a serious labor shortage developed. The planters then contracted for cheap Chinese and Japanese labor. When the treaty expired seven years later, another convention extended it for seven more years. The Senate delayed action until 1887, at that time adding an amendment that gave the United States exclusive coaling rights at Pearl Harbor. The Hawaiian government, dependent for its existence upon the revenues from the sugar industry, reluctantly acquiesced. Two years later the State Department offered Hawaii a new treaty, which would have curtailed its governmental prerogatives, but the Hawaiians declined to consider it.

THE SAMOAN ISLANDS AND INTERNATIONAL RIVALRIES

The experience of the United States in the Samoan Islands pointed up the scramble for new markets and colonies in an area as yet unclaimed by Britain or France. The ringleaders in this scramble were the United States, Germany, and soon Japan, although in this case Japan and France were not involved.

The Samoan Islands, nominally Christian since the efforts there of British Protestant missionaries early in the century, were well known to American whalers and traders, who frequently called at one of the two good harbors, Apia on Upolu or Pago Pago on Tutuila. Charles Wilkes had charted the fourteen islands of the group in 1839. Especially impressed with the harbor at Pago Pago, he appointed an acting consul there and signed a treaty of friendship and commerce with some of the chiefs. However, the effects of his visit were not permanent.

Over the next thirty years, German traders, chiefly representing Goddefroy and Son of Hamburg, dominated the islands economically. They were less successful politically because the natives were split into several warring factions, each claiming sovereignty. After the Civil War several American promoters obtained large tracts of land from some of these factions. Calling themselves the Polynesian Land Company, they failed to interest the American government in their scheme and it quickly collapsed. The promoters were followed almost at once by an agent of the successful New York shipbuilder and promoter, William H. Webb, who asked the United States government for a subsidy to establish a San Francisco to Australia and New Zealand steamship line that would call at Samoa. Webb sent reports extolling the strategic position of the islands and the harbor at Pago Pago. The American government turned down his proposal, but New Zealand granted him a small subsidy; he began service, but three years later the company failed.

Webb's reports stimulated the State Department's interest in Samoa. In 1872 an American naval officer, Commander Richard W. Meade, again surveyed the Pago Pago harbor. He signed a treaty with the chief of one of the native factions that gave the United States exclusive rights to the harbor as a coaling station. The Senate, still smarting from Grant's attempted annexation of Santo Domingo, took no action, but the intrepid President did. He sent to Samoa as his confidential agent a big six-foot-tall adventurer named Colonel Albert B. Steinberger. Much to the chagrin of the German and English in Samoa, Steinberger temporarily unified the warring factions and organized a government in 1875 of which he was prime minister. He thereupon resigned as Grant's agent. Within a year he was deposed and shipped off to Fiji aboard a British warship. But although the internal bickering continued, Steinberger had demonstrated to the

Samoan chiefs the possibility of a unified government, and two of the major groups did get together long enough to ask Britain and the United States — but not Germany — for annexation.

In 1878 Chief La Mamea negotiated in Washington the first treaty of friendship and commerce signed by the united chiefs with any government. The pact provided for the nonexclusive use of Pago Pago as a United States coaling station. Because the treaty committed the United States to very little, the Senate quickly approved it, but the House refused to appropriate enough money for the coaling facilities. The Samoan chiefs, under pressure, then made similar treaties with Britain and Germany.

By 1879 the three powers had begun to exercise an informal control over Samoan affairs. However, the various intrigues between foreign government representatives and the chiefs caused, in the words of one expert, "lethargy rather than anarchy" in the Samoan government throughout the early 1880's. By 1886 the United States and Germany, attempting to deal with the situation, met with Britain in Washington. The conference failed; the United States, with the least economic stake in Samoa, called for Samoan autonomy. However, Germany and Britain refused to consider such a proposal.

THE TWO YOUNG GIANTS.
IVAN AND JONATHAN REACHING
FOR ASIA BY OPPOSITE ROUTES.

Soon revolt and counterrevolt raised international tempers to the boiling point. By early 1889 the situation was so tense that three American warships were sent to Apia, where they came face to face with four others, three German and one British. Trouble appeared imminent, for the respective consuls of the three powers were making injudicious accusations. On March 16, 1889, a sudden hurricane struck, with disastrous effect. Of the seven warships in the unprotected harbor, only H.M.S. *Calliope* reached the open sea and successfully rode out the furious tropical storm. The American and German ships were either sunk, badly disabled, or beached, and many lives were lost.

This incident prodded another three-power conference meeting in Berlin in April 1889 to come to an agreement about Samoa. After drawn-out negotiations, the powers agreed to set up a condominium to govern the country. In reality, this merely upheld the status quo. The Senate reluctantly approved the agreement, recognizing that the United States' participation marked a fundamental departure from previous foreign policy. The solution satisfied no one; it was another decade before Samoa became entangled in nascent American imperialism.

THE UNITED STATES AND ASIA DURING THE GILDED AGE

American foreign policy in Asia was concerned with upholding and expanding the rights acquired by United States nationals in China and Japan. One exception to this pattern was Korea, where in 1882 an American diplomat signed a commercial treaty with the "Hermit Kingdom." Previous efforts, including one patterned after Commodore Perry's in Japan, had failed because of Korea's precarious position as a pawn in Far Eastern politics between China and Japan, each of whom had historical claims to suzerainty over the country. The United States' treaty recognized Korea as an independent kingdom, a fiction ended by the resounding Japanese victory in the Sino-Japanese War of 1894-1895.

During this period, American relations with Japan were far more cordial than those with China. A Japanese mission sent to the United States on the eve of the Civil War was successful in accomplishing its diplomatic ends, but it did not arouse the interest of Americans. A similar mission in 1872, however, caused a great deal of public excitement, keeping Japan in the public eye for two decades. Toward the end of the century the American essayist Lafcadio Hearn published several beautiful and laudatory books about his adopted country, and this also served to keep interest alive and well-disposed toward the distant land.

In China the story was quite different. Since the signing of the Burlingame Treaty, Chinese immigrants had poured into the United States. They were mostly landless, poverty-stricken rural peoples from south China who emigrated to work on the railroads in the West. By 1870 they numbered 63,000 and a decade later, 105,000. After the railroads were built, American workers became increasingly hostile to Chinese competition in the labor market. A series of riots in California added substance to the growing demand for exclusion of the Chinese. After several abortive attempts,

Congress passed the Chinese Exclusion Law of 1882, which suspended Chinese immigration for ten years. The law exemplified the practice of permitting unrestricted immigration from Europe while restricting it from Asia. The point was not lost on Asian governments, but there was little the Chinese could do. A particularly bloody massacre of twenty-eight Chinese miners at Rock Springs, Wyoming, in 1885 expressed the persisting ill feeling. Congress extended the Exclusion Act before it expired, in spite of protests from the Chinese government.

THE UNITED STATES AND THE CONGO

Among the least likely places reached by United States foreign policy during the Gilded Age was the Congo. The State Department became embroiled in the Congo because of the efforts of two men, the erstwhile explorer and reporter Henry M. Stanley and the wealthy American promoter and diplomat Colonel Henry S. Sanford. Both worked for King Leopold of Belgium to further recognition of his personal control over the vast tropical land. Other European powers were interested in exploiting the Congo, and Portugal had long claimed the region. However, Sanford, backed by Stanley and his high reputation, lobbied astutely, dangling before Congress the lure of a potential market. Congress and the State Department formally recognized the paper regime of Leopold on April 10, 1884. In this affair, a leading authority on the period concluded: "the United States had not risked anything except for loss of face, but it had not gained anything either."

The next year an American delegation played a prominent part at a European conference called to decide the future of the Congo. The United States was conspicuously successful in expounding and getting adopted liberal trade principles for the African country. These included free trade, free navigation, religious freedom, and a ban on the slave trade. The country now became the Congo Free State, although it was still controlled by Belgium. In the commercial race following its establishment, the United States, totally ignorant of conditions in tropical Africa, proved unable to compete.

THE SETTLEMENTS WITH GREAT BRITAIN

In spite of the United States' failure to pursue the expansionist foreign policy goals of Seward during the Gilded Age, American diplomats could cite with mixed feelings another development of comparable importance. Beginning somewhat awkwardly in the Grant administration was the slow development of an entente with Great Britain. The British actively encouraged it, fearing that Sumner's attitude toward them might be reflected in United States policy. Sumner thought so too, especially when Grant accepted his choice of John Lathrop Motley as Minister to England. But when Motley projected Sumner's ideas in preference to those of the State Department, Fish merely bypassed him. He transferred the negotiations that had long been in progress to Washington. The British proved to be very tractable, probably because they could foresee the consequences if Britain and Russia became involved on opposite sides in the short-lived Franco-Prussian War of 1870-71.

A joint commission of five British and five American negotiators then met to work out a settlement not only of the *Alabama* claims but of other differences as well. They agreed on the Treaty of Washington, which provided for international arbitration concerning the *Alabama* claims and for three additional panels to work on all or parts of three remaining problems. Britain weakened its own case by expressing regret for the escape of the *Alabama* and other raiders, an admission of guilt. Both the United States and Britain quickly ratified the Treaty of Washington, but Canada, involved in the settlement of several of the other problems, did so reluctantly.

THE *ALABAMA* SETTLEMENT

Foremost in the view of both countries was settlement of the *Alabama* claims. A distinguished international tribunal of five members met in Geneva to consider the case. At that moment, the American agent suddenly demanded that the tribunal consider Sumner's claims concerning the indirect cost of the war. The demand endangered the entire proceedings, the British having assumed during the negotiations in Washington that the matter had been dropped permanently. Secretary of State Fish had been responsible for inserting the claim; he had realized that until it was finally laid to rest other settlements would not pass the Senate.

In any case, there were sharp repercussions in England, causing embarrassment to Gladstone and the Liberals who were in office. Charles Francis Adams, the American member of the tribunal, solved the problem by having the tribunal unofficially consider Sumner's claims and rule them invalid. The tribunal then generously awarded the United States $15.5 million for the *Alabama* claims, a sum accepted by both parties.

CANADIAN FISHERIES AND OTHER ACCORDS

Two of the three problems decided by the Treaty of Washington were relatively unimportant and quickly settled; the third concerned American fishing rights off Canada and was more complex. Since the United States had ended reciprocity, Canada had retaliated by setting its own high tariffs and by restricting American fishing rights to those outlined in the Convention of 1818. In 1877, a tribunal convened at Halifax, Nova Scotia, ruled that the United States could use Canadian shores and waters for fishing purposes by paying $5.5 million for the privilege. The United States paid, but the issue was far from settled. When American fishermen complained about some parts of the agreement, Congress abrogated the settlement, effective July 1, 1885. Each side adopted retaliatory tactics toward the other until finally another arbitration was agreed upon.

In the fall of 1887 in Washington, a joint Anglo-American commission negotiated a treaty, which was signed in February but then defeated in the Senate the following August. The commissioners farsightedly adopted their findings as a two-year modus vivendi, which was renewed several times, although the situation was not permanently solved until 1912.

THE UNITED STATES AND PELAGIC SEALING

Another kind of fishing problem involving the United States and Canada concerned the pelagic, or offshore, sealing practices in the Bering Sea. Canadian seal hunters commonly killed the seals in the water as they migrated from their Pribiloff Islands breeding grounds. The sex of the animal could not be determined in the water, and it has been estimated that for every seal killed and skinned, four others died. To stop this practice, the United States in 1886 declared the Bering Sea closed. Canadian ships were seized on the grounds that they were decimating the seal herds. Britain, still responsible for Canada's external relations, protested vociferously. The tribunal set up to arbitrate the matter in 1892 found against the United States on all counts and the United States was required to pay Canada approximately $500,000 for the ships seized.

This did not save the seal herds. After 1900 the Japanese too joined in the decimation. The Russians, concerned over their own seals, joined with the United States in offering concessions to the Canadians and the Japanese in exchange for regulations. In 1911 a four-power treaty, with England still representing Canada, was signed. Subsequently, the treaty was renegotiated in 1957 and renewed in 1962. It provided for 30 percent of the kill to be divided equally between Canada and Japan, and outlawed pelagic sealing and the killing of females. In this way an awkward diplomatic problem involving both morality and profit was solved.

THE ANGLO-AMERICAN ENTENTE

By the last decade of the nineteenth century the United States had reached an entente with Great Britain. Unofficial, unexpected, and pragmatic as it

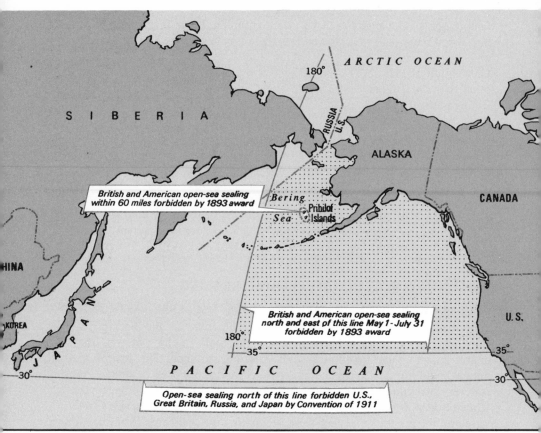

Map 7.   Bering Sea Sealing Controversy

was, it was based upon grudging mutual respect and a willingness to discuss mutual problems. Irish-Americans were still hostile and a small group still looked toward the annexation of Canada, but by and large relations and understanding steadily improved despite a rather ludicrous incident that occurred during the presidential election of 1888. Sir Lionel Sackville-West, the British Minister, privately preferred one presidential candidate, a fact which was disclosed with great fanfare. The American government demanded his recall, but the British refused until the charges could be investigated. The United States then dismissed him, which so infuriated the British that he was not replaced until after the election of another president four years later. Sir Julian Pauncefote, the new minister and an able and experienced diplomat, smoothed over the affair, serving in Washington with distinction until 1902.

By the 1890's the Gilded Age and all it connoted was fast receding. A new generation of politicians with strong convictions and forceful leadership prepared to arouse the American public from its continentalism. In transferring the emphasis from domestic to international concerns, this group paved the way for new problems and new solutions. Interestingly enough, they did this by effectively employing the rhetoric of the Gilded Age.

Further Reading

A good diplomatic overview of the entire priod is found in Foster R. Dulles, *Prelude to World Power: 1860-1900* (New York, 1968). A challenging new interpretation of the same era is *Walter La Feber, *The New Empire: An Interpretation of American Expansion, 1860-1898* (Ithaca, N.Y., 1963).

For a more detailed look at the diplomacy of the 1880's see David M. Pletcher, *The Awkward Years: American Foreign Relations under Garfield and Arthur* (Columbia, Mo., 1961). Merze Tate's study on Hawaii, *The United States and the Hawaiian Kingdom: A Political History* (New Haven, Conn., 1965), is excellent. Edwin P. Hoyt, *The Typhoon That Stopped a War* (New York, 1967) is a journalistic account of the Samoan affair.

For a look at several of the Grant appointees and other State Department problems see Frederick W. Seward's book cited at the end of the last chapter. Roy F. Nichols' volume, cited at the end of Chapter 7, is also useful here.

Asterisk denotes paperback edition.

10

The End of Continentalism, 1890-1900

The end of American continentalism did not come about in just one decade. Besides a small group of political leaders who looked beyond the boundaries of the United States, there were unmistakable signs of a change in the American public's attitude toward expansionism and colonialism. In 1883 the Republican administration of Chester A. Arthur had laid the foundations of a modern navy by building three steel light cruisers. Slowly the "white fleet," consisting of lightly armored fast ships (of several classes) designed for lightning strikes, emerged. This concept, however, was a far cry from the fleet, consisting of large, heavily armed battleships designed for offensive action, which emerged in the 1890's.

THE INTELLECTUAL BASIS OF IMPERIALISM

Contrary to their usual pragmatic and individualistic behavior, Americans at the end of the century were profoundly influenced by ideas, which became a rationale for American imperialism. By this term is meant the establishment of colonies and the attempt to dominate other peoples. Quite possibly, imperialism, as formulated in nineteenth-century America, began with the work of the English philosopher and pioneer sociologist Herbert Spencer. Applying Darwinian concepts to society, Spencer argued that the ultimate survivor — the fittest in society — was the most able businessman and that the most advanced society was Western and European. Belief in the inherent superiority of some peoples over others became one of the important bases of American imperialism. This belief was echoed by many others who, though using far different methods of reasoning, also arrived at Spencer's conclusions. The Reverend Josiah Strong, for example, in his 1885 best seller, *Our Country,* insisted that

Christianity should be the civilizing agent in all parts of the world. However, the most qualified purveyors of Christianity, in Strong's estimation, were members of the Anglo-Saxon race, whom he urged to take aggressive action both to alleviate the problems of American industrialization and to compensate for the closing of the American frontier.

THE ANGLO-SAXONS, 1885

From Josiah Strong, *Our Country*

God, with infinite wisdom and skill, is training the Anglo-Saxon race for an hour sure to come in the world's future. Heretofore there has always been in the history of the world a comparatively unoccupied land westward, into which the crowded countries of the East have poured their surplus populations. But the widening waves of migration, which millenniums ago rolled east and west from the valley of the Euphrates, meet today on our Pacific coast. There are no more new worlds. The unoccupied arable lands of the earth are limited, and will soon be taken. The time is coming when the pressure of population on the means of subsistence will be felt here as it is now felt in Europe and Asia. Then will the world enter upon a new stage of its history — the final competition of races for which the Anglo-Saxon is being schooled. . . .

If I read not amiss, this powerful race will move down upon Mexico, down upon Central and South America, out upon the islands of the sea, over upon Africa and beyond. And can any one doubt that the result of this competition of races will be the "survival of the fittest"?

Within a decade, *Our Country* had sold 175,000 copies so that, taken together with works in a similar vein by the popular homespun philosopher John D. Fiske, the impact was formidable. Fiske, who singlehandedly produced almost a five-foot bookshelf, was especially adept at popularizing the ideas of Darwin, Spencer, and other philosophers. In his most famous article, "Manifest Destiny," which he repeated innumerable times as a lecture, Fiske combined social Darwinism with Anglo-Saxonism to produce a potent concept of an elite American force whose mission was the betterment of the world.

Two others who arrived at the same conclusions from rather different directions were a naval officer, Captain Alfred Thayer Mahan, and a college professor, Frederick Jackson Turner. Mahan is better known because he was the only naval thinker and strategist of real importance that the United States ever produced. The publication in 1890 of *The Influence of Sea*

Power upon History, in which he traced and explained England's greatness in terms of its maritime supremacy, put him very much in the public eye. Mahan believed that maritime supremacy required a flourishing foreign commerce carried by a healthy merchant marine, all supported by a strong navy maintaining a chain of overseas bases. The empire forged by the English prospered because colonies supplied both raw materials and markets for the mother country.

In 1890 Mahan began a vigorous magazine campaign in which he called for the use of these ingredients in the building of an American empire. He advocated a powerful navy and an isthmian canal protected by strategically located bases in the Caribbean and the Pacific. He further suggested that overseas expansion could reduce the specter of overproduction, which had become quite real with the depression of 1893. Although Mahan spoke and lectured widely, his ultimate recognition was due to the influence he exerted over a group of young, rising politicians who eventually implemented most of his program.

Quiet, studious Frederick Jackson Turner made almost as strong an impact in academic circles. In 1893 in Chicago, he delivered his intellectual bomb, "The Significance of the Frontier in American History," which has markedly influenced the interpretation of American history ever since. Turner suggested that the western frontier, with its availability of free land, was the most significant and unique aspect of American history. It shaped the country's form of democracy and engendered certain character traits such as individualism. Further, the frontier served as a safety valve for untold thousands in the East, shaped political institutions, and promoted nationalism. When the free land was gone and the frontier closed in 1890, according to Turner, a great epoch was ended. Turner, agreeing with other ideologues, suggested the pattern of imperialism as an alternative in an 1896 article. His contention was that, even though American continental expansion had ended, to assume that:

> these energies of expansion will no longer operate would be a rash prediction; and the demands for a vigorous foreign policy, for an interoceanic canal, for a revival of our power upon the seas, and for the extension of American influence to outlying islands and adjoining countries, are indications that the movement will continue.

A final contemporary to be mentioned is Brooks Adams, a social philosopher and intellectual in his own right. As befitted the grandson of John Quincy Adams and the son of Charles Francis Adams, Brooks Adams was a fierce individualist whose ideas often ran counter to those professed by other men of the period. He eventually became a positive supporter of

American imperialism. Three of his closest friends during the 1890's were among the most persistent imperialists: Theodore Roosevelt, Assistant Secretary of the Navy in 1897; Henry Cabot Lodge, an influential long-term Massachusetts congressman and senator (1892-1924); and John Hay, Secretary of State (1898-1905).

LATIN AMERICA AND AMERICAN DIPLOMACY

While some of the problems troubling United States relations with Latin American countries were traceable to the earlier part of the century, others began or were aggravated during the 1880's and 1890's. Early in the 1880's James G. Blaine, an aggressive Republican spoilsman with a blemished record and an overweening ambition for the presidency, became Secretary of State. His first tenure of office — six months — was cut short by the assassination of President James A. Garfield, whose successor belonged to a different wing of the Republican party. But Blaine returned to the position nearly eight years later and served for the full term of Benjamin Harrison's presidency.

James G. Blaine took aggressive steps to widen the United States' sphere of influence in Latin America. He was especially interested in competing with and besting England in selling manufactured goods there. A firm advocate of reciprocity during a high tariff period, Blaine forced into the McKinley tariff bill — a high tariff measure — an amendment allowing very little reciprocity. This was the most he could achieve against a Congress which wanted no reciprocity whatsoever. The amendment was adopted but was never given a fair trial; it was prohibited by Congress in 1894.

Blaine's initial diplomatic overtures to the South and Central American countries were totally unsuccessful. At the request of Guatemala, he attempted in 1881 to mediate a struggle between that country and Mexico. Not only did he fail to help Guatemala, he succeeded in antagonizing Mexico. Far more serious were Blaine's efforts to end the War of the Pacific, which began in 1879. Chile was fighting Peru and Bolivia for possession of a guano-rich area that also contained nitrate deposits. By 1881, victorious Chile had appropriated the contested area, and the special envoy dispatched by Blaine to make peace based upon the status quo ante bellum won nothing but hostility for the United States.

In truth, Blaine earnestly desired to bring about cooperation among the nations of the hemisphere. To this end, he proposed a conference, but left office before it could be implemented. Later, he returned to act as host to the Inter-American Conference of 1889, the first of its kind since John Quincy Adams' day. The representatives of eighteen Latin American countries were taken by train on a tour of the United States; they responded by electing Blaine the presiding officer of the meetings that followed. Though the meetings accomplished little, they were the forerunner of the Pan American Union of our day, which provides for exchanges of economic, scientific, and cultural information within the Western Hemisphere.

THE UNITED STATES AND CHILE

The ill will that Chile felt toward the United States erupted in two incidents in 1891. Chile was divided by civil war, the president and his supporters opposing the members of the Chilean congress and the navy. The rebels' ship *Itata,* sent to obtain arms, was detained by American authorities on a charge of violating neutrality laws. The crew overpowered the United States marshal on board and steamed for Chile. An American cruiser gave chase but did not intercept the *Itata* before she reached Chile. After vigorous protests by the State Department, the rebels turned over the ship and cargo to the American authorities. Ironically, much later a court ruled that the ship and its cargo had not violated American law.

The rebels' accusation of American favoritism was based on fact. The United States Minister to Chile, Irish-born, aggressive Patrick Egan, openly favored the president's supporters, allegedly because they were anti-British. Egan became very unpopular with most Chileans when he harbored war refugees in the legation, an action that sparked the second incident in October 1891. Commander Winfield S. Schley of the U.S.S. *Baltimore* allowed a large number of his crew to go on shore leave in Valparaiso, long a liberty port for American naval units. Chilean tempers were high; a brawl began in the heart of the saloon district in which two sailors were killed and others beaten and knifed by an angry mob. The police allegedly aided the mob. Reaction in Washington matched the incident: President Harrison and his Secretary of the Navy, Benjamin F. Tracy, belligerently demanded an apology and an indemnity. In spite of the good intentions of Blaine, who sought to settle the affair peacefully, Chile was first dilatory and then obdurate about the matter. The United States not only prepared for war, but Harrison actually sent a war message to Congress on January 25, 1892. Chile immediately backed down, apologized, and paid an indemnity of $75,000 for the families of the dead and wounded men. The incident clarified two things concerning the United States: it pointed up the country's rising jingoistic attitude, and it demonstrated the importance of the new navy as a powerful foreign policy maker — a harbinger of times to come in American foreign affairs.

THE VENEZUELAN BOUNDARY DISPUTE

The attempts of successive secretaries of state to pursue an aggressive policy in Latin America embroiled the United States in a diplomatic wrangle with Great Britain in the mid-1890's. An area comprising approximately 50,000 square miles lying between Venezuela and British Guiana had long been in dispute. The area assumed new value when gold was discovered there, because access to it was by way of Venezuela's Orinoco River, whose mouth formed part of the disputed territory. The claimants broke off diplomatic relations in 1887; the United States then persistently offered its good offices for arbitration. The Venezuelans were always willing to arbitrate, but the British consistently refused. They maintained that the territory had always belonged to British Guiana and was not susceptible to arbitration. The affair dragged on until a lobbyist hired by Venezuela captured the attention of both the American public and Congress. In January 1895 Congress passed a resolution urging arbitration, and President Cleveland signed it. When there was no response from England, the new Secretary of State, Richard Olney, a vigorous Boston corporation lawyer, sent a strong note in which he accused Britain of violating the Monroe Doctrine by holding land claimed by Venezuela. "Today the United States is practically sovereign on this continent, and its fiat is law," Olney stated, to which the British Prime Minister replied by denying the validity of the Monroe Doctrine in international law and refusing to allow the United States to arbitrate the dispute.

With the permission of Congress, President Cleveland set up an independent commission to recommend and then enforce a boundary line. American public opinion seemed to favor such a militant action, but the British unexpectedly agreed to international arbitration. Eventually 90 percent of the disputed land was awarded Great Britain, with control of the mouth of the Orinoco River going to Venezuela. The British change of heart reflected a new understanding of the realities of international politics. Faced with worldwide competition from their former ally, Germany, the British evidently saw the necessity of building friendships and, later, ententes with their two hereditary enemies, France and the United States.

During the Venezuelan boundary argument, the German kaiser openly supported the dissident anti-British Boers in South Africa, thereby alarming other European nations who feared the outbreak of another war. The threat receded, but England moved to bolster its American ties by negotiating a general arbitration treaty in 1897. Although Congress would not approve the proposed treaty because it committed the United States in advance to a course of action, cordiality between the two countries nevertheless increased, marked by a new diplomatic departure in 1895. In that year the

United States and Britain agreed to ambassadorial rank for their ministers. Perhaps more symbolic than meaningful, the act signified not only a new token of mutual esteem but implied diplomatic equality between two of the major nations of the world.

HAWAII AND THE RISE OF AMERICAN IMPERIALISM

One of the first areas to experience the strident, growing American imperialism was the Hawaiian Islands. The McKinley Tariff Act of 1890 removed Hawaiian sugar from the protected list and, in addition, gave Louisiana sugar producers a subsidy of two cents a pound. At about the same time, a strong-willed, anti-American monarch, Queen Liliuokalani, succeeded to the throne. She soon unilaterally annulled the constitution which originally had been inspired by white American planter interests, substituting for it one which gave the monarchy and the native Hawaiians actual political power. At that juncture, January 16, 1893, the American business community instigated a revolt. Fortunately a bloodless revolution, it was aided and abetted by John L. Stevens, the American Minister to Hawaii, who favored annexation. At an opportune moment, he landed 150 Marines from the U.S.S. *Boston,* ostensibly to protect American lives and property. The next day, the revolutionists abolished the monarchy, and Stevens hastened to recognize their government.

PATIENT WAITERS ARE NO LOSERS.

Uncle Sam. — I ain't in no hurry; — it'll drop into my basket when it gets ripe!

This 1897 cartoon reflects the American attitude toward continued expansion.

Two weeks later, Stevens proclaimed the Hawaiian Islands a protectorate and hoisted the American flag. By mid-February 1893 President Harrison submitted to the Senate a treaty of annexation together with a curious statement that the United States government had not aided the revolution! The Senate, however, did not act on the treaty until the incoming President, Grover Cleveland, was again in office.

Cleveland, who did not favor an expansionist policy, acted with moral certitude and withdrew the treaty from consideration. He sent a personal representative, James H. Blount, to Hawaii to investigate. Blount disavowed the protectorate, lowered the American flag, and wrote a scathing indictment of Stevens for fostering and abetting the revolution. Cleveland not only accepted the report but planned to reestablish Queen Liliuokalani on the throne. But the business interests, who had established a republican government headed by Judge Sanford B. Dole, were firmly entrenched. Dole and his government threatened another revolution if the queen were restored. Unable to resolve the problem without the use of force, President Cleveland called upon Congress. But when Congress did nothing, Cleveland reluctantly recognized the Dole government. For the next four years the Hawaiian Islands, anticipating annexation when and if the Republicans returned to power, helped pave the way for this eventuality by employing an effective group of lobbyists.

The work of propagandizing for Hawaii caused a major debate to break out between proannexation imperialists and those who opposed the addition of any territory to the national domain. In their 1896 party platform the Republicans pledged annexation. When William J. McKinley was elected, he redeemed the pledge by signing another pact with Hawaii calling for annexation. A new factor was the supposed interest of Japan, based on the fact that one quarter of the Hawaiian population was Japanese and that this group had always suffered discrimination. Annexationists argued that Japan coveted the islands, a claim seemingly borne out by the presence there of a Japanese warship. Japan had also officially protested against the possibility of American annexation. In any case, the Senate still had a strong enough minority to prevent approval of the treaty by the two-thirds vote needed. McKinley then resorted to the tactics used by John Tyler a half-century before. He introduced the annexation treaty as a joint resolution, which needed only a majority of both houses to pass.

Even so, opposition was fierce. Only the obvious strategic value of the islands in the face of a war with Spain aided passage of the resolution. In July 1898 Congress passed the resolution, which the President signed on August 12, 1898, in time for the Hawaiian Islands to become the United States' first major overseas acquisition. The similarity of the episode to the annexation of Texas may well be noted.

CUBA AND THE AMERICAN MARTIAL SPIRIT

The growth of American imperialism and jingoism was best illustrated in Cuba. Cuba had not been in the American public eye for a decade, but it was still seething with discontent, fostered by the inept and corrupt Spanish rule. The immediate cause of Cuban insurgency was a severe depression brought on by the passage of the Wilson-Gorman Act of 1894, a generally low tariff act which paradoxically raised the tariff on Cuban sugar. As plantation workers were laid off in great numbers, many formed rebel bands, and another revolt broke out in February 1895. Both sides resorted to a scorched-earth policy, but for different reasons. The rebels felt that destroying the economic life of the island would drive out the Spaniards; the Spaniards, for their part, felt that it was the only way to deprive the rebels of the use of the land. The result was misery and privation for the Cuban people, as well as the destruction of much American property. The ability of the rebels to propagandize effectively in the United States made the difference in the volatile situation.

Since the end of the Ten Years' War, according to one recent expert's report, of the seventy-one filibustering expeditions embarking from the United States, twenty-seven had reached their destination. Although not permanently effective, this action demonstrated the ability of the Cuban exiles to gain support. Large sums of money were again raised to assist the rebels. It was indicative of the mood of the country that President McKinley, certainly lukewarm about annexing Cuba, secretly donated $5,000 to the rebel cause.

The burgeoning revolution forced Spain to take new steps. In February 1896 General Valeriano Weyler was ordered to Cuba to crush the insurgents. He instituted a harsh concentration-camp policy and resettlement program, the evils of which the American press was quick to exploit. In two years, about 200,000 Cubans — men, women, and children — died from disease, malnutrition, and battle wounds.

Two New York newspapers were instrumental in keeping the revolt constantly before the American public. William Randolph Hearst's *Journal* and Joseph Pulitzer's *World* were locked in a circulation battle, and both used sensational "yellow journalism" in their quest for stories. They did not hesitate to concoct incidents or to exaggerate others out of all proportion in order to make sensational news. Other papers throughout the country echoed the imperialist and interventionist editorials of the New York journals, but few went to such extreme lengths. Hearst's often quoted remark to an artist complaining about his inability to draw dramatic pictures because of the quiet situation was symptomatic. Hearst wired the artist: "You furnish the pictures and I'll furnish the war." Sensationalism did sell newspapers; by 1898 both New York dailies were selling about 800,000 copies each, with special editions selling over 1,000,000.

AMERICAN DIPLOMACY AND CUBA

American diplomats had also been active in Cuba's behalf. Cleveland's Secretary of State tried unsuccessfully to negotiate with Spain, and Congress then passed a joint resolution asking Cleveland to recognize Cuban belligerency as well as to try negotiation. Cleveland, very much opposed to any form of American intervention, refused. By this time, Spain was convinced that the United States wanted the island, and its intransigence mounted. The Republicans inserted a strong statement in their platform demanding that "the government of the United States should actively use its influence and good offices to restore peace and give independence to the Island."

When McKinley came to the presidency, the deteriorating situation seemed suddenly to have improved. Because in the autumn of 1897 a new liberal government in Spain had announced reforms for Cuba, he therefore moderated his strong stand. But within two months it became clear that the Spanish were unable or unwilling to effect the needed changes. McKinley was willing to intervene on a humanitarian basis, but the immediate impetus for war came from two events having little to do with humanitarianism toward the Cuban people.

The first concerned Dupuy de Lôme, a veteran Spanish diplomat and Spain's Minister to the United States. He had written an intemperate letter concerning American politics and politicians to a friend who was traveling in Cuba. A rebel sympathizer stole the missive, and it was published in sensational style on the front page of the February 9 issue of the New York *Journal.* De Lôme displayed the characteristic Spanish aristocratic arrogance toward Cuba. In evaluating the United States' role, he characterized McKinley as "weak and a bidder for the admiration of the crowd, besides being a would-be politician who tries to leave a door open behind himself while keeping on good terms with the jingoes of his party." Although de Lôme resigned and the Spanish government apologized, the incident polarized American opinion, undercutting the position of moderates who favored Spanish retention of the island together with reforms.

The situation did not have a chance to settle before the second incident occurred. A month earlier, Fitzhugh Lee, Consul-General in Havana and an ardent interventionist, had requested naval protection for American property. The light battleship U.S.S. *Maine* arrived and anchored in Havana Bay. On the night of February 15 the *Maine* was blasted out of the

DESTRUCTION OF THE U.S. BATTLESHIP *MAINE*

water by some type of undersea charge. The explosion killed 260 officers and men and sank the ship. Inflammatory articles in the American press left no doubt that the Spanish were the culprits. However, a naval inquiry held shortly after the blast and a subsequent inquiry in 1911 failed to fix the responsibility for what was called "an external explosion."

At the outset, McKinley tried to soothe the troubled waters, but he soon escalated his demands. Beginning with simple reforms, he next demanded the independence called for in the Republican platform of 1896. In early March 1898 Congress gave the President a blank check for $50 million for war preparations. There followed a short, painful period during which Spain desperately tried to extricate herself from a probable conflict that could only end in defeat. Several European countries — notably excepting Britain — halfheartedly tried to mediate on Spain's behalf, but these efforts were doomed to failure. On April 20 Congress voted to recognize Cuba as a free state; five days later it declared war on Spain retroactive to April 21. At the same time the war resolution was passed, Congress also approved an amendment by Senator Henry M. Teller of Colorado stating that the United States had no intention of annexing Cuba.

THE SPANISH-AMERICAN WAR

The ten-week Spanish-American War proved as successful as the jingoes had foreseen and even made an imperialist out of William J. McKinley! But American victories in "the splendid little war," as John Hay later termed it, could not conceal the grave deficiencies in the army any more than could American enthusiasm or Spanish ineptitude. The army's normal authorized strength of just over 25,000 men was commanded by officers who had seen little action since they were junior officers in the Civil War. Worse, the logistics of sending off three expeditionary forces, one to Cuba, another to Puerto Rico, and, later, a third to the Philippines, threatened to overwhelm the entire organization. Only rampant individualism combined with ability, enthusiasm, and good fortune saved the day. Another pitfall was yellow fever, to which the army fell prey after its notable victory at San Juan Hill. It proved to be a far greater scourge than the enemy. By July 17 the fighting in Cuba was over, and within another month, in Puerto Rico also.

The American navy, having long prepared for just such a war, decimated the enemy's obsolete fleet at Manila Bay on May 1; a comparable victory was won at Santiago. After the Manila Bay action, Admiral George Dewey landed the exiled nationalist leader, General Emilio Aguinaldo, who quickly and effectively formed a guerrilla army to fight the Spanish.

Later, the navy was forced to call for an American army to take the city of Manila. The Spanish garrison, preferring victorious Americans to Filipinos, aided the American troops, and Manila fell on August 13, 1898, one day after a preliminary peace treaty had been accepted by Spain. The treaty called for the Spanish surrender of Guam, cession of Puerto Rico and Guam, and American occupation of Manila and its environs until a final decision concerning disposition of the Philippines was made.

General Aguinaldo soon realized that American procrastination over leaving Manila meant that the Filipinos had merely exchanged one conqueror for another. His guerrilla action against the American army soon erupted into a far more costly conflict for the United States than the war against Spain had been. The Filipino nationalists were not subdued until 1902.

THE PHILIPPINES AND THE UNITED STATES

The United States had won the war convincingly; Americans seemed to reflect genuinely humanitarian attitudes toward Cuba, but the Philippines were a different matter. They were almost completely unknown to the citizenry, even to government officials. The future of the islands sparked an intense, nationwide debate of three months' duration in the fall of 1898. Naval leaders demanded annexation of the Philippines because of their strategic location as an entrepôt to the Orient and because of the covert plans the Japanese and the Germans supposedly had regarding them. Many business leaders supported annexation on commercial grounds, even though most of them had been antiwar until April. Even that portion of the religious press representing missionary activity abroad editorialized in favor of annexing the Philippines as a Christian duty.

President McKinley, certainly floating with the public tide, acceded to imperialist demands, "but only after praying for divine guidance." On December 19, 1898, a five-man American commission signed with Spain another Treaty of Paris. Providing for the terms of the earlier treaty, it called for American annexation of the Philippines in exchange for an indemnity of $20 million to be paid to Spain. Spain soon sold the remainder of its Pacific island holdings to Germany, leaving that part of the Pacific to the aspirations and competition of the new powers and Britain.

**PRESIDENT WILLIAM McKINLEY'S DECISION
TO ANNEX THE PHILIPPINES, 1899**

When next I realized that the Philippines had dropped into our laps I confess I did not know what to do with them. I sought counsel from all sides—Democrats as well as Republicans—but got little help. I thought first we would take only Manila; then Luzon; then other islands, perhaps, also. I walked the floor of the White House night after night until midnight; and I am not ashamed to tell you, gentlemen, that I went down on my knees and prayed Almighty God for light and guidance more than one night. And one night late it came to me this way—I don't know how it was, but it came: (1) That we could not give them back to Spain—that would be cowardly and dishonorable; (2) that we could not turn them over to France or Germany—our commercial rivals in the Orient—that would be bad business and discreditable; (3) that we could not leave them to themselves—they were unfit for self-government—and they would soon have anarchy and misrule over there worse than Spain's was; and (4) that there was nothing left for us to do but to take them all, and to educate the Filipinos, and uplift and civilize and Christianize them, and by God's grace do the very best we could by them, as our fellow men for whom Christ also died. And then I went to bed, and went to sleep, and slept soundly.

The Treaty of Paris had rough going in the Senate. A respected Republican senior senator from Massachusetts, George F. Hoar, led the battle against it, supported by a diverse group of Americans, many of whom had joined the Anti-Imperialist League. Its ranks included industrialist Andrew Carnegie, labor leader Samuel Gompers, politician Carl Schurz, college president David Starr Jordan, Speaker of the House Thomas B. Reed, and writers Hamlin Garland and Mark Twain. The fight for the treaty was led by the other Massachusetts senator, Henry Cabot Lodge. The role of William Jennings Bryan, titular head of the Democratic party, was unclear: on the one hand, he was strongly anti-imperialistic; on the other, he desired a clear-cut issue for the 1900 presidential race. The final vote taken on February 6, 1899, was 57 to 27, one vote more than the required two thirds needed for approval.

The most popular political satirist of the day, Peter Finley Dunne, using his characters Mr. Dooley and his friend Mr. Hennessey, expressed what a great many Americans felt. Hennessey said, "We're a gr-reat people," to which Mr. Dooley replied, "We ar-re that. An' th' best iv it is, we know we ar-re."

THE FRUITS OF VICTORY

The dictums of Mahan and other imperialists seemed to be fully borne out and reinforced by the American victory. One episode that contributed even more to Mahan's stature occurred early in the war. The battleship U.S.S. *Oregon* was stationed at Puget Sound when the commander of the

Atlantic fleet ordered her to join his fleet. Then began an epic race against time around Cape Horn to Cuban waters that both captured public attention and underscored the great need for an interoceanic canal.

The Spanish-American War also served as the catalyst that forced 76,000,000 Americans in 1900 to look outward and to accept the status of world power that their explosive economic development had brought about.

THE UNITED STATES SINCE THE MONROE DOCTRINE

In the three quarters of a century since the Monroe Doctrine was first promulgated, the United States had outgrown its adolescence, expanded, and changed. For instance, the State Department, employing thirteen clerks in Adams' day, required sixty-five in 1898; correspondingly, the number of diplomats rose from fourteen ministers and over 140 consular officials to more than double that number.

At the turn of the century the United States was still an agricultural country, but it now had the largest industrial potential of any nation. Not only had the population increased sevenfold and the economic value of manufacturing twentyfold, but a corresponding social and intellectual ferment had accompanied the development. The fabric of government had survived the Civil War; in 1900 the emphasis was on economic, political, and diplomatic concerns.

Further Reading

For an overview of the diplomatic aspects of this decade, consult the volume by Foster R. Dulles cited at the end of the last chapter. Another survey covering the next fifty years and having a different point of view is *William A. Williams, *The Tragedy of American Diplomacy*, rev. and enl. (New York, 1962).

The intellectual frame of American imperialism is presented in *Richard Hofstadter, *Social Darwinism in American Thought: 1860-1915*, rev. ed. (New York, 1959). This subject is also discussed in Ernest R. May's excellent study, *Imperial Democracy: The Emergence of America as a Great Power* (New York, 1961), with an emphasis on United States diplomatic policies in the 1890's.

A good diplomatic history of the Spanish-American War is *H. Wayne Morgan, *America's Road to Empire: The War with Spain and Overseas Expansion* (New York, 1965). For a lively account of the fighting, see *Frank Freidel, *The Spendid Little War* (Boston, 1958). An older and still valuable book on the same subject is Walter Millis, *The Martial Spirit: A Study of Our War with Spain* (Boston, 1931). For the use of the navy during the war see the book by Harold and Margaret Sprout cited earlier, and also Brayton Harris, *The Age of the Battleship: 1890-1922* (New York, 1965).

Bradford Perkins' recent study, *The Great Rapprochement: England and the United States, 1895-1914* (New York, 1968), is highly recommended for its examination of Anglo-American relations during this period.

Asterisk denotes paperback edition.

Part III • The World Without: America as a World Power, 1900-1945

11

The United States and Latin America: The Protector and the Unprotected

The United States' relationship with Latin America changed perceptibly after the acquisition of Caribbean territory in the wake of the Spanish-American War. Earlier, the American presence had been limited to economic investment, infrequent naval visits, and occasionally a diplomatic crisis. Now the United States considered itself very much a part of the area and moved swiftly to strengthen its position by an aggressive and expansive foreign policy. The first country to feel the change was Cuba. Each American president since Grant had deprecated the notion of annexing Cuba. President William McKinley repeatedly stated this view during the war; and it was buttressed by the Teller Amendment by which Congress pledged the United States not to annex Cuba.

CUBA'S STATUS AND AMERICAN IMPERIALISM

The Cuban situation quickly changed after the fighting ended. The American occupation army, commended by tough, annexationist-minded General Leonard Wood, introduced all manner of reforms, but still the Cubans were not happy. They demanded their freedom. To quiet them and also to co-opt anti-imperialistic sentiment in the coming election of 1900, Wood assembled in Havana in November 1900 a group of Cuban leaders to draft a constitution. But American leaders in Washington had also been studying the problem of how to give Cuba a little independence but not too much. Elihu Root, then Secretary of War, initiated legislation to this end. It was introduced by the expansionist-minded Chairman of the Senate Committee on Cuban Relations, Orville H. Platt of Connecticut, as a rider to the army appropriations bill. Approved in early March 1901, the provisions dealing with Cuba became known as the Platt Amendment. Cuba could draw up its own constitution, and American military occupation would be withdrawn; however, the amendment tied so many strings to the clauses that Cuban sovereignty was permanently impaired, making the country in reality an American protectorate.

Though the Cubans disliked the Platt Amendment, they reluctantly embodied its terms in the constitution they adopted in 1903. The remaining Latin American countries considered the amendment as the first step toward the annexation of Cuba, despite the temporary withdrawal of American troops in 1902. The growing prewar American economic domination of the island now became a stranglehold; investments jumped from about $50 million in 1898 to $200 million by 1911, and to over $500 million by 1920. Sugar for the American market was the commodity that fueled Cuba's governments. To safeguard these investments, American troops returned from 1906 to 1909, in 1911, and again in 1917. In 1917 they helped to keep in power a Cuban president who was at the same time the managing director of the Cuba-American Sugar Company!

THE INTEROCEANIC CANAL AND THE HAY-PAUNCEFOTE TREATY

The construction of an interoceanic canal seemed to most Americans at the turn of the century to be vital for the protection of their newly acquired overseas empire. But there were two unresolved problems: the Clayton-Bulwer Treaty of 1850, and the decision as to a route. The treaty appeared the more formidable in that England saw no reason to abrogate it and said so several times. Nevertheless, when Secretary of State John Hay gave his attention to the matter, the British proved unexpectedly amenable. The British stake in the Caribbean had diminished since 1850, and they preferred to change the pact rather than to allow it to be disregarded, as Congress had threatened it would be.

Hay and the British Ambassador, Sir Julian Pauncefote, concluded a treaty giving the United States permission to construct and to own an interoceanic canal. The treaty also banned fortifications and provided for the neutralization of the proposed canal, but the Senate changed the last two agreements and the British refused to accept the changes. Although Hay's first attempt ended in stalemate, he had no difficulty in reopening negotiations because the British were not unhappy at the prospect of having Americans and American fortifications in the area. Actually, the United States fleet had already replaced much of the British navy in the Caribbean, thus reversing their roles in the nineteenth century. The second agreement, the Hay-Pauncefote Treaty, was signed on November 18, 1901. Superseding the previous treaty, it allowed the United States to proceed unhampered. Tacit permission was granted the United States to fortify the canal, and for its part the United States undertook to charge "just and equitable" tolls. The Senate quickly approved this version; the way was now clear to build an American canal.

THEODORE ROOSEVELT AND THE PANAMA CANAL

The problem of route now assumed major importance. Presidential commissions of 1876, 1895, and one in 1899 headed by Admiral J. G. Walker had all supported a route through Nicaragua as being the least costly. One reason why this route was deemed cheaper than the much shorter one through the Isthmus of Panama was that the New Panama Canal Company, reorganized out of the old De Lesseps group, was asking $109 million for its rusty equipment and the right of way granted it by the Colombian government.

At the time Theodore Roosevelt became President, the New Panama Canal Company, afraid of losing out altogether, lowered its price to $40 million, thereby winning the President's support for the Panama route. The Nicaraguan location was all but concluded, however, after the Senate approved a bill authorizing a canal there, when two astute lobbyists and an upheaval of nature intervened to shift Congressional preferences. One of the lobbyists was a New York lawyer, William Nelson Cromwell, a good friend of Republican leaders and general counsel for the New Panama Canal Company. He reluctantly cooperated with the other lobbyist, Philippe Bunau-Varilla, the flamboyant former chief engineer of the De Lesseps company. For more than a year both men worked to promote the Panama route, but their efforts would probably have been in vain had not nature taken a hand.

At the time Congress was considering the rival routes, Mount Pelée, a volcano on the French island of Martinique, suddenly erupted. The widespread death and destruction resulting from the disaster unnerved congressmen, especially when there were reports of a Nicaraguan volcano erupting only a hundred miles from the proposed route. At that point Bunau-Varilla thoughtfully provided each congressman with a Nicaraguan stamp depicting the volcano in wild eruption. The Senate thereupon changed its mind and, with the House, voted the Isthmian Canal Act on June 28, 1902. The act provided for the purchase of the assets of the New Panama Canal Company for $40 million, to be used for the construction of a canal through the Isthmus of Panama. An agreement made with the Colombian representative in the United States was rejected by the Colombian Senate as an infringement on its sovereignty.

President Roosevelt was furious at this last development and considered taking the isthmus by force. However, he was relieved of such a necessity by Cromwell and Bunau-Varilla. With a war chest of $100,000 Bunau-Varilla departed for Panama to stir up a revolution. Using workers from the American-owned railroad as an army, he declared Panama free of Colombia on November 4, 1903. The United States navy prevented a Colombian army from landing, and, two days later, the United States extended *de facto* recognition to the new republic. Full, or *de jure*, recognition came a week later when Roosevelt officially received Panama's first Minister to the United States, Philippe Bunau-Varilla! Hay had little trouble negotiating a treaty that guaranteed Panama's independence while giving the United States a lease in perpetuity on a strip of land ten miles wide, the proposed length of the canal. Panama was to receive $10 million outright plus an annual rent of $250,000, to begin in nine years. The Hay-Bunau-Varilla Treaty was ratified in February 1904, and Panama became America's second protectorate.

"T. R."

Theodore Roosevelt later took much of the credit for the episode. He had brandished his big stick, and the short-term result was the opening of the Panama Canal a scant ten years later. However, the United States had alienated Latin American countries by its arbitrary action, Colombia in particular. In the long run, Roosevelt paid a high diplomatic price for the gain of perhaps a year or two.

THEODORE ROOSEVELT
ON BUILDING THE PANAMA CANAL

By far the most important action I took in foreign affairs during the time I was President related to the Panama Canal. Here again there was much accusation about my having acted in an "unconstitutional" manner—a position which can be upheld only if Jefferson's action in acquiring Louisiana be also treated as unconstitutional; and at different stages of the affair believers in a do-nothing policy denounced me as having "usurped authority"—which meant, that when nobody else could or would exercise efficient authority, I exercised it. . . .

No one connected with the American Government had any part in preparing, inciting, or encouraging the revolution and except for the reports of our military and naval officers, which I forwarded to Congress, no one connected with the Government had any previous knowledge concerning the proposed revolution, except such as was accessible to any person who read the newspapers and kept abreast of current questions and current affairs. By the unanimous action of its people, and without the firing of a shot, the state of Panama declared themselves an independent republic. . . .

From the beginning to the end our course was straightforward and in absolute accord with the highest of standards of international morality. Criticism of it can come only from misinformation, or else from a sentimentality which represents both mental weakness and a moral twist.

THE BIG STICK IN THE CARIBBEAN SEA

This cartoon from the New York Herald *reflects American attitudes toward T.R.'s action in the Caribbean.*

Presidents Taft and Wilson were assiduous in their attempts to improve relations with Colombia, but Colombia was recalcitrant, demanding either arbitration of the affair or a large indemnity. Every attempt to get Congress to vote an indemnity was blocked by Henry Cabot Lodge until 1921. In that year a treaty was negotiated by which Colombia was paid $25 million for the loss of Panama, a sum reluctantly approved by the Senate only after Colombia made it clear that she would otherwise discriminate against American companies in the newly discovered and extensive oil fields in that country.

THE ROOSEVELT COROLLARY TO THE MONROE DOCTRINE

Theodore Roosevelt made his most famous foray into American foreign policy with respect to Latin America as a result of an incident in Venezuela and another in the Dominican Republic. Venezuela's dictator, Cipriano Castro, defaulted on debts owed to Germany and England. After fruitless negotiations, the two countries decided, as an ultimatum to Castro, to blockade the country, disavowing in advance any territorial claims. The United States, ostensibly remaining on the sidelines, dispatched Admiral Dewey and the American fleet to keep close watch. After some tension, all parties agreed to arbitration and the case was submitted to the International Court of Arbitration at the Hague. While this ended the incident, it raised doubts as to the wisdom of allowing European powers to collect debts forcibly in the Western Hemisphere. A note to this effect was drafted by the Argentinian Minister of Foreign Affairs, Luis M. Drago, and was adopted by the 1907 Hague Conference.

The episode concerning the Dominican Republic began similarly. By 1903 the erratically governed country owed over $30 million, the repayment of which was hampered by a succession of unstable governments. To keep foreign governments from stepping in, Roosevelt announced his Corollary to the Monroe Doctrine, which stated that the United States would assume the authority to intervene to correct wrongdoing in this hemisphere. In other words, the United States would maintain order to prevent European powers from doing so. The Corollary added that American adherence to the principles of the Monroe Doctrine made such a step necessary.

However, when in 1905 Roosevelt asked the Senate's approval to take over the Dominican Republic, the Senate did nothing. The President proceeded to act under the authority of an executive agreement rather than under the terms of a treaty. For two years the navy collected taxes and duties, gave the Dominicans unaccustomed governmental stability, and regularly met payments on the country's debts. In 1907 the Senate, finding little wrong with such an arrangement, approved the treaty submitted by Roosevelt that it had ignored in 1905.

The Dominican Republic story did not end with Roosevelt; both Taft and Wilson authorized American intervention in 1912 and 1916, respectively. The troops sent by Wilson in 1916 remained for eight years, during which time they efficiently operated a dictatorial regime that all but suspended individual rights, freedom of movement, and imposed a stringent censorship. Thus America's third protectorate was little better off in terms of human development than it had been before.

Haiti had an even more constricting experience with the Roosevelt Corollary. President Wilson first sent in the Marines in 1915 to quell what amounted to anarchy, the country having had seven presidents in four years, most of whom had suffered violent deaths while in office. A small but stubborn guerrilla force, aided by the mountainous terrain, was not subdued until 1921. United States troops sustained over 3,000 casualties, and the Marines were not inclined to be gentle with the Haitians. Not until 1934, two years after the navy evacuated the Dominican Republic, did the Marines finally leave Haiti; and in both countries American governmental influence and economic domination lasted far beyond the stay of its troops.

THE AMERICAN PROTECTORATE OF NICARAGUA

In 1910 Nicaragua became another United States protectorate under the Roosevelt Corollary. The Nicaraguan dictator, José Zelaya, had been in power since 1893. Originally supported by American business interests, he shortly became a nationalist with almost imperialistic ambitions. His rule lasted longer than his strength warranted because of his incessant warfare against his neighbors and his fiery anti-Americanism. In 1909 Zelaya refinanced the national debt with a European banking syndicate, pledging the customs receipts as collateral, but before he could begin repayment, he was ousted by a private American-financed revolution. The new government, unstable even with American backing, forced Taft to take over the country. American military personnel then administered the finances of the country. When Taft asked for Senate approval of his action, as Roosevelt had done earlier, the Senate refused, citing its usual arguments against entanglements abroad. Taft then worked out a private debt arrangement by which American bankers took over the customs and began repayment of foreign debts. Nevertheless, in 1912 the President was forced to land troops there once again, and this time they stayed.

Taft also tried to solve Nicaragua's chronic debt problem by signing a treaty giving the United States the right to build a canal through Nicaragua and to establish military bases there for the paltry sum of $3 million. The Senate would not agree, and the plan failed; but when Wilson succeeded Taft he revived the idea. The Bryan-Chamorro Treaty was signed in 1914 and ratified two years later. The Marines remained until 1924, returned in 1926, and stayed on until 1933.

THE AMERICAN NAVY IN THE CARIBBEAN

One often-cited reason for the repeated occupation of Latin American countries was the need to safeguard the Panama Canal. The completion of the Panama Canal confronted the United States with an entirely new strategic problem in which these countries were vital lifelines to the canal

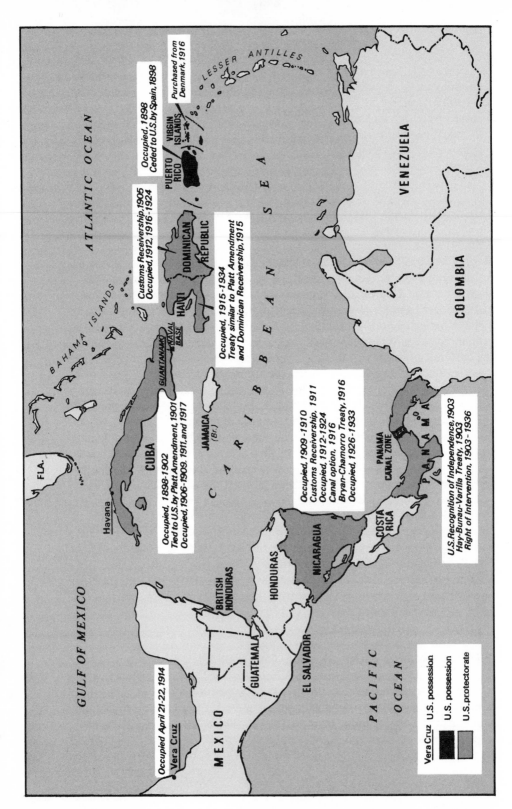

Map 8. American Possessions and Protectorates in the Caribbean

and therefore had to be protected and aggrandized. The navy moved rapidly from the theorizing of Mahan to the construction of a large and powerful battleship fleet. A small naval base at Guantánamo Bay on the southeast coast of Cuba became the center of fleet operations in the Caribbean; in 1909 Congress was asked to authorize construction of a major supply base there but delayed doing so until 1912.

An added dimension of American naval activity in the Caribbean was the use of naval officers as temporary rulers of occupied Latin American countries. They executed and originated foreign policy to such an extent that by the early 1920's some had far more experience in the area than did trained diplomats.

CENTRAL AMERICA AND THE UNITED STATES

The difficulties experienced by the United States in Nicaragua were typical of those faced throughout the remainder of Central America. Honduras, Costa Rica, Guatemala, and El Salvador all had unstable governments which engaged in interminable wars with each other. With more zeal than common sense, the State Department early in the century attempted to combine these countries and Nicaragua into a league, but the plan never became effective. Instead, the small republics all nurtured bitterness toward the United States because of its alleged highhandedness. One example of the American attitude could be found in the terms of the Bryan-Chamorro Treaty. Costa Rica, El Salvador, and Honduras protested that this treaty infringed on their territorial rights because it provided for a Nicaraguan route through territory that was disputed land among these countries. However, the United States blithely ignored their protests, since to have considered them would have cast doubt on the transaction with Nicaragua for use of the land for the projected canal. In addition, the Central American republics were influenced in their actions by Mexico, their neighbor to the north, who was also attempting to dominate the isthmus area.

MEXICO AND THE UNITED STATES

A discussion of Mexico in the early 1900's must begin with a résumé of Mexican governments after Maximilian's overthrow in 1867. Following a short-lived republic lasting only a decade, a new dictator, Porfirio Díaz, took over the government. He was not only the most powerful Latin American strong man but the most durable, retaining power for thirty-four years. In that time Díaz stabilized the government and attracted large amounts of foreign capital by exploiting the poverty-stricken lower classes. Americans had by 1910 invested over $1 billion in Mexico, mostly in oil and mining, and were receiving an excellent return on their investments. Approved by Americans for his zealous protection of their financial interests, Díaz aroused just the opposite reaction when he sought to establish a Mexican sphere of influence in Central America. He supported revolutionary factions in several countries; and when the United States convened a conference in 1907, with the aim of creating stability in the area, a Mexican representative attended but did not sign the final protocol.

Despite these flaws, the ability of Díaz to keep order in Mexico commended him first to Theodore Roosevelt and then to William Howard Taft. Unfortunately, in 1910 a decade-long revolution erupted, passing through several stages before it resulted in radical and permanent governmental and social changes. At the outset, the goal was to overthrow the elderly Díaz; this was accomplished by 1911. The rebel leader who succeeded Díaz was Francisco Madero, an idealistic reformer who had once studied briefly at the University of California. Madero represented the disenfranchised and the landless; he had a somewhat impractical plan for the complete reconstitution of Mexican society along representative democratic lines. The United States promptly recognized his government. As a matter of fact, certain American oil interests aided him financially to keep Díaz from granting the British major oil concessions. However, Madero was brutally murdered in February 1913, leaving his followers leaderless.

Madero's successor and erstwhile chief lieutenant, General Victoriano Huerta, had already deposed Madero before his murder. Americans, shocked by the murder, blamed Huerta — who denied it — and withheld recognition from the regime. Huerta represented the reactionary Mexican landed class; his government was quickly recognized by Britain, France, Germany, and other countries. President Woodrow Wilson was in office before the final decision was made, although the United States Ambassador to Mexico recommended immediate recognition.

Wilson had already decided on a policy — in fact, a new policy. He refused to recognize the new Mexican government because of the brutal way in which it had achieved power. He claimed Huerta did not represent the Mexican people and that American policy would be one of watchful waiting. Privately, President Wilson wrote to a friend: "I am going to teach the South American republics to elect good men." In fact, Wilson was reversing the historic policy of *de facto* recognition, based upon a government's ability to govern, that had first been clearly enunciated by Jefferson a century earlier. According to Wilson's formula, the moral quality of a regime would also weigh in determining whether it should be recognized or not. Wilson backed up his policy by supporting another follower of Madero, General Venustiano Carranza, who had raised a revolt in northern Mexico. The President tried to pressure European governments into disavowing Huerta and supporting Carranza, but he was unsuccessful because Huerta was still favored by foreign business interests.

Carranza, understanding its effect on Mexican public opinion, looked upon Wilson's support as the kiss of death. Only Britain shifted its allegiance to Carranza, and not for reasons of Mexican politics. The British wanted to ensure American friendship in the coming struggle with Germany that they now foresaw. But, practical as ever, the British also demanded something in return for changing their loyalties. They had long claimed that the American law exempting coastwise vessels from Panama Canal tolls violated that part of the Hay-Pauncefote Treaty which called for nondiscrimination against any nation's shipping and which required "just and equitable" charges. For his part, Wilson persuaded Congress to remove the exemption, thus fulfilling the bargain.

Huerta still thrived, but the need for munitions in his struggle against Carranza was urgent. In early April 1914 a paymaster and seven sailors from the U.S.S. *Dolphin*, one of the blockading ships in Mexican waters, were arrested on shore by Huerta's men. On Huerta's order they were quickly released and an apology tendered, but the American admiral demanded, in addition, a twenty-one-gun salute. Huerta refused to comply unless the United States should give him a similar salute, which he knew was impossible as long as the American government did not recognize his regime.

President Wilson then asked Congress for authority to use force to compel proper respect for the American flag. While Congress was in the act of approving the request, Wilson ordered the navy to occupy Vera Cruz to prevent the German steamer *Ypirango* from landing a load of ammunition. The city was captured only after sharp fighting in which nineteen Americans and more than a hundred Mexicans were killed. Public opinion in Latin America was so aroused against the United States that Wilson was forced to halt his offensive actions. Even Carranza blasted the landing as another foreign intervention.

At that juncture — and to Wilson's obvious relief — Argentina, Brazil, and Chile (called the ABC powers) offered to mediate. Both sides promptly accepted. The conference was fruitless except insofar as it gave Wilson more time to work against Huerta. A month later the Mexican leader lost his business backing and, weakened by Wilson's policies against him, fled the country. Carranza succeeded to the government but proved unable to unite all the factions.

The United States, having retreated from Wilson's unilateral declaration on the policy of recognition, now attempted to work through an alliance of six Latin American states. This group, in an endeavor to shore up Carranza, extended *de facto* recognition to him in October 1915, a premature act in light of the turmoil which persisted in Mexico over the next five years.

Most of the problems during this period revolved around two generals who continued to oppose the government. The armies of Pancho Villa and Emiliano Zapata pillaged, raped, and robbed in the process of fighting Carranza. Villa murdered sixteen American engineers traveling by train in northern Mexico. He proceeded to compound this felony by raiding Columbus, New Mexico, where he killed nineteen Americans and burned the town. Wilson dispatched 8,000 men under the command of General John J. Pershing to hunt down Villa. To Carranza's consternation, Pershing pushed deeper and deeper into Mexico, engaging Villa and other guerrilla forces. However, when Villa remained elusive, Carranza used the opportunity of the American invasion to solidify his hold on the central government. A series of informal meetings were held between the United States and Carranza regarding Villa, Pershing, and other problems, but little was accomplished.

Wilson realized that the strong possibility of American intervention in World War I necessitated a withdrawal from Mexico. In January 1917, therefore, he began to recall the American troops despite the fact that Villa was still unpunished. On March 11, 1917, Carranza promulgated a new constitution, which proved to be a significant event in his career. Elected president under its terms, he thereafter ignored his own creation. Early in 1920 he was ousted by General Álvaro Obregón.

Although Wilson extended *de jure* recognition to Carranza's government after the adoption of the constitution and his election as president, Carranza became bitterly anti-American. This attitude toward the United States may have been a decisive factor in the adoption of Article 27 of the constitution, which by giving the government all subsoil rights in Mexico immediately jeopardized foreign oil and mining interests. For the next two decades the United States tried diplomatically to protect American investments in the face of increasing Mexican social and economic demands to confiscate foreign holdings.

LATIN AMERICA: FACT AND FICTION

The Woodrow Wilson-versus-Mexico imbroglio was symptomatic of American relations and attitudes toward Latin American countries for at least the first three decades of the twentieth century. Wilson's moralistic approach and his change of direction in policy toward Mexico were responsible for the altered relationship of the South American countries with the United States. Hereafter, those nations played either passive or hostile roles in dealing with the United States and responded only to economic or political coercion.

The State Department itself did not contribute to a better understanding. Having only a few experienced Latin American experts, the department did not give even these men positions of importance until the 1920's. Before then, not only did presidents meddle, but they sent their secretaries of state on goodwill or fact-finding trips like that taken by Elihu Root in 1906. In this instance, Root's enthusiastic accounts, reflected in those of the newspapermen who accompanied him, differed markedly from the meager foreign policy results.

To Latin Americans, during the period from the end of the Spanish-American War to the outbreak of World War I, the United States remained the country whose motives were the most suspect. The appellation "Colossus of the North," used by its southern neighbors to denote the United States, was particularly descriptive and apt.

Further Reading

Two general histories that span the progressive era satisfactorily are *George E. Mowry, *The Era of Theodore Roosevelt: 1900-1912* (New York, 1958) and *Arthur S. Link, *Woodrow Wilson and the Progressive Era: 1910-1917* (New York, 1954).

The diplomatic history of the United States during roughly the same period is treated by Julius W. Pratt in *America and World Leadership: 1900-1921* (New York, 1970). An excellent book dealing with the United States in the Caribbean is Dana G. Munro, *Intervention and Dollar Diplomacy in the Caribbean: 1900-1921* (Princeton, N.J., 1964). For United States-Mexican affairs, see *Howard F. Cline, *The United States and Mexico*, rev. ed. (Cambridge, Mass., 1963) and *Robert E. Quirk, *An Affair of Honor: Woodrow Wilson and the Occupation of Veracruz* (New York, 1967).

Two books about Theodore Roosevelt are listed at the end of the next chapter, while a third, *Howard K. Beale, *Theodore Roosevelt and the Rise of America to World Power* (New York, 1966), is pertinent here. Books cited earlier by Bradford Perkins and William A. Williams are also helpful.

Asterisk denotes paperback edition.

12

Worldwide Interests and International Rivalries, 1900-1914

The twentieth century was ushered in by Americans and their news media with only slightly less ceremony than that accorded Queen Victoria during the celebration of her Diamond Jubilee in 1897. Albert J. Beveridge, a popular senator known to support expansion, keynoted the event in a burst of enthusiasm, declaring:

> God has made us master organizers of the world to establish system where chaos reigns. . . . He has made us adept in government that we may administer government among savage and senile peoples. . . . . He has marked the American people as His chosen nation to finally lead in the regeneration of the world.

THE CONFIDENT AMERICAN

Buoyed by their accomplishments of the past century and fueled by the mass labor of the very immigrants they often assailed, most Americans were self-confident and assertive — even bumptious — naive, and emphatically moral. The citizen of the turn of the century was mirrored in his leaders. Compared to Civil War and post-Civil War politicians, the new breed, which included such colorful personalities as Theodore Roosevelt, Robert M. LaFollette, and "Golden Rule" Jones, was both dynamic and progressive. They tended to turn to the new social sciences to solve social problems. The reform legislation began first at city and state levels, but by Theodore Roosevelt's presidency had reached the national government. The aura of progressivism permeated Washington; its effect on the conduct of American foreign policy was also exemplified by Roosevelt. His personal moral values became his criteria for evaluating international affairs. Nations, as well as people and businesses, were measured by his yardstick, judged good or bad and treated accordingly. Possessing a wide-ranging acquaintanceship with the world's leaders, Roosevelt could often ignore diplomatic channels in favor of direct communication with, say, the German kaiser or the British prime minister. Americans applauded his efforts to simplify foreign affairs, not realizing that on many occasions he complicated matters.

THE RISE OF THE ESTABLISHMENT

American government became much more complex after the turn of the century, but it was not until 1909 that the State Department was reorganized. Four divisions were set up along political-geographical lines: Western European, Near Eastern, Latin American, and Far Eastern (already in operation). At the same time, the top echelon of assistant secretaries was realigned and expanded.

By 1909 a relatively small group of men dominated American foreign policy so completely that it made little difference who was president. The interests of finance capital were preponderantly represented; this included some of the best-known internationally minded industrialists. Railroad tycoon E. H. Harriman and financier J. P. Morgan worked with W. W. Rockhill, Willard Straight, and Dr. Horace N. Allen, who were simultaneously practicing diplomats and businessmen. (Allen was a former missionary as well.)

Secretary of State Elihu Root (1905-1909) was a corporation lawyer who earlier, as Secretary of War, had reorganized the army. He and his successor, Philander Knox (1909-1913), also a lawyer, supported and were part of the rise of the establishment. But other organizations as disparate as the navy and several Protestant missionary societies backed the diplomacy of the establishment because it coincided with their interests.

This led to a staggering increase in American foreign investments, which rose from $0.7 billion in 1897 to $7 billion by 1919, with a corresponding increase in diplomatic participation. The culmination was reached with President William Howard Taft's policy of "dollar diplomacy," which sought to substitute dollars for bullets. In the words of Willard Straight, Acting Chief of the Division of Far Eastern Affairs in 1908-1909, it was "the alliance of diplomacy with industry, commerce and finance."

PRESIDENT WILLIAM H. TAFT ON DOLLAR DIPLOMACY, 1912

In Central America the aim has been to help such countries as Nicaragua and Honduras to help themselves. . . . The national benefit to the United States is twofold. First, it is obvious that the Monroe doctrine is more vital in the neighborhood of the Panama Canal and the zone of the Caribbean than anywhere else.... Hence the United States has been glad to encourage and support American bankers who were willing to lend a helping hand to the financial rehabilitation of such countries because this financial rehabilitation and the protection of their customhouses from being the prey of would-be dictators would remove at one stroke the menace of foreign creditors and the menace of revolutionary disorder.

The second advantage of the United States is one affecting chiefly all the southern and Gulf ports and the business and industry of the South. The Republics of Central America and the Caribbean possess great natural wealth. They need only a measure of stability and the means of financial regeneration to enter upon an era of peace and prosperity, bringing profit and happiness to themselves and at the same time creating conditions sure to lead to a flourishing interchange of trade with this country.

IMMIGRATION AND AMERICAN SOCIETY

The 75,000,000 Americans in 1900 represented more than ever a polyglot. In the next decade, immigration soared to more than twice that of the preceding decade. By 1910 it totaled 8,795,000, mostly from the central, eastern, and southern parts of Europe. Entry into the United States remained virtually unrestricted to Europeans in spite of continuing agitation for limitation. The two most vocal groups were the American Protective Association, founded in 1887, which was militantly anti-Catholic, and the Immigration Restriction League, organized in Massachusetts in 1894. The latter campaigned for literacy tests and constantly warned of the perils of diluting America's Anglo-Saxon strain. This kind of propaganda combined with the threat of cheap labor to arouse hostility toward immigrants which frequently erupted in bloody clashes. Two such were the Haymarket Riot of 1886 and the New Orleans affair of 1891. The Haymarket Riot was sparked by a labor dispute, but it also had strong antiforeign overtones.

The trouble in New Orleans began in March 1891 when unknown assassins killed the police superintendent. Suspicion fell on the Sicilians and other Italians in the city who were members of secret societies known to advocate violence. A number of these men were arrested and tried, but then acquitted by the court. Before the suspects could be released, however, a mob numbering in the thousands, unhampered by the police, broke into the jail and lynched eleven men. The Italian government was incensed, although only three of the eleven men were still Italian citizens. The Italian minister was recalled amid a growing clamor over national honor exacerbated by the press in both countries. The Federal government was virtually helpless in the face of state and local laws. Eventually, the State Department paid an indemnity of $25,000 from its own contingency fund in reparation for actions for which New Orleans was responsible.

JOHN HAY AND THE OPEN DOOR

The Orient was the first international arena in which the United States tested its new world status after the Spanish-American War. The results of that test, apparent to all, were interpreted in widely different ways. The term "Open Door" referred to the policy under which the Western nations and Japan carved out economic interests for themselves in China on a nonexclusionary and equal basis. This situation, existing since the days of Anson Burlingame in the 1860's, ended with the Japanese victory over China in 1895. After that, the Japanese as well as Russia, France, Germany, and Great Britain became more rapacious in their demands. By the late 1890's the complete political and economic dismemberment of China seemed at hand.

Several influential American interest groups which deplored the possibility of dismemberment, although for different reasons, joined forces in a strange alliance. Business interests professed to see a great threat to their almost nonexistent market of 400,000,000 Chinese. American missionary societies believed that their half-century of work would be wasted if they were forced out by other powers. Naval officers pointed out the strategic value of obtaining bases on the coast of China. (The Chinese government was willing to grant these, but other foreign powers objected.) Finally, the State Department was alarmed by the rapid domination of a large part of northern China by the Japanese. The confluence of these groups and their demands for action led to one of the most quixotic episodes in American diplomatic history.

John Hay, who became McKinley's Secretary of State in 1898, was the central voice in enunciating American policy. Hay had begun public service as Lincoln's secretary, going on to serve in several legations before being appointed an assistant secretary in 1879. Wealthy, cultured, moving in Washington's highest social circles, he strongly espoused the imperialism of the 1890's. To secure the United States' commercial rights and to prevent dismemberment, Hay continued Burlingame's successful policy of forcing predator nations in China to respect treaty obligations. These guaranteed equal commercial rights and Chinese territorial integrity. The British in 1898 suggested just such a policy, to be implemented by an Anglo-American alliance. But Hay rejected this proposal and instead drafted a note with the aid of two advisers that accomplished the same purpose unilaterally. His aides were Alfred E. Hippisley, an Englishman who had served the Chinese as a customs official, and William W. Rockhill, a wealthy American expert on Asia.

The result was the first Open Door Note, sent to Great Britain, Germany, and Russia on September 6, 1899, and later to France, Italy, and Japan. The note asked these nations to accept nondiscriminatory practices within their spheres of influence in regard to duties, harbor charges, and railroad rates. Mild in phraseology, it made no mention of guaranteeing Chinese territorial integrity or of the question of sovereignty.

All six nations responded evasively in diplomatic language. Hay thereupon announced publicly on March 20, 1900, that all six had accepted his Open Door policy. For a variety of reasons, none of the nations involved called his bluff; thus the Open Door quickly became a successful *fait accompli* as far as the American public was concerned. However, the countries to whom the note had been addressed reacted in much the same way they had to the Monroe Doctrine in 1825: they ignored it.

THE BOXER REBELLION

Before Hay had time to attempt other ploys, an insurrection broke out in China. It was initiated in June 1900 by a fanatical antiforeign group called the Boxers. They captured much of Peking, murdering and pillaging as they

JOHN HAY

advanced. Then they besieged the foreign compound of the city, which contained most of the foreign legations. Poorly organized and armed and ineffectually led though they were, the Boxers nevertheless proved a formidable foe. They were secretly aided by the Chinese dowager empress, who hoped to bolster her rapidly decaying regime. The siege lasted until August when an international rescue force of 14,000, 2,500 of whom were Americans, raised the siege and crushed the uprising.

It was obvious that foreign powers might once again seize on such an opportunity to permanently emasculate China. With the dual purpose of averting this possibility and of upholding American interests, Hay sent a circular note on July 3, 1900, to the governments concerned. Often called the Second Open Door Note, it and the first note together comprised the United States' Open Door Policy. More specific and more stringent than the first, the second note insisted on the preservation of Chinese territorial integrity and administrative control as well as on the necessity of safeguarding "the principle of equal and impartial trade with all parts of the Chinese Empire." Hay did not request or expect replies to this note; its purpose rather was to attest publicly to America's idealism in international affairs. During the election year it served to counter much of the criticism leveled by the Democrats and anti-imperialists at the government because of the continued fighting in the Philippines.

THE OPEN DOOR NOTES, 1899-1900

Circular Letter of September 6, 1899

...the Government of the United States would be pleased to see His German Majesty's Government give formal assurances and lend its coöperation in securing like assurances from the other interested powers that each within its respective sphere of whatever influence—

First. Will in no way interfere with any treaty port or any vested interest within any so-called "sphere of interest" or leased territory it may have in China.

Second. That the Chinese treaty tariff of the time being shall apply to all merchandise landed or shipped to all such ports as are within said "sphere of interest" (unless they be "free ports"), no matter to what nationality it may belong, and that duties so leviable shall be collected by the Chinese Government.

Third. That it will levy no higher harbor dues on vessels of another nationality frequenting any port in such "sphere" than shall be levied on vessels of its own nationality, and no higher railroad charges over lines built, controlled, or operated within its "sphere" on merchandise belonging to citizens or subjects of other nationalities transported through such "sphere" than shall be levied on similar merchandise belonging to its own nationals transported over equal distances.

Circular Letter of July 3, 1900

... The purpose of the President is, as it has been heretofore, to act concurrently with the other powers, first, in opening up communication with Pekin and rescuing the American officials, missionaries, and other Americans who are in danger; secondly, in affording all possible protection everywhere in China to American life and property; thirdly, in guarding and protecting all legitimate American interests; and fourthly, in aiding to prevent a spread of the disorders to the other provinces of the Empire and a recurrence of such disasters. It is, of course, too early to forecast the means of attaining this last result; but the policy of the government of the United States is to seek a solution which may bring about permanent safety and peace to China, preserve Chinese territorial and administrative entity, protect all rights guaranteed to friendly powers by treaty and international law, and safeguard for the world the principle of equal and impartial trade with all parts of the Chinese Empire.

Not so widely heralded, but of more lasting importance, was the American disposition of the huge Boxer indemnity China was forced to pay. Of its share of $25 million, the United States remitted nearly $17 million to the Chinese government, which used $10 million of the amount to set up scholarships for young Chinese for study in China and in the United States.

JAPAN AND FAR EASTERN POWER POLITICS

In spite of Hay's efforts, American investors in China were frustrated in their efforts to materially enlarge their holdings by the power politics of the European nations and Japan. The problem became more acute after the Russo-Japanese War of 1904-1905. Enmity between Japan and Russia had begun in the 1890's when Japan attempted to secure an economic foothold in Manchuria, only to be rebuffed by Russian troops who had stayed beyond the time of their promised departure. Japan concluded a naval alliance with Great Britain in 1902 (expanded in 1905 and renewed in 1911) which recognized Japanese naval primacy in the Pacific. The alliance freed the bulk of the British Pacific fleet to join the Atlantic fleet as a bulwark against Germany in the anticipated showdown.

The Russo-Japanese War began with a surprise Japanese attack on the Russian fleet at Port Arthur. Because the Japanese were considered the underdogs in the war, the American public enthusiastically supported their efforts. Even Theodore Roosevelt thought, "Japan is playing our game," but his attitude changed when the Japanese decisively defeated the Russians on both land and sea. He soon came to feel that a victorious Japan — not Russia — was the real threat to America's Open Door Policy.

Japan secretly asked Roosevelt to use his good offices to end the war, which, although they were winning, was seriously overtaxing their resources. The Treaty of Portsmouth (New Hampshire), mediated by Roosevelt, was concluded in September 1905. By its terms, the Japanese received a free hand in Korea and southern Manchuria and acquired half the Russian island of Sakhalin, which lay north of the Japanese homeland island of Hokkaido. The Nobel Peace Award was later conferred on Roosevelt for his efforts. Actually, however, he aroused Japanese enmity when he refused to agree to a large indemnity that they desperately needed, and his decision called forth anti-American riots in Tokyo.

The Japanese occupation of Korea closed the country to Western exploitation. The United States not only concurred but secretly agreed in September 1905 to recognize Japanese control over Korea in exchange for a Japanese disavowal of intentions toward the Philippines. The pact was negotiated by Roosevelt's Secretary of War, William Howard Taft, and Count Taro Katsura. Never publicly acknowledged, it became known as the Taft-Katsura Agreement. Shortly afterwards, the United States withdrew its minister and closed its legation in Seoul. Korea endured five more years, but its existence was a farce. When Japan formally annexed the Hermit Kingdom in 1910, the United States said nothing.

THE JAPANESE SCHOOL CRISIS

However, from this time until the outbreak of World War I, United States-Japanese relations were not smooth. Much of the difficulty lay in the continued prejudice shown by Americans toward Orientals, in this case the Japanese. Discriminatory patterns similar to those against the Chinese were displayed in the San Francisco school incident in 1906. The school board passed an ordinance segregating the comparatively few Japanese children. Japan protested to Roosevelt, who had no jurisdiction in a city matter. Nevertheless, he replied that he would resolve the problem. Using judicious pressure and personal charm, Roosevelt persuaded the city to suspend action. On the other hand, during 1907 and 1908 he worked out a series of executive agreements with the Japanese Ambassador by which Japan voluntarily ceased issuing exit permits to her nationals to come to the

United States. In return, Roosevelt promised that the United States would not stigmatize them by passing laws barring their entrance. This compromise became known as the Gentlemen's Agreement.

Nevertheless, anti-Japanese sentiment on the West Coast increased rather than diminished, and relations between the United States and Japan continued to be strained. About this time, Roosevelt illustrated his dictum to "Speak softly but carry a big stick." He sent a strong naval contingent to Pacific waters in December 1907, and on around the world. While the fleet was being employed as an adjunct of foreign policy, Roosevelt in May 1908 concluded a five-year arbitration treaty with Japan.

Even more important, Secretary of State Root was negotiating with the Japanese Ambassador, Baron Kogoro Takahira. Signed on November 30, 1908, the Root-Takahira Agreement resolved several of the outstanding differences between the two countries. It also established the status quo in Asia — meaning recognition of Japan's hegemony over southern Manchuria — while the United States gained an undisputed hold on the Philippines. By the terms of the agreement, the United States retreated even farther from its own Open Door Policy.

THE STATE OF CALIFORNIA VERSUS JAPAN

While the Japanese government and the Roosevelt administration were easing tensions through realistic diplomatic negotiations, California's attitude remained obdurate, hostile, and discriminatory. Each year, beginning with 1907, legislation restricting the rights of Japanese residents was introduced and only defeated by strenuous political effort. But public hostility was not to be gainsaid. In 1913 the state legislature passed a bill, signed by the governor, prohibiting Japanese from owning land and declaring them "ineligible for citizenship."

The Japanese government protested vigorously, the Japanese populace became violently anti-American, and for a time hostilities appeared possible. President Wilson, who emphasized that California did not speak for the nation, and his pacifist Secretary of State William Jennings Bryan were able to ease the tension. Shortly after, World War I began and Japan turned to carving out a larger share of China than its southern Manchuria holdings. But the California law remained in force, and the Japanese people and their government were not reconciled to the United States until after the war.

THE UNITED STATES AND THE OPEN DOOR IN CHINA

The period between the second Open Door Note and the outbreak of World War I tested the Open Door Policy and found it severely wanting. In

1905 Roosevelt supported E. H. Harriman's plan to buy the South Manchuria Railroad from Japan. When the plan was not realized, Harriman and Willard Straight decided to build their own line, only to abandon the idea at the onset of the financial recession of 1907. The next year Straight, now a State Department official, formed a group of bankers to invest in Chinese railroads. This group strongly protested in 1910 when it was not included in a consortium of English, French, and German bankers which obtained rights to build railroads in south and central China. The foreign bankers reluctantly admitted the Americans, but the advantage quickly became a liability; the consortium loan was the spark that ignited the revolution which overthrew the Manchu dynasty in 1911. Taft's Secretary of State, Philander Knox, tried to use American capital in Manchuria to forestall additional Japanese and Russian expansion; but he only succeeded in antagonizing both countries and in slamming the door on American investments.

The United States, following the lead of the European powers, did not immediately recognize the Chinese republican regime. The European governments stated, and Knox concurred, that recognition would follow if the new Chinese government guaranteed the safety of foreign investments. However, when Bryan succeeded Knox and Wilson followed Taft, they immediately reversed this policy. Thus, on May 2, 1913, the United States became the first major power to recognize the Republic of China. The two Democrats also repudiated dollar diplomacy by turning down a request from American bankers that the government back their investment. Thus, at the outbreak of the war, the American presence in China was marginal, to say the least, and, for the American public, far more imagined than real.

THE UNITED STATES AND EUROPE

Much of this chapter has chronicled American foreign policy in Asia, but the fact remains that the entire nation looked first to Europe. The ambitions of Germany in the period between the Boer War and the outbreak of World War I caused uneasiness, punctuated by several crises involving the United States. The first incident concerned the occupation of Morocco, in dispute between Germany and France. In 1880 Germany, as well as the United States and Great Britain, had acquiesced in allowing France a stronger hand in Morocco. By 1904 France had agreed to allow Great Britain control over Egypt in exchange for French control of Morocco. This began the entente between France and England by which they reversed their historic competition in an effort to thwart German aspirations.

Germany opposed the take-over in Morocco; Kaiser Wilhelm visited the Sultan at Tangier, where he delivered a warlike speech demanding a voice in any decision that concerned Morocco. Although the British supported the

French position, the French were forced to agree to a conference — a diplomatic victory for Germany. The Kaiser persuaded Roosevelt to attend the conference as a moderating influence, much to the annoyance of the Senate, which felt that inasmuch as the United States was not directly concerned, there was no need to meddle. During the conference, held at Algeciras in January 1906, the Germans were chagrined to discover that with the exception of Austria-Hungary, the other participants all supported France. Roosevelt persuaded the participants to accept a compromise treaty, the Act of Algeciras, which nevertheless constituted a diplomatic victory for France since it left her in actual control of Morocco. The Senate consented to the Act of Algeciras with the strong reservation that adherence was not to be interpreted as a departure from the traditional American policy of no foreign entanglements.

THE BIG STICK AT ALGECIRAS

This cartoon comments on T.R.'s intervention in the Franco-German dispute over control of Morocco.

THE CEMENTING OF THE BRITISH-AMERICAN ENTENTE

One of the first diplomatic problems facing the United States after the Spanish-American War was the question of the correct attitude to adopt in the Boer War (1899-1902), then being fought in South Africa between the British and the Boers. The American public seemed solidly pro-Boer, but Hay and Roosevelt were pro-British. In addition, the State Department was chary of possible anti-British moves because of its desire to negotiate an end to the Clayton-Bulwer Treaty. So, while opposition to British imperialism in South Africa was heard, it was muted and never officially expressed.

The only serious problems before World War I to test Anglo-American friendship were those concerning Canadian-American relations. The most important one involved the boundary of Alaska along the panhandle. When gold was discovered on the banks of the Klondike River, Canada claimed a portion of the contested area, which thereby gave its citizens access to the gold region. The thousands of rough-and-ready gold seekers from both nations pouring into the area made for a highly flammable situation. Because a British-American commission had failed to solve the problem in 1898, a temporary and shaky modus vivendi operated until 1902. But with his characteristic bluntness, President Roosevelt took up the dispute. The next year both sides agreed to submit the question to "six impartial jurists of repute," three British and three American. Roosevelt, who did not consider the Canadians to have a case, had already sent troops to the scene to protect American rights. He now appointed the three Americans to the panels, two of whom were not impartial or even jurists! England complied with the agreement and appointed jurists. When the results of the commission's work favored the United States, the Canadians were so incensed that they refused to sign the agreement. They felt that Britain had once again sacrificed Canadian interests for the sake of American friendship. The boundary settlement, together with the fisheries case discussed in a previous chapter, resulted in a Canadian antipathy toward the United States that did not subside until America's entry into World War I.

PEACE CONFERENCES AND WORLD PARTICIPATION

While the Senate tried to prevent America's entanglement in Europe, the executive branch participated more and more often in Continental concerns. In 1899 the United States was fully represented at an international peace and disarmament conference held at the Hague. Called by Czar Nicholas II of Russia, the conference was attended by representatives from twenty-six countries; but hopes for disarmament were soon dashed, and the conference broke up after three months of fruitless discussion. Its sole noteworthy accomplishment was the establishment of a Permanent Court of Arbitration to be composed of a panel of expert and impartial members. But even the countries that signed the final report did not bind themselves to use the Court. During the conference the United States delegation consistently attempted to separate national and international issues, declaring that the former could not be considered negotiable. The Senate supported this view, which became its legislative position for the next four decades.

Czar Nicholas, slightly encouraged by the first conference, called a second at the Hague in 1907. This time, forty-four nations participated, including, for the first time, several Latin American countries. The results were negligible and disappointing to a growing number of Americans educated in the new social sciences who favored a legalistic approach to international problems.

Despite the overall failure of the conferences, both Hay and Roosevelt attempted to make use of the Permanent Court of Arbitration. But when Hay negotiated treaties with individual countries binding both parties to use the Court, the Senate insisted upon a minute examination. Hay, who had little regard for that body, demurred, and it remained for Root to submit treaties that accorded with the Senate's wishes. They were amended to provide for five-year renewable terms and then passed. Most were renewed, but their scope was so narrow that in 1911 President Taft, himself an eminent lawyer, instructed Knox to make model treaties with France and Great Britain that would realistically support his desire for peace as well as the principle of arbitration. Knox tried to do this, but the Senate so truncated the treaties that Taft would not ratify them in their final form.

BRYAN'S PEACE ATTEMPTS

When Woodrow Wilson succeeded Taft as President in 1913, he appointed William Jennings Bryan as his Secretary of State. Bryan was a three-time Democratic presidential candidate and a Midwestern agrarian radical. He was also a religious fundamentalist and antievolutionist who would suffer much cynical abuse at the hands of journalists during his later years. Because American history is usually written by urban-oriented liberal historians, his reputation has never recovered.

Bryan himself considered that the outstanding achievement of his mature career was his work on behalf of peace. He signed over thirty conventions with countries providing for a year's cooling-off period between signatories while an international commission investigated the disagreements. Since these pacts bound the United States to little, the Senate approved them. By November 1914 all the major countries except Germany had signed. None of the conventions were ever invoked, but the idea that nations could be rational in disputes with each other found positive form first in the League of Nations and then in a series of similar pacts negotiated by Secretary of State Frank B. Kellogg a quarter of a century later.

THE EVE OF WORLD WAR I

When the war erupted in the summer of 1914 the United States had already passed through its imperialistic phase. Public opinion deplored the war, and Congress repeatedly attempted to ensure neutrality through legislation. The Senate, in fact, called for disengagement from all foreign involvement. Yet ever since the McKinley era, the executive branch had felt compelled to mount an aggressive American foreign policy in a much changed world. Thus the conflict between the executive and the legislative branches over American foreign policy, which was to culminate in the defeat of the League of Nations in 1919, was clear and well developed by the eve of World War I.

Further Reading

The two general histories by George E. Mowry and Arthur S. Link cited at the end of the last chapter are very helpful. A pair of interesting books dealing with American foreign policy in the first half of this century are *George Kennan, *American Diplomacy: 1900-1950* (New York, 1952) and Walter Lippmann, *United States Foreign Policy: Shield of the Republic* (Boston, 1943).

The role of Theodore Roosevelt is evaluated in Charles E. Neu, *An Uncertain Friendship: Theodore Roosevelt and Japan* (Cambridge, Mass., 1967) and *Raymond A. Esthus, *Theodore Roosevelt and the International Rivalries* (Waltham, Mass., 1970). For further reading on Japan, see William L. Neumann's work cited at the end of Chapter 7. The American role in China during this period is treated in *John K. Fairbank, *The United States and China,* rev. ed. (New York, 1962) and in Paul A. Varg, *The Making of a Myth: The United States and China, 1897-1912* (East Lansing, Mich., 1968).

The voyage of the American fleet around the world is well told in Robert A. Hart, *The Great White Fleet* (Boston, 1965). Good biographies of Henry Cabot Lodge, William H. Taft and others are available and may be read with profit. One especially pertinent study is *Richard W. Leopold, *Elihu Root and the Conservative Tradition* (Boston, 1954). Many of the books mentioned at the end of the last two chapters are helpful.

Asterisk denotes paperback edition.

13

World War I: The Scars of Victory

Americans reacted with disbelief when one of the several crises after 1910 led to the beginning of the most horrendous war the world had ever experienced. There seemed little reason to suspect that the assassination of an Austrian archduke by a Serb nationalist would bring on anything more than another tense period. In fact, the Balkan wars of 1912 and 1913 had appeared far more likely to precipitate a crisis.

Historians and statesmen later professed to see a pattern of secret treaties, alliances, and frictions that made the coming of war inevitable. This may have been a realistic assessment as far as Europeans were concerned, but it was not true for Americans. The people of the United States were still very much imbued with their conception of progress and the perfectibility of man. Their own pragmatism reinforced these beliefs, which dated back a century or more. Thus, when international crises occurred, most Americans were optimistic about reaching peaceful solutions, and until late July 1914 this optimism was borne out by events.

WOODROW WILSON AND "THE GREAT COMMONER"

President Wilson's appointment of William Jennings Bryan as Secretary of State was a political recognition of the Great Commoner's strength in the Democratic party. But Bryan was by this time a somewhat anachronistic representative of the Western populists who were usually both isolationist and pacifist; earlier they had been the backbone of the anti-imperialist movement. Woodrow Wilson, on the other hand, represented the urban, liberally oriented Democrats who were concerned with continuing the progressive movement haltingly begun during Theodore Roosevelt's term. Because of Bryan's personal identification with the cooling-off pacts, he rapidly lost authority and influence as the war intensified, and Wilson more and more concerned himself directly with foreign policy.

NEUTRALITY AND THE AMERICAN PEOPLE

The majority of America's 98,000,000 people in 1914 were pro-Ally, which meant that they favored Great Britain, France, Italy, and Russia as opposed to the Central Powers (Germany, Austria-Hungary, Turkey, and Bulgaria). About 32,000,000 Americans were either foreign born or the children of foreign born. This included 8,000,000 German-Americans and over 4,500,000 Irish-Americans, who were pro-German at the outset. These "hyphenated," Americans were often resented by the bulk of the American people because they retained and promoted Old World languages and cultural ties. Nevertheless, they were important politically, especially to the Democrats, Wilson's election in 1912 having been made possible only by a split in the Republican party. As a minority President, he faced the task of converting his following into a majority by the time of the 1916 election. Wilson moved with vigor on domestic programs and within the Western Hemisphere, but he approached the war in Europe with much more caution.

But Wilson could not prevent the belligerents from attempting to win over American public opinion. The British, masters of propaganda and psychological warfare, succeeded in keeping the United States pro-Ally by emphasizing the Anglo-Saxon American cultural debt to England and playing on American antiforeign emotions. One effective method was to spread horror stories of German atrocities; another was the spy scare, which brought undeserved accusations against and even violence to many German-Americans. Also, the British carefully censored the war stories written by correspondents accompanying the Allied armies to give them a pro-British tone. The Germans at first paid little attention to propaganda in the United States, and incidents such as the execution of Edith Cavell, a British nurse, in October 1915 cost them many friends.

NEUTRALITY AND WOODROW WILSON

At the outbreak of the war, President Wilson immediately proclaimed American neutrality, saying, "We must be impartial in thought as well as in action." But except for Bryan, Wilson and his cabinet were pro-Ally, so that while professing impartiality, Wilson was more neutral toward some countries than toward others.

On various occasions during the first three years of the war, Wilson attempted to mediate the conflict through the person of Colonel Edward M. House, a wealthy Texan and strong supporter who served as the President's unofficial counselor and alter ego. On his third trip abroad in January 1916, House signed a memorandum with the British Foreign Secretary, Sir

Edward Grey, which offered to stop the war at an "opportune time" and let Woodrow Wilson mediate. But both sides were confident of victory, so the opportune time never came.

AMERICAN PROSPERITY AND FREEDOM OF THE SEAS

The United States had been in a business recession on the eve of the war, but prosperity returned quickly as war orders started flowing in from the belligerents. Just as rapidly, however, the United States became involved in the problems of a neutral trading with belligerents during wartime. In the interim since the Paris meeting of 1856, several futile attempts had been made to codify rules relating to neutrals in wartime. More recently, the subject had been discussed at the two Hague conferences and at the London Naval Conference in 1909.

The United States reverted to its liberal interpretation of maritime rights, as it had with the Plan of 1776, rather than to the more constricting position it had adopted during the Civil War. But the three years before American intervention in 1917 represented a sharp attack on this position, mostly at the hands of Great Britain. The British began an unannounced blockade of Germany in March 1915; all ships trading with the Central Powers were stopped and detained, the British now interpreting as contraband even foodstuffs and other items not usually so considered. American shipping was markedly affected because the British navy forced American merchant ships into British ports, confiscating their cargoes or in other ways delaying their sailing, so that the cargo was of little value to the customer. By the summer of 1915 American trade with the Central Powers was virtually nonexistent. The United States protested in vain; a series of notes was sent beginning in September 1914, culminating in a sharply worded one in October 1915. The British, however, understood exactly to what lengths they dared go without jeopardizing American friendship.

Ambassador Walter Hines Page was so pro-British that he personally softened the tone of one of the notes before delivering it. Similarly, Sir Cecil Spring-Rice, the British Ambassador to the United States and a lifetime supporter of Anglo-American unity, did much to smooth over the difficulties caused by Britain's confiscation of American cargoes and the censorship of mail.

Great Britain's increasing control of the seas tended to maneuver the Wilson government toward the Allies, since American businessmen had little choice but to do business with them. From 1914 to 1916, when trade with the Allied countries of Russia, France, England, and Italy jumped from $0.75 billion to $3.2 billion, trade with the Central Powers correspondingly decreased from over $150 million to less than $1.2 million. This dramatic rise in trade with the Allies converted the United States within a short time from a debtor to a creditor nation. The Allies not only spent their available cash, but they soon liquidated their assets in the United States to pay for war material. By 1915 it had become obvious to Wilson that they would require loans. Early in the war Bryan, backed by the President, had forbidden private loans to belligerents, but Wilson reversed Bryan's position to allow short-term commercial credits to Britain, France, and Russia.

ROBERT LANSING AND WOODROW WILSON

By June 1915 Bryan felt that the administration was too harsh in its dealings with the Central Powers and at the same time too soft with the Allies. He thereupon resigned, having been already bypassed in decision making by Wilson. His successor was an urbane, cosmopolitan lawyer, Robert Lansing, who earlier had been a protégé of Elihu Root. Lansing was pro-Ally, his ideas closely paralleling those of Wilson, who took an increasingly larger part in formulating foreign policy.

One of Lansing's first steps was to formulate a new policy on loans. In September 1915 the Allies were permitted to float loans on the American market. Thus, by the time the United States finally entered the war in April 1917, public subscription loans together with those from private banking amounted to over $2 billion, as against about $27 million lent to Germany. Indisputably, and regardless of Wilson's neutrality charade, the Allies effectively linked continued American prosperity to their cause.

THE CENTRAL POWERS AND THE UNITED STATES

The Central Powers, led by the mighty German army, at first rolled victoriously through Belgium and part of France; but after the first battle of the Marne River, the Germans were brought to a standstill on the Western Front. Both sides became deadlocked in trench warfare and settled down to a war of attrition. Until Germany began its all-out submarine warfare in early 1915, its relations with the United States were far smoother than were those of Britain. On February 4, 1915, Germany retaliated against the British blockade by declaring a zone around Great Britain in which all shipping, including neutral shipping, would be subject to attack. Wilson issued a stern warning to Germany — in contrast to the mildly worded note he sent England about the same time — protesting the German blockade as a violation of international law.

German U-boats began to take a heavy toll of Allied shipping. Beginning with the torpedoing of the British liner *Falaba* in late March 1915, American lives were lost. Bryan urged Wilson to ban American travel on ships of belligerents, but Wilson sided with Lansing, who insisted that Americans had the right to travel freely. Loss of American lives prompted German officials to place advertisements in approximately forty American newspapers warning Americans against traveling on British ships carrying munitions. That same day the *Lusitania*, a Cunard liner, sailed from New York with a full passenger list and carrying a cargo partly composed of munitions. On May 7 she was torpedoed in the Irish Sea and sank in eighteen minutes; casualties amounted to 1,198 men, women, and children, 128 of whom were Americans.

Feeling in the United States ran high against Germany, and Wilson sent a strong note demanding disavowal of the act. When Germany's reply was felt to be unsatisfactory, Wilson drafted an even stiffer note. Bryan's opposition to this note was the immediate cause of his resignation, and Lansing's first act as Secretary of State was to deliver Wilson's second *Lusitania* note. German public opinion was likewise aroused, but the German government was not inclined to antagonize the United States government to the point of jeopardizing relations.

In early June the German admiralty issued secret orders to spare large ocean liners and American ships, but on August 19 the British liner *Arabic* was sunk, with the loss of two Americans. The German Ambassador in Washington, Count Johann von Bernstorff, expressed regret for the sinking and offered an indemnity. Von Bernstorff exceeded his cabled instructions, and in a note of September 1, called the *Arabic* pledge, promised that U-boats would not sink unarmed passenger ships without warning. President Wilson had won an important concession from the Germans which, except for the sinking of the Italian liner *Ancona,* was kept until March 1, 1916. In February Germany finally apologized for sinking the *Lusitania* and agreed to pay an indemnity.

However, the pressure of the German war machine was too great for German civilian leaders to long withstand it. On the heels of the *Lusitania* apology came another note informing neutrals that after March 1 German submarines would sink all merchant ships without warning. This note coalesced Congressional sentiment around Bryan's position, which would have prohibited American travel on belligerents' ships. Wilson responded by drafting an open letter to the Democratic chairman of the Senate Foreign Relations Committee supporting Bryan's position. In private, however, he conveyed to key congressmen the political facts necessary for reelection — just six months away — and the entire scheme was quietly shelved.

At about the same time, on March 24, a U-boat sank the unarmed French liner *Sussex* in the English Channel. Although no Americans were lost, the act completely contradicted the *Arabic* pledge. President Wilson threatened to sever diplomatic relations "unless the Imperial Government should now immediately declare and effect an abandonment of its present method of submarine warfare." The German leaders, weighing the cost of alienating the United States against the gains that could be expected from continuing unrestricted submarine warfare, decided for the second time to restrain their U-boats. In the *Sussex* pledge of May 4, Germany promised not to sink merchant ships and passenger liners without warning. Wilson had won another diplomatic victory, but at the cost of narrowing the scope of diplomacy between the two countries.

THE ELECTION OF 1916

The apparent settlement of the U-boat controversy made Wilson's reelection slogan, "He kept us out of war," a potent factor with the American electorate. Wilson waged a forceful campaign against the distinguished but colorless former New York governor and Supreme Court

PREPAREDNESS DAY PARADE

President Wilson marches down Pennsylvania Avenue as war rages in Europe, June 1916.

justice, Charles Evans Hughes. On the one hand, Wilson stressed his successful diplomacy, while on the other he called attention to the nation's preparedness. Large appropriations had been passed by the last session of Congress to increase the strength of the army and navy, although Wilson was forced to rely on Republican support to get the bill passed.

During the election campaign in the summer of 1916, Lansing arranged to purchase the Danish West Indies for $25 million, a feat that neither Seward in 1867 nor Roosevelt — who could have had them for as little as $5 million — in 1902 was able to achieve. Now Lansing stressed to Congress the possibility that the islands might fall into European hands, and the Senate quickly approved the purchase as an aid to preparedness.

Nevertheless, despite Wilson's efforts, preparedness fell far short of that demanded by militant opposition leaders such as Theodore Roosevelt. Roosevelt's militancy and his demands for immediate intervention were an embarrassment to Hughes, who was a moderate and close to Wilson's position on foreign affairs. The election was very close. Wilson was reelected by a narrow margin, but the Democratic majority in Congress was greatly reduced, a portent of disenchantment with the Democratic brand of progressivism.

After his victory Wilson made a last attempt in December 1916 to end the war by mediation. He called on both sides to state their war aims clearly. The replies indicated that each side demanded total victory. Wilson thereupon delivered one of his most famous speeches to the Senate, calling for a lasting peace based not on military victory but on the equality of all nations and "made secure by the organized major force of mankind."

THE ROAD TO WAR

Wilson's pleas fell on deaf ears. The German military machine proceeded with unrestricted submarine warfare, expecting thereby to break the stalemate on the Western Front. Count von Bernstorff transmitted the German statement announcing this on January 31, 1917, at the same time bringing his government's answer to Wilson's war aims message.

The American government's reaction, given Wilson's threats at the time of the *Sussex* pledge, left little choice but to sever diplomatic relations, which Lansing did on February 3. The period from that date until the American declaration of war two months later enabled the American public to become psychologically prepared for war.

When unrestricted submarine warfare resulted in the sinking of American ships, Wilson asked Congress for authority to arm merchant vessels. The House approved, but the measure was defeated by a filibuster in the Senate, thus inspiring Wilson's description of the antiwar senators as a "little group of willful men." He was able to accomplish his purpose, however, by invoking a precedent based on a 1797 law, and by mid-March merchant ships were being armed.

The single incident that most hastened the coming of war was the Zimmerman telegram affair. Alfred Zimmerman, the German Foreign Minister, sent a coded telegram to von Bernstorff for relay to a German official in Mexico. In case of war with the United States, the official in Mexico was instructed to approach the anti-American Carranza with an offer of Texas, Arizona, and New Mexico as a reward for a Mexican alliance with Germany. British Intelligence intercepted and decoded the message but waited over a month before transmitting it to the State Department. Wilson released it to the public on March 1; the outcry was enough to convince him that Americans were ready to intervene. A month later he called for war, telling Congress that "the world must be made safe for democracy." On April 6, 1917, the United States declared war against Germany.

Hoping to cause division within the Central Powers, Wilson did not include Austria-Hungary in the declaration of war against Germany. But Austria was too much influenced by Germany and too weakened by its shaky internal structure to respond. In December 1917 the United States declared war on the Austro-Hungarian Empire.

In retrospect, the decision to declare war seems to have been based not so much on German actions during February and March as on certain other factors. One factor was the Russian Revolution of March 1917, which at first promised the replacement of autocracy by a more broadly based socialistic democracy. Another factor was the pro-Ally sentiment within the United States government and among the American people. While a minority opposed and remained opposed to participation in the war, a study of sixty-eight leading newspapers shows that all but one were vociferously interventionist after the beginning of March. Finally, both Wilson and Lansing concluded that a German victory would destroy any hope for a postwar world based on democratic institutions.

THE CHANGING AMERICAN PEOPLE AND THE STATE DEPARTMENT

The United States mobilized its industrial might and its human resources with a speed that had not been believed possible by either friend or foe. Unfortunately, a comparable marshaling of diplomatic resources did not follow. Wilson did turn to the universities to appoint a group of scholars — numbering as many as 150 — to investigate and advise on policies to be implemented after the war. The Inquiry, as the group was called, was useful but did not significantly affect American policies then or later. Rather, Wilson made his own decisions and announced them personally.

The State Department underwent little change. The size of the department was enlarged from 208 in 1914 to 440 in 1918 to meet the need for increased diplomatic exchanges. For example, in 1914 the department telegraphed 28,091 words; by 1918 the total had risen to 217,597. Unfortunately, the American diplomats of World War I were much like their predecessors. They proved almost impervious to the radical changes in American life that had been engendered by a generation of reform and several years of unequaled prosperity. New modes of behavior, new forms of dress, new moral attitudes were advanced by a literate and growing minority of young people to whom the President and his advisers seemed old-fashioned and conservative.

A pertinent illustration of this conservative bias was the failure of American diplomacy to adjust to the Russian Revolution. By early November 1917 the Bolsheviks, extreme Communists, had overthrown the democratic socialist regime in parts of Russia. Led by Nikolai Lenin, the Bolsheviks won control of the cities and, despite considerable remaining opposition, determined to end Russian participation in the war by making peace with Germany. Because he disapproved of the radical Bolsheviks, Wilson refused to recognize the new Soviet government, a policy the United States maintained until 1933. On November 8, in his Decree on Peace, Lenin called for a democratic peace that would not involve exchange of territories or indemnities. The Allies protested the Russian's unilateral action, but worse was yet to come. Later in the same month the new head of Russian foreign affairs, Leon Trotsky, published the texts of the so-called secret treaties. These consisted of five agreements among the Allies that had been negotiated over a two-year period beginning in March 1915. They specifically spelled out territorial awards to be given the Allies once the Austro-Hungarian and Ottoman empires were dismembered. The agreements had not been made public, although the contents were known to the United States government. Wilson refused to comment, diametrically opposed to his peace-without-victory ideal though the agreements were. After the secret treaties were published, Lenin proceeded to sign a humiliating — for Russia — peace treaty with Germany, completely disregarding earlier treaty obligations to the Allies.

THE UNITED STATES AND THE SPECTER OF COMMUNISM

The sudden shift of government in Russia did as much as the war to shake America's faith in the ideal of exporting democratic institutions. One result was a domestic fear of Bolshevism that far outweighed its contemporary importance. Wilson contributed to this fear by sending a small detachment of troops to Murmansk and Archangel in 1918 to join British and French contingents fighting against the Bolsheviks. This act was undertaken in the face of the President's contention that the Russian people should be allowed to form their own government without outside interference. The American troops were withdrawn in June 1919, eight months after the end of the war. The Allies, however, succeeded in one of their objectives; they carved out of Baltic Russia three buffer states to which the Treaty of Versailles subsequently gave life.

During the same period, an American army of 9,000 landed at Vladivostok. Officially, its purpose was to aid in extricating a Czech army that had been caught in Eastern Europe, but the Czechs, busy fighting the Bolsheviks, appeared in no hurry to leave. Wilson also attempted to use this American army to curb Japanese ambitions in the area, but was unsuccessful.

The American troops remained in Siberia until April 1920, although the war ended in November 1918! Wilson thus backed the Whites against the Reds during the civil war that followed Russia's change in government. It was not until 1920 that Lenin, aided by his war minister Leon Trotsky, was able to defeat the armies of the major contenders. Only then was the American army withdrawn. But American interference left a legacy of suspicion as to America's motives and in the long run served to consolidate support for the Bolsheviks against a foreign invader in time of crisis.

THE UNITED STATES, CHINA, AND JAPAN

The United States experienced new foreign policy difficulties with Japan as early as 1915. When the Allies in Europe declared war in 1914, Japan, although not bound by its pact with Great Britain, followed suit. The Japanese navy swiftly seized German possessions in the Pacific that Germany had acquired some fifteen years earlier from Spain. These islands included the Carolines, the Marshalls, and the Marianas, with the exception of Guam. Equally efficiently, the Japanese army captured control of the Shantung Peninsula, in the process ousting German concessionaires there and blatantly violating China's sovereign rights.

China protested to the United States, claiming that Japan had violated the American Open Door policy. Wilson's administration at first did nothing, on the grounds that it did not want "to allow the question of China's territorial integrity to entangle the United States in international difficulties." Japan took advantage of its favorable position in January 1915 by presenting China with the so-called Twenty-One Demands. Had China agreed to these concessions, she would have ended by subordinating her sovereignty to Japan, just as Korea had after 1895. Secretary of State Bryan protested Japan's demands in a conciliatory note; Japan withdrew the most onerous of them but still required China's immediate acceptance of the remainder. On May 25, 1915, despite another note from Bryan, the Chinese complied. From that time on, Japan held the major economic and political whip hand in China.

Japan took advantage of Europe's preoccupation with the war to replace Allied investments with its own. The Allies suggested to Wilson a revival of the consortium as a means of thwarting the Japanese. The Japanese sent one of their able diplomats, Viscount Kikujiro Ishii, to Washington to prevent this and to define specifically the relationship of both countries to China. Ishii arrived in the fall of 1917, by which time the countries involved — the United States, China, and Japan — were allied in fighting the Central Powers. The Lansing-Ishii Agreement reaffirmed the Open Door policy, once again guaranteeing the territorial integrity of China. But by the terms of a secret protocol, the special rights and privileges of the countries already in China were confirmed. However, the agreement as a whole was so ambiguously worded that both sides claimed a victory. In any event, the agreement mollified somewhat the Japanese anti-Americanism that had arisen as the result of California's laws and the American stand on the subject of China.

Wilson did not hesitate to try to block the gains Japan was making in northern Manchuria and parts of Mongolia at Russia's expense. He hoped to use the army he had sent in 1918, but failed because of the proximity of a far larger Japanese force. He then tried the consortium, which made little headway and was abandoned in 1920. In this case, he reversed his own policy against dollar diplomacy without gaining anything. By the time the war ended, President Wilson's only diplomatic achievement in Asia was that China still survived at all.

WOODROW WILSON AND THE FOURTEEN POINTS

Still concerned with the objectives of the war, President Wilson found it necessary to answer the Russians' publication of the secret treaties. With the help of Colonel House and the Inquiry, he dramatically presented his reply to Congress on January 8, 1918. In it, he specified fourteen points whose realization he believed would be the foundation of a sound and democratic postwar world. Five of the points were international in scope: (1) an end to secret diplomacy; (2) freedom of the seas in peace and in war; (3) the reduction of armaments after the war; (4) removal of international trade barriers; and (5) an impartial adjustment of colonial claims. The next eight points involved the principle of national self-determination: (6) the German evacuation of Russian territory; (7) restoration of Belgian freedom; (8) the

REMEMBER
·BELGIUM·

Buy Bonds
Fourth
Liberty
Loan

WORLD WAR I

*This poster reflects America's
commitment to national self-
determination. Wilson included
the restoration of Belgian
freedom in his Fourteen
Points.*

restoration of Alsace and Lorraine to France; (9) establishment of an independent Poland; and (10-13) the self-determination of the different peoples of the Austro-Hungarian and Ottomon empires. Point 14, Wilson's most cherished one, called for the establishment of a world association of nation-states, regardless of size, to guarantee the independence and territorial rights of all.

As many of the Fourteen Points conflicted with Allied treaties, the program as a whole received a much warmer reception in the United States than elsewhere, though some Americans considered that a provision for hanging the Kaiser ought to be added. Undoubtedly Wilson hoped to influence Germany and Russia as well as the Allies, but his hopes were in vain. Germany imposed harsh terms on Russia under the Peace of Brest-Litovsk signed on March 3, 1918. This included annexing about one third of Russia's European population, in contravention of the self-determination principle set forth in Wilson's message.

THE END OF THE WAR

The collapse of Russia released nearly half a million German soldiers for a concerted drive on the Western Front. By July 1918 the Germans were a scant forty miles from Paris, facing an exhausted Allied army. At this juncture the influx of fresh American troops helped turn the tide. The German army slowly retreated toward its borders; by September the German military leaders asked the United States for peace based on the Fourteen Points, to which the other Allies reluctantly agreed. Before a peace could be implemented, however, the internal situation of the Central Powers disintegrated. The Austro-Hungarian Empire dissolved and ceased fighting on November 3. In the interim the German navy mutinied, the Kaiser abdicated, and the republican government which replaced him agreed to end the war. The armistice ending the fighting was signed in the French commander's private railway car on November 11, 1918.

WOODROW WILSON AND THE PEACE CONFERENCE

The week after the armistice was signed, President Wilson announced that he would participate in the peace conference to be held at Versailles. As he was the first President to leave the United States during his term of office, Wilson's decision aroused controversy on all sides. With him went a five-man commission and a mass of experts, but only one Republican of minor standing was included in the party. President Wilson was greeted in Europe by tumultuous and enthusiastic crowds wherever he went in England, France, and Italy.

Representatives of thirty-two states attended the Versailles Conference. Most of the work in drafting the peace treaties was done by small groups under the supervision of the Big Four: Wilson of the United States; Georges Clemenceau, Premier of France; David Lloyd George, Prime Minister of England; and Vittorio Orlando, Prime Minister of Italy. Wilson believed that the implementation of a world organization was the single most important facet of the negotiations and that other problems, no matter how pressing, could be solved later. The other leaders, clearly speaking for their own countries, demonstrated a thirst for vengeance, a strong interest in territorial acquisition, a passion for security, and a demand for large reparations.

But if their demands ran counter to Wilson's announced objectives, his ideas were equally anathema to them. Europeans had suffered staggering devastation for four years and in the process lost almost an entire generation of young men. While American dead in the war amounted to about 117,000, France had lost 1,300,000, Russia, 1,700,000, Germany, 1,700,000, Austria-Hungary, 1,200,000, Italy, 650,000, and England, 462,000. Little wonder that Wilson was forced first to moderate and then to abandon several of his Fourteen Points in exchange for a world organization! The Allies reluctantly acceded to Wilson's most cherished desire; yet to many

Europeans the concept of a League of Nations seemed to herald a new age in international cooperation.

Some Americans did not agree; Wilson was greeted on his return from Versailles with the Round Robin, a statement from the Senate. Signed by over a third of the senators, it called for postponing action on a world organization until after a peace treaty had been negotiated. The Senate's chief complaint, now and later, concerned Article X of the Covenant to the League, which provided for the collective security of all League members. An attack on one member was to be considered an attack on all, an international aspect that clearly would deprive the Senate of a measure of its national sovereignty. But without Article X, the League of Nations would have been merely an organization of sovereign states not essentially different from the organizations proposed as early as William Ladd's time in 1840.

Wilson returned to Europe and the conference a second time. During his absence many of the decisions concerning the partitioning of Europe had been made. The final document, signed by Germany on June 28, 1919, was a far cry from Wilson's doctrine of leniency. Germany retained its independence but lost its African and Pacific holdings and its concessions in China. Alsace and Lorraine were returned to France; the Saar Basin along the Rhine was to be occupied and exploited by the French for fifteen years, after which a plebiscite would determine the future of the area. New countries such as Poland and Czechoslovakia were carved out of former enemy territory and borders were realigned in the same way. Germany declared its war guilt, agreeing to immediate reparations of $5 billion, with the remainder to be set later. Wilson's only imprint on the final Treaty of Versailles was the inclusion of the League of Nations. But establishment of the League encouraged him to believe that many of the battles he had lost could be retrieved by the successful operation of the world organization. He returned to the United States in July and promptly submitted the treaty to a special session of the Senate for approval.

WOODROW WILSON AND THE NEW CONGRESS

During Wilson's sojourn in Paris, the Congress that had been elected the previous November had convened. The Republicans won a narrow majority in both houses, although Wilson had campaigned strenuously for the Democrats, endeavoring to link a Democratic victory to the success of his Fourteen Points and his program for peace without victory. The new Republican majority, small though it was, foreshadowed the growing conservative temper of the nation. Senate majority leader Henry Cabot Lodge now became chairman of the Senate Foreign Relations Committee, where the treaty would first be received. Lodge's statesmanship, as reflected

Map 9. Europe in 1920

in his handling of the Treaty of Versailles, was unfortunately prejudiced by his personal dislike for Wilson, a feeling the President returned in kind.

Insulated from public opinion though the senators were, they divided into several groups that were very much a microcosm of American attitudes. Most of the Democrats could be counted on for support of the treaty despite some privately expressed doubts. The Republicans were more divided: a group of about twenty, led by Lodge, were strong reservationists; that is, they would vote approval of the treaty only if major changes were made in Article X of the Covenant. Republican Frank B. Kellogg of Minnesota represented a dozen or so members who were mild reservationists desiring only minor changes. Finally, fourteen irreconcilables opposed the treaty and the League in any form. They were more important than their numbers indicated; among them were several of the best-known progressives, including Robert M. LaFollette of Wisconsin, Hiram Johnson of California, and William E. Borah of Idaho. Because of their seniority they held six seats on the Foreign Relations Committee.

LEAGUE OF NATIONS COVENANT AND ARTICLE X

THE HIGH Contracting Parties,
In order to promote international co-operation and to achieve international peace and security
    by the acceptance of obligations not to resort to war,
    by the prescription of open, just and honourable relations between nations,
    by the firm establishment of the understandings of international law as the actual rule of conduct among Governments, and
    by the maintenance of justice and a scrupulous respect for all treaty obligations in the dealings of organized peoples with one another,
Agree to this Covenant of the League of Nations.
Article X. The Members of the League undertake to respect and preserve as against external aggression the territorial integrity and existing political independence of all Members of the League. In case of any such aggression or in case of any threat or danger of such aggression the Council shall advise upon the means by which this obligation shall be fulfilled.

Lodge began committee hearings on the treaty, confiding to friends that he hoped to delay action until the American public could be counted on to oppose it solidly. Through the summer, some sixty witnesses, representing all shades of opinion and all degrees of expertise, testified, while public opinion little by little began to build in favor of Lodge's major reservations.

President Wilson hoped to counter Lodge's stratagem by going directly to the people, a tactic he had used successfully in the past in a battle over tariffs. Despite his physician's warning that the trip might overtax his physical powers, the sixty-three-year-old President undertook an arduous journey through the Midwest to California, giving thirty-two major speeches and eight minor ones. His eloquence moved the large crowds to displays of enthusiasm but probably changed few opinions. A group of Republican senators who followed behind Wilson likewise drew large crowds who listened to them attack the treaty. On October 2, 1919, after speaking to an audience and receiving a wild ovation, Wilson suffered a complete physical breakdown. He was rushed back to Washington where he had a stroke that paralyzed one side of his body and from which he never fully recovered. During the crucial months ahead, he was for all practical purposes no longer a factor to be reckoned with.

Lodge's committee voted out the treaty, at the same time attaching so many recommendations and reservations to it as to render it worthless. The Senate threw out the committee recommendations and began debate on the original treaty. Lodge then introduced a series of amendments from the floor, most of which were inconsequential but one of which would have freed the United States from responsibility to act under Article X unless Congress first approved. Wilson adamantly opposed the Lodge reservation as destroying the League's chances for preserving world peace. Without the Lodge reservation, the treaty was defeated on November 19, 1919. A reconsideration of the treaty in March 1920, this time with the Lodge reservation, likewise lost by a margin of seven votes, 49-35.

Two months later Congress endeavored to end the impasse by passing a joint resolution declaring hostilities at an end, but a presidential veto was quickly forthcoming. Although Wilson had only partially recovered his health, he determined to make the presidential election of 1920 "a great and solemn referendum" on the support of the League. The Democratic candidates, James M. Cox of Ohio and Franklin D. Roosevelt, former Assistant Secretary of the Navy, were pledged to support League membership. The Republican nominee, Warren G. Harding of Ohio, assumed a chameleon-like position on the League issue. Before one group he would favor some kind of League, but not the one proposed; with another he would oppose the idea entirely! In any case, Harding won a smashing victory, defeating Cox by a plurality of 7,000,000 votes.

Harding interpreted his mandate as one of opposition to the League of Nations, and the United States decisively withdrew from membership. Almost as a footnote, the new, solidly Republican Congress ended the war officially by a joint resolution, at the same time reserving the benefits that the Allies had gained under the treaty settlement. The following month Secretary of State Charles Evans Hughes negotiated separate treaties with Germany, Austria, and Hungary, deriving the benefits of the Versailles agreements without assuming the comparable responsibilities.

The United States at long last was at peace with the Central Powers, nearly three years after the last gun had ceased fire on the Western Front. Ever since, historians and observers in general have painstakingly scrutinized every aspect of Wilson's idealism for its relationship to America's failure to join the League and the effect this momentous decision ultimately had on the outbreak of World War II. Postmortems are always hazardous, but in this instance we have expected the right answers to the wrong questions.

The United States in Woodrow Wilson's era was psychologically and temperamentally unsuited to engage in reordering the nation-state system. Achieving the status of a world power earlier in the century without the necessity of having to test its physical and moral strength, the United States was still a relatively unsophisticated member of the world community. Too, the proposed League of Nations was little more than an attempt to freeze the existing status quo within a traditional balance of power setting. Such a concept was compatible with the world as it had existed in the late nineteenth and early twentieth centuries but made little sense after the World War began. Vast technological and social changes had by 1920 brought into being world problems of a magnitude never before conceived. Under such circumstances, neither Wilson nor Lodge nor Roosevelt could hope to impose their ideas on a transformed world.

Further Reading

An excellent book on the diplomacy of World War I is *Daniel M. Smith, *The Great Departure: The United States and World War I, 1914-1920* (New York, 1965).

Woodrow Wilson has been the subject of many able biographies. Three, which are especially relevant here and which offer differing interpretations, are *John M. Blum, *Woodrow Wilson and the Politics of Morality* (Boston, 1956); *Herbert Hoover, *The Ordeal of Woodrow Wilson* (New York, 1961); and *Arthur S. Link, *Wilson the Diplomatist: A Look at His Major Foreign Policies* (Chicago, 1965).

The American attitude toward the war before 1917 is explored by *Ernest R. May, *The World War and American Isolation: 1914-1917* (Chicago, 1966). A longer time period is spanned by Selig Adler who deals with the same subject in *The Isolationist Impulse: Its Twentieth Century Reaction* (New York, 1966).

The story of the American army in Siberia is well told in a recently reprinted study by Betty M. Unterberger, *America's Siberian Adventure, 1918-1920* (Westport, Conn., 1969). The difficulties at Versailles are detailed in *Arno J. Mayer, *Politics and Diplomacy of Peacemaking: Containment and Counterrevolution at Versailles 1918-1919* (New York, 1969).

In addition to these, check references in earlier chapters to books on the armed services. Finally, good biographies of the following men should prove useful here: William E. Borah, William J. Bryan, Robert Lansing, and Charles E. Hughes.

Asterisk denotes paperback edition.

14

The Diplomacy of a
Creditor Nation, 1920-1933

The United States in Warren G. Harding's day, and for the next decade, was a disunited country. Outwardly it bore the appearance of uniformity, reinforced by a strident nationalism that pervaded most of America's relations with the rest of the world. Beneath the surface, however, there was a marked reaction to the war as well as to the continued crumbling of the fixed beliefs of an earlier time. The 1920's were, in part, an era of intellectual and social radicalism: a great literary outpouring was accompanied by disharmonious public outcries to such episodes as the Sacco-Vanzetti case (1921-1927) and the Tennessee "monkey" trial (1925).

But the temper of most Americans was conservative and oriented toward recreating the ideal small town or urbanized society. Sinclair Lewis exaggerated both these conservative ideals, first in *Main Street*, where the narrow bigotry of small-town mores was held up to mockery, and later in *Babbitt*, a sarcastic stricture on American supersalesmanship and the urban middle class. Americanism was lauded by conservatives as the most important value, but decried by liberals as just another word for reaction and overt materialism. An unreasoning fear of Communism swept the country immediately after the war. In 1920 over 6,000 arrests were made of suspected Communists in the United States; eventually 556 aliens were deported for their political beliefs.

THE DANGER OF IMMIGRATION, 1916

From Madison Grant, *The Passing of the Great Race*

It is evident that in large sections of the country the native American will entirely disappear. He will not intermarry with inferior races and he cannot compete in the sweat shop and in the street trench with the newcomers. Large cities from the days of Rome, Alexandria, and Byzantium have always been gathering points of diverse races, but New York ... will produce many amazing racial hybrids and some ethnic horrors that will be beyond the powers of future anthropologists to unravel.

One thing is certain; in any such mixture, the surviving traits will be determined by competition between the lowest and most primitive elements and the specialized traits of Nordic man; his stature, his light colored eyes, his fair skin and light colored hair, his straight nose and his splendid fighting and moral qualities, will have little part in the resultant mixture.

One of the notable "anti" aspects of Americanism in the 1920's was its antiforeign bias, a combination of dislike of foreigners per se with the current hysteria over Communism. The result was two restrictive immigration acts passed in 1921 and 1924. The latter, the National Origins Act of 1924, permanently choked off large-scale immigration by basing annual entry quotas on the percentage of nationals of any one country in the United States in 1890. This effectively barred great numbers of southern and eastern Europeans from immigrating, because the largest quotas belonged to English, Irish, and northern Europeans.

THE SECRETARY OF STATE AND THE DEPARTMENT

Harding's Secretary of State, Charles Evans Hughes, was an extremely able administrator. His reorganization of the State Department lasted until nearly the end of World War II and gave it the stamp it bears today. Most important to the execution of foreign policy was the passage of the Rogers Act of 1924. This merged the diplomatic and consular services, provided for a system of merit promotion within the Foreign Service for grades from vice-consul to counselor, and set up stiffer requirements for career Foreign Service officers. The act solidified the Foreign Service and gave it an esprit de corps that was noticeably lacking before. On the other hand, charges of elitism and undemocratic behavior became common before the decade was over.

Hughes also expanded the number of bureaus. For the first time he brought experienced career men from the field to staff them. Perhaps the most eloquent testimony to the change came about after the death in 1924 of Alvey A. Adee, who had served twenty-two secretaries of state. His work was now taken over by an entire bureau! Unfortunately, although peacetime diplomacy entailed more paper work than that of wartime, the department was continually understaffed due to the insufficient funds voted by Congress. While such indicators as quantity of mail and volume of cables increased during the 1920's, personnel actually decreased.

THE WORLD CREDITOR AND THE DEBTORS

The great unsolved dilemma of American foreign policy in the 1920's and early 1930's was how to balance the American involvement in Europe necessary to protect the country's large loans with the growing demand for isolationism. The Allies owed the United States a total of $10.3 billion, which included over $3 billion borrowed after the end of the war. The interest amounted to 5 percent, the money having been raised by the sale of United States Treasury bonds to Americans at 4¼ percent interest. Most of the Allied loans had helped pay for war material and foodstuffs purchased in the United States; hence the money never left the country and measurably contributed to the great wartime prosperity.

Woodrow Wilson had refused to discuss the debt question at Versailles. He probably recognized the strength of the Allied contention that the loans ought to be scaled down or canceled outright because, since they were incurred fighting the war, they could rightly be considered as subsidies. The American attitude on the subject was expressed in President Calvin Coolidge's terse remark, "Well, they hired the money didn't they?"

In 1922 Congress created a World War Foreign Debt Commission that was empowered to negotiate the terms of repayment with the debtor countries. The commission renegotiated the interest rate according to a nation's supposed ability to pay. England was charged 3 to 3.5 percent interest, with payments spread over 62 years; France, 1.6 percent; and Italy, 0.4 percent. Therefore, the actual amount of the debts before funding was reduced considerably, ranging from 30 percent for England to 80.2 percent for Italy.

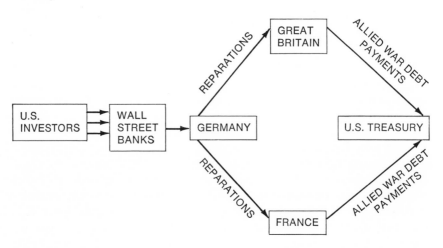

THE FLOW OF PRIVATE INVESTMENTS AND WAR DEBTS AFTER WORLD WAR I

In spite of the commission's work, a sort of Alice-in-Wonderland atmosphere pervaded Congress and other areas of policy making. In contrast to most economists and other financial experts, Congress refused to admit a relationship between Allied debts, reparations, and high tariffs. The Allies had thought to repay their debts to the United States with reparations exacted from Germany, but Germany defaulted on its payments in 1922. French troops then occupied the Ruhr, the principal seat of German industry, and the German economic plight became truly desperate. Although not officially a member of the Allied Reparations Commission, the United States suggested a less stringent reparations agreement in 1924. The Dawes Plan — named for the banker Charles G. Dawes — was succeeded by an even more modest program in 1928, the Young Plan, named for industrialist Owen D. Young. Beginning with the Dawes Plan, American investment was allowed in Germany. As this money flowed in, the rampant German inflation came to an end and industry quickly recovered. The profits from the revived German industry allowed the Germans to pay scaled-down reparations to the Allies, who in turn repaid the United States. The entire system depended upon American investments abroad, and the year 1929 brought American investments to a dead stop.

To make matters worse, the United States enacted tariff bills in 1922 and 1930 that raised an almost impenetrable protective wall around American-produced goods, thus making it virtually impossible for the Allies, who were also heavily industrialized, to sell manufactured products in the United States. By 1929 the total American investment abroad since 1920 had exceeded debt repayment by about three times.

AMERICA, JAPAN, AND THE WASHINGTON NAVAL CONFERENCE

Despite the nationalistic attitude that was so much a part of Americanism in the 1920's, Americans and their Congress were most reluctant to support a large military and naval establishment. The navy had experienced only temporary financial cutbacks since Theodore Roosevelt's presidency, but in 1919 and again in 1920 funds for new shipbuilding were sharply curtailed. Yet the navy represented a strong arm of State Department policy, especially in the Pacific. Since neither the British nor the Japanese showed a disposition to reduce their fleet strengths, the obvious recourse was either a new naval race or an attempt to persuade the different powers to limit their fleets. The lesson of the pre-World War I naval race between Great Britain and Germany, with the United States lagging behind, was not lost on Congress. Certain Congressional leaders began to urge international disarmament. Interestingly, it was Senator William E. Borah who first introduced a resolution in 1920, asking the President to invite Great Britain and Japan to negotiate an arms limitation agreement. The resolution passed both houses in June 1921.

A month later, at a Commonwealth meeting in London, the British decided that Canada and the other dominions would not soften their hostility toward a renewal of the Anglo-Japanese Alliance, which had been extended another ten years in 1911. Since the Japanese insisted on renewal, the British had to decide whether to mollify the Japanese or their own dominions. Prime Minister Lloyd George tried to solve the problem by inviting the United States and Japan to a conference on Far Eastern affairs and arms limitation. About the same time, President Harding, in response to the joint resolution of Congress, invited these countries together with France and Italy to meet in Washington to discuss the limitation of armaments. The scope of the proposed Washington meeting was broadened to include, at Lloyd George's request, Far Eastern problems.

Against this tangled backdrop of motives, the Washington Conference convened on November 12, 1921. Unlike Versailles, the meetings were soon open, and a throng of newspapermen and observers kept the American public minutely informed of the proceedings. The American delegation, headed by Hughes, was composed of distinguished members of both political parties, obviating any charge of partisan politics no matter what the outcome. Hughes immediately upset conference protocol by coming directly to the point of disarmament in his opening remarks.

Hughes called for a ten-year moratorium on the construction of battleships, plus the scrapping of those built or under construction, so that the ratio of the three largest naval powers in tonnage built or under construction would be: Great Britain, 5, the United States, 5, and Japan, 3. He added that the United States would be prepared to scrap thirty ships already built, building, or planned. He then suggested by name those ships that Great Britain and Japan should scrap. The startled delegates adopted his suggestions almost as stated, after some private maneuvering by Japan. However, it was France, not Japan, which became the stumbling block. France based its demands for a higher naval ratio on its past record, not on its present strength. When France and Italy were each assigned a ratio of 1.7, French representatives angrily rejected the figure, thereby threatening to scuttle the conference. Only the combined weight of world opinion together with a direct appeal to the French premier forced France to capitulate and join with the other four Allies in signing the Five-Power Treaty on February 6, 1922. This pact was the crux of the conference: it provided for the Hughes plan for a ten-year period and included limits on the size and armaments of battleships, battle cruisers, and aircraft carriers; it also froze fortifications in the western Pacific. The pact was to remain in force until December 31, 1936, and could thereafter be abrogated by giving two years' notice.

THE AMERICAN DELEGATES TO THE WASHINGTON, D.C., DISARMAMENT CONFERENCE
Left to right: Elihu Root, Oscar W. Underwood, Charles Evans Hughes,
and Henry Cabot Lodge.

The Japanese acceded to the ratio because they were more interested in settling other problems relating to the United States and in renewing the Anglo-Japanese Alliance. These three powers negotiated privately during the conference and agreed upon the Four-Power Treaty, which included France. It abrogated the Anglo-Japanese Alliance, substituting for it consultation among the four signatories should any one of them be threatened. Each power was bound to respect the others' possessions in the Pacific, which thereby safeguarded the Philippines.

At the end of the conference the conferees also agreed to a Nine-Power Treaty, which was a personal diplomatic triumph for Charles Evans Hughes. The signatories agreed to recognize the provisions of the United States Open Door policy. In this way, twenty years after it was originally enunciated, the Open Door policy became international law — at least to the signatories at the Washington Conference. Unfortunately, the conference did not include Russia. The trio of pacts took up the major part of the conference and attracted the most publicity. Americans were excited by the prospect of cooperative arms limitation, and the Senate approved all three pacts with only mild dissent. In reality, however, the pacts were but a weak and belated substitute for a world organization, such as the League of Nations, which the United States had so irrevocably rejected. And arms limitation and disarmament, attractive ideas though they were, proved to be more and more elusive of attainment as the 1920's wore on.

THE SEARCH FOR WORLD PEACE AND ARMS LIMITATION

Arms limitation was considered a vital first step toward disarmament; yet because the Five-Power Treaty said nothing about building smaller naval craft, Britain, Japan, France, and Italy quickly turned to developing and building cruisers, destroyers, and submarines. The United States did not match their building pace, preferring to try to end the race by diplomacy. In 1927 President Coolidge called for a five-power meeting in Geneva, but only Britain, Japan, and the United States attended. The conference proving fruitless, the United States entered the naval race with appropriations for fifteen cruisers.

The coming of Herbert Hoover to the presidency in 1929 coincided with a new attempt at naval limitation. Hoover first negotiated an informal limitation agreement with Prime Minister Ramsey MacDonald, who then called for another five-power conference. The London Conference, in session from January to April 1930, wrestled with the plan to extend the earlier ratio to all classes of naval ships. The final pact, the London Naval Treaty, extended the proposed ratio, but since neither France nor Italy signed, the treaty was measurably weakened. The Japanese, who only accepted the pact after considerable domestic difficulty, never enforced its provisions and soon joined France and Italy in the naval race. The London Naval Treaty did, however, extend the ban on battleships for another five years.

Arms limitation was of course not confined to naval ships. A strong movement for arms limitation and world peace resulted in the Geneva Protocol of 1924, which proposed using the World Court, established at the same time as the League, to enforce compulsory arbitration. The United States strenuously opposed the protocol; even such an internationalist as Hughes predicted dire consequences were it to be enacted. When Britain also opposed it, the protocol died. However, several European nations met the following year in Locarno, Switzerland, to sign regional agreements embodying most of the ideas of the Geneva Protocol. The meeting was so harmonious that the "spirit of Locarno" seemed to indicate that world peace was indeed attainable.

In the United States many groups and organizations were pledged to work for world peace, arms limitation, and disarmament. By 1927 their efforts had convinced the French Foreign Minister, Aristide Briand, of the utility of an antiwar pact, and France offered to sign one with the United States. Secretary of State Kellogg adopted the idea and extended it to other countries. In late August 1928 fifteen nations signed the Kellogg-Briand Pact renouncing war as an instrument of national policy. Kellogg then negotiated some twenty-eight individual conciliation treaties under the pact, all outlawing war and providing for arbitration. The Senate approved each treaty, adding a clause reserving the right to approve any problem that was to be submitted to arbitration. Kellogg, recipient of the Nobel Peace Prize in 1929 for his efforts, realistically evaluated his work as having little "practical importance." Nevertheless, the United States' attempt to exert leadership was reassuring to the advocates of peace.

KELLOGG PEACE PACT, 1928

The President of the German Reich, the President of the United States of America, His Majesty the King of the Belgians, the President of the French Republic, His Majesty the King of Great Britain, Ireland and the British Dominions beyond the Seas, Emperor of India, His Majesty the King of Italy, His Majesty the Emperor of Japan, the President of the Republic of Poland, the President of the Czechoslovak Republic,

Deeply sensible of their solemn duty to promote the welfare of mankind;

Persuaded that the time has come when a frank renunciation of war as an instrument of national policy should be made to the end that the peaceful and friendly relations now existing between their peoples may be perpetuated;...

Have decided to conclude a treaty and for that purpose have appointed as their respective plenipotentiaries:...

Who, having communicated to one another their full powers found in good and due form have agreed upon the following articles:

Article 1. The high contracting parties solemnly declare in the names of their respective peoples that they condemn recourse to war for the solution of international controversies, and renounce it as an instrument of national policy in their relations with one another.

Article 2. The high contracting parties agree that the settlement or solution of all disputes or conflicts of whatever nature or of whatever origin they may be, which may arise among them, shall never be sought except by pacific means.

Article 3. The present treaty shall be ratified by the high contracting parties named in the preamble in accordance with their respective constitutional requirements, and shall take effect as between them as soon as all their several instruments of ratification shall have been deposited at Washington.

The last major effort to achieve both disarmament and world peace was the World Disarmament Conference held in Geneva in 1932. Fifty-nine nations, including a strong United States delegation, attempted to deal with the disarmament of land forces. However, European national jealousies foredoomed the outcome. After listening to the wrangling for five months, the American delegation suggested that all land armaments be reduced by a third. The plan was greeted enthusiastically by the press and public, but not by most of the delegates. The plan was abandoned and the conference dragged on into the presidency of Franklin D. Roosevelt, finally breaking up in dismal failure in June 1934 after Hitler had come to power and Japan had invaded Manchuria.

Though disarmament talks had failed, one more effort at limitation was made at the London Naval Conference in late 1935. The results were negated by the failure of Italy and Japan to participate. Already in 1934 Japan had given notice of abrogating the Five-Power Pact, and the naval race continued.

THE UNITED STATES AND THE WORLD COURT

Another hope for peace seen by certain articulate groups in America was membership in the Permanent Court of International Justice — the World Court. This judicial arm of the League of Nations had been established under a separate statute so that a nation would not have to join the League in order to become a member of the World Court. From the first time the question of membership was submitted to the Senate in 1923 until its final defeat in January 1935, its history was frustratingly repetitive. All the presidents, all the secretaries of state, and (after the mid-1920's) probably a majority of Americans supported the United States' backing of the court. Moreover, Elihu Root had helped draft the original statute and other internationally oriented American lawyers served as judges on the World Court. They included John Bassett Moore and, later, Charles Evans Hughes and Frank B. Kellogg. But the irreconcilables, led by Borah, disapproved of even sending observers to League meetings and succeeded in blocking approval of the enabling pact. The final blow came during Franklin D. Roosevelt's administration when public pressure to join grew clamorous.

Passage seemed assured, but the aging Borah and his allies were joined by the dynamic Senator Huey P. Long and the popular radio priest Father Charles E. Coughlin in opposition. After a display of verbal pyrotechnics bolstered by a large amount of mail against the court, the Senate voted down the pact by seven votes, 52-36. This ended hopes of American participation in the World Court until after World War II and the creation of a similar body within the United Nations.

THE UNITED STATES AND ASIA

After World War I the United States encountered particular difficulties with both China and Japan. Much of the conflict with Japan concerned America's efforts to guarantee the security of the Philippine Islands, though the initial disagreement in 1919 was over maintenance of a cable station on Yap in the Caroline Islands. When the Carolines were awarded to Japan as a mandated territory, Wilson objected in vain.

This disagreement became intertwined with other American-Japanese problems. The Japanese were especially sensitive to American moves, and the 9,000 American troops stationed in the Far East, ostensibly to combat the Bolsheviks, did nothing to allay Japanese suspicions of American motives. Also, Wilson helped to defeat a statement on racial equality in the League Covenant which Japan had strongly favored. The effect of this slight was heightened by the rising sentiment, particularly vocal in California and other Western states, in favor of excluding Orientals. An act passed by California in 1920 forbade the Japanese even to rent land in the state. Congress also was under considerable pressure to end immigration of Orientals. In 1921 Hughes renegotiated the Gentlemen's Agreement, considerably tightening immigration from Japan; however, Senate hostility obviated its submission. Instead, by the Quota Act of 1921, Congress excluded Japanese immigration entirely, causing a further deterioration in relations between the two countries.

The problems were intensified by the rampant anti-Americanism expressed by the Japanese public; in 1921 particularly, relations were very tense. However, the settlement of some other problems at the Washington Conference paved the way for ameliorating the mutual hostility; for example, the United States received the cable station on Yap in exchange for recognizing the Japanese mandate of the Carolines.

In 1923 Japan suffered a devastating earthquake in the Tokyo region. The rapid and generous American response to the disaster temporarily eased tensions. However, the West still enforced its discriminatory laws. Later in the decade Japan signed the Kellogg-Briand Pact; it also faithfully lived up to the Five-Power Treaty on naval limitation until the early 1930's.

UNITED STATES POLICY AND CHINA

During the 1920's the United States again experienced difficulties with China. The Chinese revolution had disintegrated and large portions of the country were governed by avaricious warlords in command of mercenary armies. In the south, Sun Yat-sen, the heir of the revolution, controlled less than a third of China. Nevertheless, at the Washington Conference the Chinese delegates were unanimous in demanding the end of foreign leaseholds and extraterritoriality, demands which went unanswered.

Sun Yat-sen died in 1925; shortly afterward, his party, the Kuomintang, reorganized in the face of rioting and gave control of the army to the wealthy young Moscow-trained general, Chiang Kai-shek. Chiang so strengthened the fighting ability of the Nationalist army that by 1927 he had effective control of the entire country except for Manchuria. Much of his early success was due to his antiforeign, anti-Western attitude. At Nanking on March 24, 1927, Nationalist soldiers violently attacked both Westerners and Japanese, and only quick action by a British and an American gunboat averted a worse disaster. The United States and other countries whose nationals were involved protested vigorously but to no avail; the United States, however, refused to join a projected international punitive expedition to collect reparations and an apology, so the plan was abandoned.

In the meantime, Chiang, in a series of bloody massacres, purged the Communist element of his party and severed diplomatic relations with Russia. The next year, when he occupied Peking, Chiang began to reverse his hostile policy toward the West, but despite repeated attempts he was unable to end foreign spheres of interest in China. The United States did make small concessions in 1928, but the other countries would do nothing. Being a signatory of the Kellogg-Briand Pact did not keep China from becoming increasingly involved with two other signatories, Russia and Japan. Between 1929 and 1931, when Chinese troops were attempting to retake Manchuria, they fought pitched battles with both countries.

THE MANCHURIAN INVASION CRISIS

By 1931 Manchurian interests accounted for almost half of Japan's foreign investments. When the Nationalists tried to reimpose their historic sovereignty over the province, the Japanese reacted sharply, using the contrived incident at Mukden as an excuse to escalate a war. They drove the Chinese out of Manchuria and in February 1932 set up the puppet state of Manchukuo with a Manchu as emperor. China appealed to the United States to invoke the Kellogg-Briand Pact and to the League of Nations for its help. Because the League was unequal to the demand, it fell to Secretary of State Henry L. Stimson to deal with the crisis. Unfortunately, although a large American fleet was in the Pacific during the crisis, Stimson could not make use of it because President Hoover, a Quaker and a pacifist, would not countenance either economic or military sanctions.

JAPAN SEIZES MANCHURIA

This 1931 cartoon reflects American bitterness over Japan's warlike actions in the face of international efforts for peace.

On January 7, 1932, Stimson, in anticipation of coming events, had attempted to use diplomacy by reverting to the Wilsonian policy of nonrecognition of Manchukuo. He informed China and Japan that the United States would not recognize any government "which may impair the treaty rights of the United States . . . or the international policy relative to China, commonly known as the open door policy." This statement, later names the Hoover-Stimson Doctrine, proved to be woefully inadequate as a deterrent. Japan remained completely unconcerned by Stimson's statment; its troops attacked Shanghai in January 1932 and the next month set up Manchukuo. The tortuous diplomacy of the United States was not backed up by either France or Great Britain, who refused to respond. The Japanese, to the revulsion of the American public, indiscriminately bombed and terrorized Shanghai, occupying it until the following May.

Secretary Stimson had meanwhile invited other nations to uphold his policy of nonrecognition of Manchukuo. The Assembly of the League of Nations adopted the doctrine after a League commission corroborated the Japanese invasion of China. But the overall effect of the League's support, far from deterring Japan, simply caused it to notify the League in March 1933 that it would withdraw its membership after the prescribed two years. Not only did the victorious Japanese army continue to enlarge its holdings in Manchuria but it also moved to control territory in Mongolia that had long been disputed by both China and Russia.

The Russians had increased their military strength in that area during the previous few years, a far more effective deterrent to Japan than the Hoover-Stimson Doctrine. In May 1933 Japan finally made a truce with China according to which a large part of the area south of the Great Wall was to be demilitarized but dominated by Japan. The next year Japan established monopolistic business practices in Manchukuo, forcing out all other concessionaires. This sounded the death knell of both the Open Door policy and the Hoover-Stimson Doctrine, although the Roosevelt administration tried to continue them by diplomatic means. In any case, Roosevelt kept most of the major units of the American fleet in Pacific waters.

THE UNITED STATES AND LATIN AMERICA

For fifteen years after World War I, United States policy in Latin America was a curious mixture of imperialism and democratic concern heavily larded with paternalism. During World War I, Latin American reactions to American intervention in Europe had ranged from antipathy in Mexico and Colombia, through the indifference of most of the states, to the positive support of Brazil (who became an ally). Sixteen Latin American republics joined the League of Nations, but the prevailing attitude toward the United States remained mistrustful.

The United States made certain ameliorative efforts. In 1921, as noted, the United States agreed to pay Colombia $25 million for the loss of Panama, but required recognition of the Panamanian government as part of the bargain. At other times during the decade, attempts were made to remove troops from the American protectorates, but without success. One expert, Graham H. Stuart, has pointed out that in 1924 only six Latin American republics out of twenty were completely free of United States domination, while another six were subject to American armies of occupation!

Another method of conciliation was the hemispheric conference. Although historically conferences had accomplished little, a fourth was scheduled for 1914 but was not convened until 1923. This conference, meeting at Santiago, Chile, and another, held five years later in Havana, Cuba, both signed hemispheric peace-keeping pacts but were unable to create effective machinery to enforce them. Another postwar conference, held just after Roosevelt came into office, accomplished more, but it was not until the Latin American states were convinced of American intentions to withdraw rather than to intervene that such meetings became meaningful.

Beginning in the late 1920's, the United States did attempt, with varying degrees of success, to extricate itself from Latin America. Both Coolidge and Hoover made goodwill trips, but it was not until after President Hoover repudiated the hated Roosevelt Corollary to the Monroe Doctrine, in 1930, that real improvement could be seen. At first, any change was more than offset by the ultrahigh Smoot-Hawley Tariff of 1930, which nearly bankrupted the larger republics. They defaulted on their debts, causing resentment among the American people.

Nevertheless, a change for the better was evident. In spite of revolutions in Brazil in 1930 and in Panama, Cuba, and Honduras in 1931, Hoover stayed out of their affairs. He also pledged to remove American troops from Nicaragua and Haiti as well. By 1933 the American protectorate had all but ended except for the abrogation of the Platt Amendment, which came the next year. But although Hoover was responsible for initiating what became the Good Neighbor policy, it did not reach fruition until Franklin D. Roosevelt's administration.

THE UNITED STATES AND MEXICO

In the 1920's and early 1930's American policy makers' greatest difficulties within the hemisphere were in coping with the continuing Mexican revolution. From 1920 to 1934 Mexico was governed by leaders who moved slowly with regard to the land distribution and subsoil rights provided for in the 1917 constitution. American oil companies pressured the State Department in 1920 not to recognize President Obregón unless some guarantee of subsoil rights were forthcoming. Secretary of State Hughes negotiated the Bucareli Agreements, by which foreign oil companies were allowed to retain properties owned before 1917; the agreements also called for compensation for appropriated land, which affected fewer Americans than did the oil issue.

However, in 1924 Obregón was succeeded by Plutarco E. Calles (1924-1928), who promptly repudiated the Bucareli Agreements. The Mexican Congress then passed legislation limiting to fifty years all oil rights acquired before 1917. Calles also supported anti-Catholic legislation. When he supported a revolutionary regime in Nicaragua in 1927, Secretary of State Kellogg warned Congress that Russian agents were active in Mexico, but even though American business interests urged strong action, the Senate contented itself with urging arbitration of the disagreement. President Coolidge appointed Dwight W. Morrow, a Bowdoin classmate, as Ambassador to Mexico. Morrow, a wealthy banker without diplomatic experience, ably represented American interests while developing a great deal of empathy with the Mexican people. Quickly winning government support, Morrow tangibly contributed to the growth of a new respect for the United States by his own personality and by the popular visits of his son-in-law, Colonel Charles A. Lindbergh, and of the humorist Will Rogers. A new Petroleum Code passed in 1927 embodied the features of the Bucareli Agreements. Calles' successors supported the action taken by his regime, and until 1934 relations between the two countries were as amicable as those during the Porfirio Díaz regime.

THE GREAT DEPRESSION AND AMERICAN FOREIGN POLICY

The Great Depression, which began with the stock market crash in 1929, was worldwide in scope. Undoubtedly, the reparation and debt problems contributed to its severity, as did the tariff wall erected by the United States to isolate itself economically. The majority of Americans favored any action tending to increase America's isolation from Europe; however, the difficulty of safeguarding American investments abroad without becoming involved diplomatically became more apparent as the depression lengthened. The handwriting on the wall was plainly to be seen, but the American people and their leaders still thought, talked, and acted in the spirit of the victors at Versailles nearly a generation before.

Further Reading

An excellent diplomatic survey of this period is L. Ethan Ellis, *Republican Foreign Policy: 1921-1933* (New Brunswick, N.J., 1968). Equally useful here and with the next chapter is *Selig Adler, *The Uncertain Giant: 1921-1941* (New York, 1969). The knotty problem brought about by war debts and reparations is discussed in *Herbert Feis, *The Diplomacy of the Dollar: First Era, 1919-1932* (New York, 1966).

An invaluable study of American-East Asian relations covering a longer time span is *Akira Iriye, *Across the Pacific: An Inner History of American-East Asian Relations* (New York, 1969). An earlier work specifically on this decade is his *After Imperialism: The Search for a New Order in the Far East, 1921-1931* (Cambridge, Mass., 1965). Two other books that specifically cover events in the 1920's and early 1930's are by Robert Ferrell: *Peace in Their Time: The Origins of the Kellogg-Briand Pact* (New York, 1969) and *American Diplomacy in the Great Depression: Hoover-Stimson Foreign Policy, 1929-1933* (Hamden, Conn., 1969).

Memoirs have been cited before, but from this period onward they are especially valuable. For this chapter two excellent volumes are Henry L. Stimson and McGeorge Bundy, *On Active Service in Peace and War* (New York, 1948) and Charles W. Thayer, *Diplomat* (New York, 1959). Also refer again to books cited earlier by William A. Williams, George Kennan, Walter Lippmann and William L. Neumann.

Asterisk denotes paperback edition.

15

American Foreign Policy in the New Deal Era

The beginning of Franklin D. Roosevelt's administration was not auspicious in the realm of foreign policy. President Roosevelt arrived in office with impressive credentials; a Wilsonian liberal, he had served during World War I as Assistant Secretary of the Navy. He struggled unsuccessfully to be elected Vice President in 1920 on the pro-League platform Wilson had forced on the Democratic party. Wealthy, handsome, well-traveled, Roosevelt returned to New York where he was considered one of the young leaders of the party. In 1921 he suffered a polio attack that crippled him permanently and seemed at first to have ended his promising political career. However, just three years later, he was again a major force in New York state politics. Elected governor in 1928, Roosevelt — and the mildly liberal policies he followed — gave little indication of his policies as President. Neither did his campaign speeches to the depression-ridden country in 1932 betray a statement of direction.

THE HUNDRED DAYS

FDR began his term with an electrifying inaugural address that promised action to combat the devastating effects of the depression. There were 12,000,000 jobless and the gross national product had fallen from $104 billion in 1929 to $74 billion in 1932. The hundred days of special legislation, the beginning of the New Deal, reflected an economic nationalism that gave the country hope and the new vision it so desperately needed. However, the effect of the program on foreign policy — with two exceptions — was quite the opposite. Cordell Hull, Roosevelt's choice for Secretary of State, shared many of the President's theories, but he never temporized for the sake of political expediency as did FDR. As a long-time Congressional leader from Tennessee, Hull assumed the role of an international Wilsonian liberal whose particular goal was low tariffs.

AMERICAN FOREIGN POLICY AND DOMESTIC POLITICS

One of FDR's first foreign policy decisions concerned the type and extent of United States participation in the World Economic Conference meeting in London in June 1933. The month before, the United States had gone off the gold standard, as had Great Britain and Japan. However, at the conference the stabilization of currency seemed to be the most pressing problem, so Secretary Hull, leader of the American delegation, agreed to participate in a temporary plan to support it. Hull was hoping for an agreement on tariff reciprocity, authority for which Roosevelt had promised to ask Congress. But FDR not only reneged on the reciprocity pledge, he scuttled the conference by refusing to join any plan for international stabilization.

The following year Hull managed to convince Roosevelt of the economic possibilities of reciprocal trade agreements. An agreement would be negotiated item by item with a given country, allowing a tariff concession for the item in question in exchange for a similar concession on an American item exported to that country. A most-favored-nation clause would permit the same reduction on the same item regardless of trading partner, provided only that that particular country had signed a reciprocity agreement. The Reciprocal Trade Agreements Act of 1934, passed in March, embodied these features, allowing the President to reduce existing tariffs up to 50 percent. The overall effect of the legislation in the 1930's was negligible both as a foreign policy factor and as an economic factor. Fearful of unduly antagonizing Congress, FDR and Hull concluded few agreements that allowed foreign goods to compete with American goods or that seriously undercut the Smoot-Hawley Tariff of 1930 — even with a 50 percent reduction. The act was renewed at three-year intervals; it marked an innovative approach to a very old problem whose results would be much more important after the end of World War II.

Another foreign policy foray with negligible results concerned an old foe of Woodrow Wilson. On November 16, 1933, the Roosevelt administration recognized the USSR. In retrospect, it is ironic to note that it was American business interests, hoping for new markets, who pushed the lukewarm Roosevelt. The hope never really materialized and Russia's theoretically vast markets remained as untapped by Americans as had those of China a quarter of a century earlier.

LATIN AMERICA AND THE GOOD NEIGHBOR POLICY

One conspicuous success in early New Deal diplomacy was in Latin America. FDR's inaugural address, echoing Hoover's policies, dedicated the nation to being a good neighbor both to the north and the south. After a shaky start, in which the United States refused to recognize a radical Cuban government after a bloody revolution, Roosevelt proved true to his pledge. Troops were withdrawn from Haiti, and for the first time since World War I there were no American troops in Latin America. Next, the United States recognized the more moderate Cuban government which succeeded the earlier radical one and on March 29, 1934, abrogated the Platt Amendment, retaining only the naval base at Guantánamo Bay. Similarly, new agreements with Panama in 1936 returned much of the sovereignty the United States had exercised there, although the Senate, fearful for the safety of the Panama Canal, did not approve the pact until 1939.

As the 1930's unfolded, FDR's personal popularity increased in Latin America. His New Deal seemed to place him in the mainstream of social reform to which most South and Central American countries aspired but few achieved. His reputation was enhanced when he visited Buenos Aires in December 1936 to open a Latin American conference called to discuss the maintenance of peace in the hemisphere. Long experience had taught Secretary Hull that the United States could not interfere in attempting to keep peace among warring Latin American countries, no matter how unselfish its motives. He therefore worked at Buenos Aires and at Lima in

FDR DURING A FIRESIDE CHAT

Roosevelt was one of the first presidents to effectively exploit the communications media to reach the American people.

1938 to get a collective security principle accepted. By 1938 acceptance was even more important because Nazi influence had made large inroads in Argentina. The adoption of the Declaration of Lima in late December 1938 was a compromise victory for Hull. It did provide for consultation on a collective basis should an outsider endanger peace in the hemisphere, but Hull had hoped for a far stronger statement. However, the suspicions and hostility of Argentina forced the compromise.

The new consultative machinery met its first test when World War II broke out in September 1939. The foreign ministers of each country in the hemisphere met in Panama to declare their neutrality. They set up a security zone of 300 miles around the hemisphere from which they hoped to exclude the belligerents. The security zone proved unenforceable, however, as both sides violated the Declaration of Panama with impunity.

THE DECLARATION OF PANAMA, 1939

The republics of America, meeting in Panama have solemnly ratified their position as neutrals in the conflict which disturbs the peace of Europe. But as the present war may reach unexpected derivations, which by their gravitation may affect the fundamental interests of America, it is hereby declared that nothing can justify that the interests of belligerents prevail over the rights of neutrals, causing upsets and sufferings of peoples who, by their neutrality in the conflict and their distance from the scene of the happenings, should not suffer its fatal and dolorous consequences.

There is no doubt that the governments of the American republics ought to foresee these dangers as a means of self-protection and to insist upon the determination that in their waters and up to a reasonable distance from their coasts no hostile acts may be engaged in or bellicose activities carried out by participants in a war in which the said [American] governments do not participate.

For these considerations the governments of the American republics resolve and herewith declare:

1. As a measure of continental protection, the American republics, as long as they maintain their neutrality, have the undisputed right to conserve free from all hostile acts by any belligerent non-American nation those waters adjacent to the American continents which they consider of primordial interest and direct utility for their relations, whether such hostile act is attempted or carried out by land, sea or air.

2. The governments of the American republics agree to make an effort to seek observance by the belligerents of the dispositions contained in this declaration through joint representations to the governments actually participating in hostilities or those that may participate in the future.

This procedure will in no wise affect the exercise of the individual rights of each state inherent in its sovereignty.

3. The governments of the American republics further declare that, whenever they consider it necessary, they will consult among themselves to determine what measures they can take individually or collectively for the purpose of obtaining fulfillment of the dispositions of this declaration.

4. The American republics, as long as there exists a state of war in which they themselves are not participating and whenever they consider it necessary, may carry out individual or collective patrols, whichever they may decide through mutual agreement or as far as the elements and resources of each one permit, in waters adjacent to their coasts within the zone already defined.

The first real test of hemispheric solidarity occurred when France and the Netherlands, both of whom had colonies in the Western Hemisphere, fell to the Nazis. In June 1940 Congress reiterated the "no transfer" part of the Monroe Doctrine; most of the Latin American countries agreed to this policy since they had been assured of consultation before the United States took action. In July the foreign ministers convened in Havana to approve and reinforce the American policy. Formal military alliances were begun at this meeting, and the ideas of the Monroe Doctrine were embodied in the Declaration of Havana requiring collective action. The move was appropriate — if a century late! Military ties rapidly emerged; by December 1941 the United States had various kinds of military missions in eleven countries and was helping to arm several others.

THE UNITED STATES AND MEXICO

Mexico constituted a special problem for Roosevelt and Hull in the 1930's. The new Mexican President, Lázaro Cárdenas, in 1934 began an ambitious land reform program based on the constitution of 1917. Land reform and possible nationalization of foreign-owned industry caused concern abroad to the Catholic Church — a large landowner — and to business interests. FDR, despite pressure from these groups, continued to maintain good relations with Cárdenas. However, in 1938, when foreign-owned oil companies in Mexico refused to meet workers' demands for higher wages and improved benefits, the Mexican government stepped in and expropriated all the holdings.

Cárdenas pledged compensation but branded as exorbitant the American oil companies' demand for $260 million. The argument dragged on, but FDR refused to heed newspaper and Congressional calls for strong action.

Instead, he renewed his pledge of nonintervention. Negotiations began anew in 1940 when Manuel Camacho became President. Finally, just a month before Pearl Harbor, President Roosevelt pressured the oil companies into accepting about $42 million in settlement, well below the actual worth of the property. At the same time, land ownership claims were also settled in northern Mexico. As a result, although the interests of business were temporarily sacrificed, Mexico entered World War II as a staunch ally of the United States, a far different situation than that existing during World War I.

THE PEACE MOVEMENT AND ISOLATIONIST POLICIES

During the 1920's and continuing through most of the 1930's, a prominent feature of American life was the number of organizations devoted to world peace. Of the more than 1,200 groups dedicated to this cause, many had solid financial backing. These included the Carnegie Endowment for International Peace, the World Peace Foundation, and the Council on Foreign Relations. However, they were never able to agree among themselves as to whether to support the League of Nations and World Court or even as to the best way to attain their goal. The combined impact of these groups contributed to two major themes in American foreign policy during the interwar period: disarmament and isolationism (which was more representative of the majority opinion than was internationalism).

Possibly because of the disillusionment that accompanied the failure of international disarmament conferences, many groups chose an alternative: to make the manufacture and sale of armaments unprofitable. Another alternative was to isolate the United States in order to minimize outside contacts and therefore to lessen the possibility of involvement in foreign affairs. These and comparable antiwar solutions were kept before the American public through the medium of literature and the arts: for instance, in literature, Ernest Hemingway's *A Farewell to Arms* (1929); in drama, Robert Sherwood's *Idiot's Delight* (1934); in motion pictures, *The Big Parade* (1925) and *All Quiet on the Western Front* (1930). Large-scale advertising in popular periodicals and on radio programs kept the subject of peace in the consciousness of the American people. In 1934 several books and an article in *Fortune* indicted munitions makers for the exorbitant profits they had acquired from the war. Variations on this theme made an international arms cartel responsible for prolonging World War I and for attempting to sabotage world peace efforts. As one expert has pointed out, this view was so pervasive that "even the American Legion wanted to harness the munitions tycoons."

The weight of public opinion contributed to the Senate's holding a much-publicized hearing on the munitions industry. The Munitions Investigating Committee (the Nye Committee), headed by an isolationist senator from North Dakota, Gerald P. Nye, was heavily weighted with isolationists who had little difficulty in producing evidence of the excessive profits enjoyed by the arms industry. The findings of the committee led to the unwarranted conclusion that World War I had been the result of a "great conspiracy." Those who were convinced of the existence of a conspiracy readily accepted the corollary that to avoid a repetition the United States should isolate itself from the world as a safeguard against involvement with any belligerents. According to nonscientific contemporary polls, a majority of Americans agreed with the findings of the Nye Committee and believed that American intervention in World War I had been a mistake.

NEUTRALITY BY LEGISLATION

With monumentally poor timing because of the rise of fascism in Europe, Congress from 1935 to 1939 passed a series of Neutrality Acts which attempted to implement isolationist and antiwar views. Roosevelt and Hull, unable to prevent the passage of such bills, sought broad executive discretionary powers in their use. The first Neutrality Act provided for a tight arms embargo against belligerents and warned Americans that they traveled on belligerent ships at their own risk. FDR invoked this act when Italy invaded Ethiopia in October 1935, but the embargo in effect militated against Ethiopia, which sorely needed arms, and favored Italy, which did not.

The United States refused to cooperate with the League in applying sanctions against Mussolini, the Italian dictator. Instead, in early 1936 Congress passed the Second Neutrality Act, which extended the provisions of the first act for a year, stiffened its provisions, and forbade loans to belligerents. The same year, civil war broke out in Spain; Roosevelt, anticipating strong isolationist sentiment in Congress, asked for an even more stringent law. The Neutrality Act of 1937 extended the ban on loans, prohibited Americans from traveling on belligerent ships, and allowed arms purchases on a cash-and-carry basis for two years provided that purchases were carried on ships owned by the belligerents. This act marked the high point of isolationist sentiment as expressed through legislation.

The Spanish Civil War soon became far more than a localized insurrection. Mussolini's Italy and Hitler's Nazi Germany, having signed a nonaggression pact in 1936, aided the rebels under General Francisco Franco with massive air and war material support. The Soviets provided some support for the Loyalists, and about 2,000 Americans fought for the

Loyalists as members of the Abraham Lincoln Brigade. However, by 1939 Franco had triumphed, and another European dictatorship was established.

FDR AND THE ISOLATIONIST IMPULSE

The reasons that led some Americans to fight against Franco in Spain highlighted the foreign policy dilemma that vexed FDR and Hull until the end of the decade. Both men were aware of the threat posed by Hitler's rise in Germany and of the dictator's plans for liquidating German Jewry and for abridging the rights of individual Germans. (The League proved helpless to prevent Hitler's take-over of the Rhineland in 1936 or to keep Mussolini from withdrawing from the League in 1937.) FDR and Hull faced formidable obstacles in attempting to develop a more international foreign policy. Not only Congress but the American public forced Roosevelt to delay any overt moves toward dealing with the deteriorating situation in Europe until after the 1936 election.

The first indication of a change in policy toward European events came in Chicago on October 5, 1937, when FDR told a large audience that world peace was being threatened by 10 percent of the world's population. He contended that the remaining 90 percent needed to work together to quarantine the culprits. He was referring not only to Italy and Germany but to Japan as well. The Japanese had again invaded northern China, in the process bombing Shanghai and causing great loss of life. Roosevelt's meaning was clearly illustrated to Americans on December 12, 1937, when Japanese bombers bombed, strafed, and sank a naval river boat, the U.S.S. *Panay*, which was escorting oil tankers up the Yangtze River. Public indignation, however, was not so much directed at Japan as at the United States government for protecting private enterprise in a war zone. Reflecting isolationist sentiment, Representative Louis Ludlow of Indiana introduced a bill for a constitutional amendment that would have prohibited Congress from declaring war until a national referendum had been held. The bill was defeated only because FDR used his influence and authority to oppose it.

Diplomacy continued to be helpless to check Japanese, Italian, or German aggression. Just before the *Panay* incident, nineteen nations, including the United States, but not Italy or Germany, had met in Brussels to try to stop Japan's aggression in China. The conference was a failure and the invasion continued unabated. The well-trained Japanese armies spread out through China after capturing Shanghai, Nanking, Peking, and other major port cities. On November 3, 1938, Japan heralded the new order in Asia, the Greater Asia Co-Prosperity Sphere, based upon its rule in

Manchuria and domination of China. According to a recent student, Professor Akira Iriye, Japanese leaders believed the United States would not declare war regardless of Japanese actions in Asia.

THE UNITED STATES AND THE PHILIPPINES

This belief may have been well-founded until that time, but American diplomats and strategists were becoming increasingly alarmed at the vulnerability of the Philippines. America's Pacific outpost had proved a distinct liability because of the prohibitive cost of fortifying the islands. American businessmen were disappointed too. In spite of large-scale investment, the Philippines had never developed either the market or a sufficient surplus of exports to enable them to pay their way. Disenchantment had begun in 1916, as illustrated by the Jones Act, which promised the Philippines independence as soon as a stable government could be established. Stable government had in fact become part of the administrative contribution of the United States, but the islands were to wait another eighteen years before realizing any degree of self-government.

In 1932 pressure from several groups forced Congress to consider Philippine independence once again. Labor unions were protesting the influx of cheap Filipino labor which was competing with the already hard-pressed American labor. Also, duty free tobacco, sugar, and coconut oil caused American producers to agitate for a change in Philippine status so that these items could be given tariffs, thereby lessening competition. Congress passed the Hare-Hawes-Cutting bill in December 1932, which provided for independence after a ten-year waiting period. During the interim the Philippines would enjoy commonwealth status and self-government, but would remain under American foreign policy. President Hoover vetoed the bill because he felt the Filipinos were not ready for independence and would not, in any event, be able to maintain it in the face of Japanese aggression. Congress overrode his veto, but the Philippine legislature then rejected the bill. Filipinos feared economic disaster should their exports be subjected to tariffs, and they also opposed taking on the expense and burden of nationhood while the United States still maintained military bases there.

In 1933 FDR backed and signed a similar law, the Tydings-McDuffie Act, which deleted the permanent base section of the earlier bill. The Philippine legislature reluctantly accepted its terms and in November 1935 inaugurated the self-governing Commonwealth of the Philippines. Complete independence was slated for July 4, 1946. The Filipinos themselves were uneasy spectators of the aggressive moves of the Japanese, their main island of Luzon being only a few hundred miles south of Japan.

The Japanese continued their aggrandizement in Asia and, thanks to the European crises of 1938 and 1939, were left relatively undisturbed. By 1938 Secretary of State Hull clearly recognized the possibility of a Berlin-Tokyo agreement. The Japanese began to indicate a move southward toward the oil of the Dutch East Indies. In early 1939 they seized Hainan, a Chinese island, and then the Spratley Islands, some 400 miles west of the Philippines. The United States showed its disapprobation of Japanese conduct by publicly supporting Chiang Kai-shek and lending him $25 million. But the American public demanded stronger action and a "moral embargo" from airplane manufacturers. Congress, in fact, threatened to abrogate the Japanese-American Treaty of Commerce and Navigation signed in 1911. Secretary Hull took the threat seriously and on July 26, 1939, gave Japan the required six-months termination notice. In turn, this gave President Roosevelt a freer hand to impose economic sanctions against Japan, though he temporarily held them in abeyance.

THE FIRE IN EUROPE

From the end of 1937 on, the situation in Europe rapidly deteriorated. Early in 1938 Hitler marched into Austria, annexing that helpless state. Next he turned to the Sudetenland, the western part of Czechoslovakia, which contained over 3,000,000 Germans. President Eduard Beneš mobilized the Czech army, called upon France and Russia to honor their alliances with Czechoslovakia, and prepared to meet the expected German aggression. Neville Chamberlain, the British Prime Minister, in a desperate attempt to stave off what appeared to be imminent war, twice visited Hitler with plans to ameliorate the crisis. But Hitler would concede nothing; at this juncture, FDR wired all the countries involved asking them to hold a conference to discuss the Czech problem. On September 28-29, 1939, at Munich, Britain and France backed down when Hitler refused all compromise. Thus, Czechoslovakia was doomed. Roosevelt's part in the Munich agreement was minimal. Although he was disappointed with the outcome, polls showed that a majority of Americans believed that the Munich agreement meant a lasting peace.

AMERICA AND THE FATE OF GERMAN JEWRY

The systematic and continued oppression of the nearly 3,000,000 Jews in Germany began with Hitler's rise to power in 1933. Many thousands fled, leaving everything behind in exchange for exit papers. As anti-Jewish laws became more and more harsh, hundreds of thousands were sent to concentration camps. Americans, appalled by the revelations in such books as John Gunther's *Inside Europe* (1936), began to sympathize with their plight. In 1938 a new wave of terror began after a young Polish Jew murdered a Nazi official in Paris. In retaliation, the Nazis burned synagogues in Germany, fined the Jews a billion marks, forbade their attending high schools and universities, barred them from cultural events, and even prohibited them from driving cars. Prominent Americans of all faiths, including Herbert Hoover and Harold Ickes, went on the air to broadcast their horror and outrage. Although many well-known German and Austrian Jews had escaped to America during the decade, there was never enough agitation to force Congress to amend the quota system to permit a greater influx. The State Department was also far from aggressive, partly because of a long-standing anti-Semitism. The inescapable conclusion, in the words of one historian, is that "For every refugee who came to this country, many more who could have been saved died in Hitler's extermination chambers."

THE PEAK OF ISOLATIONISM

FDR had long taken an almost patriarchal interest in the navy, and he was also concerned about the deteriorating state of the army. Even before the fall of Czechoslovakia he submitted a large rearmament measure to Congress. After a four months' wrangle, the Vinson Naval Expansion Act was passed, and then only because the isolationists could not agree as to whether rearming would aid or hamper America's isolationism. The Vinson Act was limited; it did not fortify Guam, as the navy wanted and as Congress would never do, but it did add enough units to enable the navy to operate at least minimally after the Pearl Harbor attack.

When FDR viewed the newly elected Congress that met in 1939, he found that isolationist sentiment, far from dying, seemed actually to be increasing. His suggested repeal of the neutrality laws touched off a six-months' debate that ended in the defeat of the proposed legislation. When Congress adjourned on August 5, 1939, the elderly isolationist leader, Senator William E. Borah, confidently predicted that there would be no war. But this marked the last time that Congressional isolationist sentiment would keep FDR from a foreign policy course he and Cordell Hull had charted.

THE BEGINNING OF WORLD WAR II

In March, while Congress debated the neutrality laws, Hitler occupied the remainder of Czechoslovakia and began to demand the reannexation of

Danzig and the Polish Corridor. Shortly after this, Mussolini's army seized Albania. The question now became: "When will the war begin?" The key to the European situation lay in the Soviet Union. Britain and France had made overtures to Josef Stalin, but the Soviet dictator was deeply suspicious of the Western democracies partly as the result of France's failure to honor her pledge to Czechoslovakia and her reluctance to stand up to Hitler. At the same time, Stalin wanted territory in Eastern Europe that had in the past belonged to Russia and that would now provide an added safeguard for Russia's long, exposed western border.

In August the Nazis offered Stalin a nonaggression pact together with a promise to try to restrain Japan from invading Mongolia, an area long disputed between China and Russia. By the terms of a secret protocol, the Germans also promised to remain neutral should the Soviets decide to occupy certain territories within their "sphere." The announcement of the pact reverberated like a thunder clap. England retaliated by immediately signing an alliance with threatened Poland. On August 29, 1939, Hitler delivered an ultimatum to Poland, and three days later German armies invaded the country. On September 3, having failed to get a response from Germany to their ultimatums to withdraw, Britain and France declared war. This precipitated World War II, although some maintain that the war really started in 1931 when the Japanese invaded Manchuria.

THE RETREAT FROM ISOLATION

Almost immediately, President Roosevelt and Secretary Hull began to attack American isolationist policies, leaving no doubt as to the direction of their sympathies. Roosevelt declared the United States neutral, but, as he put it in a radio address, "I cannot ask that every American remain neutral in thought as well." According to a public opinion survey, Americans did not: 84 percent favored an Allied victory. Next, FDR called for a special session of Congress to modify the stringent neutrality act which had banned the sale of arms to belligerents. After a hectic six-weeks' debate, Congress passed the Fourth Neutrality Act; this provided for cash-and-carry arms sales to belligerents, forbade Americans to sail on belligerent ships, and prohibited American merchant ships from using belligerent ports or combat zones. Initially, the act aided the Nazis by clearing the seas of over ninety American cargo carriers, thus freeing Nazi U-boats from any restraint they might have exercised in attacking shipping destined for blockaded England. But after the defeat of Poland, the war settled down to a static "sitzkrieg" during which the Nazis in their Siegfried fortifications stared across at the Allies in the French Maginot Line, and there was minimum contact between the armies.

During the fall and winter Stalin devoured a large portion of Poland and the Baltic republics, the latter conceived at Versailles in 1919 and composed of Latvia, Lithuania, and Estonia. He also invaded Finland to realign his vulnerable borders. The American public was strongly pro-Finnish, but FDR refrained from voicing strong objections. After initial reverses, the Russian army forced the Finns to cede a large portion of their eastern frontier.

In April, Hitler's blitzkrieg rapidly overran Denmark and Norway. On May 10 the Germans invaded the Low Countries and within a week had captured Holland, Luxembourg, and much of Belgium. When the King of the Belgians surrendered on May 27, the British army in Flanders was encircled on three sides and looked as if it would be lost to England for the duration; miraculously, it was evacuated almost intact from Dunkirk by the stubborn determination and courage of the British navy and volunteer civilian helpers. By June 11 the Nazis were approaching Paris. The French government, after declaring Paris an open city, fled to Bordeaux and appealed to Roosevelt for aid.

FDR, powerless to give immediate assistance, had been trying among other things to keep Mussolini out of the war. He failed, and Italy declared war on June 10, an act which Roosevelt bitterly attacked, saying that "the hand that held the dagger has struck it into the back of its neighbor." After France surrendered on June 22, 1940, FDR decided to continue diplomatic relations with the puppet regime headed by the eighty-year-old World War I hero, Marshal Henri Philippe Pétain. Roosevelt was criticized for this decision, but it seems clear that the President considered diplomatic relations with Vichy more important to American interests than the recognition of Charles de Gaulle's Free French group in London. Vichy became a useful listening post and the United States could at least attempt — unsuccessfully, however — to mitigate the Pétain government's anti-Semitic and fascist tendencies.

The Nazi victories changed American attitudes markedly. Congress was still debating FDR's request for a modest increase in the defense budget when the German legions marched across Europe. Immediately, Congress granted the President more than he asked for; by September it had voted defense appropriations of $10.5 billion, more than five times the amount for the preceding year. Opinion polls clearly demonstrated that the American people favored increasing aid to England, but about the same percentage insisted that aid stop short of war. At the time of the French debacle in June, two congressmen — not supporters of FDR — introduced the first peacetime conscription in the nation's history. With only the slightest suggestion from Roosevelt, the bill was passed after a summer's heated battle, becoming law on September 16, 1940, as the Burke-Wadsworth Act.

Another indicator of America's change toward a position of

nonbelligerency was the immediate popularity of a group organized by editor William Allen White — the Committee to Defend America by Aiding the Allies. Within six weeks of its founding, the organization had over 300 local chapters which sponsored rallies, radio broadcasts, newspaper advertisements, and social functions to pressure Congress and FDR for more aid to England. During the summer another group met to oppose these pressures and present an isolationist alternative. The America First Committee had the backing of such public figures as Colonel Charles A. Lindbergh and Robert E. Wood, head of Sears, Roebuck and Company. It used the same techniques as the White Committee but with less effect.

THE DESTROYERS DEAL AND THE ELECTION OF 1940

The election of 1940 pitted Roosevelt, who was challenging the "no third term" dictum of Jefferson, against an unknown utilities magnate, Wendell Willkie. Willkie agreed in principle with FDR's foreign policy, thereby repudiating the large segment of the Republican party which leaned toward isolationism or nonparticipation. Roosevelt was actually helped by the nature of the European war, which led many voters to support him as a tested leader.

A major foreign policy step taken by Roosevelt in September could have hurt him politically but did not. In May, Winston Churchill, the new British Prime Minister, had asked FDR to sell Britain forty or fifty destroyers of World War I vintage so that she could protect vital shipping lines. Roosevelt hesitated, fearing isolationist repercussions in Congress and the danger of providing Willkie with a ready-made issue. Nevertheless, in early September, by an executive agreement, he traded fifty destroyers in exchange for sites for eight Western Hemispheric bases in British possession from Newfoundland to British Guiana. Willkie had approved the transaction and, despite the hostility of isolationists and others who felt that Congress should have been consulted, the affair helped FDR. Many Americans viewed it as a positive step to aid the sorely pressed Allies. In any event, FDR won the election by 5,000,000 votes — not the 1936 landslide, to be sure, but still an impressive showing.

LEND-LEASE AND THE ROAD TO BELLIGERENCY

By the fall of 1940 the United States had shifted from a position of legislated neutrality to one of nonbelligerent participation on the side of the Allies. In a letter to Roosevelt written in December, Churchill described Britain's critical need for foodstuffs and war material, adding that England would be unable to pay should the supplies be forthcoming. FDR's response was the concept of lend-lease, by which England would be given the munitions and other supplies necessary to sustain life. According to Roosevelt, England's survival was vital for America's own security. The American people, receiving the news in one of the President's homey fireside chats, evidently agreed. Congress passed the enabling act, labeled H.R. 1776 in the House, by wide margins, despite the fervent pleas made against the measure by Lindbergh and other isolationists. The President signed the historic act on March 11, 1941. An appropriations bill that followed gave FDR \$7 billion to begin the program, an amount equal to the total of the controversial loans of World War I. The United States cemented the agreement by holding joint military talks with the British, entering, as one writer expressed it, "a common law alliance." A series of military discussions produced a joint agreement that should America become involved in a war with Japan and Germany, the Allies would concentrate on defeating Germany first.

THE LEND-LEASE ACT, 1941

Be it enacted That this Act may be cited as "An Act to Promote the Defense of the United States."
Section 3.
(a) Notwithstanding the provisions of any other law, the President may, from time to time, when he deems it in the interest of national defense, authorize the Secretary of War, the Secretary of the Navy, or the head of any other department or agency of the Government—

(1) To manufacture in arsenals, factories, and shipyards under their jurisdiction, or otherwise procure, to the extent to which funds are made available therefor, or contracts are authorized from time to time by the Congress, or both, any defense article for the government of any country whose defense the President deems vital to the defense of the United States.

(2) To sell, transfer title to, exchange, lease, lend, or otherwise dispose of, to any such government any defense article, but no defense article not manufactured or procured under paragraph (1) shall in any way be disposed of under this paragraph, except after consultation with the Chief of Staff of the Army or the Chief of Naval Operations of the Navy, or both. . . .

(4) To communicate to any such government any defense information, pertaining to any defense article furnished to such government under paragraph (2) of this subsection.

(5) To release for export any defense article disposed of in any way under this subsection to any such government,

(b) The terms and conditions upon which any such foreign government receives any aid authorized under subsection (a) shall be those which the President deems satisfactory, and the benefit to the United States may be payment or repayment in kind or property, or any other direct or indirect benefit which the President deems satisfactory. . . .

(d) Nothing in this Act shall be construed to authorize or to permit the authorization of convoying vessels by naval vessels of the United States.

(e) Nothing in this Act shall be construed to authorize or to permit the authorization of the entry of any American vessel into a combat area in violation of section 3 of the Neutrality Act of 1939. . . .

Section 8.

The Secretaries of War and of the Navy are hereby authorized to purchase or otherwise acquire arms, ammunition, and implements of war produced within the jurisdiction of any country to which section 3 is applicable, whenever the President deems such purchase or acquisition to be necessary in the interests of the defense of the United States. . . .

Section 9.

The President may, from time to time, promulgate such rules and regulations as may be necessary and proper to carry out any of the provisions of this Act; and he may exercise any power or authority conferred on him by this Act through such department, agency, or officer as he shall direct.

In April the Nazis intensified their submarine warfare, successfully using the wolf-pack technique, whereby a group of eight or ten submarines would make surface attacks on convoys in the evening. FDR countered by ordering the navy to occupy Greenland and to patrol the western part of the Atlantic. Nevertheless, he was forced to tell the American public at the end of May that the Allied cause was desperate: Hitler had captured the Balkans, defeating the British in Greece and on Crete, while in North Africa, the British army was being driven back to Egypt.

The American occupation of Iceland temporarily slowed submarine attacks, but by September the Nazis were again wreaking havoc on the seas. On September 4 the American destroyer *Greer* was attacked; a week later FDR announced that henceforth American ships would shoot on sight. Until then, Americans had merely notified the British of the position of sighted submarines.

The President edged closer to belligerency by asking Congress to repeal the Fourth Neutrality Act. An attack on the destroyer *Kearney* and the sinking of the *Reuben James*, with a loss of 115 lives, induced Congress not only to repeal the neutrality act but to pass an amendment arming American merchant ships. Thus, by November 1941, FDR had led the country to a definitely pro-Allied position, a fact recognized by the Nazis. They delayed massive attacks on American shipping; and when the stunning surprise attack came, it was not from the Nazis but from the Japanese in the Pacific.

THE FAR EAST, 1939-1941

After the abrogation of the 1911 treaty with Japan in January 1940, Cordell Hull continued to permit trading with the Japanese on a day-to-day basis. While the so-called Phony War went on in Europe, tensions in the Far East eased slightly. But after Hitler's startling victories in the spring, Japan demanded and received limited concessions from France, the Netherlands, and England. The militarists in Japan were not content with these concessions; they engineered a change of cabinet in July that brought to power Prince Fumimaro Konoye as Prime Minister, Yosuke Matsuoka as Foreign Secretary, and General Hideki Tojo as Minister of War. The moderate Konoye was overshadowed by Tojo, who sought closer ties with the Axis Powers and an expansion of the Japanese empire to the south.

FDR reacted to the change in the Japanese cabinet by instituting a licensing system for exports to Japan. He had already moved the Pacific fleet from northern California to Pearl Harbor. The astute and experienced American Ambassador to Japan, Joseph C. Grew, who had long opposed the imposition of economic sanctions, now conceded that such a position was untenable. In September 1940 Japan announced that its Greater Asia Co-Prosperity Sphere now included "the former German islands under mandate, French Indo-China and Pacific Islands, Thailand, British Malaya, British Borneo, Dutch East Indies, Burma, Australia, New Zealand, India, etc."

On September 27 Japan became an Axis partner, signing an alliance with Hitler and Mussolini which, in American eyes, made Japan a part of the world fascist threat. FDR responded to news of the alliance with an embargo on all iron and steel scrap.

While neither country gave ground, tensions did lessen during the fall and winter of 1940-1941. Then on April 13, Japan, to the consternation of its Axis partners, signed a neutrality pact with Russia; this relieved Japan's exposed border in Manchuria, but it also allowed the Russians to transfer troops to the west in time to meet the German invasion of Russia which began in June 1941. The Japanese now demanded that the Vichy government give them control of the southern half of Indochina. In a futile effort to restrain the Japanese from taking this step, the United States froze Japanese assets and embargoed most exports, the most important of which was oil.

The Japanese predicated their policies on oil, of which, according to the experts, they had only an eighteen-months' supply. While most officials in both countries did not want war, each country either misread or misunderstood the other's actions, so that during the summer of 1941 tensions again increased. For its part, the United States demanded guarantees of no further expansion in Asia; Japan, however, not only wanted the oil embargo lifted but insisted on a free hand in Asia. In August the Konoye cabinet, after being reshuffled to bring in more moderates, offered fresh proposals, one of which was a summit talk with FDR in the Pacific. But Hull distrusted Konoye and persuaded Roosevelt to refuse unless prior agreement on basic terms could first be obtained. This was probably an error in judgment.

In retrospect, this refusal proved to be the point of no return for the Japanese in deciding on war with America. In September their top leaders decided on a timetable for war, to be adhered to unless their demands were met. In mid-October Prince Konoye resigned in favor of the militant General Tojo, who implemented a plan to submit two proposals to the United States. Should these be rejected, the Japanese would launch an attack before the end of the year. However, thanks to having broken the Japanese naval code, the State Department was fully aware of the plan. Hull counseled delay to enable heavy bombers to reach the Philippines and to allow time for improving the general state of defense. A special Japanese envoy arrived in mid-November bearing both of the plans. Saburo Kurusu was an able, pro-American diplomat who was married to an American. Hull rejected both plans but made a counteroffer to gain time. Critics of Hull have since been harsh with him for his seeming inflexibility, but Hull's ten-point manifesto does not seem unreasonable in light of the eighteen months of fruitless negotiations that had preceded it, his knowledge of how far the Japanese were prepared to go, and his support of FDR. Nevertheless, Hull's reply, taken with the stunning Nazi victories in Russia, allowed the militarists on November 29 to obtain the consent of the reluctant Emperor Hirohito to attack the United States.

PEARL HARBOR — DAY OF INFAMY

The Japanese had decided months before on an audacious surprise attack on Pearl Harbor to destroy the American fleet. They gambled on the belief that America's desire to defeat Hitler would outweigh its reaction to a Japanese attack and that a quick peace would be forthcoming. On November 25 the Japanese striking force set out in deep secrecy. Although American policy makers realized that Japan was about to strike, they believed it would be toward southeast Asia. FDR spent a week drafting a personal message to Hirohito, but it was not sent until December 6.

On December 7, 1941, the Japanese attacked Pearl Harbor. As one expert has written, it was devastatingly effective "because of skillful planning, superb execution and unbelievably good luck." Five American battleships were sunk or seriously damaged, Pearl Harbor was considerably impaired as a naval base, and half the planes in Hawaii were destroyed. Casualties amounted to more than 3,000 American sailors, soldiers, and marines killed.

Ever since that date, which FDR called "a day of infamy," the question of ultimate responsibility has been debated. While no single answer will please more than a few, one answer at least has little to do with individual responsibility. The attitudes of American decision makers, shaped in the interwar period or earlier, simply did not prepare them, with but few exceptions, to understand the Japanese or to accept the responsibilities of global diplomacy.

When Franklin D. Roosevelt went before Congress the day after the Pearl Harbor holocaust bearing a declaration of war, it was passed with hardly a dissenting vote. He could be certain of one difference between this war and World War I: Americans were not only united against the Axis powers — after Pearl Harbor they believed they were fighting for their country's very life.

Further Reading

*William E. Leuchtenburg, *Franklin D. Roosevelt and the New Deal, 1932-1940* (New York, 1963) surveys this period well. A more diplomatically oriented survey is *John E. Wiltz, *From Isolation to War: 1931-1941* (New York, 1968). Selig Adler's *The Uncertain Giant*, cited at the end of the last chapter, is equally useful here. FDR's Latin American policy is mentioned in the books cited above. *Bryce Wood, *The Making of the Good Neighbor Policy* (New York, 1967) delves into this subject. The problems of the depression and American diplomacy are discussed in Lloyd C. Gardner's challenging *Economic Aspects of New Deal Diplomacy* (Madison, Wisc., 1964).

The literature about isolation is extensive, but Selig Adler's *The Isolationist Impulse*, cited previously, is outstanding. Two other excellent analyses are *The Challenge to Isolation: 1937-1940* (New York, 1952) and *The Undeclared War: 1940-1941* (New York, 1953), both written by William L. Langer and S. Everett Gleason. A more general work dealing with the late 1930's and continuing through Pearl Harbor is *Robert A. Divine, *The Reluctant Belligerent: American Entry into World War II* (New York, 1965).

For the Far East in the 1930's, see Akira Iriye, *Across the Pacific*, cited earlier, as well as Edwin O. Reischauer, *The United States and Japan*, 3rd ed. (Cambridge, Mass., 1965). Dorothy Borg, *The United States and the Far Eastern Crisis of 1933-1938* (Cambridge, Mass., 1964), covers the mid-1930's thoroughly. Of the many books published about the events leading up to and including Pearl Harbor, the three cited here are especially readable and authoritative: *Herbert Feis, *The Road to Pearl Harbor* (New York, 1962); Walter Millis, *This Is Pearl! The United States and Japan, 1941* (New York, 1947); and *Roberta Wohlstetter, *Pearl Harbor: Warning and Decision* (Stanford, Calif., 1962) are highly recommended.

Memoirs by Henry L. Stimson (cited earlier), Joseph Grew, William Phillips, Cordell Hull, Husband E. Kimmel, and George F. Kennan are useful. The latter's *Memoirs, 1925-1960* (Boston, 1968) is applicable to the next several chapters.

Biographies are numerous for men of the period. One model of a good political biography is *James M. Burns, *Roosevelt: The Lion and the Fox* (New York, 1957). Others include studies of Cordell Hull, Joseph Grew, Gerald P. Nye, and Henry L. Stimson.

Asterisk denotes paperback edition.

16

World War II and the Shaping of Global Diplomacy

When the Japanese attacked Pearl Harbor on December 7, 1941, they strengthened rather than weakened American determination to defeat Germany first. Most major wartime decisions were made at top-level conferences by Roosevelt, Churchill, and Stalin, or their foreign ministers. The first conference dated back to a meeting between FDR and Churchill off Newfoundland in mid-August 1941. There they had adopted the Atlantic Charter, which contained eight points, several of them vague but all disavowing territorial aims and all supporting self-determination. Subsequent meetings spelled out the Atlantic Charter. The sum of the wartime conferences represented the most extreme position even taken by the executive branch in actually formulating and implementing American foreign policy without Congressional consultation.

THE STATE DEPARTMENT AND CONGRESS IN WORLD WAR II

The advent of war saw a State Department little changed since World War I. During the 1930's Congress was particularly niggardly with appropriations for the department, and not until after the war began did the situation change. Early in the war Secretary Hull set up a committee headed by Under-Secretary of State Sumner Welles to gather material relating to both the long-range and the immediate goals of a global war. From this group came much of the impetus for the Dumbarton Oaks Conference of 1944 and the Charter of the United Nations. The onrush of wartime responsibilities saw the department increase to more than 1,600 members and overflow its home in "foggy bottom."

American wartime diplomacy and the making of foreign policy were taken over by FDR to an astonishing degree. Also, since military decisions took precedence over diplomatic considerations, many of the latter decisions were made by military men who had had little diplomatic experience. The role of the State Department was further reduced by the welter of overlapping authority assumed by temporary agencies. To cite one example, the State Department claimed jurisdiction over the lend-lease program, but so did three other agencies! Despite periodic attempts to set up and implement coordinating committees, jurisdictional disputes were endemic, serving further to weaken the role of the State Department.

Many of the same statements regarding a diminution of authority applied to Congress as well. FDR governed by virtue of being Commander-in-Chief of the armed forces. Many important executive agreements that he made in the course of wartime conferences committed the nation to foreign policy decisions. Congress could only look on impotently, though it did assume its role as public watchdog and, far more effectively than in the past, used its authority to investigate domestic war preparations.

THE UNITED STATES AND LATIN AMERICA DURING WORLD WAR II

For the first time in history, the belligerents, using air and sea power, could wage total war almost anywhere in the world. Because sources of strategic materials as well as populations were in danger from the Axis powers, Latin America thus became involved in a way that had not been possible in World War I. After Pearl Harbor, out of twenty Latin American republics, nine immediately declared war and three severed diplomatic relations with the Axis. In January 1942 the hemispheric foreign ministers· met at Rio de Janeiro to consider what action to take regarding the war. The United States hoped that a strong and unanimous statement calling for the severing of relations with the Axis would result; but Argentina and Chile insisted on a weaker version that permitted each republic to make its own choice, although they were the only countries that did not end diplomatic relations with the Axis immediately. To maintain the fiction of hemispheric solidarity, the American representative, Under-Secretary of State Sumner Welles, reluctantly accepted their alternative. But in so doing, he incurred the lasting enmity of his chief, Cordell Hull, who strongly opposed such a compromise.

In June and in August, Mexico and Brazil, respectively, declared war, but Argentina and Chile still refused to break with the Axis. Within a year Chile joined the Allies, but Argentina remained adamant, partly because of its trade patterns and partly because of its sizable German and Italian population. For example, the United States bought almost everything the Latin Americans had to sell, with the exception of Argentine beef and wheat, both commercially competitive items between the two countries.

It was not until January 1944, when the outcome of the war was evident, that Argentina severed relations with the Axis, and another fifteen months passed before it declared war on Germany, Italy, and Japan. Even at that late date Argentina's compliance came about through diplomatic pressure, not a change of heart. In July 1944 a pro-Nazi officer clique led by Colonel Juan Perón took over the Argentinian government. The Perón regime sought recognition by the United States; with this in mind, a special inter-American conference held at Chapultepec in February 1945 made a declaration of war the price of recognition and promised Perón that by doing so he could participate in the United Nations Conference at San Francisco scheduled for the following April.

The conferees at Chapultepec then turned their attention to a more far-reaching consideration. They adopted the historic Act of Chapultepec, which turned the Monroe Doctrine into a joint hemispheric defense pact by declaring that an attack against one country represented an attack against all.

The participation of the Latin American republics in World War II was the culmination of the Good Neighbor policy. The United States not only bought vast quantities of their goods but also aided in financing their industrial expansion. At the same time, although only Mexico and Brazil sent armed contingents overseas, the United States sent military missions and quantities of military stores to most of its southern neighbors. By the time the war ended, only Argentina marred the sentiments of mutual goodwill and respect that prevailed.

THE FIRST YEAR OF THE WAR

In the first year of the war the Allies suffered a series of positively catastrophic military defeats. Only occasionally was the gloom relieved by diplomatic announcements of great importance, which were, even so, predicated solely on victory. The situation was bad for the United States, worse for Great Britain, but desperate for Russia. The Soviets were retreating before the lightning offensive of the Nazis, who had invaded Russia on June 22, 1941. Now the Soviets were being pushed back to the Moscow suburbs. FDR had embraced the USSR as an ally with full lend-lease privileges, but Stalin complained about the amount of aid actually received. Nazi U-boats were so effective that merchant ships were being sunk faster than the Allies could replace them. A few days before Pearl Harbor the German army breached Moscow's outer defenses and the fall of the city seemed certain.

Across the globe the Japanese followed up their attack on Pearl Harbor by capturing Guam and Wake Island. In the winter of 1941-1942 they seized

Thailand, Malaya and Singapore, Hong Kong, the Dutch East Indies, Borneo, New Britain, the Solomons, part of New Guinea, and were threatening Australia. On February 27 and 28 the Japanese fleet inflicted a stunning defeat on the Allied fleet in the Java Sea, thus sealing the fate of the Dutch East Indies. But this was the last major Japanese naval victory of the war.

In this atmosphere of disaster Winston Churchill and his staff arrived in Washington in late December 1941 to confer with Roosevelt. The chief result of the meeting was the announcement on January 1, 1942, of a twenty-six nation pact, the Declaration of the United Nations. The participating nations were pledged to uphold the terms of the Atlantic Charter and not to make a separate peace. FDR had signed and issued the pact as an executive agreement. Public opinion polls showed that Americans concurred wholeheartedly with the President's action.

THE ATLANTIC CHARTER, 1941

The President of the United States of America and the Prime Minister, Mr. Churchill, representing His Majesty's Government in the United Kingdom, being met together, deem it right to make known certain common principles in the national policies of their respective countries on which they base their hopes for a better future for the world.

First, their countries seek no aggrandizement, territorial or other;

Second, they desire to see no territorial changes that do not accord with the freely expressed wishes of the peoples concerned;

Third, they respect the right of all peoples to choose the form of government under which they will live; and they wish to see sovereign rights and self-government restored to those who have been forcibly deprived of them;

Fourth, they will endeavor, with due respect for their existing obligations, to further the enjoyment by all States, great or small, victor or vanquished, of access, on equal terms, to the trade and to the raw materials of the world which are needed for their economic prosperity;

Fifth, they desire to bring about the fullest collaboration between all nations in the economic field with the object of securing, for all, improved labor standards, economic advancement and social security;

Sixth, after the final destruction of the Nazi tyranny, they hope to see established a peace which will afford to all nations the means of dwelling in safety within their own boundaries, and which will afford assurance that all the men in all the lands may live out their lives in freedom from fear and want;

Seventh, such a peace should enable all men to traverse the high seas and oceans without hindrance;

Eighth, they believe that all of the nations of the world, for realistic as well as spiritual reasons, must come to the abandonment of the use of force. Since no future peace can be maintained if land, sea or air armaments continue to be employed by nations which threaten, or may threaten, aggression outside of their frontiers, they believe, pending the establishment of a wider and permanent system of general security, that the disarmament of such nations is essential. They will likewise aid and encourage all other practicable measures which will lighten for peace-loving peoples the crushing burden of armaments.

FRANKLIN D. ROOSEVELT
WINSTON S. CHURCHILL

The seriousness of the military situation assured close cooperation among the Allies. This was especially true in the case of the United States and Great Britain because of the genuine admiration and respect Roosevelt and Churchill felt for one another, though FDR and his staff soon assumed the paramount role. The task of cooperating with the USSR and its leader was infinitely more difficult. Stalin was persistently suspicious of the motives of his Western partners, and he especially suspected bad faith when supplies were not immediately forthcoming or when the Allies did not quickly mount a cross-channel invasion to relieve the German pressure on Russia. Too, he sought guarantees that any postwar settlement would ensure his possession of the Baltic states and the parts of Finland and Poland he had taken in 1939-1940. Churchill refused this assurance and was able to convince FDR that the Declaration of the United Nations, which the Russians also had signed, made no mention of postwar political plans.

In May the Soviet Foreign Minister, Vyacheslav Molotov, demanded the opening of a second front in Europe before the end of the year. Roosevelt assented, but a few months later, when Churchill was again conferring with the President, the Prime Minister refused to support a second front, arguing that at best it could be no more than a diversionary tactic. Alternatively, Churchill proposed that the Americans land an army in North Africa to combine with the British army in an offensive against the Germans and Italians. Churchill flew to Moscow personally to announce this decision to the dubious Josef Stalin.

The winter of 1942 aided the Russians in halting the Nazis in the Moscow sector, but to the south the Germans advanced nearly to Stalingrad and by October were menacing the city.

The North African invasion (TORCH) was successfully mounted on November 8, 1942. Although it announced the American military presence, its initial success was due in large measure to the effective diplomatic

Map 10. World War II in Europe and North Africa

neutralization of the threat of intercession by the Vichy government, which still controlled Algeria, Morocco, and Tunisia. At the urging of the State Department, General Dwight D. Eisenhower, the overall commander of the invasion, made a deal with Admiral Jean Darlan, the number two man in the Vichy government. Darlan ended French resistance in North Africa in exchange for being recognized by the Allies as the French representative in authority there. British and American public opinion reacted adversely to the idea of a Vichy turncoat being in charge of French North Africa, and FDR was placed on the defensive in explaining the move. Before the year was over, however, Darlan was assassinated and the previously selected and popular General Henri Giraud took over. Meanwhile, another French officer, General Charles de Gaulle, head of the Free French government in London (recognized by the British but not by the Americans), awaited an opportune moment to advance his cause.

THE TURNING OF THE TIDE

De Gaulle's time came shortly. He vigorously advanced his claims at the conference held by Churchill and Roosevelt in Casablanca, January 14-23, 1943. Despite FDR's personal distaste for de Gaulle, the Free French spokesman was recognized by both Churchill and Roosevelt as a co-leader with Giraud. Soon Giraud was eased out and thereafter de Gaulle alone spoke for France.

Another decision made at Casablanca involved demanding unconditional surrender from the Axis. FDR claimed that "unconditional surrender" referred only to ending fascism, but Axis propaganda declared it would mean the destruction of their populations. Most authorities feel that the Axis propaganda on the subject served to stiffen enemy resistance as time passed. The policy also put off a discussion among the Allies of their postwar political plans for more than eighteen months. At the time, Stalin concurred in the unconditional surrender policy.

Roosevelt and Churchill also decided at Casablanca on the plan to invade Sicily. In July 1943 the defeat of the Italian army in Sicily knocked Italy out of the war. The Italian homeland was invaded in early September, but the Allies were soon stalled by the German armies, which quickly occupied the whole of the country, replacing the Italians. In the meantime, the Italians had overthrown Mussolini, but Hitler, hoping to use the Duce as a political pawn, sent German paratroopers to remove him to the comparative safety of northern Italy. Allied armies attempting to move up the Italian peninsula were contained by fierce resistance during the winter of 1943-1944, in spite of a large-scale amphibious landing at Anzio, south of Rome. With the coming of spring, the Allies pushed northward once more, capturing Rome on June 4, 1944. Although the Allied timetable for victory had been upset by the German defenders, the Allies had kept better than twenty enemy divisions occupied and therefore unavailable for defending Normandy against a cross-channel invasion.

A cross-channel invasion, Stalin's primary demand, was planned in May 1943 in Washington at another conference between FDR and Churchill. The Nazi submarine menace had subsided and the Allies expected to take the offensive. The Allies' most notable current victory was the heroic Russian defense of Stalingrad, which had withstood an incredible pounding by the German army until late in 1942 when the Russians counterattacked. On February 2, 1943, the surrounded besieging Nazi army of 90,000 surrendered. From this time on, the Soviets began to force back the German armies, and by the time of the Washington conference (TRIDENT) the Russians were counterattacking along the entire eastern front. The two leaders in Washington set June 1, 1944, as the date for the cross-channel invasion (OVERLORD).

Stalin was furious to learn that the invasion had been postponed for still another year. He accused the Western democracies of perfidy and canceled a projected meeting with FDR in July. The tension was relieved by the combination of the Allied success in Sicily and the Russian counteroffensive, and Stalin planned to meet FDR and Churchill in Teheran in December 1943.

THE WAR IN THE PACIFIC, 1942-1944

The conduct of the war in the Pacific produced the least amount of friction among the Allies. After the catastrophic winter of 1941-1942 an American naval force stopped a Japanese offensive in the Battle of the Coral Sea, fought May 7-8, 1942. Although the engagement ended in a draw rather than in an Allied victory, it did protect Australia from invasion. Far more important was the Battle of Midway, June 3-6, 1942; here, the Japanese lost four aircraft carriers, while the Americans lost only the *Yorktown*. In both these engagements aircraft participation demonstrated that both fleets were highly vulnerable to air torpedo attack.

The Japanese now shifted their operations southward, capturing Port Rabaul in New Guinea and the large airfield on Guadalcanal in the Solomons. From both bases Australian cities were vulnerable to bombing attacks. In August 1942 American marines invaded and captured the Guadalcanal airfield, but the Japanese quickly landed reinforcements, threatening, in turn, to wipe out the American invaders. A series of small naval engagements culminated in the Battle of Guadalcanal, November 13-14, 1942. The Americans won a decisive victory at small cost, sinking two battleships, three destroyers, and eleven transports, and damaging three cruisers and six destroyers. The victory safeguarded and consolidated American holdings on Guadalcanal.

General Douglas MacArthur, named supreme commander in the Pacific theater after his evacuation from the Philippines, was able by January 1943 to retake New Guinea. MacArthur began to use an island-hopping procedure, bypassing and isolating strongly fortified Japanese-held islands. Island hopping was not entirely successful — American casualties at Tarawa in the Gilberts were heavy — but in the main it was effective enough

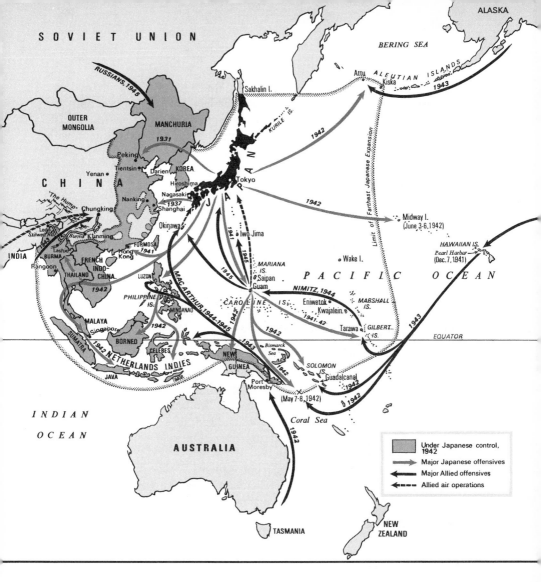

Map 11. World War II in the Pacific

to advance the invasion of the Philippines from December to October 1944, with the aid of another naval victory. In the Battle of the Philippine Sea, June 19-20, 1944, the Japanese had one carrier sunk and four others heavily damaged, which significantly reduced their strength.

Nevertheless, when the invasion of Leyte threatened to cut off the Japanese in the southwest Pacific, they risked another naval battle for control of the Philippines. The Battle of Leyte Gulf, fought on October 24-25, 1944, was the greatest naval engagement in history and a crushing defeat for the Japanese fleet. In it, the Japanese lost their four remaining carriers, three out of nine battleships, nine cruisers, and nine destroyers. American losses were one light carrier, two escort carriers, two destroyers, and one destroyer escort. By late fall 1944, although much fighting lay ahead, including the invasion of the Japanese homeland, the Allies could look with certainty to eventual victory in the Pacific.

CHINA IN WORLD WAR II

China was a source of both frustration and disagreement among the Allied leaders during the war. FDR truculently demanded — and eventually won — a wartime role for China that was not warranted either by her position or leadership. The President was undeniably handicapped by having to deal with long-standing Chinese problems, some of which dated back to the nineteenth century. At the time of Pearl Harbor, the Chinese army was demoralized and dangerously close to disintegration. Chiang Kai-shek, for a decade the most powerful leader in China, moved the government to Chunking in southwest China as a safety measure against Japanese incursions. FDR planned to give massive military aid to Chiang, but his Allies and his priorities reduced the actual amount to a trickle. To shore up the remnants of Chiang's army, Roosevelt sent his personal emissary, General Joseph "Vinegar Joe" Stilwell, to act as chief of staff to Chiang and head of American military operations and lend-lease. Chiang also received a loan of $500 million.

Stilwell, a good soldier but an inept diplomat, was soon at odds with Chiang. The Allied loss of Burma with its overland supply route to China forced the Allies to make use of an airlift from India over the Himalayas to Chunking. The difficulties were many and supplies were scarce during 1942, the total delivered averaging only about a hundred tons a month.

Concerned over the paucity of supplies for Chiang, FDR resorted to diplomacy to make other concessions to China. Near the end of the year he offered a treaty, signed in January 1943, by which the United States relinquished all rights of extraterritoriality in China. The British signed a similar treaty the same day, so that theoretically China regained the sovereignty she had lost more than a hundred years before. Next, FDR introduced legislation to end Chinese exclusion from the United States. The Senate unenthusiastically passed the bill and FDR signed it on December 7, 1943.

Two weeks earlier, while FDR and Churchill were in Cairo for another conference, they had been joined by Chiang and his wife. Madame Chiang Kai-shek, an American-educated member of an aristocratic Chinese family, had made a goodwill tour of the United States and had addressed Congress in February. Roosevelt and Churchill, and later Stalin, agreed that China was to be given every chance to become a major power. To that end, all

Chinese territories would be returned and aid to China would continue and increase.

However, despite the Allies' good intentions, the Chinese government remained weak as the result of runaway inflation and widespread corruption. The Chinese Communists in the north seemed to be more effective. In early 1944 the United States State Department sent a mission to evaluate their ability to fight and govern. The report was glowing, reflecting in part a growing disenchantment with Chiang, which even Roosevelt was forced to acknowledge. Chiang's Nationalist forces enjoyed an uneasy truce with the Communists that dated back to 1937 when the Japanese threatened to overrun the country. Each side was deeply suspicious of the other, and real cooperation between the two never materialized.

By the time the State Department submitted its report, the strategic importance of China to the Allies had diminished considerably. Chinese air bases were originally valuable for their proximity to Japan, but island hopping rapidly obviated this factor. During the darkest days of the war a daring American air raid over Tokyo had been launched from a carrier, although FDR implied that it came from a base in China. Later, B-29's operating from Guam offered a better solution than Chinese seaboard bases.

In the fall of 1944 FDR sent Chiang a stern note, but this produced little effect on the Chinese government. Stilwell was recalled and replaced by General Albert C. Wedemeyer for the military and Patrick J. Hurley as Ambassador to China. Roosevelt's final effort on Chiang's behalf was his insistence at the Yalta Conference, held in early February 1945, that China receive a permanent seat on the important Security Council to be established as part of a world organization. Stalin, little interested in the Chinese Communists, also pledged support for Chiang's government. Nevertheless, recognizing China's weakness, FDR made a secret treaty with Stalin at Yalta to bring Russia into the war against Japan.

By that time a serious split had developed between Hurley and Wedemeyer, on the one hand, and the State Department, on the other. Hurley and Wedemeyer wanted to aid only Chiang; the State Department, feeling that Chiang's government was hopelessly corrupt, preferred to support the Communists. FDR backed Hurley and Wedemeyer, but the situation did not improve. By early summer of 1945 all attempts to unite the Nationalists and the Communists had failed, presaging either civil war or the continued presence of a strong third force.

THE WAR AND AMERICAN ANTI-IMPERIALISM

Throughout World War II one source of continuing friction between Roosevelt and Churchill was FDR's often expressed anti-imperialistic sentiments. His views, well publicized, affected India, parts of the Middle

East, the French colonies, and, to a lesser extent, those of the Netherlands. However, FDR placed his main emphasis on freeing India. Unfortunately, he had little more than the average American's understanding of the deep cultural and religious rifts within the country. The antagonism between the Hindu majority and the sizable Moslem minority had been a major factor in hampering British efforts to raise India's status. Churchill, for his part, was unwilling to contemplate a British empire shorn of India; mention of the subject was so patently distasteful to him that FDR was forced to resort to memos in preference to speech.

Early in the war the Moslem minority began to agitate for a separate state, and although the British sent a special mission in 1942 to survey the problem, the impasse continued. Later in that year Indian jails overflowed with Hindu leaders, including Mahatma Gandhi, head of the Congress Party, who insisted that the war against the Japanese did not concern India. An American diplomat tried to work out a solution, but he too failed. By the end of the war India was a giant powder keg ready to explode; the explosion was touched off in 1947.

The focus of Rooseveltian anti-imperialism also included the Middle East. The United States had had minor diplomatic, economic, and religious ties there since the 1820's. Extensive oil fields were discovered in Iran before World War I, but the United States had no substantial interest in them until 1928 when the sheik of neighboring Bahrain granted a concession to Standard Oil of California. In 1934 an Arabian-American Oil Company was formed to exploit fields in Saudi Arabia, but compared to the British stake, American holdings were insignificant.

When the war began, Allied planners assigned responsibility for the Middle East to the British, but soon American leaders were objecting to British heavy-handedness. The British in Iran, Iraq, and Egypt were accused of suppressing local nationalist aspirations, but by the end of the war the British attitude had softened and American thinking more nearly matched that of the British. Both countries condemned and threatened the Free French for endeavoring to keep Syria and Lebanon. The American threat to end lend-lease was a factor in forcing de Gaulle to withdraw French troops and end French domination of these countries.

Of all the difficulties in the Middle East, those in Palestine loomed largest, and because they were unsolved posed a major problem for the future. British Foreign Secretary Arthur Balfour had in 1917 published the Balfour Declaration, promising to support the Zionist desire for a national Jewish homeland in Palestine. The Arabs in Palestine had responded acrimoniously, and in fact only a few Jews came during the 1920's. During the next decade, Hitler's persecutions and the rise of anti-Semitism in Europe produced a flow of Jewish emigrants. Arabs resisted the influx with force, and the British had to cope with a full-scale rebellion. In 1939, with the war imminent and Arabian oil concessions more important than ever, the British issued a White Paper which in effect abrogated the Balfour Declaration. This restricted Jewish immigration and promised eventual independence to Palestine under the Arab majority. Both Arabs and Jews were suspicious of this wartime ploy, and during the war the Arabs tended to be pro-Nazi, while many Jews fought for the British. The official American policy remained one of nonintervention, but the majority of Americans were clearly and vociferously pro-Jewish. This was even more the case after 1942 when Hitler's extermination campaign came to light.

By 1944 both American political parties included pro-Zionist planks in their party platforms and FDR personally favored a Jewish state. Illegal Jewish immigration increased during the war and the British were faced both by increased Jewish terrorism and the implacable hostility of the Arabs, who were rapidly being displaced in Israel. The new President, Harry S. Truman, wrestled with this problem, but an expedient answer came only after three more years of strife.

Of the Middle Eastern countries only Turkey escaped the ravages of World War II. Turkey maintained its neutrality by bargaining first with one side and then with the other, using control of the Dardanelles as a trump card. Besides being a center of spy activities for both sides, Turkey supplied the Axis with needed chrome and the Allies with less needed and overpriced supplies. An Allied ultimatum eventually forced Turkey to declare war on the Axis in February 1945, just in time for the Turks to participate at the United Nations meeting in San Francisco.

THE STATE DEPARTMENT AND THE ATOMIC BOMB

The state of American preparedness and Allied needs dictated a complete and rapid change in the domestic economy. FDR, with considerable experience from the days of World War I and the attempts of the New Deal to manage the economy, implemented the conversion, often at the cost of efficiency. He was often impatient with the advice offered by career diplomats, and he tended to denigrate the work of the department. In the governmental bureaucracy, the State Department was little changed organizationally, although its personnel mushroomed with the addition of several wartime agencies. FDR became estranged from Cordell Hull after the war began and turned more often to Sumner Welles and Harry S. Hopkins, a former social worker, for advice. As the war progressed, Hull became even more isolated, although Welles had resigned in August 1943. Finally, in December 1944, the aging, exhausted, and embittered Hull resigned, blaming the British and domestic commercial interests for undercutting his authority.

Roosevelt's new Secretary of State, Edward R. Stettinius, Jr., was a successful businessman and a loyal supporter. He had been the first Lend-Lease Administrator in 1941 and two years later he replaced Welles as Under-Secretary of State. His new appointment marked the first time that any but a career diplomat had been chosen. As Under-Secretary, Stettinius devoted much thought to the reorganization of the State Department. On January 15, 1944, the department began its first major reorganization since 1909. Having helped with the basic plan, Stettinius made two radical changes, effective December 10, 1944, after his confirmation as Secretary of State. The administrative and executive hierarchy was completely redesigned. Agencies established since 1941 were integrated, including the Office of Foreign Relief and Rehabilitations Operations, the Office of Lend-Lease Administration, the Office of Foreign Economic Coordination, and the Office of Public Information, to name but a few. While the reorganization made for better planning and coordination, in the long run many other deficiencies were revealed.

One of the many new wartime agencies, the Office of Scientific Research and Development, had evolved from a governmental research program, but it was not connected with the State Department. The agency developed or improved such military hardware as the proximity fuse, rockets, and radar; it also discovered DDT and antibiotics. But its most spectacular feat was the development of the atomic bomb, based upon nuclear fusion of uranium. Despite the vast expense and the numerous scientists and personnel required for the project, its existence was otherwise a well-kept secret known only to a few top leaders. On July 16, 1945, the bomb was successfully tested near Alamogordo, New Mexico, and made available for military purposes. Although Hull and even Welles were aware of the existence of the bomb, Vice-President Harry S. Truman, elected in 1944, was not. The Alamogordo test heralded a new age, but the bomb made little real impression until its use on Japan.

THE UNITED NATIONS IN SPIRIT AND ACTION

Both FDR and Hull cherished the dream of a strong world organization to succeed the powerless League, and they wanted the United States to take the lead in its development. Welles' committee for postwar planning, which had been set up in the State Department, was expanded to include the leaders of both political parties. In June 1943 a resolution introduced by Representative J. William Fulbright committing the nation to support a world organization overwhelmingly passed the House, 360 to 29. The Republican party had already held a summit meeting on Mackinac Island,

Michigan, at which such former isolationists as Senator Arthur H. Vandenberg of Michigan and Governor Thomas E. Dewey of New York also declared their support for a world organization. The Senate now passed, 85 to 6, a similar resolution introduced by the Texas Democrat, Senator Tom Connolly. The idea of a world organization seemed to be wholeheartedly endorsed by the American public, especially after the implementation of the newly created bipartisanship in the passage of the resolutions.

At the meeting of foreign ministers in Moscow in October 1943, Hull obtained agreement from the Soviets and the British to sponsor such an organization. He also persuaded them to allow China to become a sponsor. Thus, the four countries signed the Declaration of Moscow on October 30, 1943, calling for a world organization to maintain "peace and security."

THE TEHERAN AND QUEBEC CONFERENCES

FDR flew to Teheran after his Cairo meeting with Chiang and Churchill to confer for the first time with Stalin. Although Roosevelt counted on a personal diplomatic success with Stalin, he actually achieved little more than a measure of cordiality. Nevertheless, the meeting went smoothly because FDR and Churchill coordinated their plans for OVERLORD with the Russians' spring offensive. Stalin reiterated his pledge to Hull that Russia would fight Japan. The Big Three also discussed the future of Germany but made no firm decisions.

The fate of Germany occupied the attention of various governmental agencies during 1943 and part of 1944. The army and the State Department favored a comparatively mild treatment of Germany, but Secretary of the Treasury Henry M. Morgenthau, Jr., a close friend of Roosevelt, disagreed. He submitted a plan whereby German industry would have been dismantled and the country reduced to an agricultural economy. Roosevelt endorsed the Morgenthau plan, as did Churchill at a meeting in Quebec in mid-September 1944.

After the cross-channel invasion was successfully mounted in June 1944 and Germany appeared closer than ever to defeat, the top-level conferences became more concerned with the political structure of the postwar world than with military strategy. Also, Roosevelt was running for a fourth term in 1944 and wanted to emphasize Allied cooperation to the voters. He easily won the election, probably because Governor Dewey was a "me too" candidate. But Allied cooperation ended over the problems of postwar Germany and Poland, which came to represent the failure of the wartime coalition.

THE YALTA CONFERENCE

The abrupt end of Allied cooperation may have startled FDR, but not Churchill or Stalin. The Big Three met at Yalta in February 1945 to discuss four major postwar issues. The first, concerning the voting makeup of the United Nations, did not prove a substantial problem. Most of the plans for a world organization had been drawn up under American leadership at the Dumbarton Oaks Conference held outside Washington from late June to early October 1944. The only major unresolved problem was the Soviet demand for a veto power in the proposed Security Council, the body that would have jurisdiction in world security matters. At Yalta the Big Three readily agreed to a compromise: each would have a veto power, but the veto could not be used on purely procedural matters. A date in late April 1945 was set for a meeting in San Francisco to implement the Dumbarton Oaks plan.

A second problem disposed of at Yalta was the Russian promise to enter the war against Japan after the defeat of Germany. Stalin agreed to do so only after FDR and Churchill acceded to his demands. These included:

1. Control of all concessions Russia had held in China before the Russo-Japanese War of 1904-1905.
2. The internationalization of Dairen.
3. Confirmation of Port Arthur as a Russian base.
4. Certain Manchurian railroad concessions.
5. Russian acquisition of the southern half of Sakhalin and the Kurile Islands.

These concessions were embodied in secret executive agreements which, later, were those most attacked by critics of the administration and by historians. FDR's advisers were divided about the necessity for Russian intervention, but in February it was still five months before the successful atom bomb test. Chiang Kai-shek was forced to accept the projected rape of China's newly acquired sovereignty — a point that critics would also make much of.

Although the entry of the Soviets into the Far East struggle would later cause the most controversy, the other two questions — the fate of Germany and the fate of Poland — were far more crucial to Allied postwar relations. Shortly after the Quebec talks, both FDR and Churchill realized that the Morgenthau Plan for Germany was unrealistic, and it was shelved. However, neither the State Department nor other governmental agencies were able to agree on a viable alternative. American policy proved to be one of trial and reaction, even though a European Advisory Commission had been set up by the foreign ministers at Moscow to deal with the problem. It had been decided in advance that Germany would be divided into three zones for occupation purposes. At Yalta FDR would not agree to Stalin's plans for permanent dismemberment but neither would he accept Churchill's total opposition. He did agree to a temporary division for purposes of occupation, postponed the issue of Germany's future, and pressed for the establishment of a French zone. FDR only supported de Gaulle after General Eisenhower and others had convinced him that de Gaulle truly represented France. A zone was finally given to France, but it was carved out of those assigned England and the United States.

At Yalta FDR refused to force a showdown concerning Western access to Berlin, which was to be occupied jointly by the Allies although an enclave within the Russian zone. One group of American advisers, including veteran diplomat Robert D. Murphy, strongly urged a settlement, but others suggested that rather than incur Soviet displeasure at that moment, it would be better to postpone the decision. This was the position FDR adopted.

As to the question of German reparations, Roosevelt stood between Stalin, who demanded a minimum of $20 billion, and Churchill, who opposed setting a specific amount, though he agreed in principle to

CHURCHILL, ROOSEVELT, AND STALIN AT YALTA, 1945

reparations. A compromise allowed the Russian figure to stand as a working estimate but turned over the general subject to a reparations commission to ascertain the exact amount to be levied. When the committee met in Moscow after Germany's defeat, it was unable to agree on standards for imposing reparations; thus each ally treated its zone of occupation differently.

If the fate of Germany represented decisions that had been postponed during the war, that of Poland could be compared to an iceberg of which only the top was visible. Anxious to legitimize the Soviet occupation of Polish territory taken over at the beginning of the war, the Russians repeatedly pressed for a settlement of this point. The border in this case roughly coincided with the one suggested for Russia at the Paris Peace Conference in 1919, the Curzon Line, which was based on ethnic and geographical considerations. But at that time the new Polish state had attacked the weak Bolshevik regime and successfully acquired about a third more territory than was encompassed by the Curzon Line. The Soviets accepted this boundary in the Treaty of Riga (1921).

The 1921 boundary obtained until the dismemberment of Poland in 1939. The situation was complicated by the centuries-long enmity between the two countries. In any event, the Polish government-in-exile demanded a Russian guarantee of its prewar boundary. The Polish-Americans, representing a potent political force, kept the subject well publicized in the United States.

The Polish-Americans were unexpectedly aided by the Nazis, who in April 1943 disclosed that some 8,000 Polish officers had been slaughtered by the Russians in Katyn forest three years earlier. They pressured the Polish government-in-exile to demand an investigation. The Soviets angrily broke off diplomatic relations with the exiled government and began to support the Communist partisans in Poland. By the time of the Yalta meeting, the Russian army had sealed Poland's fate by backing the pro-Soviet regime in Lublin. In one of the most unfortunate episodes of an incredibly brutal story, the Soviet army camped on the outskirts of Warsaw in August 1944, passively watching the underground uprising that lasted until October. Meanwhile the Nazis slaughtered thousands of inadequately armed Poles and further decimated the ranks of Polish anti-Communists.

A major decision of the Big Three at Yalta revolved around support for the anti-Communist Polish government-in-exile versus support for the Lublin government — already accepted by the Soviets. As a compromise, the Lublin government was enlarged by the addition of a few members from the government-in-exile, and free but unsupervised elections were scheduled to be held as soon as possible. But by not spelling out the rules for a democratic election, FDR and Churchill, who both had evidence of the widespread intimidation by Russian agents in Poland, practically assured a Communist victory.

After FDR's death, President Truman sent the long-time presidential troubleshooter, Harry Hopkins, to negotiate the issue with Stalin. By early June 1945 he had committed the United States to recognition of the Lublin regime in return for Western permission to observe the coming election. Truman recognized the Lublin government on July 5, 1945; later in the month, at the Potsdam meeting of the Big Three, July 16-26, the Polish election question appeared to have been resolved.

THE BALKAN STATES IN WORLD WAR II

By the time of the Yalta Conference the future of the Balkans was apparently resolved. Churchill had long considered the area the strategic key to Europe. At every wartime meeting he urged American attention to the area, but United States military men did not share his views. The only concession made to Churchill was Operation ANVIL; the military forces were to capture the French Mediterranean port of Marseilles and then march northward to effect a junction with the armies coming from the west. This plan was successfully carried out in August 1944 with the use of American and Free French troops. Even so, Churchill had wanted the attack to be made on the Istrian Peninsula, at the very gateway to Central Europe. By the time the war ended, the Soviets had bested Britain everywhere in the Balkans except Greece. At Yalta little was said about the Russian *fait accompli.*

THE UNITED NATIONS AND THE END OF THE
WAR IN EUROPE

After Yalta the Allied armies began their final drive against Germany. Not even the sudden death of FDR at Warm Springs, Georgia, on April 12, 1945, slowed the advance of the military juggernaut. In early May, Hitler committed suicide, and on May 7 the Nazis surrendered unconditionally.

During the same fateful period, the United Nations was born in San Francisco on April 25, 1945. When the Charter of the United Nations was signed by the participants on June 26, it marked the full circle the United States had come since 1917. The United States not only pledged to participate in the world body, which was markedly similar to its predecessor, but it also joined the ancillary organizations such as the World Court. Deepening its commitment, the United States offered to provide the headquarters for the United Nations in New York City, an offer which the other members accepted.

But while the euphoria of peace pervaded part of the world, the war against Japan continued. The bloody invasion of Iwo Jima in February and that of Okinawa in April bore out the military contention that invading the Japanese homeland would be not only costly in lives but could not be mounted before the fall of 1945. American military experts badly overestimated the Japanese war potential, although earlier they had underestimated it. Thus, when President Truman attended the final wartime meeting at Potsdam, he carried this information as well as knowledge of the successful atomic bomb test. At Potsdam Stalin met for the first time both Truman and the new British Prime Minister, Clement Attlee.

The Potsdam Conference was typical of other wartime meetings in that, despite strong British objections, Truman postponed almost all political decisions until the peace settlements. This was true concerning the problems of Germany, Poland, and the Balkans, as well as of Stalin's demand for a North African colony formerly belonging to Italy. Potsdam's most signal accomplishment was the creation of a Council of Foreign Ministers, representing the Big Three plus France, which was to draw up peace treaties that would settle the long-postponed political problems.

The other was President Truman's Potsdam Declaration, issued on July 26, calling on the Japanese to surrender unconditionally. This, however, had no more effect on the Japanese than had the earlier declaration on the Germans. Truman then decided to employ the atomic bomb against Japan. On August 6 the first bomb, equivalent to 20,000 tons of TNT, was dropped on Hiroshima, leveling four square miles in the center of the city and killing 80,000 people. Three days later a second bomb was dropped on Nagasaki, with similar results; the Japanese will to resist was crushed. In the time between the dropping of the two bombs, the Soviets declared war on Japan and marched into Manchuria. Stalin legitimized his invasion of China by signing a treaty with Chiang.

On August 14 the Japanese government surrendered, accepting the Allied terms of unconditional surrender. The formal document that restored peace to the world was signed aboard the battleship *Missouri* on September 2, 1945. World War II, the worst in history, was over; only the peace, enforced by the United Nations, needed to be maintained.

Further Reading

Two excellent surveys of the diplomacy of the war years are *John L. Snell, *Illusion and Necessity: The Diplomacy of Global War, 1939-1945* (Boston, 1964) and *Gaddis Smith, *American Diplomacy during the Second World War: 1941-1945* (New York, 1965). A more controversial book is Lloyd C. Gardner's recent *Architects of Illusion: Men and Ideas in American Foreign Policy, 1941-1949* (Chicago, 1970).

For detailed accounts of wartime diplomacy, three titles by Herbert Feis are worthwhile: *Churchill, Roosevelt, Stalin: The War They Waged and the Peace They Sought* (Princeton, N.J., 1966), *Between War and Peace: The Potsdam Conference* (Princeton, N.J., 1967), and *The Atomic Bomb and the End of World War II* (Princeton, N.J., 1967). Two different and important interpretations of the use of the atomic bomb are expounded in *Gar Alperovitz, *Atomic Diplomacy: Hiroshima and Potsdam* (New York, 1965) and Gabriel Kolko, *The Politics of War: The World and United States Foreign Policy, 1943-1945* (New York, 1968).

Military analyses of the war are numerous, but *Dwight D. Eisenhower, *Crusade in Europe* (New York, 1948) remains among the best. Many of the memoirs listed at the end of the last chapter are useful. To these add *Robert D. Murphy, *Diplomat Among Warriors* (New York, 1969) and memoirs by Sumner Welles, William D. Leahy and Edward R. Stettinius, Jr. The edited works of Henry Morgenthau, Jr., James V. Forrestal, David E. Lilienthal, Arthur Vandenberg and Joseph Stilwell should be consulted as well.

Asterisk denotes paperback edition.

Part IV • The Nuclear Age: America as a World Leader Since 1945

17

The Revolution in American Foreign Policy: Cause and Effect, 1945-1947

A sharp decline in the operation of American diplomacy coincided with the rapid demobilization of the army and the removal of United States military personnel from Europe and parts of Asia. Both the new President and his Secretary of State contributed to this hiatus until the early spring of 1947.

Harry S. Truman, before being elected Vice-President in 1944, was an undistinguished Democratic senator from Missouri. In many ways, the career of his Secretary of State, James F. Byrnes, was similar. Byrnes was a South Carolina politician with administrative experience but no diplomatic background. Like his chief, he had excelled in loyalty to the Democratic party and had risen through the party ranks to the position of senator.

THE ATOMIC BOMB AND AMERICAN FOREIGN POLICY

The effect of World War II on American foreign policy and diplomacy was cataclysmic, though this fact was not immediately perceived. The United States had accepted the wartime leadership of the Allies, but it did not take the same attitude toward that leadership in peacetime. The rapid demobilization of the armed forces reduced them from 12,000,000 in 1945 to 3,000,000 a year later and to less than 1,000,000 by early 1950. Reasons abounded as to why the United States no longer needed a large standing army, the two most cogent in popular thinking being the American monopoly of the atomic bomb and faith in the successful operation of the United Nations. The atomic stockpile seemed to ensure that the United States would be the most powerful nation in the world for a long time. At Potsdam, President Truman did not capitalize on the bomb's effectiveness as a tool of foreign policy; rather, he joined with England and Canada in proposing that control of atomic weapons be vested in a United Nations authority. The Soviets opposed this because, while it would take control away from those countries possessing the weapon, it would prevent the others from learning the secret of making the bomb. The plan would also have provided for international inspection as one of its basic features.

By August 1946, when it became apparent that the United Nations would not be able to resolve the problem satisfactorily, Congress passed the Atomic Energy Act of 1946, which established the United States Atomic Energy Commission. While not entirely closing the door on international cooperation, the commission was subject to Congressional control in the area of exchange of information on atomic energy. During this period President Truman had been advised that the USSR would not be capable of building an atomic bomb for from five to fifteen years. When the Russians produced a bomb in less than four years, the confrontation remained unchanged, though it had assumed global proportions by that time.

THE UNITED NATIONS AND THE HOPE FOR WORLD PEACE

When in late July 1945 Congress overwhelmingly accepted the United Nations Charter, the United States became the first nation to join the new world organization. The American people not only enthusiastically supported a leading role for the United States in the United Nations, but they automatically credited a world attitude toward peace that never existed. In fact, the disillusionment over the inability of the world body to solve major problems was rooted in a lack of understanding about international affairs that had characterized American thinking since World War I.

The United Nations had been conceived as a league of sovereign states which, working through the Security Council, could use force to keep the peace. The council was composed of five permanent members — the United States, Great Britain, the USSR, France, and China — plus six other members elected for two-year terms. The five permanent members had a veto over any substantive matters, a system which enabled them to block action on many problems. All nations were to be represented in the General Assembly, which originated more as a forum than as a body with the strong advisory powers it later developed. The United Nations also comprised many agencies that were direct counterparts of League of Nations bodies or that had been suggested or tried earlier.

The Charter of the United Nations was a great improvement over its predecessor; nevertheless, it still largely reflected the old balance of power concept. The Charter also allowed regional collective security pacts to help keep the peace. As with the League, the United Nations proved most successful in dealing with the social, cultural, and economic problems of less advanced states and in handling minor political disagreements not involving the major powers or their satellites.

EUROPE AND ASIA, 1945-1947

The fact that American diplomacy faltered in 1945-1946 did not mean that it was inoperative. The problem of keeping millions of Europeans alive during the winter of 1945-1946 fell squarely on the United States. At the height of the war, the United States and its allies set up the United Nations Relief and Rehabilitation Agency (UNRRA), which began operation in April 1945, with the United States supporting about three quarters of the entire budget as well as furnishing food and supplies. The job was gigantic: much of Europe and Britain were devastated; civilian deaths were conservatively estimated at 15,000,000, including 6,000,000 Russians and 5,000,000 million Poles. (The 6,000,000 Jews liquidated by Hitler were not included in the totals.) In addition, millions of "displaced persons" were uprooted and destitute. Congress was implored to ease the plight of displaced persons by relaxing immigration quotas, but it did not respond until 1948 and then allowed only 205,000 additional refugees to be admitted.

For the second consecutive generation the flower of European manhood had been killed or maimed by a world war. The United States suffered a total loss of 293,986 dead, the Soviets, nearly 7,000,000, and the other Allies, 2,000,000 more. In the Axis countries, the German war dead totaled 3,255,000, and the remainder, 300,000. These figures illustrate the problem faced by UNRRA; by vast donations of foodstuffs it did succeed in preventing major outbreaks of epidemics. After only one year of operation with UNRRA the United States had spent $3 billion, for which it distributed 6,000,000 tons of food and returned about 6,000,000 displaced persons to their homes. Other private relief agencies, including the Red Cross, more than doubled the public contribution. Unfortunately, UNRRA soon became unpopular in the United States because some Eastern European governments used the relief supplies as a political weapon. The result was that the American government withdrew from the agency at the end of 1946; thereafter, relief became the responsibility of the individual country, causing a marked slow down in recovery because of the lack of foodstuffs needed to keep the caloric count high enough to begin physical rebuilding projects.

The situation in Asia, particularly in parts of China and Japan, was much the same as in Europe as far as devastation was concerned, and comparable as to war casualties. Physical destruction seemed less because of the generally underdeveloped conditions and low living standards of Asia. Nevertheless, the Chinese had lost 1,300,000 men and the Japanese, 1,862,499, and millions of civilians were killed or missing. UNRRA assistance was confined to Europe, but from mid-1945 until early 1947 the United States supplied $2 billion to Chiang alone. In Japan the Allied occupation force under General Douglas MacArthur effectively helped the Japanese population through the first postwar year. Other areas — the Philippines, the Dutch East Indies, and French Indochina — also received aid in varying amounts. However, up to 1947 all relief had been strictly on a stopgap basis; the ability of the stricken nations to help themselves to survive still lay in the future.

THE END OF LEND-LEASE AND POSTWAR LOANS

A week after Japan surrendered, President Truman ended lend-lease, as he had been authorized to do by Congress. During its life the act had provided about $50 billion worth of supplies. The chief beneficiaries had been: Great Britain, $31 billion; USSR, $11 billion; France, $3.2 billion; and Latin America, nearly $0.5 billion. Great Britain had reduced its indebtedness by supplying services to the United States valued at $6.8 billion.

While termination of lend-lease was expected by the Allies, its abrupt cancellation forced Britain to seek a loan to stave off financial ruin. After three months of negotiations the United States agreed to lend England $4.4 billion on favorable but not interest-free terms. However, Congress did not approve the transaction for seven months, during which time its value shrank 23 percent; worse yet, it proved to be but a stopgap like UNRRA.

If the British, America's closest wartime ally, had difficulties obtaining loans from the United States, the position of Soviet Russia was far worse. In January 1945 the Russians asked for a $6 billion loan, but dropped the request when the State Department sought to link it with cooperation on political matters. In the late fall of the same year Stalin asked for a $1 billion loan. The State Department did not answer the Soviet request during the winter, which coincided with the failure of the Council of Foreign Ministers to reach agreement on the peace treaties. Finally in March the State Department offered the loan with only those controls that applied to all loans. Stalin refused, shortly afterwards announcing another Five Year Plan to rebuild heavy industry. This marked the final effort of the Soviets to borrow directly from the United States.

GERMANY, THE USSR, AND THE ESSENCE
OF THE COLD WAR

The increasing Allied disenchantment with the Soviets was especially evident in regard to Germany. The foreign ministers had agreed on the various zones of occupation, the general level of reparations, and the treatment of all zones as a single economic unit in order to enable Germany to survive. The French were the first to refuse to be bound by these requirements, since they had had no part in making them. They attempted to separate the industrial areas of the Saar, the Ruhr, and the Rhineland in order to levy reparations, reaffirming their action through their representative to the governing Allied Control Council.

Map 12.   Allied Occupation of Germany and Austria

Shortly after this the USSR became an even greater obstacle. The Soviet army had dismantled and taken to Russia all of the German industry in the Russian zone plus thousands of skilled workers as well. In addition, the Russians demanded the agreed-upon reparations from the other zones but would not allow the agricultural surplus from their zone to supply the remainder of Germany. By the end of 1945 the disagreements were irreconcilable, and in May 1946 the United States, Great Britain, and

France jointly suspended reparations to the Soviets from their respective zones. In essence, this action began the Cold War.

For a better understanding of the major factors causing such a breach, let us quickly examine the Soviet Union. It was a totalitarian state dominated absolutely by an old-line Communist revolutionary, Josef Stalin. Stalin had an ingrained distrust of the Western democracies, and he viewed each of their actions with dark suspicion. To the chagrin of Western statesmen, who had occasionally taken him at his word, he simply did not abide by the usual standards of international morality. The quick recovery of the Soviet Union from the effects of the war seemed improbable to experts because, in addition to manpower losses, one fourth of its capital equipment, 70,000 villages, 1,700 towns, and nearly 100,000 collective farms had been destroyed. Therefore, to Stalin the domination of Eastern Europe, with its industrial capability and strategic location, was absolutely necessary.

The United States and Great Britain, for their part, retained a healthy and long-standing distrust of the USSR and Stalin, despite FDR's belief in the power of personal diplomacy. Opinion surveys showed that at least a third of all Americans continued to be hostile to Russia during the war. The most vociferous American critics of friendship with Russia were in Congress or were high-ranking military officers. Rash and warlike speeches made by these leaders were not conducive to meaningful diplomacy. Other ploys, such as the lure of loans and the threat of the atomic bomb, were attempted by the United States in dealing with the Soviets, but to no avail. In 1946 the strength of the American forces in Europe stood at less than 2,000,000 men as compared with the Soviets' 6,000,000, a number large enough to overrun all of Europe.

Against this power struggle was spelled out the political settlements of Eastern Europe and the attempts to negotiate peace treaties with the former Axis powers. Agreement was general among the Allies that the former Axis satellite countries — Austria, Italy, Rumania, Hungary, Bulgaria, and Finland — should be independent. But when the time came for implementing the agreement, the Council of Foreign Ministers meeting in London in September 1945 could not agree. Only a concession by Secretary of State Byrnes in December to recognize the Russian satellite governments in Rumania and Bulgaria allowed the peacemaking to continue. The council had met in Paris, before a twenty-one-nation peace conference opened in July 1946, to draft peace treaties for all the countries except Austria, where a zone arrangement similar to that for Germany had been worked out. The Soviets steadfastly refused to allow a democratically elected government to take over from their occupation troops, who had dismantled and removed the industry and oil resources that remained intact. Having the best farmland in their zone, the Russians exported the agricultural surplus to Russia, thereby forcing the United States to make massive donations of food to keep the Austrians from starvation. Austria did not finally regain its sovereignty until December 1955, when a peace treaty recognizing its neutrality with regard to the Cold War was signed and executed.

The Paris Conference met from July until October, making recommendations which were then incorporated into the final treaty versions by the Council of Foreign Ministers meeting in New York. By the terms of the treaties, approved in early 1947, Rumania, Hungary, and Bulgaria became Soviet satellites; Italy, stripped of its colonies and the Adriatic port city of Trieste, began an uncertain future as a democratic constitutional monarchy. Finland lost only the territory won by the Russians in 1940. Poland had not been the subject of a peace treaty, the Russians having insisted on a western border at the Oder-Neisse line, formerly well within German territory. In addition to signing a treaty with the Lublin government recognizing this border, the Soviets also displaced about 9,000,000 Germans to the west. The election agreed to by the Big Three at Moscow was held in January 1947, and without international control, the Lublin government easily won. From that time, Poland kept to its new borders, soon becoming an important Soviet satellite.

One of the few areas of agreement among the Allies during this period concerned the fate of the Axis war leaders. An Allied War Crimes Commission set up a tribunal at Nuremberg, Germany, where the twenty-two top Nazis were tried from November 1945 to October 1946 for crimes against humanity. Of the nineteen convicted, ten were hanged. Hermann Goering, former head of the Luftwaffe, committed suicide before his sentence could be carried out. The debate still rages as to whether the trials violated basic American principles of jurisprudence and were *ex post facto*, or whether they merely represented the carrying-out of the Kellogg-Briand pacts signed nearly two decades earlier for the purpose of setting a standard of international morality.

CHINA, JAPAN, AND THE ASIAN PROBLEM

While the Council of Foreign Ministers dealt mostly with Europe, it also made several significant agreements affecting the Far East. An early agreement, made at Cairo and confirmed at Potsdam, affirmed that Korea would be independent. The Soviets entered Korea first and agreed to an American plan to divide the country arbitrarily at the 38th parallel, the Russians to the north and the Americans to the south. Both countries expedited the surrender of the Japanese armies in Korea; then the Allies found themselves in opposition, and the 38th parallel became a dividing line between the two. At Moscow, in December 1945, the Council of Foreign Ministers had agreed to a united provisional government, after which the

Koreans would manage their own affairs. Nothing came of the agreement, however, because, although the Koreans demanded unification, the United States and the Soviet Union could not agree on a modus vivendi.

The United States was more successful in its discussions regarding Japan. Also at the Moscow meeting, the foreign ministers set up a Far Eastern Commission, to be located in Washington, and an Allied Council, in Tokyo, both of which would set policy for Japan. In fact, however, all policy was made unilaterally by General MacArthur, Supreme Commander of the Allied Powers (SCAP). He soon controlled Japan so tightly that the Soviets and the other Allies were forced out, so that Japan became an American satellite to the same degree that Eastern European countries were Soviet-influenced.

MacArthur faced staggering problems: in addition to the military losses and the civilian dead, about 40 percent of Japanese urban areas had been destroyed, leaving millions homeless and facing starvation. There were also 6,000,000 Japanese soldiers to be repatriated. The original American idea of limiting Japan's industrial recovery proved impractical and MacArthur was soon urging the opposite course. He ordered war-crimes trials comparable to those at Nuremberg. They lasted from May 1946 to November 1948. Twenty-five men were convicted, seven of whom were hanged.

MacArthur forced Emperor Hirohito to disavow his divinity, although the Emperor still retained his great cultural influence over the Japanese people. The armed forces were disbanded and MacArthur granted comprehensive personal liberties never before known. These changes and educational reforms were embodied in a new constitution that went into effect on May 3, 1947. The only major failure of American policy in Japan was the inability to obtain agreement on a Japanese peace treaty, an event that waited until 1951. Overall, Japan represented America's most conspicuous foreign policy success between 1945 and 1947.

THE UNITED STATES AND CHINA, 1945-1947

At the opposite pole of effectiveness was the United States' policy in China during the same years: vacillating, procrastinating, and indecisive. The State Department kept a close watch on the Soviets in China, but the Russians played a comparatively small role there until March 1946. The Chinese Communists at Yenan were sufficiently strong by the end of the war that they threatened to move into Manchuria and the cities of north China ahead of Chiang's Nationalist armies from the south. To prevent this, the United States ordered the Japanese to surrender only to Chiang's army. While an abortive conciliation attempt between Chiang and Mao Tse-tung, leader of the Communists, occurred in mid-August 1945, American planes airlifted Chiang's armies to occupy the key cities in eastern and central China, including Nanking and Shanghai. In addition, about 50,000 American marines occupied strategic sites in north China. They accepted the Japanese surrender there and forestalled the Communists.

United States policy toward China was clouded by dissension and conflicting advice. Patrick Hurley resigned on November 27, 1945, blasting the seeming American indifference to the fate of the Nationalist government. President Truman called General George C. Marshall out of retirement to serve as his personal emissary. Marshall made two trips to China in 1946; he was momentarily successful in arranging a truce between Chiang and Mao; but the Soviets, who had been inactive in China until March 1946, withdrew their troops from Manchuria, thus enabling the Chinese Communists to obtain quantities of surrendered military equipment. From that time on, Mao's armies met the Nationalists frontally, beginning a counterattack in the fall that eventually defeated Chiang. By December 1949 the remnants of Chiang's army and the Nationalist leaders were forced to flee to Taiwan, leaving Mao free to take over the government of all mainland China.

One factor that aided the Communists was the rampant inflation that doubled prices sixty-seven times in a two-and-a-half-year period after the war. For most of this period, the United States continued its token support of Chiang in spite of reports that he faced imminent disaster. By the time the Truman administration decided to aid China, the problem had reached staggering proportions and American policy makers were facing new and even more immediate commitments in Europe.

THE PHILIPPINES AND THE FORMER ALLIED COLONIES IN ASIA

During the fateful first two years after the war, the Philippines attained the long-sought freedom that most of them desired, although it seemed to the Filipinos that there were strings attached. The Philippine Trade Act of 1946 gave American interests preferential treatment even beyond the independence date of July 4, 1946. Another act provided for an immigration quota and allowed Filipinos to become American citizens. The United States retained fifteen army and naval bases on a ninety-nine-year lease and agreed to train the Philippine army and to take responsibility for the defense of the islands. Compensation for war damage was paid to property owners. In brief, the islands were granted independence, but at the same time they remained an economic fief and a strategic bastion of the United States.

Even so, the Philippines were more fortunate than the colonies of the other Allies. In the Dutch East Indies, for example, a well-developed nationalist movement fought the Dutch when they returned to the islands. The Indonesian nationalists complained that American lend-lease material was being used against them by the Dutch at the same time that Americans professed sympathy for the nationalist cause. After several years, the United States, using the auspices of the United Nations, was able to pressure the Dutch to give up the rich colony. A truce and an agreement leading to independence were signed aboard an American warship in January 1948.

The French were not so easily displaced from Indochina, their major holding in Asia. FDR and, later, Truman favored some form of self-government or United Nations supervision for the region. However, despite a nationalist revolt that began in the area known as Vietnam in 1946 and gained strength after 1949, the French reestablished themselves there. They had less difficulty in the other parts of Indochina, Laos and Cambodia. The indigenous populations of the three countries had little in common with one another, and ties were maintained through the French and their administration. In Vietnam the French found themselves engaged in a debilitating conflict that would last for more than seven years.

India's independence had been assured by Attlee, Churchill's successor, even before the end of the war. This promise was fulfilled on August 15, 1947, by splitting the subcontinent into Hindu India and Moslem Pakistan. Unfortunately, an orgy of killing swept those areas where there were minorities of either religion, and at least 12,000,000 people fled their homes. The United States remained aloof, but each of the new countries afterward predicated its relations with America on the basis of what one country received as compared with the other.

THE MIDDLE EAST IN THE POSTWAR ERA

Pakistan's oil-rich neighbor to the west, Iran, was occupied by the Soviets after the war in spite of Russian promises to the contrary. The Soviets went so far as to aid a revolt in the northern part of the country, whereupon Iran complained to the United Nations in January 1946. The Russians finally agreed to negotiate and thereby acquired large-scale oil concessions, but in the spring of 1946 the United States forced them to withdraw from the country, although they retained their oil concessions. Later that year the Iranian government crushed the northern dissidents; since that time Iran has remained oriented toward the West.

Earlier, the Soviets exerted similar pressure on Turkey, which responded by mobilizing its army. After a strong protest from the United States in August 1945, combined with the deployment of an American fleet to the area, the Russians backed down.

In other Middle Eastern countries where British influence had predominated, the British reasserted their authority without great difficulty. And except for North Africa, the British replaced the French as the major power in the Arab world. The single exception to British hegemony was Palestine, where the demand to admit 100,000 European Jewish refugees was anathema to the Arab population. Nevertheless, the plan was popular in the United States and received the support of President Truman in both 1945 and 1946. The State department advised moderation in the face of Arab hostility because of its fear of adverse effects on American oil investments, which had greatly increased after 1945. In Palestine the British were attempting to turn back the tide of illegal refugees and at the same time cope with the well-organized Jewish terrorist organizations. In April 1947 the British gave notice that they intended to turn over the Palestinian mandate, granted them by the League of Nations, to the United Nations. In November they announced that they would withdraw by May 15, 1948. On that date the Jews proclaimed the state of Israel; eleven minutes after receiving the news, President Truman extended *de facto* recognition, making the United States the first country to do so.

PRESIDENT TRUMAN ON RECOGNITION OF ISRAEL, 1948-1949

1. STATEMENT May 14, 1948

This Government has been informed that a Jewish state has been proclaimed in Palestine, and recognition has been requested by the provisional government thereof.

The United States recognizes the provisional government as the *de facto* authority of the new State of Israel.

2. STATEMENT, January 31, 1949

On October 24, 1948 the President stated that when a permanent government was elected in Israel, it would promptly be given *de jure* recognition. Elections for such a government were held on January 25th. The votes have now been counted, and this Government has been officially informed of the results. The United States Government is therefore pleased to extend *de jure* recognition to the Government of Israel as of this date.

1947: THE YEAR OF AMERICAN FOREIGN POLICY DECISION

From its record during the 1946 Council of Foreign Ministers, it was apparent that United States policy had been one of reaction and response to Soviet moves rather than one of aggressive innovation and leadership.

However, changes were taking place in policy formation, diplomatic personnel, and in the organization of the State Department itself. Not necessarily an immediate cause of change, but important in the long run, was the Foreign Service Act of 1946, which brought about the most far-ranging restructuring in the department since the Rogers Act of 1924. Among other provisions, the act permitted lateral transfer within the Foreign Service from one classification to another and established a long-needed educational and training institute, the Foreign Service Institute. Also instituted was the navy's system of weeding out weak officers, "promotion up" or "selection out" of personnel being the goal. Officers were reviewed annually, allowed only a specified number of years in each grade, then either promoted or dismissed. In addition, the Hoover Commission, in 1949, recommended that a number of changes be made in the State Department. Some were, and by now change in the department has become endemic, although two major difficulties remain: coordination with other agencies responsible for foreign policy and recruitment of superior young Americans for Foreign Service and State Department careers.

The first shift in foreign policy with respect to the Soviets became evident shortly after the appointment of General George C. Marshall as Secretary of State on January 21, 1947. President Truman, who relied heavily on the advice of military men during his first administration, enlisted Marshall's services as a leader he could trust. When Marshall took over the State Department, one of his first acts was to set up a Policy Planning staff under the experienced diplomat George Kennan. The interaction of planning with the restructuring of the department proved a powerful catalyst; historic policies were conceived and implemented that altered or more sharply focused many aspects of American foreign policy.

A NEW AMERICAN POLICY: THE TRUMAN DOCTRINE

The change in American policy was first felt in Greece, where the British had restored the constitutional monarchy after the war. The Greek government was sorely tried by Communist guerrillas in the north, trained usually in Yugoslavia and Bulgaria. Aided by British troops, the Greeks succeeded in holding off the Communists, but the financial burden impelled the British in February 1947 to warn Marshall that they would have to forego their commitment to Greece as of March 31. The Greeks had earlier asked for American help, and it now seemed clear that if the United States did not assume the British role there, the country would fall to the Communists. On March 12 President Truman asked Congress for an appropriation of $400 million to save Greece and Turkey. He outlined the use of American military and economic advisers to assist the two governments. Congress debated the new Truman Doctrine, but the outcome was never really in doubt; on May 22, the measure, representing the first peacetime policy change toward Europe, was passed. The new policy, although a stopgap, paved the way for the Marshall Plan, America's major postwar foreign policy program.

THE MARSHALL PLAN

The Marshall Plan was developed in George Kennan's Policy Planning Staff in the late winter of 1947. Much of the groundwork had been laid by Marshall's Under-Secretary for Economic Affairs, William L. Clayton, who wrote perceptive memos on the desperate plight of Europe in the winter of 1946-1947. In Churchill's words, Europe at that time was "a rabble-heap, a charnel house, a breeding ground of pestilence and hate." But the galvanizing force was Marshall himself, who returned in late April from a Council of Foreign Ministers meeting in Moscow. He had been shaken by

GENERAL GEORGE C. MARSHALL RECEIVES THE NOBEL PEACE PRIZE, DECEMBER 1953

the seeming implacability of Russia at a meeting which produced little but discord over the drafts of treaties for Germany and Austria. Within six weeks of his return, a comprehensive program emerged from Kennan's group, made up of its ideas, those of Clayton, certain military studies, and statements by such influential people as the columnist Walter Lippmann. The composite was a policy statement delivered by Marshall at Harvard University on June 5, 1947. There he outlined the Marshall Plan for the recovery of the European economy and, as part of it, the United States commitment to an ideological struggle with the Soviet Union. It was after this pronouncement that Lippmann's term, "the Cold War," became most appropriate.

THE MARSHALL PLAN, 1947

From Secretary of State George C. Marshall's speech at Harvard, June 5, 1947

The truth of the matter is that Europe's requirements for the next 3 or 4 years of foreign food and other essential products—principally from America—are so much greater than her present ability to pay that she must have substantial additional help, or face economic, social, and political deterioration of a very grave character.

The remedy lies in breaking the vicious circle and restoring the confidence of the European people in the economic future of their own countries and of Europe as a whole. The manufacturer and the farmer throughout wide areas must be able and willing to exchange their products for currencies the continuing value of which is not open to question.

It is already evident that, before the United States Government can proceed much further in its efforts to alleviate the situation and help start the European world on its way to recovery, there must be some agreement among the countries of Europe as to the requirements of the situation and the part those countries themselves will take in order to give proper effect to whatever action might be undertaken by this Government.... The initiative, I think, must come from Europe. The role of this country should consist of friendly aid in the drafting of a European program and of later support of such a program so far as it may be practical for us to do so. The program should be a joint one, agreed to by a number, if not all, European nations.

Marshall suggested to Europe a policy of recovery through self-help. The United States, he said, would pay the bill "against hunger, desperation, and chaos." Although not stressing the political aspects of the program, he did not in reality expect the Soviets to mix their economy with that of the West. Nevertheless, at a mid-July meeting in Paris to implement the plan, the

USSR attended, though its staellites did not. When the other European nations decided to back joint recovery efforts in preference to individual ones, the Russians walked out, making irreconcilable the split between East and West.

The sixteen countries remaining at the conference set up the Committee of European Economic Cooperation, which by September presented a four-year recovery program to be supported by massive American aid. Even so, Truman was forced to ask Congress for interim assistance for these countries and Germany, the latter reluctantly admitted to participation in the plan. Congress received the bill for the Marshall Plan in December — following another fruitless meeting of the Council of Foreign Ministers. The issue was debated during the winter, and the Communist take-over in Czechoslovakia in February probably reinforced the resolve of the Republican Congress. On March 21, 1948, Congress overwhelmingly approved the bill, and it was signed by President Truman on April 3. The act established an Economic Cooperation Administration separate from the State Department to administer the $12.5 billion appropriated for the initial three years of the plan. The overall program was designated the European Recovery Program (ERP).

MR. "X" AND THE POLICY OF CONTAINMENT

Only slightly less momentous in its long-range effect was an article by a Mr. "X" in the July 1947 issue of *Foreign Affairs*. (The author was later identified as George Kennan.) He predicated future American foreign policy toward the Soviets on the basis of ideological containment by all means short of atomic war. Kennan believed that the world had become polarized, with Russian policies dictating a permanent clash with the Western democracies that could be forestalled only by a strong unilateral American policy. These ideas became the rationale for much of the United States policy toward the Soviet Union after 1947.

THE SOVIET REACTION

Whether the Russian response was in fact a reaction to the attempt on the part of the Allies to encircle the Soviet Union is a point authorities still debate. In any case, the Soviets welded their satellites into an effective political unit and took steps to offset American moves. First, they created an agency to stimulate the economic development of the countries in the Russian bloc. Second, in September 1947 they resurrected the Comintern, a hard-line international Communist organization that attempted to spread

Stalin's ideology and policies throughout the world. Finally, in 1948 the Soviets initiated a series of harassments (see Chapter 18).

By the end of 1947 the United States had embarked on a series of actions designed to improve the welfare of democratic states while restraining the tide of Communism. This demanded an articulate and far-reaching foreign policy that would in turn necessitate a sharp change in America's historic attitude toward alliances and interdependence among nations. The United States government and the American people had committed themselves to effecting change abroad, but would they now accept continuation of the status quo at home?

Further Reading

A lively review of major events since 1945 appears in *Eric F. Goldman, *The Crucial Decade and After: America, 1945-1960* (New York, 1960). Two good surveys of American diplomatic history since 1945 are *Paul Y. Hammond, *Cold War Years: American Foreign Policy Since 1945* (New York, 1969) and *Walter La Feber, *America, Russia, and the Cold War: 1945-1966* (New York, 1967). The books by William A. Williams and Lloyd C. Gardner cited before are also useful.

All of these books treat American difficulties with Russia and with Asia. For particulars relating to Germany, see Eugene Davidson, *The Death and Life of Germany* (New York, 1959).

The failure of the United States to prevent the Communist takeover in China is explained in *Herbert Feis, *The China Tangle: The American Effort in China from Pearl Harbor to the Marshall Mission* (New York, 1965) and *Tang Tsou, *America's Failure in China: 1941-1950* (Chicago, 1963). The struggle over Japan is admirably related in *Herbert Feis, *Contest Over Japan: The Soviet Bid for Power in the Far East, 1945-1952* (New York, 1968). For an examination of the situation in the Philippines, see Theodore Friend, *Between Two Empires: The Ordeal of the Philippines, 1929-1946* (New Haven, Conn., 1965).

Memoirs for the period abound. The most important include *Harry S. Truman, *Memoirs: Volume I, Year of Decision* (New York, 1965); James F. Byrnes, *Speaking Frankly* (New York, 1947); and Dean Acheson, *Present at the Creation* (New York, 1969). Others cited earlier are pertinent, and those by Marshall Knappen, Arthur Bliss Lane, James G. McDonald, W. Bedell Smith, Albert C. Wedemeyer and John Leighton Stuart are also enlightening. A biography of George Marshall is useful here.

Asterisk denotes paperback edition.

18

World Challenge and
American Response, 1947-1955

The American government and people responded to basic changes in foreign policy in various and sometimes unfortunate ways. An additional and greatly disturbing factor was the Soviet detonation of an atomic bomb in late September 1949. This acted as another catalyst which, added to all that had taken place between the United States and the Soviet Union since Yalta, intensified the deep political and ideological cleavages within American society. From a national wartime unity and a continued economic prosperity came a period of disillusionment that began almost as early as the first Soviet veto in the Security Council of the United Nations in 1946. By the end of the decade, although the Communist tide had been turned abroad, Americans were not sure they had conquered it at home.

ANTI-COMMUNISM, CONGRESS, AND FOREIGN POLICY

In Canada in 1946 a large Soviet spy ring was uncovered, in the process of which high officials were implicated. Two years later a well-known New Deal diplomat, Alger Hiss, was accused by a former Communist, Whitaker Chambers, of having passed official secret documents to Soviet espionage agents before the war. Hiss sued for libel, was tried twice for perjury, and was convicted on that charge after the second trial in 1950. If Hiss were guilty, Americans speculated, was it not possible that the State Department harbored other disloyal employees in sensitive positions? Secretary of State Dean Acheson's strong statement of support for Hiss, in fact, did little to enhance the Secretary's stature with Congress.

Most disturbing of all was the revelation in February 1950 by Klaus Fuchs, an English atomic scientist turned spy, that four Americans were part of an elaborate espionage ring that had helped the Soviets develop the atomic bomb. All four were convicted; two were sentenced to long prison terms, while Julius and Ethel Rosenberg were electrocuted in the mid-1950's.

The age of suspicion resulted in two phenomena, both initiated in Congress. One was the most stringent peacetime security measure passed since 1798, the McCarran Internal Security Act, approved in 1950 over President Truman's veto. This act banned Communists in defense industries, forced Communist and Communist-front organizations to register with the Attorney-General, and barred aliens who had been Communists from entering the country. In conjunction with an earlier law, the McCarran Act was used to outlaw and bring to trial members of the fast-shrinking American Communist party.

Repressive as this measure was, it was routine compared to the second phenomenon. An obscure junior senator from Wisconsin, Joseph R. McCarthy, claimed in a speech in Wheeling, West Virginia, in February 1950, that he had proof that the State Department was riddled with Communists. In response to demands for numbers and names, he variously cited 205, 57, 81, 10, 116, and finally only one, a Far Eastern expert on the faculty of Johns Hopkins University, Owen Lattimore.

Thus began a most unfortunate period in which well-known men such as FDR, Marshall, Acheson, and Lattimore were slandered and many others denied access to classified information on the grounds of being security risks. McCarthy rose meteorically, and within two years was one of the most influential men on Capitol Hill. His accusations served to weld together those Republicans, as well as a few Democrats, who blamed Roosevelt for knuckling under to Stalin at Yalta, with a vocal minority who charged that Truman and Acheson had allowed the Chinese Communists to take over China, forcing Chiang to flee to Taiwan. The Congressional rhetoric in large measure represented the frustrations of a people who, for the second time in the century, had won a war only to lose the peace. One example was the close vote in Congress on the Bricker Amendment in 1953. First introduced in 1951 by Senator John W. Bricker of Ohio, the proposed constitutional amendment would have limited the President's authority to make executive agreements and required such agreements to be approved by the Senate. President Eisenhower at first approved, but later was influential in defeating the measure — but not before such groups as the American Medical Association, the Daughters of the American Revolution, and others had testified in its favor.

The supercharged atmosphere of suspicion in Congress and among the American people affected foreign policy in the early 1950's. Incalculable harm was done to the State Department by the myriad investigations and the singling out of a few men with long diplomatic service. The shock waves caused by this, added to those growing out of the frequent departmental reorganizations in which merit often got lost in the shuffle, together with the rise of other agencies as foreign policy makers, caused a continued decline in the department's importance in terms of its ability to sponsor and execute foreign policy.

OTHER MAKERS OF FOREIGN POLICY

By the early 1950's several new governmental agencies had prominent roles in formulating and executing American foreign policy. The two most important — but not the only ones — were the National Security Council (NSC) and the Central Intelligence Agency (CIA), both products of a 1947 act. The NSC was a superadvisory group to the President composed of the secretaries of State and Defense, the Joint Chiefs of Staff, and representatives of other high governmental agencies, such as the Atomic Energy Commission. The NSC advises the President on matters pertaining to national defense and foreign policy. In recent years this set up has served to increase the authority of the Secretary of Defense in determining foreign policy.

The CIA was organized as an adjunct of the NSC to coordinate domestic and foreign intelligence and to advise the NSC of its findings. The CIA has taken over much of the function once provided, however inadequately, by the State Department. A major difficulty in using the CIA as an agent of policy has been its secrecy and cloak-and-dagger tactics, which often keep American diplomats in an area very much in the dark as to its activities.

When other factors in policy making, such as party politics, public opinion, and pressure groups, are added, it is no wonder that the State Department has had great difficulty in accommodating itself to the rapid changes that have characterized postwar American foreign policy.

Any discussion of the State Department must include mention of the professional diplomats, those whom Truman characterized as the "striped pants boys." Basic changes in American foreign policy have effected concomitant changes in the role of the diplomat. Since the end of World War II the heads of embassies have become responsible for directing or coordinating economic aid programs, military assistance programs, information services, the Peace Corps, and so forth. Now the top American diplomat functions more as a business executive in charge of multifaceted operations who holds the entire operation together by a staff and line relationship. Although many more diplomats have achieved the rank of career minister or career ambassador, political parties still reserve about one third of the top posts abroad for patronage. Congress has continued to take an ambivalent attitude toward the State Department and the diplomats, on the one hand making increasing demands, on the other often echoing Truman's remark. In addition, Congress has passed acts reorganizing the State Department in 1949, 1956, and 1965, but has not improved the minimal allowance given to diplomats to aid their functioning overseas. The result is that the department has had increasing difficulty in recruiting first-rate applicants and practically no success in attracting minority groups. In 1968, for example, of 3,363 Foreign Service officers, only 26 were black!

RUSSIAN HARASSMENT AND AMERICAN REACTION

An effective tool used by the Soviets after 1947 to weaken American foreign policy was harassment. One of their first attempts, in June 1948, was to cut off Berlin from the West by a tight blockade. Ostensibly, this was in reaction to the proposed currency reform for Berlin that had been agreed to by the West, but more plausibly it was because the Allies, with the exception of the Soviets, had decided to merge their occupation zones and create a democratic West Germany. The Soviet blockade was thwarted for nearly a year by an Allied airlift. At its peak, the airlift supplied the city with an average of 8,000 tons a day, and on some days supplies reached a total of 13,000 tons. The West German government was constituted and drafted a constitution in May 1949, just after the Russians lifted the blockade. The episode convinced the Allies of the need for a military force capable of countering the Soviets' strength of about twenty-five divisions in central Europe.

PRESIDENT TRUMAN AND NATO

The Berlin airlift crisis coincided with the 1948 presidential election. Truman was not favored because his opponent, Governor Thomas E. Dewey, also supported the administration policy and his party had won a Congressional majority in 1946. Both parties had approved the Senate resolution of Senator Arthur H. Vandenberg calling for the negotiation of collective defense pacts within the United Nations Charter. This paved the way for the United States to negotiate a series of such pacts, of which the North Atlantic Treaty Organization (NATO) was the most important.

The election was an unexpected victory for Truman and the Democrats. Truman, acceding to Marshall's wish to retire, elevated Dean Acheson to Secretary of State. Acheson was a brilliant lawyer who had served the State Department in several capacities, most recently as Under-Secretary. His public personality was somewhat glacial and at times served to antagonize members of Congress. Acheson had long supported Kennan's containment theory and even surpassed the latter in his avowal of the Soviet threat. Even before Acheson became Secretary of State, talks had been held with the Western countries of Europe regarding a military alliance that would commit the American presence to Europe. The first draft of the treaty, completed about the time of the election, was not released until early in 1949. It included the United States and eleven other nations: England, France, Canada, Belgium, Italy, the Netherlands, Luxembourg, Portugal, Norway, Iceland, and Denmark. By the terms of the pact, signed for a ten-year period and renewable, the signatories promised to develop their capacities for self-defense and to consider an attack against one nation as an attack against all. The NATO pact was overwhelmingly approved by the Senate on July 21, 1949, and became operative in September. Greece and Turkey joined in 1951, and in 1954 West Germany was admitted to membership. NATO represented the end of the century-and-a-half American policy of "no entangling alliances." An entire organizational structure under a NATO Council came into being, supported by the United States with an intial outlay of $1.4 billion for 1949.

THE NORTH ATLANTIC TREATY ORGANIZATION, 1949

The Parties to this Treaty reaffirm their faith in the purposes and principles of the Charter of the United Nations and their desire to live in peace with all peoples and all governments.

They are determined to safeguard the freedom, common heritage and civilization of their peoples, founded on the principles of democracy, individual liberty and the rule of law.

They seek to promote stability and well-being in the North Atlantic area.

They are resolved to unite their efforts for collective defense and for the preservation of peace and security.

They therefore agree to this North Atlantic Treaty:

Article 3. In order more effectively to achieve the objectives of this Treaty, the Parties, separately and jointly, by means of continuous and effective self-help and mutual aid, will maintain and develop their individual and collective capacity to resist armed attack.

Article 4. The Parties will consult together whenever, in the opinion of any of them, the territorial integrity, political independence or security of any of the Parties is threatened.

Article 5. The Parties agree that an armed attack against one or more of them in Europe or North America shall be considered an attack against them all; and consequently they agree that, if such an armed attack occurs, each of them, in exercise of the right of individual or collective self-defense recognized by Article 51 of the Charter of the United Nations, will assist the Party or Parties so attacked by taking forthwith, individually and in concert with the other Parties, such action as it deems necessary, including the use of armed force, to restore and maintain the security of the North Atlantic area. . . .

Article 6. For the purpose of Article 5 an armed attack on one or more of the Parties is deemed to include an armed attack on the territory of any of the Parties in Europe or North America, on the Algerian departments of France, on the occupation forces of any Party in Europe, on the islands under the jurisdiction of any Party in the North Atlantic area north of the Tropic of Cancer or on the vessels or aircraft in this area of any of the Parties.

Article 7. This Treaty does not affect, and shall not be interpreted as affecting, in any way the rights and obligations under the Charter of the Parties which are members of the United Nations, or the primary responsibility of the Security Council for the maintenance of international peace and security.

Article 9. The Parties hereby establish a council, on which each of them shall be represented, to consider matters concerning the implementation of this Treaty. The council shall be so organized as to be able to meet promptly at any time. The council shall set up such subsidiary bodies as may be necessary; in particular it shall establish immediately a defense committee which shall recommend measures for the implementation of Article 3 and 5.

Article 10. The Parties may, by unanimous agreement, invite any other European state in a position to further the principles of this Treaty and to contribute to the security of the North Atlantic area to accede to this Treaty. Any state so invited may become a party to the Treaty by depositing its instrument of accession with the Government of the United States of America. The Government of the United States of America will inform each of the Parties of the deposit of each such instrument of accession.

THE HUMANITARIAN IMPULSE: AMERICA'S POINT FOUR PROGRAM

One of the most quoted parts of President Truman's inagural address in January 1949 was his outline of an American commitment to help underdeveloped countries by "making progress available." But the idea was easier to propose than to implement; Congress did not appropriate money for the program for more than a year, and then it was only a token amount. The Point Four program never realized its potential, except perhaps as a vocal self-congratulatory exercise.

THE UNITED STATES AND REGIONAL ALLIANCES

Between the beginning of NATO and the year 1955 the United States pursued a policy of defensive alliances with friendly nations. The treaties usually contained a promise of aid should any one country be attacked and of United States military assistance to help the member countries build up their armed forces. By these provisions the various regional alliances bound their members to the West, in line with the American policy of containment.

The earliest pact, developed at about the time of NATO, was with the

Latin American states, the Organization of American States (discussed in Chapter 19). The next two after NATO were negotiated in 1951 and 1954. The first was an alliance between Australia, New Zealand, and the United States (ANZUS). More important for containment was the multilateral treaty negotiated with certain Asian nations in Manila, September 1954. The Southeast Treaty Organization (SEATO) included Pakistan, the Philippines, and Thailand, Australia, New Zealand, Great Britain, France, and the United States. However, this grouping did not include some of the most important Asian countries, for example India and Indonesia. Both ANZUS and SEATO differed from NATO in that they were paper alliances rather than operating multinational organizations.

Another multilateral treaty was urged by the United States upon several countries in order to shore up the defense of the Middle East. The Baghdad Pact of 1955 included Turkey, Pakistan, Iran, Iraq, and Great Britain, but not Egypt or Israel. The United States did not join, thinking to quiet hostility in the Arab-Jewish conflict, but when this hope proved vain and Iraq withdrew in 1958, America joined the alliance, which was then renamed the Central Treaty Organization (CENTO).

By the mid-1950's the United States had made, in addition to the regional alliances, several individual defense treaties. While negotiations were for the most part carried out by diplomats, the actual alliances ultimately involved the military. This resulted in military men rather than diplomats making the actual decisions as to what was best for national defense against Communist expansion, which superseded all other considerations. The problems that could arise when field commanders made their own foreign policy were well illustrated in the Korean War.

THE UNITED STATES, CHINA, AND KOREA

When the United States and Russia failed to agree on a united Korea, Secretary of State Marshall asked the United Nations to intervene. In 1948, UN-supervised elections were boycotted by the North, which set up its own state. The South inaugurated the Republic of Korea, electing the elderly nationalist Syngman Rhee President. By June 1949 all foreign troops had left Korean territory. During the following year both North and South claimed the entire country, the 38th parallel proving to be a very weak boundary. The United States gave military aid to South Korea but withheld offensive weapons such as tanks and planes because of Rhee's belligerency. In February 1950 Congress appropriated $110 million toward the economic recovery of South Korea.

Suddenly in June the well-trained and well-equipped North Korean army struck across the 38th parallel, completely routing the surprised South

Koreans. President Truman requested and received from the United Nations a condemnation of the act. The absence during the next few crucial days of the Soviet delegate, who had boycotted the Security Council since January in protest to the seating of the delegate from Nationalist rather than Mainland China, negated the certainty of a veto. After an anguished plea from Rhee, the President ordered air and sea support for the South Koreans south of the 38th parallel.

On July 7, 1950, the Security Council took over the war in the name of the United Nations, appointing General Douglas MacArthur commander. By early September, while American forces were being built up, the North Koreans had captured the entire peninsula except for the enclave around the southern city of Taegu extending southward to the port of Pusan.

By then American forces in Korea numbered 210,000, about half the total of troops fighting for the United Nations. Most of the remainder were supplied by South Korea, although eventually some sixteen nations sent token forces. The United States financed the entire war effort and supplied more than 93 percent of the air force and 85 percent of the naval strength.

President Truman had originally committed American forces to action without consulting Congress. As the conflict continued and casualties rose, the concept of a limited war emerged. Attitudes shifted as frustration mounted, caused in part by the 23,000 dead and the 116,000 wounded. Another important factor was the removal of General MacArthur in April 1951.

MacArthur waged a brilliant offensive which began September 15 when he launched an amphibious attack on Inchon, just below the 38th parallel. He cut across the peninsula, trapping a major part of the North Korean army, which surrendered in large numbers. The remnants fled north beyond the parallel boundary, the United Nations forces in hot pursuit. Although President Truman had announced in June that the United States was interested in maintaining the status quo in Korea, the United Nations advance changed his views. Soon his planning encompassed the future of the entire country. The UN General Assembly also approved MacArthur's northward push.

During the summer most American diplomats were more concerned with Communist China's reaction to MacArthur's drive than with the Soviets. The Chinese delivered a series of warnings that culminated in a flat statement to India by Foreign Minister Chou En-lai on October 2, 1950, that the Chinese would intervene if the United Nations army continued north of the 38th parallel. However, other factors, headed by the consideration that the Chinese were using threats as a means of gaining entrance into the United Nations, convinced United States policy makers that Red China was only bluffing.

Less comprehensible was the breakdown in American intelligence.

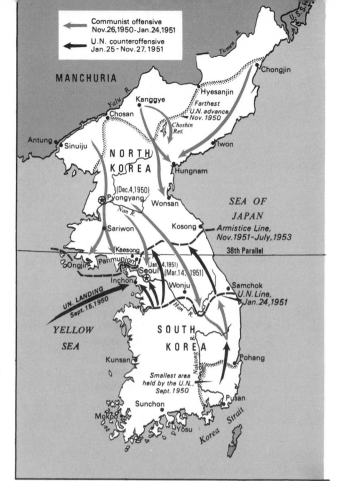

Map 13.
The Korean War,
1950-1953

MacArthur had advised President Truman that the Chinese could move only about 50-60,000 troops across the Yalu River, the northern boundary of Korea, when in fact 320,000 troops were massed there. Many members of the United Nations, and most of the veteran State Department experts, decried the decision to continue northward. They suspected MacArthur's motives when he asked for — but was refused — permission to bomb targets in China.

The Chinese "volunteers" who were occasionally captured in October became more frequent in November. As the United Nations army moved up the Yalu River for a final drive, the Chinese attacked in force, inflicting heavy casualties and forcing MacArthur's forces southward once more. By Christmas 1950 the Chinese had retaken Seoul and Chou En-lai was talking about the reunification of Korea to be sponsored by *his* nation. In early December President Truman had held a strategy meeting with Prime Minister Clement Attlee, who disagreed with the American view that Red China, Soviet Russia, and North Korea constituted one monolithic enemy to be treated as equal threats to the free world.

THE PRESIDENT AND THE GENERAL

General MacArthur had his own concept of waging war; willing to accept nothing less than total victory, he could not envisage a non-victory or a limited war. At various times he had pressed President Truman and the Joint Chiefs of Staff for permission to blockade Communist China's coast, to bomb coastal cities and supply routes, or to allow Chiang's army on Taiwan to make diversionary strikes on the mainland. These requests were denied, and by January 1951 MacArthur was warning that he might be forced to withdraw from the Korean peninsula. However, before the situation deteriorated further, the United Nations' Eighth Army, commanded by General Matthew B. Ridgway, regained the initiative and slowly pushed the Chinese and North Koreans northward.

In February the General Assembly branded Communist China the aggressor. However, Secretary of State Acheson indicated his willingness to negotiate a cease-fire. After the President's public statement to this effect, MacArthur negated it by publicly threatening to attack China. Shortly after, the Republican House leader released a letter from the General that flatly contradicted the limited-war concept advocated by the Truman administration. MacArthur added: "There is no substitute for victory." Retribution was swift: on April 11 President Truman relieved MacArthur of both his United States and United Nations commands.

MacArthur returned posthaste, to be greeted by tumultuous crowds on his way to Washington. He spoke eloquently to Congress, reiterating his views. While the public may at first have supported MacArthur, Congress did not. A Congressional inquiry strengthened the administration's hand, correspondingly weakening MacArthur's. The episode was an effective illustration of the President's authority as Commander-in-Chief and it also helped increase President Truman's prestige abroad.

By late June 1951, the opposing armies in Korea had reached a stalemate just north of the 38th parallel. The Soviets now indicated that truce talks would be acceptable. The talks began in July in an atmosphere of mutual distrust; negotiations were conducted by military men rather than by diplomats. A painful, twenty-two-month period followed, during which time the fighting, often fierce, continued. Casualties were moderately high, but neither side was able to alter its position significantly.

Naturally, the war in Korea influenced Americans in the 1952 presidential election. The Republican platform sharply attacked the negative aspects of the containment policy. The Republican nominee, General Dwight D. Eisenhower, pledged himself, if elected, to effect a truce. After his sweeping victory, this pledge was fulfilled in April 1953 when truce talks were resumed. By July an armistice was agreed upon, calling for the 38th parallel as the boundary between the two Koreas, the repatriation of prisoners, and an international conference on Korea to be held at Geneva.

The probable reasons that North Korea acceded to the armistice would include (1) the heavy cost of the war to Communist China; (2) the American threat to use atomic weapons; and (3) the policy shift in the Kremlin after Stalin's death in March 1953. Syngman Rhee made a spectacular effort — fortunately unsuccessful — to sabotage the truce by freeing 27,000 North Korean soldiers before they could be repatriated. The United States by the summer of 1953 had made containment work, at least temporarily, but at a high cost.

THE JAPANESE PEACE TREATY

United Nations forces, mostly American, still occupied the Japanese homeland in the late 1940's. The rebuilding of Japan's industry, a goal espoused by MacArthur in 1947, continued despite Soviet protests. However, the need to conclude a long-range defense pact that would allow the United States air and naval bases in Japan necessitated a peace treaty. A Far Eastern expert and consultant to the State Department, John Foster Dulles, was sent to Tokyo by President Truman in June 1950 to discuss treaty terms with MacArthur. In February Dulles was officially appointed to represent the United States in negotiating a peace treaty with Japan. He was able to obtain prior commitments of approval from all the Allies except Russia, who continued to protest the presence of American troops in Japan. The treaty was offered to a fifty-two-nation conference meeting in San Francisco, September 4-8, 1951, on a take-it-or-leave-it basis. Only Russia and two of its satellites refused to sign the final document. The treaty provided for mild reparations and restriction of Japan to the home islands, which forced Japan to relinquish the Kuriles and the lower part of Sakhalin. Japan retained sovereignty over the Ryukus and the Bonin Islands, but agreed to temporary American control. Shortly after, a defense treaty was signed between Japan and the United States. In March 1952 the Senate approved the treaties and on April 28, 1952, the war with Japan officially ended.

PRESIDENT EISENHOWER AND SECRETARY DULLES

When Dwight D. Eisenhower was nominated by the Republican party in the summer of 1952, he was in a certain sense a political question mark. He soon proved to be the most popular man in the United States and confounded many in his party by his progressive outlook and internationalist stance. Although he alienated a number of the more conservative Republicans by his policies, Eisenhower completely dominated the party. His status was such that he was eventually able to silence McCarthy once and for all after the latter persisted in attacking Marshall and other men whom Eisenhower respected. Nevertheless, a sizable minority of congressmen, led by the Senate minority leader, William F. Knowland — nicknamed "the Senator from Formosa" — continued to support Bricker's and McCarthy's desire to limit the American role abroad.

President Eisenhower chose as his Secretary of State John Foster Dulles. An experienced diplomat, Dulles was also authoritarian and highly moralistic. He believed in personal diplomacy and junketed over 350,000 miles during his six-year tour of duty. His reaction to the Soviet and the Red Chinese threat was as rigid as Acheson's. Dulles emphasized the role of the atomic bomb and talked of "massive retaliation," supporting the use of air power and missiles as a means of defense rather than the concept of limited war that had characterized the Korean conflict. He believed in using these deterrents in bargaining, and he was convinced that the United States must go to the "brink of war" in dealing with the Communists. Such policies did not endear him to all Americans or to some Western nations. Finally, Dulles was so firm a proponent of regional pacts to contain Communism that he was often caricatured for his "pactomania."

THE UNITED STATES AND THE TWO CHINAS

While the Japanese peace treaty was being considered, the Soviets and the Communist Chinese in February 1950 signed a thirty-year mutual aid agreement to protect them from the West and Japan. The pact underlined the dilemma the United States faced in dealing with the problem of China. Chiang had been written off militarily when he took the remnants of his army to Formosa — promptly renamed Taiwan. But on the other hand, the Chinese Communists had so alienated the Americans by their antagonistic and hostile actions that the United States had not extended *de facto* recognition to the regime.

With China's entry into the Korean War, the American attitude stiffened further, blocking China from admittance to the United Nations. American aid propped up Taiwan until early 1954 when a defense treaty, comparable to that with the Philippines, was signed. Massive military and economic assistance allowed Chiang to maintain an army of about 600,000. During the 1952 election the Republicans promised to unleash Chiang's forces; this was done, but to little avail. The small-scale landings the Nationalists mounted on the mainland were disastrous and they were forced to make Taiwan a defense bastion. By 1954 the two Chinese governments were hurling invective at each other so forcefully that some congressmen feared the defense pact between the United States and Chiang would trigger a war.

This fear was intensified when the Chinese Communists shelled two tiny

Nationalist-held offshore islands, Quemoy and Matsu, which were only five miles from Amoy. The Reds invaded and took other offshore islands in January 1955, leading to the belief that an attempt to take Quemoy and Matsu as well as the Pescadores and possibly Taiwan itself was imminent. President Eisenhower asked Congress for a resolution that would enable him to cope with any situation arising from the threat to Chiang's holdings in the Formosa Straits. Congress passed the Formosa Resolution on January 28, 1955, giving the President an unprecedented carte blanche to deal with the situation. Matters were temporarily eased when Chiang was forced to tone down his invective and to withdraw from some of the islands, although not from Quemoy and Matsu. The United States then discussed the issue at Geneva with the Communists; no agreement was reached, but the status quo was maintained until 1958.

NEW ASIAN NATIONS AND THE UNITED STATES

The Philippines, being staunch allies of the United States, had increasing difficulty with terrorist guerrilla forces, Communist or Left-oriented, that hoped to overthrow the popularly elected government and bring about a social and economic revolution. The initial success of the Hukbalahaps (or Huks) led the United States to offer economic as well as military assistance. In 1950 an American report had called for Philippine governmental reforms, but little was done. In 1954 Ramón Magsaysay, the most effective leader the infant republic had yet produced, was elected President. Within a year he turned the tide against the Huks and promoted nationalistic feeling by renegotiating a more equitable trade agreement with the United States.

The Philippines' neighbor to the south, the new state of Indonesia, caused the State Department some concern. Receiving independence from the Dutch after a prolonged conference lasting from August 23 to November 2, 1949, Indonesia officially proclaimed its independence on August 15, 1950. However, the Dutch retained economic control of the new nation as well as ownership of West New Guinea (called West Irian by the Indonesians). Both these facts were causes of friction. Although Indonesia's leaders, Achmed Sukarno and Mohammed Hatta, had quelled a pro-Communist uprising in late 1949, they still considered themselves neutral. They espoused an anticolonial policy that prevented acceptance of direct American military and economic aid and thus refused to align themselves with either side in the Cold War.

The high tide of Indonesia's policy and influence came with the Bandung Conference, held at Bandung, Indonesia, April 18-24, 1955. Sponsored by Indonesia and four other Asian nations, the conference attracted top-level diplomats representing one and a half billion Asians and Africans. It accomplished little save to demonstrate the size of a third and unaligned force in the world. The State Department offered to extend long-term loans to Sukarno, but so did the Soviet Union and Communist China.

INDOCHINA AND THE GENEVA ACCORDS

Across the South China Sea, France was trying to salvage its Asian colonies, but continued warfare in Vietnam proved a serious drain on French resources. The Chinese Communists aided the rebels, but to what extent remained unknown. In May 1950 the United States recognized a French-sponsored puppet regime in Vietnam. Secretary of State Acheson offered military and economic aid to the French in their struggle to defeat Ho Chi Minh, the nationalist leader. But in spite of massive assistance and the American funding of over 75 percent of the French war effort, the French not only failed to subdue the Viet Minh but were by 1954 bottled up in a fortified stronghold in the northern part of the country. After a fifty-five-day siege, Dien Bien Phu fell on May 7, 1954. During the latter stages of the battle, the French had requested American air strikes, but the Eisenhower administration, failing to get British backing and supported by American public opinion, refused. On this occasion President Eisenhower referred to the "domino theory": if Vietnam fell to the enemy, the remaining independent nations of Asia would fall like a row of dominoes.

At the same time that Dien Bien Phu was under siege, the United States, the Soviet Union, Great Britain, France, and Communist China were meeting with other Asian states at the Geneva Conference, April 26-June 21, 1954, in an attempt to end the fighting and stabilize the situation in southeast Asia. The Geneva Accords were made at the expense of the West, whose diplomatic hand was weak as the result of the military standoff in Korea and the French loss in Vietnam. No decisions were made regarding Korea; Vietnam, however, was divided at the 17th parallel, the north going to Ho Chi Minh's Viet Minh and the south to the French puppet government. An election supervised by the United Nations was to be held within two years to reunite the country; Laos and Cambodia were also scheduled to hold free elections and were confirmed as independent states.

The United States did not participate in this part of the conference and did not sign the Geneva Accords. In fact, within a year the Americans began replacing the French in South Vietnam, sending in teams of military advisers and planners and financially supporting the South Vietnamese government. The French puppet was shortly replaced by Ngo Dinh Diem, who quickly turned dictatorial, and the French influence rapidly disappeared.

INDIA AND PAKISTAN

The pattern of American relations with India and Pakistan had changed little since 1949. India charted a neutral course, soliciting aid from both sides, although the amount given by the Soviets was small compared to that offered by the United States. In 1950 India and the United States signed a Point Four agreement, by which the Americans promised to supply financial and technical assistance to develop agriculture. To avert a famine in 1951, the United States also sent to India wheat valued at $190 million. Nevertheless, the Indian government under Jawaharlal Nehru remained unreconciled to the United States as the result of difficulties dating back to 1948 over the northern province of Kashmir, claimed by both India and Pakistan. The United States, while not publicly admitting the fact, preferred to have Pakistan control Kashmir, and India was quick to discover this. Thus, when the United States offered to mediate, Indian sensibilities were inflamed, so that any short-run gains American diplomacy had been able to make were canceled.

Pakistan took a strongly pro-American, anti-Communist stand, first receiving military assistance from the United States in 1953. Later, Nehru refused such assistance, even though he believed the Pakistanis would use their military aid toward acquiring Kashmir. In any case, the United States continued to support Pakistan militarily and economically as a staunch ally against the spread of Communism.

THE MIDDLE EAST

Between 1948 and 1955, both revolution and counterrevolution were played out in the Middle East against a background of abject poverty and strident nationalism. Israel, victorious over the Arabs in the summer of 1948, consolidated its borders, in the process forcing out of 600,000 Arab residents. These refugees, now landless and poverty-stricken, lived in camps supported by the United Nations. The Arab states would not assist them because Israel insisted that the refugees be resettled in Arab lands; but to agree to that, the Arabs felt, would be to relinquish their claims on the territory occupied by Israel, a state whose existence they refused to recognize. The United Nations kept a truce team in Israel, but, as the future would show, the situation remained explosive.

Israel's success helped spark revolutions elsewhere. In 1952 a group of Egyptian army officers led by Colonel Gamal Abdel Nasser overthrew a weak and corrupt monarchy, after which they pledged themselves to social reform and continued anti-Israeli action. Upheavals also occurred in Jordan and Syria. In Iran the situation was complicated by the clandestine efforts of the West. In 1951 a nationalist government took over the vast Anglo-Iranian Oil Company during a dispute over Iran's share of the profits. The British tried to dislodge the government by applying economic sanctions. Then, in August 1953, an American-supported coup toppled the recalcitrant government, and a new international oil consortium, which allowed the British oil companies 40 percent, the United States 40 percent, and the Dutch and the French the remainder, was formed. Profits were to be divided equally between the consortium and Iran. This move, together with the Baghdad Pact, seemed to offer more stability to the area than had existed for some time, but this proved illusory after the Suez Canal crisis in 1956.

THE REBUILDING OF EUROPE, 1949-1954

To 150,000,000 Americans, the focus during this period was not on the Middle East or the Far East — except for Korea — but on Europe. Again excepting Korea, more news and information about Europe were disseminated in the United States than about all the rest of the world combined. At the same time that the United States was implementing NATO, Europe was making a spectacular economic recovery under the Marshall Plan. For example, France's industrial output by 1950 exceeded her 1938 capacity by nearly 40 percent. Italy and England lagged slightly, but by the mid-fifties they too were exceeding their prewar levels. Most incredible was the rise of West Germany; by 1952 the Federal Republic ranked second to Britain in European industry. But production of consumer goods lagged, and Europe did not recover its prewar standard of living until nearly a decade after the war.

To United States policy makers, one of the most intriguing ideas involved the possibility of Europe's economic and political unity, at this time apparently more attainable than ever before. Several months before the NATO pact was signed, ten Western European countries had created a Council of Europe to serve as a forum for unification ideas. The two major obstacles at the outset were the reluctance of member states to surrender any meaningful amount of sovereignty to a supranational body and the deep-seated French fear of allowing West Germany to become a full member with the right to rearm. The first obstacle eventually doomed the possibility of and superstate, but to contemporary Europeans the specter of a strong Germany seemed to pose an even more insoluble problem.

In May 1950 French Foreign Minister Robert Schuman proposed a scheme for the control of European coal and steel by a supranational authority. This led, in September 1952, to the creation of the European Coal and Steel Community (ECSC), the participating members being Belgium,

WEST GERMANY JOINS NATO

President Dwight D. Eisenhower signs the historic agreement ending
Allied occupation of West Germany as Secretary of State
John Foster Dulles looks on, April 1955.

France, Luxembourg, the Netherlands, and West Germany. Great Britain was not a member. In a most auspicious beginning, the ECSC abolished tariffs and quotas throughout the community.

At the time the Schuman Plan was effected, the United States was attempting to implement NATO so that Europe would be able to defend itself militarily. To that end, especially after the Korean War began, the United States reinforced its troops in Europe and pressed for the inclusion of a German force within NATO. The French protested, suggesting instead the formation of a European Defense Community which would employ German troops at a divisional level but from whose top councils the Germans would be barred. President Eisenhower and Secretary Dulles accepted the plan, but then the French National Assembly voted it down. Dulles hoped to prevent this by threatening France with an "agonizing reappraisal" of America's European commitments. Although the Secretary painted a rather bleak picture of NATO's future, the French scuttling of the European Defense Community, as it turned out, made little difference.

A new stratagem was devised to admit Germany as a troop-contributing European member, although not within NATO. An old military alliance, the Brussels Pact of 1948, was refurbished, and with the addition of Germany and Italy, renamed the Western European Union (WEU). WEU forces were to be controlled by NATO; the United States and Great Britain pledged continuing support in Europe to allay France's fears of German domination. The preliminary treaties were signed in late October 1954, and by the end of the year the French Assembly had narrowly ratified it.

West Germany was eventually admitted to full partnership in the West, becoming a full member of NATO in 1955. But despite this accomplishment, the European members of NATO failed to meet their troop quotas, and have not done so since. Because of this and the increasing commitments of the United States, American policy makers decided to arm NATO components with nuclear weapons, under United States control, to increase their offensive power. This in turn spurred the Soviets to develop an intercontinental missile, a project which was successful three years later.

THE SOVIET UNION AND GERMAN REUNIFICATION

Stalin's death in March 1953 resulted in Soviet changes in foreign policy. A loosening of external controls set off explosions in three of Russia's Eastern European satellites. The uprisings in Hungary and Poland occurred later and will be discussed in the next chapter; but the first, an uprising in East Germany in June 1953, had to be quelled by Soviet troops.

A temporary thaw in the Cold War occurred when the Soviets agreed to discuss German reunification, something they had not been willing to do since 1949. The foreign ministers met in Geneva in January and February and again from April to June 1954, but an Austrian treaty was their only accomplishment.

The Soviet Union countered NATO and WEU by a comparable arrangement, the Warsaw Pact of May 1955, with its eight satellites. By its terms, the Eastern European countries — minus Yugoslavia — established joint command of their armed forces and set up pact headquarters in Moscow. Another deterrent to harmony between the United States and Russia was the development and testing by each country of a more powerful atomic weapon, the hydrogen bomb.

Even so, President Eisenhower took the initiative by proposing a program, to be called Atoms for Peace, by which the United States would supply nuclear materials for peaceful use to an international commission. Widely heralded in early 1954, the plan was not implemented for several years, and then in a limited way, because it depended upon the international control of the materials. President Eisenhower also proposed to the Soviets in 1955 an "open skies" plan: each side would exchange complete plans of their military establishments and permit reconnaissance flights over each other's territory to minimize the possibility of a surprise attack. The Soviets later rejected the proposal; in any case, the plan had not been approved by either Congress or NATO.

Eisenhower's proposal was made, significantly, at the first Big Four meeting in a decade. Held in Geneva, July 18-23, 1955, the conference was so friendly that a new "spirit of Geneva" seemed to have appeared. However, nothing was accomplished either on the future of Germany or on disarmament. A foreign ministers' meeting in the fall faltered over the same problems that had existed since Potsdam.

By 1955 Europe was still divided into two armed, hostile camps. But for the first time since the end of the war a rapidly growing Western European community of nations was becoming aware of the rumbling behind the iron curtain, and through the development of NATO, ECSC, and WEU, Europeans were sensing new bonds that had not existed before in modern times.

Further Reading

The surveys cited earlier by Eric F. Goldman, Paul Y. Hammond, Walter La Feber, and William A. Williams are equally appropriate for this chapter.

Also pertinent is *Ronald Steel, *Pax Americana* (New York, 1968), which expresses a most interesting viewpoint. The Marshall Plan and its genesis are presented in *Joseph M. Jones, *The Fifteen Weeks* (New York, 1965). A moving portrayal of Europe in 1950 is found in *William L. White, *Fire in the Ashes: Europe at Mid-Century* (New York, 1953).

For American policy in Indochina after the war, see the excellent study by *Ellen J. Hammer, *The Struggle for Indochina: 1940-1955* (Stanford, Calif., 1966). Two fine books dealing with the Korean War and the removal of MacArthur are *Glenn D. Paige, *The Korean Decision* (New York, 1968) and *Allen S. Whiting, *China Crosses the Yalu: The Decision to Enter the Korean War* (Stanford, Calif., 1968).

A good guide to postwar clandestine activities is *Allen Dulles, *The Craft of Intelligence* (New York, 1965). *Kim Philby, *My Silent War* (New York, 1967), is the sensational book by a Soviet double agent. A biography which helps to explain the entire era is *Richard Rovere, *Senator Joe McCarthy* (New York, 1960).

Supplement the period with memoirs such as *Harry S. Truman, *Memoirs:* Volume II, *Years of Trial and Hope* (New York, 1965) and *Dwight D. Eisenhower, *White House Years: Mandate for Change, 1953-1956* (New York, 1965). Other appropriate memoirs are by Henry S. Villard, Ellis Briggs, Francis Sayre, Edwin F. Stanton and Chester Bowles.

Asterisk denotes paperback edition.

19

The Resurgence of Europe and the Problem of the Middle East

By the mid-1950's the countries of Western Europe had recovered their prewar production and living standards, and problems relating to European economic recovery could be considered solved. Thereafter, the efforts of the United States shifted from supplying direct economic aid to giving more military assistance. For this, the Defense Department was responsible, though it coordinated its efforts with a semiautonomous section of the State Department that had been responsible since 1955 for other kinds of government aid. This agency has been known by several names, but is at present called the Agency for International Development (AID).

THE UNITED STATES AND FRANCO'S SPAIN

Although the economic commitments of the State Department did not include military assistance, the department was nevertheless preoccupied with the defense of Europe. For this reason an agreement with Spain became necessary. Spain had long been a target of the Western democracies because it was a tightly run dictatorship headed by the fascist General Francisco Franco. In 1950 the United States belatedly recognized the Franco regime and began secret negotiations for American bases in Spain. In 1953 an executive agreement confirmed these negotiations, and Spain thus joined those European countries to which the United States provided both economic and military assistance. The military and naval installations in Spain were especially important because American nuclear weapons were stationed there; they also bolstered European security at a time when the number of NATO ground forces supplied by European members lagged considerably behind commitments.

THE HUNGARIAN REVOLT

While the United States was trying to augment the defense of Western Europe, the Soviets were having difficulties with two of their Warsaw Pact satellites. In Poland and Hungary troubles arose during the period of looser Soviet controls that resulted from the power struggle following Stalin's death. In June 1956 workers in Poznan, Poland, set off a three-day riot aimed at liberalizing the regime. The riot was quelled and some of the workers were arrested and tried, but the revolt did result in a more liberal government, although one still operating within the prescription of Soviet demands. Under the leadership of Wladyslaw Gomulka, Poland won considerable autonomy even while remaining a member of the Warsaw Pact.

Hungary was not so fortunate. Students in Budapest began an uprising on October 23, 1956, which at first forced the Soviets to withdraw. Imre Nagy formed a government that went far beyond the reforms envisaged in Poland. Most unforgivable from the Soviet viewpoint was the new government's announcement of Hungary's withdrawal from the Warsaw Pact. Almost as bad was Nagy's addition of several non-Communists to the cabinet. The uprising spread throughout the country, directed as much against the Soviet presence in Hungary as against old-line Stalinists within the government. Russia responded by sending in large numbers of reinforcements and armor, ruthlessly crushing the revolt.

The United States officially played little part in the affair, but the consequences of unofficial action had grave repercussions. President Eisenhower in his election campaign of 1952 had held out hopes that the United States would assist peoples struggling to free themselves from Communism. Then, during the Hungarian uprising, propaganda broadcasts from a privately owned American station, Radio Free Europe, led the revolutionists to believe that American aid would arrive. Such an interpretation was never intended by either Eisenhower or Dulles, but since the major source of support for Radio Free Europe was later shown to be the CIA, the episode left bitterness that has not yet entirely subsided. At the height of the uprising the United States was also involved in the Suez Canal crisis, and Secretary Dulles was undergoing surgery for cancer. Perhaps these factors explain the indecisiveness exhibited by the United States government, which confined itself to introducing a resolution in the General Assembly calling for the withdrawal of Soviet troops from Hungary. Later, Congress authorized admittance of a quota of Hungarian refugees to the United States; 38,248 people availed themselves of the opportunity.

EUROPE, THE UNITED STATES, AND THE SUEZ CRISIS

Although European influence in the Middle East had waned since the war, British and French ownership of the Suez Canal, combined with their heavy investments in oil, made their continued presence in the area important. In late 1955 Britain joined the United States in announcing aid to Colonel Nasser's government to build a gigantic dam on the Nile at

Aswan, 800 miles south of Cairo. Besides the requisite technical skill, the dam was expected to cost an estimated $1.3 billion, but it would increase Egypt's arable land by one third. However, as Nasswe was purchasing arms from Soviet satellites for use against Israel, he refused to have anything to do with the pact that Dulles wanted to negotiate — later the Baghdad Pact. Because of Nasser's hostility, the United States and Britain on July 19, 1956, jointly and precipitously withdrew their offer to finance the Aswan Dam.

Nasser reacted by seizing the Suez Canal, a move he had undoubtedly planned far in advance of the Aswan decision. He stated that the tolls from the canal would be used to finance the dam and, in fact, with Soviet technical and financial assistance, the huge project was completed in 1970. The British and French had no intention of losing their investments and a vital oil supply route as well. Thus, they secretly joined Israel in an attempt to retake the canal, oust Nasser, and win a seaport on the Sinai peninsula for Israel. On October 29, 1956, the Israelis invaded the peninsula, within three days capturing it and destroying the Egyptian army there. The British and French presented Nasser with an ultimatum on October 30, demanding return of the Suez Canal; Nasser ignored the demand. British and French forces then occupied Port Said and the canal area, but Nasser had effectively closed the canal by sinking vessels at various strategic points.

Although the Soviet Union was preoccupied with the Hungarian revolt, it reacted angrily by threatening to send volunteers to aid Egypt. However, the key to the affair was the unexpectedly hostile reaction of President Eisenhower. Although in midst of a reelection campaign, which might have been expected to dampen controversial policy statements, he unequivocally demanded that Israeli-British-French aggression stop. On October 30 the United States introduced a cease-fire resolution in the Security Council, but the British and French promptly vetoed it. The next day a determined Eisenhower went before the American people on radio and television, pledging himself to keep the peace. On November 2 the General Assembly adopted a motion by Dulles calling for an immediate cease-fire and the withdrawal of foreign troops. The three aggressors were thus forced by the combined weight of their friends and enemies to accede without having ousted Nasser. A United Nations force supervised the withdrawals, which were completed by the following March.

In the interim, British Prime Minister Anthony Eden had been forced to resign and British and French prestige received a blow in the Middle East from which they never recovered. Nasser, on the other hand, won the canal and, after the crisis ended, was in a much stronger position than before.

THE UNITED STATES, LEBANON, AND IRAQ

After the Suez fiasco the United States found its position in the Middle East increasingly untenable. American public opinion favored support for

Israel, but American oil interests demanded friendly relations with the Arab states. The result was a series of incidents, beginning with Nasser's Suez Canal triumph, that weakened the American position in the Arab world. In June 1957 President Eisenhower tried to achieve more flexibility of action in the area: he asked Congress for authority to use American forces in the Middle East to fight Communism should any country request help. Economic and military assistance would also be proffered. This "blank check" paralleled the Formosa Resolution; after a two-month debate Congress passed the Eisenhower Doctrine.

THE EISENHOWER DOCTRINE, 1957

Resolved, That the President be and hereby is authorized to cooperate with and assist any nation or group of nations in the general area of the Middle East desiring such assistance in the development of economic strength dedicated to the maintenance of national independence.

Section 2. The President is authorized to undertake, in the general area of the Middle East, military assistance programs with any nation or group of nations of that area desiring such assistance. Furthermore, the United States regards as vital to the national interest and world peace the preservation of the independence and integrity of the nations of the Middle East. To this end, if the President determines the necessity thereof, the United States is prepared to use armed force to assist any such nation or group of nations requesting assistance against armed aggression from any country controlled by international communism: Provided, That such employment shall be consonant with the treaty obligations of the United States and with the Constitution of the United States.

Section 6. This joint resolution shall expire when the President shall determine that the peace and security of the nations in the general area of the Middle East are reasonably assured by international conditions created by action of the United Nations or otherwise except that it may be terminated earlier by a concurrent resolution of the two Houses of Congress.

In early 1958 Nasser formed the United Arab Republic by taking over the governments of Syria and Yemen. In July a nationalist revolt in Iraq, led by General Abdel Karim Kassem, overthrew the government and established an anti-Western regime that cooperated with Nasser. This event increased the pressure on nearby Lebanon, which had a large Christian population. On July 14, 1958, the Christian president of Lebanon urgently requested help from the United States to prevent a Moslem, pro-Nasser coup.

President Eisenhower, invoking the Eisenhower Doctrine, sent 14,000 troops into Lebanon. At the same time, Britain deployed a contingent of paratroopers in Jordan to keep the pro-Western government of King Hussein in power. The Soviets did little but protest these occupations, both of which were peaceful. In October American troops were withdrawn from Lebanon; their net effect was negative because Lebanon now turned from the West toward Nasser. However, for the moment, the United States continued to supply military and economic aid to Nasser's United Arab Republic.

THE MISSILE GAP AND SPUTNIK

On October 4, 1957, the Russians launched Sputnik, the world's first successful space satellite, in the process affecting American foreign policy as they had not been able to do since detonating their first atom bomb. Almost immediately, experts in Europe and America raised questions concerning Western vulnerability to long-range Soviet missiles utilizing the large rocket that had boosted Sputnik into orbit. Now began the myth of the "missile gap," which, according to Soviet propaganda, became wider and wider. Soviets proudly hailed their new intercontinental ballistic missile (ICBM), which had a far greater range than the American counterparts based in Europe. Several strategic redeployments of NATO forces did little to offset the European fear of Soviet strength.

Actually, Russian propaganda was the only tangible evidence of such a missile gap. The United States had been flying reconnaissance missions along Soviet borders and bringing back photographs which directly refuted the Russian claims to superior missile development. The evidence was confirmed by the new U-2, a plane that could fly at altitudes of over 60,000 feet and photograph with great accuracy. In early 1960, flights over Russia, although confirming the earlier proof, did little to allay European fears, since the United States could not disseminate its information for fear of sacrificing the secrecy of its missions.

KHRUSHCHEV, THE UNITED STATES, AND "SUMMITRY"

The supposed relaxation of the Cold War, which had offered hope for the settlement of a German peace treaty and other problems, was rudely shattered in September 1958 when Premier Khrushchev demanded an end to the Allied occupation of Berlin within six months. But the Western powers refused and Khrushchev temporarily dropped the threat. Instead, he reversed his position and asked for a summit meeting, the first since Geneva in 1955. Dulles, who was ill again, and Eisenhower himself were reluctant to agree to a conference without assurances of good faith on Khrushchev's part. The two meetings of the foreign ministers accomplished little, but when Eisenhower invited Khrushchev to visit the United States, the Soviet Premier quickly accepted.

Khrushchev flew to Washington in September 1959. At the United Nations he extolled the virtues of disarmament and then took a widely publicized thirteen-day tour of the country. After a two-day conference with Eisenhower at Camp David, Maryland, the two leaders announced that they had agreed to discuss major problems, including Berlin and the German peace settlement, and that the President would visit Russia the following spring. Later, a summit meeting was planned for May 16, 1960, in Paris, to precede Eisenhower's trip to Russia.

THE U-2 INCIDENT

By spring the so-called "spirit of Camp David" was dead; both the United States and the Soviet Union had reverted to rather inflexible positions on the German peace settlement. Then, on the eve of the summit meeting — May 5 — Khrushchev dramatically announced that an American U-2 had been shot down 1,500 miles inside Russian territory and the pilot captured. In a diplomatic debacle, the United States at first denied that the plane had been spying; but when Khrushchev produced both the film from the plane and the pilot, Francis Gary Powers, Secretary Christian Herter, Dulles' successor, compounded the confusion by admitting that reconnaissance flights had in fact been taking place for some time!

President Eisenhower intervened at this point and took full responsibility; he stopped further U-2 flights before leaving for the summit meeting. In Paris, Khrushchev sharply attacked Eisenhower for the incident and left the meeting abruptly. The President not only did not visit the Soviet Union, but so unfavorable was the climate of world opinion, he was also forced to cancel a trip to Japan. Khrushchev returned to New York shortly after to harangue the United Nations, which refused to brand the United States an aggressor. But his boorish behavior there alienated some of his friends and helped dissipate part of the hostility toward the United States that the incident had aroused.

THE NEW PRESIDENT AND HIS SECRETARY OF STATE

The new President of the United States in 1961 was a forty-three-year-old Democratic senator from Massachusetts, John F. Kennedy. He won a narrow victory over Richard M. Nixon, Eisenhower's Vice-President. Both had waged strenuous campaigns that stressed internationalism and differed only slightly in details. Kennedy, who was from a wealthy family long active in politics, seemed to have a charisma for younger Americans. Energetically, if not too successfully, he embarked on an ambitious domestic program that he called the New Frontier.

Soon after his election, Kennedy appointed as Secretary of State a former diplomat, Dean Rusk. During the Korean War Rusk had risen to the rank of Assistant Secretary of State for Far Eastern Affairs. He was very much a partisan of the Kennan containment thesis and consistently supported this position throughout his long tenure in office, which only ended in 1968.

THE COMMON MARKET AND THE BALANCE OF PAYMENTS

One of the foreign policy goals embraced by both Kennedy and Rusk was a West European economic union. They hoped that economic union would lead eventually to political union. Should this happen, they were prepared to offer full partnership to such a union in what Kennedy termed the Grand Design. This hope was premature, but the European countries did prove that they could cooperate economically; in 1957 the Treaty of Rome saw the beginning of the European Economic Community (EEC). Its members were France, Italy, West Germany, Belgium, the Netherlands, and Luxembourg. The pact provided for a common tariff, a customs union, and the free flow of capital among participating nations; the Common Market began to function in late 1958 and achieved solid economic gains. Within a decade intracountry trade had more than tripled and total trade had doubled. All other economic indicators pointed to real gains in the standard of living, except possibly in Italy.

Great Britain would not join the Common Market because of its special trade arrangements with the countries comprising the British Commonwealth. Instead, Britain organized a group of countries into the looser European Free Trade Association (EFTA) at the end of 1959. However, the success of the Common Market overshadowed the more modest gains of EFTA. In 1961, to Kennedy's delight, Great Britain applied for admission to the Common Market. Britain had negotiated for sixteen months with the EEC when de Gaulle announced in January 1963 that he would veto the application. Four years later Britain applied again, only to have the same thing happen in late November 1967. However, after de Gaulle's fall from power in 1968, observers felt that Britain would be admitted on a third try.

The Common Market soon began affecting the United States by causing a dollar deficit that grew yearly. Dollars were being paid out to EEC countries in military assistance, foreign investments, services, and other items, all of which were converted into gold, causing a serious gold drain from the United States. By the end of the 1960's the average annual deficit for the decade amounted to $2 billion. Sharp cuts in overseas spending plus insistence that Europe assume some of the foreign aid burden helped, but by 1970 the dollar gap and the gold drain still constituted serious problems.

The Common Market also affected the United States with regard to tariffs. The competition of Common Market-produced goods forced President Kennedy to ask Congress for a replacement of the Reciprocal Trade Agreement Act of 1934, which had been renewed eleven times and was again due to expire. The Trade Expansion Act, passed in October 1962, gave the chief executive sweeping authority to negotiate tariffs to meet European competition. Thus began the so-called Kennedy Round, a series of negotiations on tariff concessions that lasted until 1967 and went into effect the following year.

Less important, but widely heralded at the time, was the Common Market's creation of the European Atomic Energy Commission (EURATOM), planned as a common research and development effort in the use of atomic power. EURATOM proved a disappointment because France refused to permit effective leadership to be exercised over French plans.

BERLIN AND THE BUILDING OF THE WALL

While the United States tried to encourage a united Europe, it also worked for German reunification. Khrushchev refused to deal with Eisenhower after the U-2 affair, but he did not show the same reluctance to meet with President Kennedy. In June 1961 the two men met in Vienna for a seemingly harmonious conference; but Khrushchev delivered a warning on Berlin with a six-months' proviso stating that if the Allies did not agree on a German peace treaty, the Soviets would negotiate one with East Germany. The United States refused unequivocally to give West Berlin to Khrushchev — which would place it under East German control following a peace treaty — and reiterated its pledge to guarantee the freedom of West Berlin. President Kennedy, after reporting the difficulties to the American people and to Congress, received from Congress the funds necessary to move 45,000 troops to Europe.

The uncertain situation resulted in a mass exodus of East Berliners to the West, which by early August 1961 reached a level of 2,000 per day. On August 13, without warning, the Communists began sealing the border between East and West Berlin. They erected a wall twenty-eight miles in length, that effectively choked off the crossings. The United States protested, but the wall remained. In October, Khrushchev withdrew his six-months' deadline, but Soviet planes then began to harass other planes flying the air corridor to Berlin. This continued for a few months and then stopped unaccountably. Tension eased between the two countries from that time until the fall of 1962, when the Cuban missile crisis (discussed in the next chapter) produced a near-war that gave pause to both nations.

THE NUCLEAR TEST BAN TREATY AND ITS CONSEQUENCES

The idea of disarmament and the banning of nuclear weapons had long interested the United Nations as well as individual countries. President Eisenhower had assigned a diplomat with sub-cabinet rank to work on disarmament, but various obstacles always stood in the way of progress. The Soviets, for their part, first insisted that all foreign troops be repatriated, which would have forced the United States to withdraw its troops from Europe. Americans, on the other hand, demanded some form of on-site inspection to ensure that weapons so designated were destroyed, but the Soviets rejected this demand. After the Cuban missile crisis, when Khrushchev agreed to serious talk about a nuclear test ban treaty, both sides shelved their objections. Khrushchev's willingness to negotiate was based on the growing friction between Russia and Communist China, which was reported close to successful detonation of an atomic bomb.

The foreign ministers of the United States, the USSR, and Great Britain — the three nuclear powers — met in Moscow in 1963. On August 5 they agreed to a treaty that banned nuclear testing in the atmosphere, under water, and in outer space — places where detection could be made without the necessity of on-site inspection. Underground tests were not included because they were more difficult to monitor; later, both the United States and Russia made use of this loophole. The Senate promptly approved the treaty and President Kennedy ratified it on October 7. Most other nations also signed, the three exceptions being Communist China, France, and Cuba. The first two countries continued testing, France having joined the nuclear power ranks in February 1960, while China's first successful detonation was in October 1964. Both nations exploded hydrogen bombs in 1967.

After the initial treaty two others were negotiated in the 1960's. The first provided for the peaceful use of outer space and was signed on January 27, 1967, by the original three nuclear powers plus fifty-seven other countries. In April the Senate unanimously approved the treaty. On July 4, 1968, the United States, the USSR, and Great Britain signed a United Nations-inspired nonproliferation pact binding the signatories not to supply atomic weapons to countries not already possessing them. President Johnson hailed this treaty as a great gain for world peace.

Talks also continued on other aspects of disarmament. The development of the intercontinental ballistic missile with a nuclear warhead that could strike targets thousands of miles away made such talks especially urgent. However, not until April 1970 did specific discussions begin on missiles; the Strategic Arms Limitation Talks (SALT) opened in Vienna. At about the same time the Chinese orbited their first satellite, demonstrating that they too were acquiring sophisticated nuclear capability.

DE GAULLE AND THE UNITED STATES

While there were several disagreements and policy differences among America's allies, these did not assume significance before 1958 when General Charles de Gaulle became France's head of state. For the next decade his leadership was firmly imprinted on the countries of Western Europe as well as on France. De Gaulle pursued a historic policy of attempting to make France the dominant power in Europe outside of Russia. To this end, he developed France's nuclear capability, at the expense of Kennedy's plan for a multilateral nuclear force (MLF) to be placed at the disposal of the NATO countries jointly. At the same time, de Gaulle charted as independent a course as was possible, given France's commitments to NATO and the Common Market. In twice vetoing England's bid to enter the Common Market, de Gaulle put the French fear of British competition ahead of the benefits that would otherwise have accrued to all the member countries. To solidify his continental position, he signed treaties with both West Germany and the USSR.

The United States was de Gaulle's target even more than was Britain. He early rejected the Anglo-American control of NATO forces that denied France an equal voice. To emphasize his demands he began forcing NATO nuclear weapons out of France. In 1962 de Gaulle settled the Algerian revolt, greatly increasing France's internal stability and prosperity. By 1967 France had forced NATO headquarters to move to Belgium, although by then NATO had long since outlived its usefulness. Thus, through the 1960's, the United States discovered that an ally such as de Gaulle could be almost as much of a problem as Russia.

However, the de Gaulle era ended abruptly early in 1969. First, the French franc, stable for a decade, was weakened by the stronger German mark, forcing de Gaulle to devalue it. Then a wave of student and worker demonstrations in May 1968 forced the government to hold elections the next year, on which the general staked his political future. Repudiated at the polls, de Gaulle retired, turning over the government to men of like mind but less ability. With his departure and a change of administration in Washington, the future appeared to promise less French truculence and greater cooperation within NATO and the Common Market.

De Gaulle was not NATO's only trouble in the 1960's. Successive conferences managed to save the defense concept, but there was increasing likelihood that the United States would cut its troop and dollar commitments, as Canada did in 1970. Also, the members of NATO were so hamstrung by mutual pledges that when a coup brought a military dictatorship to power in Greece in 1967, the organization disapproved but could do little else. The United States faced the same problem but elected to continue its economic and military assistance to the new Greek government.

THE MIDDLE EAST IN THE 1960's

After the withdrawal of American troops from Lebanon in October 1958, the United States continued to support anti-Communist factions in the face of rising pro-Communist Arab nationalism. Nasser continued to lead the attack on the United States for its support and recognition of Israel, but American oil interests remained almost intact until 1967. Arab hostility toward Israel, fueled by Soviet arms, was supported by a new generation of Arab refugees who had come of age in the United Nations camps. They became the backbone of the growing and more effective guerrilla forces that struck Israel in hit-and-run raids.

By spring 1967 Nasser felt that his army was strong enough to overrun Israel. At his insistence, the United Nations peace-keeping force withdrew from the Sinai peninsula. Nasser then closed the Gulf of Aqaba, limiting Israel's access to its back-door port of Elath. On June 5 the Israelis suddenly launched a simultaneous attack on Egypt, Syria, and Jordan. In six days the Israelis destroyed the Egyptian air force, overran the Sinai peninsula, captured the Jordanian part of Jerusalem, and gained the valuable Golan heights in Syria overlooking Israel's northern border. The Suez Canal was again blocked, but this time it did not reopen, thus cutting off an important source of revenue for Nasser. Otherwise, the canal's importance for oil shipments to Europe had declined; gigantic tankers, too large for the canal, could now round the Cape of Good Hope for less money than it cost older tankers to negotiate the canal. After the Six Days' War the Israelis refused to withdraw from the occupied areas unless Nasser agreed to negotiate directly, but this he would not do. The USSR again began rearming Egypt. France reversed its policy of friendship for Israel, forcing the United States to continue its attempts to accomplish its own paradoxical objectives while trying to keep peace in the area.

Other Arab states continued to line up, not for or against Communism, as the United States thought they would, but for or against Nasser. Hardly a year passed without a crisis directly attributable to Nasser's influence. For instance, in September 1969 the pro-Western monarch of oil-rich Libya was ousted by a group of army officers who gave every indication of supporting Nasser.

SOVIET PROBLEMS WITH CZECHOSLOVAKIA AND CHINA

Following a series of poor harvests and ideological difficulties with China, Khrushchev was ousted in October 1964, to be succeeded by the team of Aleksei Kosygin as Premier and Leonid Brezhnev as First Party Secretary. Symptomatic of the changed atmosphere in Russia since Stalin's time, Khrushchev merely retired to his country home near Moscow.

Similarly, when Czechoslovakia attempted to liberalize as had Hungary earlier, though the Soviets did not hesitate to move in an army and take over the country in August 1968, the Czech leaders were only removed from office; few were arrested and none was executed. Nevertheless, the liberal regime was effectively purged and replaced by one subservient to Moscow. The United States protested Soviet action, but the Russians claimed the Czechs had asked them to intervene.

Although Russia was able to keep up its diplomatic pressure in the Middle East and in parts of Europe, it had considerable trouble with its former ally China. In 1958 the two leading Communist countries began to air their ideological differences. Historically, the two countries had been at odds over Mongolia and certain northern ports on the China Sea. A series of border clashes reached large-scale proportions in the winter of 1969. Accordingly, the Soviets were forced to moderate their pressure on the West, at least temporarily. Such a respite, while only that, gave the West Germans a chance to attack obliquely the problem of reunification. By early 1970 the West German chancellor had visited his East German counterpart, and an exchange of recognition seemed to be only a matter of time. Although the subject of reunification was not mentioned specifically, both leaders have at least kept the possibility alive.

A quarter of a century of United States foreign policy helped transform Western Europe from a starving and war-torn land into a healthy and rehabilitated competitor. As of the 1970's, the future of NATO, of the Common Market, or of a European political union was, for better or for worse, no longer in America's hands.

Further Reading

Add *Charles L. Robertson, *International Politics Since World War II: A Short History* (New York, 1966) to the diplomatic surveys by Paul Y. Hammond and Walter La Feber. Ronald Steel, *Pax Americana,* cited at the end of the last chapter also discusses this period.

As regards the Middle East, *Robert Engler, *The Politics of Oil* (Chicago, 1967) and *John S. Badeau, *American Approach to the Arab World* (New York, 1968) are useful.

However, for events there since 1955 the student would do better to consult *The New York Times* and weekly newsmagazines.

The literature on atomic warfare with all of its ramifications is vast. Two books which should begin this study are Herman Kahn, *On Thermonuclear War,* 2nd ed. (Princeton, N.J., 1961) and *Henry A. Kissinger, *Nuclear Weapons and Foreign Policy,* abr. ed. (New York, 1969).

Again memoirs are particularly helpful, especially *Dwight D. Eisenhower, *White House Years: Waging Peace, 1956-1961* (New York, 1965). Also see those by Charles W. Thayer, Sherman Adams, and Theodore Sorensen. A biography of John Foster Dulles is important for the period.

Asterisk denotes paperback edition.

20

The United States and Latin America:
Old Fears and New Concerns

The euphoria that characterized most of the Latin American countries' economically profitable relations with the United States during the war culminated in the Act of Chapultepec in 1945. But within a few years this feeling had nearly disappeared, a victim of America's preoccupation with the European demands of the Cold War. In the immediate postwar world comparatively little attention was paid to neighborliness within the Western Hemisphere. The dollar surpluses accumulated by selling raw materials to the United States were quickly dissipated and led to a Latin American demand for a hemispheric Marshall Plan.

THE LAND AND ITS PEOPLE

Much of the estranged attitude toward the Colossus of the North could be ascribed to a basic lack of communication between North and South Americans. Life styles within Latin America also contrasted markedly among the twenty republics so that mutual understanding was difficult. For example, while eighteen of the twenty republics were Spanish-speaking, hundreds of Indian dialects were spoken throughout the continent too. Only in Argentina, Brazil, Uruguay, and Mexico was there a middle class of any size. The gulf between the upper classes, whose basis of wealth was land ownership, and the poor was more characteristic of feudal Europe than it was of the twentieth century. In 1950 it was estimated that 60 percent of the land was owned by 10 percent of the people. From figures gathered after 1965, a random statistic such as the percentage of illiterates over the age of ten ranges from 13 percent in Argentina to 89 percent in Haiti as compared to 2 or 3 percent in the United States and Canada. One author has pointed out that according to recent figures, the average student in the United States spends about nine years in school, while his Latin American counterpart spends only about two!

THE RIO PACT AND THE ORGANIZATION OF AMERICAN STATES

The United States response to Latin American problems was not the equivalent of a Marshall Plan, but rather a hemispheric defense system along the lines of NATO. In 1947 this was brought into being by implementing the Act of Chapultepec. American delay had, in part, been due to the abortive attempt to oust Perón in Argentina. But after Perón's convincing victory in a free election in February 1946, the United States reluctantly accepted his government. A conference of Latin American states, including Argentina and the United States but not Canada, met in September 1947 outside Rio de Janeiro and there signed the first regional pact under the provisions of Article 51 of the Charter of the United Nations. This pact, called the Inter-American Treaty of Reciprocal Assistance, is better known as the Rio Pact. It required a two-thirds vote of the signatories, binding on all members, to combat an attack, but no member would be forced to use its armed services without its consent. President Truman considered the treaty so important that he flew to Rio to address the conference. He suggested a loan of $500 million from the Export-Import Bank in lieu of a Marshall Plan, an offer the delegates accepted only reluctantly. The United States Senate speedily approved the Rio Pact, which became the model for other regional alliances.

The following year at Bogotá, Colombia, the same countries, meeting at the Ninth International Conference of American States, created a permanent organization to carry out the terms of the treaty. This was the Organization of American States (OAS), of which the previously existing Pan American Union became the permanent secretariat. Another provision was that within the organization each country was to be allowed but one vote. OAS differed from NATO in that it was as much concerned with settling quarrels among its members as in dealing with external threats.

The OAS began operating in December 1951, but by the time of its first major test in 1954 it had neither materially improved living standards nor helped spread democracy. Continued military assistance tended rather to support dictators or to encourage military cliques. By 1954 there were in all thirteen military-type governments in Latin America. Nevertheless, American military assistance was put on a regular basis by Congress beginning in 1951. By 1954 a total of $882 million had been provided. The total was not indicative of the distribution of the money; for example, Brazil, especially friendly to the United States, received $228 million, while Argentina, dominated by Perón, received only $41 million.

GUATEMALA AND THE OAS

The OAS received its first test in 1954 with Guatemala. This Central American republic had elected as President three years earlier a Communist sympathizer, Colonel Jacobo Arbenz Guzmán. At first not overly concerned about Guatemala, the Eisenhower administration nevertheless made several attempts to get the OAS to adopt a stringent anti-Communist statement. But as the other members were lukewarm, American efforts were only minimally successful. In 1953 the President sent his brother, Milton Eisenhower, a noted educator, on a goodwill trip to Central America. Mr. Eisenhower's report stressed the need for immediate economic assistance to these countries.

The Guatemalan crisis began when the State Department demanded that Arbenz pay for lands confiscated from the powerful, American-owned United Fruit Company. Arbenz, having neither the money nor the inclination to meet American demands, refused to submit the problem to the United Nations Court of Arbitration in the Netherlands. In March 1954 Secretary Dulles brought the issue to the OAS at the Tenth Inter-American Conference in Caracas, Venezuela. Dulles finally won a strong anti-Communist measure by a 17-1 vote, which he used as a yardstick for judging the Guatemalan situation. But at best the victory was only partial; Mexico and Argentina both abstained, and even the delegates who voted for the measure privately expressed sympathy for Guatemala.

In May the crisis escalated when Guatemala received a shipment of 1,900 tons of military weapons from Czechoslovakia. The United States reacted — in fact overreacted — by hurriedly signing individual defense pacts with Nicaragua and Honduras and by airlifting military supplies to them. Further, the American Ambassador to Guatemala plotted openly against Arbenz. When an army trained by the CIA in Honduras invaded Guatemala in July, the ambassador aided it, using the embassy as a command post! Arbenz was overthrown, another man unsuccessfully sought to take his place, and finally Colonel Carlos Castillo Armas, leader of the American-backed troops, became head of the government.

The diplomatic importance of this rather minor foray cannot be overemphasized. At one stroke the goodwill that the United States had attempted to nurture in Latin America after 1934 disappeared. It marked the first time in twenty years — although there have been two occasions since — that the United States took unilateral action involving the internal affairs of a hemispheric country. This act led to renewal of the old fears of the Colossus of the North and marked a return of Yankeephobia. A more tragic effect was that the incident polarized the political situation in Guatemala; left-wing forces reorganized into guerrilla bands, some of which have operated continuously from that time until the present.

At about the same time, the Soviets attempted to take advantage of

American inattention to the area by negotiating a series of trade agreements. By 1955 they had eighteen, and Latin American trade with Russia rose sharply just at the moment when American exporters were beginning to feel the competition from Japan in foreign markets.

Nevertheless, during the next few years, political events in Latin America seemed to favor the United States. In 1955 Perón was deposed, to be followed by a military junta. In 1957 Castillo Armas was assassinated, but his successor, Miguel Ydígoras Fuentes, was also strongly anti-Communist. He worked closely with the United States, which continued to pour in large amounts of economic aid.

THE APEX OF YANKEEPHOBIA

These events proved illusory; for when President Eisenhower sent Vice-President Richard M. Nixon on a goodwill tour of eight South American countries in 1958, the result was anything but good neighborliness. Beginning with his hostile reception by the people of Montevideo in April, Nixon received frightening proof of the United States' deteriorating relations with Latin America. At subsequent stops Nixon and his wife were subjected to angry mobs who threw stones and eggs and shouted uncomplimentary remarks. In Lima, Peru, and again in Caracas, Venezuela, where the tour ended, the Vice-President's safety was imperiled. President Eisenhower airlifted a thousand troops to Caribbean bases to protect Nixon, but by then the Vice-President had already left for the United States. The event was important because, despite Secretary Dulles' avowals that due attention had been paid to the area, the remainder of the government acted as if it had not. First, Milton Eisenhower made a three-week tour of Central America in July; then, the next month, Dulles flew to Rio de Janeiro to confer about a conference of foreign ministers scheduled to be held in Washington in September 1958.

The Washington conference acted on a proposal submitted by President Juscelino Kubitschek of Brazil to set up a long-range hemispheric development plan. At first cool toward the project, President Eisenhower by 1958 strongly supported it. The plan called for the formation of an Inter-American Developmental Bank to provide low-interest, long-term loans to member countries. The United States subscribed $1 billion to the bank, which began operation in December 1959. As a full-fledged member, the United States thus reversed the policy it had followed since 1945 of unilaterally aiding Latin American countries to develop economically and plan social welfare projects. The policy of cooperative planning and assistance was reiterated at a meeting in Bogotá, Colombia, in September 1960, where a group of experts developed a plan for social and economic advancement to be financed by the bank as well as by the United States. The Act of Bogotá marked the beginning of a tardy hemispheric type of Marshall Plan — for which Congress later appropriated a paltry $500 million.

CUBA, CASTRO, AND THE UNITED STATES

Another reason for the marked change in American policy toward Latin America was the dramatic new situation in Cuba. Long an economic fief of the United States, Cuba had endured two dictators since the abrogation of the Platt Amendment in 1934. Finally, in June 1959, Fidel Castro, the leader of a guerrilla force that had once been reduced to a handful of men, overthrew and drove into exile the second of the two dictators, Fulgencio Batista. Trained as a lawyer, Castro was a charismatic leader who promised the Cubans a thoroughgoing social revolution. Initially he received wide support from Cubans in business and the professions; he was also a popular figure among Americans, for he had often been interviewed by the press and appeared on American television. The United States recognized his regime, but diplomats were soon dismayed by his actions. Castro began by executing Batista henchmen with great celerity. Next he nationalized industries — including an American oil facility — and expropriated property — usually American-owned sugar plantations. The American business and governmental community began to voice anti-Castro feelings, suggesting that he was a Communist. At that date this was highly unlikely. Castro, however, was a revolutionary socialist without a firm ideology, who was subsequently pushed into the waiting grasp of the Soviets. By late 1959 Castro was vociferously anti-American; he concluded a $100 million trade credit agreement with Russia the next year. The Soviets also contracted for some Cuban sugar, but at a lower price than that paid by the United States for what it purchased. The quantity bought by the United States was fixed by Congress so as to protect American sugar producers, but although it enriched the American-owned plantations, it had resulted in little gain for the Cuban workers. Cubans therefore found it easy to believe Castro when he told them that the United States was a threat to the revolution. In July 1960 Congress embargoed Cuban sugar, and Castro informed the United Nations that America was guilty of "economic aggression." He was supported by Premier Khrushchev, who offered Cuba military protection.

Cuba quickly became a totalitarian state; Communists, led by Argentine-born Ernesto "Che" Guevara, were Castro's closest advisers. Hundreds and then thousands of Cubans fled to Miami, Florida, landing with little but their lives. Most of the refugees were from the middle and upper classes, so that with their departure Castro was able to consolidate the most complete revolution Latin America had seen since Mexico's, which had taken some three decades to reach fruition.

Meanwhile, the United States was in the midst of a presidential election campaign. Republican Richard M. Nixon and Democrat John F. Kennedy both denounced the Castro regime, now steadily drawing nearer the Soviet orbit. Castro recognized Communist China and, defying the OAS, accepted Khrushchev's offer of protection. Kennedy's election was generally applauded in Latin America because he had called for a new policy in the area. Castro, however, reacted by demanding — even before Kennedy's inauguration in January 1961 — that the United States reduce its embassy staff in Havana from 130 to 11 within forty-eight hours. President Eisenhower thereupon broke off diplomatic relations with Cuba and President Kennedy did nothing to restore them after he took office.

PRESIDENT KENNEDY AND THE BAY OF PIGS

The new President inherited from the outgoing administration a program by which Cuban exiles were being helped to plan an invasion of their homeland. Castro publicly complained to the United Nations about the refugee camps in which the training was taking place, but nothing was done. Kennedy, acting on faulty advice, rejected his own negative inclinations and allowed the training to continue and the invasion to be mounted. On April 17, 1961, some 1,443 anti-Castro Cubans — armed, trained, and transported by the United States — landed at the Bay of Pigs on the

"PASS THE HAT!"

Americans reacted bitterly to the Bay of Pigs and its aftermath.

southern side of central Cuba. Castro was well prepared; the landing force was killed or captured within three days. The expected uprisings, of which the CIA and others had assured the President, never occurred, partly because of quick action by the Communists and partly because of the unpreparedness of the clandestine groups that remained in Cuba.

When the facts about the unilateral action became known, American prestige was seriously damaged in Latin America. In the face of the often violent anti-American demonstrations there, President Kennedy accepted full responsibility for the affair. Castro made the most of the episode, charging the United States with aggression. Nevertheless, Secretary of State Dean Rusk refused to have any dealings with Castro, labeling his government as Communist. An expensive footnote occurred when the President allowed private negotiations with Castro for the release of the 1,100 captives, for whom a ransom of $53 million in food and medical supplies was paid by private donations.

THE BEGINNING OF THE ALLIANCE FOR PROGRESS

During the two years before the Bay of Pigs fiasco, the State Department, under Dulles' successor Christian Herter, made a strong beginning in a hemispheric aid program with the Inter-American Developmental Bank. In addition, President Eisenhower made a goodwill trip to the southern countries of Latin America in February 1960. In his turn, President Kennedy made a dramatic and popular gesture on March 13, 1961, when he unveiled before Latin American diplomats his *alianza para el progreso,* the Alliance for Progress. This program was modeled after Eisenhower's but considerably expanded. It envisioned great social and economic accomplishments in the 1960's and constituted a positive response to the export of Fidelista, Castro's brand of socialism. Later in the year, financial and other experts met at Punta del Este, Uruguay, and signed into being a genuine Latin American Marshall Plan. In exchange for $20 billion from the United States over the next decade, the Latin American republics, except Cuba, committed themselves to fundamental social and economic changes, including land reform and the restructuring of inequitable tax laws. The OAS was to serve as a clearing house for the coordination and development of long-range plans submitted by each country. The foreign ministers met again at Punta del Este in January 1962 to approve and implement the pacts. However, a portent boding ill for the future was their refusal to agree on a strong executive body to direct and guide the plan. At the same meeting, on the urging of the United States, Cuba was formally ousted from the OAS by a large vote; but Argentina, Brazil, Bolivia, Chile, Ecuador, and Mexico all abstained.

PREAMBLE TO THE ALLIANCE FOR PROGRESS CHARTER, 1961

We, the American republics, hereby proclaim our decision to unite in a common effort to bring our people accelerated economic progress and broader social justice within the framework of personal dignity and political liberty.

Almost two hundred years ago we began in this Hemisphere the long struggle for freedom which now inspires people in all parts of the world. Today, in ancient lands, men moved to hope by the revolutions of our young nations search for liberty. Now we must give a new meaning to that revolutionary heritage. For America stands at a turning point in history. The men and women of our Hemisphere are reaching for the better life which today's skills have placed within their grasp. They are determined for themselves and their children to have decent and ever-more-abundant lives, to gain access to knowledge and equal opportunity for all, to end those conditions which benefit the few at the expense of the needs and dignity of the many. It is our inescapable task to fulfill these just desires — to demonstrate to the poor and forsaken of our countries, and of all lands, that the creative powers of free men hold the key to their progress and to the progress of future generations. And our certainty of ultimate success rests not alone on our faith in ourselves and in our nations but on the indomitable spirit of free man which has been the heritage of American civilization.

Inspired by these principles, and by the principles of Operation Pan America and the Act of Bogotá, the American republics hereby resolve to adopt the following program of action to establish and carry forward an Alliance for Progress.

THE PEACE CORPS AND LATIN AMERICA

Somewhat more altruistic was Kennedy's concept of a Peace Corps. During the election campaign he had proposed sending skilled young Americans to underdeveloped countries to work on small-scale projects ranging from teaching and nursing to farming and carpentry. Achieving almost immediate success, the Peace Corps proved especially effective in Latin America and in parts of Africa. In fact, nearly half of the total enrolees (about 18,000 by 1970) were sent to Latin American countries (with the exception of Argentina, Cuba, Haiti, Mexico, and Nicaragua). By the end of its first decade of operation, Peace Corps volunteers were serving in over fifty countries throughout the world.

THE MISSILE CRISIS

After the Bay of Pigs affair Castro kept up a barrage of propaganda to the effect that the United States was once more about to invade Cuba. To prevent this, he built up and armed the second largest army in the hemisphere. But in the process, and while trying to bolster Cuba's lagging economy, Castro became almost completely dependent on Soviet aid. At this juncture — the summer of 1962 — occurred one of the strangest and most dangerous episodes of the twentieth century. Khrushchev began furnishing Cuba with atomic missiles and technical experts to build launching sites for the intermediate range (up to 2,200 miles) weapons. He made this decision in order to counteract recent Soviet frustrations in Europe as well as to capitalize on an unparalleled opportunity to embarrass the United States diplomatically; he hoped thereby to gain concessions relating to American nuclear armament in Europe. Early in the summer a New York congressman charged that the Soviets were shipping nuclear rockets to Cuba. Then, on September 4 President Kennedy warned that he would not permit the installation of intercontinental missiles in Cuba. The Russians disclaimed any such intentions but continued meanwhile to send Cuba the weapons and the technicians to set them up. On September 24 Congress, agreeing with the President, passed a resolution authorizing the use of all necessary means to block the expansion of Fidelista.

By October 14 proof of Soviet duplicity had been gathered in the form of photographs showing a missile launch pad under construction. Between that date and October 22, when he revealed the situation to Americans on television, Kennedy held innumerable conferences with advisers ranging from the NSC to Dean Acheson. Kennedy decided, he told the television audience, to "regard any nuclear missile launched from Cuba as an attack by the Soviet Union on the United States, requiring a full retaliatory response upon the Soviet Union." He imposed a blockade on military equipment being shipped to Cuba, coupling this with an appeal to Khrushchev to remove the missiles under United Nations supervision. The next day Kennedy gained unanimous approval from the OAS for his actions. On October 24, the blockade, which Kennedy called a "quarantine," forced two Soviet ships to stop and remain where they were.

During the next few days, as messages went back and forth between Kennedy and Khrushchev, much of the world literally held its breath. The United Nations asked both sides to suspend action pending negotiations. Both sides agreed, but Kennedy insisted on continuing the blockade pending removal of the launching sites. At this point, Khrushchev backed down, indicating that the missiles would be removed. Kennedy, for his part, pledged not to invade Cuba and to lift the blockade when the United

Nations verified by an inspection that the weapons had been removed. The Soviets thereupon dismantled the missiles and sailed away, escorted by American naval vessels.

Castro was left out in the cold by Khrushchev's action; he reacted by refusing to allow on-site inspection by the United Nations, which enabled the United States to declare later that the bargain had not been kept. The Soviet-United States confrontation restored American prestige throughout the world, especially in Latin America. And it provided statesmen and politicians with a close and terrifying look at atomic brinkmanship. At any rate, both Kennedy and Khrushchev were sufficiently sobered by the episode to install a "hot line" to ensure rapid communication between the two leaders. Not entirely coincidentally, a new thaw began in the Cold War; in August 1963 a partial atomic test ban treaty was signed by the United States, Russia, and Great Britain.

THE UNITED STATES AND MEXICO

A discussion of recent United States foreign policy in Latin America would be incomplete without mention of the steady growth of respect between Mexico and the United States. When President and Mrs. Kennedy visited Mexico in the summer of the missile crisis, they were greeted by unprecedentedly large and enthusiastic crowds. The same spirit prevailed when the presidents of the two countries reached an accord on the division of Colorado River water, an issue that had been debated but unresolved for many years. Mexico, however, has continued an independent foreign policy course. Its relations with Castro, disapproved of by the OAS, have made diplomatic intercourse between Latin America and Castro on such matters as airplane hijacking measurably easier.

While Mexico has maintained and even strengthened its democratic outlook, other hemispheric nations have seen their democracy eroded. The rise of military dictatorships throughout Latin America has been steady; by 1970 fewer than five nations enjoyed democratically elected governments.

PANAMA AND THE DOMINICAN REPUBLIC

One reason for the failure of democratic regimes in Latin America was the stress engendered, especially among conservative groups, by Fidelista, which by the mid-1960's seemed a real threat. Venezuela and Bolivia both complained about the smuggling of Cuban arms and leaders to guerrilla forces operating in the interior.

The United States established a counterinsurgency training school in the

Canal Zone, and by 1966 was training OAS contingents. Unexpectedly, in the Republic of Panama surrounding the Canal Zone, trouble erupted in January 1964. Historically, the United States had sought to ensure the stability of the country by training its constabulary and by maintaining a large American military force in the Canal Zone. A riot broke out in Panama City, ostensibly over a flag incident but actually because of resentment against American residents whose standard of living made the Panamanians feel like second-class citizens. The rioting was quelled, but Panama demanded control over the Canal Zone and a larger share of profits from and control over the canal. President Lyndon B. Johnson, Kennedy's successor, was basically in accord with these demands, but he delayed negotiations until tempers had cooled and Panama had elected a new president. In 1965 and 1967 three pacts incorporating concessions to the Panamanians were negotiated. However, before the pacts were submitted to the Senate for what would probably have been major changes, they were shelved by Panama as unsatisfactory. Since then the situation has remained highly charged.

In the Dominican Republic one of the longest-lasting dictators in Latin America, Rafael Trujillo, absolute ruler since 1930, was assassinated in May 1961. When his family attempted to continue the regime, the United States blocked them. In company with the OAS the United States set up a shaky provisional government to govern the 3,300,000 Dominicans, who were among the poorest in per capita income in the hemisphere. In December 1962 the electorate chose President Juan Bosch, a leftist leader with great personal appeal but less governmental ability. But after eight months Bosch was overthrown by an army coup, the United States having refused to aid him.

Unstable government continued as army leaders contested for power, and a popular election was scheduled for June 1965. In April rioting broke out between pro-Bosch followers and the military. Within four days the military seemed to have the upper hand and casualties numbered in the thousands. The American Ambassador asked for military intervention both to protect American lives and to forestall what he considered to be a Castro-type revolt. President Johnson, reluctantly at first, flew in several hundred troops, later increasing the number to nearly 25,000. He still insisted that "people trained outside the Dominican Republic are trying to gain control." Thus, for the third time since the end of World War II, the United States intervened unilaterally in the internal affairs of a Latin American country.

At the same time, the administration enunciated the Johnson Doctrine, which stated that no Communist government other than Cuba's would be tolerated in the Western Hemisphere. But though the House approved the doctrine, the Senate did not, thus further weakening the OAS. American troops in the Dominican Republic were soon replaced in part by those of other countries and an Inter-American Peace Force set up. In June 1966 a new election was held under OAS supervision. When a Trujillo lieutenant, Joaquín Balaguer, was elected, the Peace Force gradually withdrew, leaving an impoverished country with a legacy of distrust toward the United States.

NEW NATIONS, NEW PROBLEMS, AND NEW HOPE

Rising nationalism and a growing sense of frustration among the impoverished unleashed new forces in Latin America. Fidelista has not been successfully exported, although well-organized guerrilla forces did fight against the governments of Venezuela and Bolivia. In Bolivia Che Guevara personally led the rebels, but American-trained troops pursued and finally captured him on October 7, 1967. Che was executed the following day; nevertheless, the end is not in sight. Many left-wing groups plot revolt throughout Latin America. Besides murder and sabotage, a favorite weapon has been the hijacking and flying of planes to Cuba. By the late 1960's, the Castro government, under international pressure, began to discourage these acts. Terrorist groups then returned to the old ploy of kidnapping envoys — including Americans — and holding them as hostages in exchange for political prisoners or for ransom.

Another aspect of rising nationalism is apparent in the new Latin American nations that have emerged from the British Empire, including Jamaica, Guyana (British Guiana), and Trinidad. They are plagued by the same problems that face their Latin American neighbors. They too exist on the edge of dire poverty while struggling to build democratic societies.

The United States has attempted by the Alliance for Progress to restructure, reform, and rebuild Latin American society. The result, a decade later, has been a dismal failure to raise living standards or to ameliorate social injustice. Nevertheless, the Alliance for Progress and the Peace Corps have brought at least hope for the future. The alternative would be Fidelista or something comparable, and that the United States cannot allow to happen.

Further Reading

American relations with Latin America are covered in the surveys by Paul Y. Hammond and Walter La Feber recommended earlier. An excellent book treating only this topic is Donald M. Dozer, *Are We Good Neighbors?: Three Decades of International Relations, 1930-1960* (Gainesville, Fla., 1961). See also *Bryce Wood, *The Making of the Good Neighbor Policy,* cited at the end of Chapter 15. Appraisals and evaluations of American policies in the 1950's and early 1960's are in Milton S. Eisenhower, *The Wine Is Bitter: The United States and Latin America* (Garden City, N.Y., 1963) and *Arthur M. Schlesinger, Jr., *A Thousand Days* (New York, 1967).

The Cuban missile crisis is chillingly recalled by a participant, the late Robert F. Kennedy, in

Thirteen Days (New York, 1969). A recent review of the Alliance for Progress after almost a decade is Jerome Levinson and Juan de Onis, *The Alliance That Lost Its Way: A Critical Report on the Alliance for Progress* (Chicago, 1970). Memoirs by Earl E. T. Smith and John B. Martin are helpful. Do not overlook the coverage in *The New York Times* which has been both comprehensive and perceptive.

Asterisk denotes paperback edition.

21

American Policy in Africa and Asia:
The Problems of Leadership

The United States has played an ever-increasing role over the past twenty years in parts of both Africa and Asia. These areas have been the scene of ideological conflicts that have resulted in wars, internal revolutions and uprisings, and a host of other related economic and social problems.

THE UNITED STATES AND UNKNOWN AFRICA

While the American public's general knowledge of Africa is based upon much misinformation, fostered by literature and later by movies and television, official State Department knowledge, while fuller, is still sadly deficient in terms of the complexities of the continent. Historically, in spite of its large minority of black Americans, the United States maintained only sporadic and slight contacts with Africa. Even Liberia, founded as a haven for freed slaves in 1822 and emerging as a nation in 1847, did not have a regular and continuous pattern of trade and contact with the United States. Diplomatically, the State Department extablished some trade and consular posts in the early nineteenth century. In the middle of the century other posts were located in the interior of Africa to protect American missionaries and other interests.

It was not until 1937 that the State Department extablished a Bureau of African Affairs, and not until 1949 that an assistant secretary was designated to head an enlarged Bureau of Near Eastern, South Asian, and African Affairs. Even after public attention had turned toward Africa following the independence of the Sudan, Morocco, and Tunisia in 1956 and of Ghana in 1957, the department still maintained more foreign service officers in West Germany than in all Africa!

AFRICA AND THE AFRICAN PEOPLE

Most of the generalizations applied to South America are even more true of Africa. There is a greater diversity of languages — according to one expert, "between one and two thousand different languages — most of them *very* different." Statistics cited in 1965 placed the per capita income for the 200,000,000 inhabitants of the continent at $120 a year. But in some parts of Africa this figure was as low as $40, while in South Africa in reached $1,380 for whites. Health standards are low — one out of every five African children dies of disease. The literacy rate of the continent is also low; not only are about 85 percent of the African people illiterate but there is a crucial lack of trained people in all fields, including government.

AFRICAN FREEDOM AND INDEPENDENCE

In the 1950's many parts of Africa seemed far from nationhood. Yet there were local leaders, often more anticolonial than nationalist, who began to organize for independence. After Morocco and Tunisia were reluctantly freed by France in 1956, the number of independent states mushroomed. By 1970 there were forty-two. United States foreign policy has for the most part consisted of attempting to counteract Soviet ideology through a minimal amount of economic aid. American governmental aid averaged about $500 million per year in the 1960's, less than a quarter of the total foreign

THE PEACE CORPS IN GHANA, 1961

investment there. Far more productive in terms of foreign policy has been the work of the Peace Corps. Although corpsmen in certain African countries, such as Ghana in 1966, have become political pawns, they are the exceptions. The second largest contingent of Peace Corps volunteers, some 5,000, have gone to Africa, where they have had extraordinary success in such fields as secondary education. They have had much to do with giving the United States a broader outlook than it would have acquired diplomatically.

American private investment has lagged except in a few areas. For example, Liberia had always attracted some capital; but since the mid-1950's United States oil companies have invested over $1 billion in Libya. South Africa, too, has garnered a large percentage of the total American investment. However, for the continent as a whole, American private industry's stake (1961-1967 inclusive) was $2.7 billion, one fourth of its investment in South America. The continuing pattern appears to be a smaller proportional investment in Africa, the continent with the most acute needs and probably the greatest potential. One of the chief factors inhibiting further investment has been the governmental instability of the new nations. As a matter of fact, the Soviets and the Chinese — both Communist and Nationalist — have experienced the same problem. This was well illustrated by the two major African crises of the 1960's — involving the Congo and Nigeria.

THE UNITED STATES AND THE CONGO

The Congo, a vast and richly endowed central African country inhabited by 14,000,000 people of varying languages and tribes, was a Belgian colony for over half a century. The Belgians exploited the Congo's mineral and other resources and operated a tightly controlled paternalistic colonial administration. On the eve of independence in the late 1950's there were fewer than 15,000 Congolese enrolled in secondary schools and only a handful who had completed a university education. Nevertheless, the Belgians quickly acceded to the demand for independence, in the expectation of retaining their economic influence and of becoming the power behind the untrained Congolese. Independence was proclaimed on June 30, 1960, but a week later the Congolese army mutinied and the new government was unable to restore order. Belgian paratroopers, a symbol of repression to the Congolese, were flown in to stop the killing and looting. The United Nations responded to an appeal from the Congo government, replacing the Belgians with a peace-keeping force. The Congo was further divided by the secession of Katanga, the wealthiest of the six provinces.

Backed by the Belgians, with suspected United States collusion, this area set up a strong anti-Communist government under Moise Tshombe. With good reason, the Tshombe government was accused of complicity in the murder of the single most popular national hero, Patrice Lumumba, who was pro-Soviet. Katanga employed a mercenary army, much of it white, and enjoyed initial success against the central government. However, the United States publicly supported the United Nations peace-keeping force, and by 1964 the rebellion had been crushed and Tshombe exiled. As soon as the United Nations forces left in June 1964 other uprisings in other provinces occurred, often with Communist Chinese or Soviet backing.

CLEARANCES AND THE STATE DEPARTMENT, 1961

From G. Mennen Williams, *Africa for the Africans*
(Used by permission Wm. B. Eerdmans Publishing Co.)

In the State Department, I quickly learned what clearances meant. Because the Congo crisis affected Belgium, the European Bureau cleared our decisions. Because it affected the UN, so did the Bureau of International Organization Affairs. As the Congo required special intelligence, the Bureau of Intelligence and Research and, to a lesser degree, the Central Intelligence Agency, both had to help. The Public Affairs Bureau, the USIA and the Bureau of Congressional Relations all had a hand in the clearance procedure. The Congo entailed long-term as well as short-term problems, so the State Department's Policy Planning Staff and the White House, among others, advised us of their policies. The Defense Department and the Agency for International Development were involved, too. And, of course, the American and foreign press and the Congress had a strong interest in what we did, although they played no role in the clearance process.

For the second time, the central government was unable to control the situation, but this time it called back Moise Tshombe from exile to become prime minister. Other African nations angrily accused the United States of duplicity in Tshombe's return, but the State Department appeared surprised and discomfited. The revolt spread, and Tshombe's old mercenary army aided the rebels and ended the possibility of help from other African states. The rebels soon captured Stanleyville, endangering the lives of some 2,000 people — mostly white — of many nationalities. To prevent a massacre, the United States ferried in the same Belgian paratroopers who had been there in 1960. Although some people had already been murdered, most were saved, and the West hailed the good-samaritan efforts of the troops. But to Africans the episode represented just another example of imperialist intervention, and the image of both Belgium and the United States was worsened. Afterwards, Tshombe recaptured most of the territory held by the rebels and eventually ended the revolt, Within a few months he was deposed, to be succeeded in November 1965 by General Joseph Mobutu. Since then, a somewhat repressive and uneasy peace has returned to the Congo.

The results of the United States' attempts to support Congolese unity have been mostly negative. On the debit side were a bill for $400 million for the peace-keeping operations, a wary acceptance of economic aid by the current military ruling group, and the hostility — somewhat dissipated by time — of surrounding African nations, particularly the Sudan and Tanzania.

THE UNITED STATES AND NIGERIA

Of all the countries in Africa that have recently gained their independence, Nigeria, with a population of nearly 60,000,000, was believed to have the best potential for success. Long a British colony, Nigeria had developed a local bureaucracy comparable to that of pre-World War II India. Education and living standards were high compared to those of neighboring countries. Yet it was here that the major African problem of tribalism — long imperfectly understood by Americans — arose in spectacular and horrifying fashion. The Nigerians who were the best educated and who held the best government positions were usually members of the Ibo peoples from eastern Nigeria. By 1966 they had spread everywhere, even to the northern part of the country where they came into conflict with the Yoruba peoples, many of whom were Moslems. Late in the year an uprising began in the north with the avowed intention of forcing the Ibos out of the area. Thousands were massacred, and a civil war resulted when the eastern region seceded and set up a republic called Biafra.

The United States worked with the British and the United Nations in an effort to bring about a cease-fire. Nominally supporting the central government under the military regime of northerner General Yakubu Gowon, the United States supplied neither military assistance nor advisers. The Biafrans, led by General Olumegwu Ojukwu, were aided by mercenary troops and by clandestine help from France. Both sides fought hard in the bloody three-year struggle during which it was estimated that over 1,000,000 Ibos were killed or died of war-related causes. By early 1970 the rebels had been defeated and mass starvation was only averted by large-scale assistance from the United States, the United Nations, and private relief agencies.

The Ibos, guaranteed amnesty by the central government, gradually returned to the mainstream of Nigerian life. Only a few leaders, including the exiled General Ojukwu, were punished. As American private investments in Nigerian oil and other resources are increasing and are expected to become substantial in the next several decades, the maintenance of good relations remains an important part of the United States' African policy.

THE UNITED STATES AND SOUTH AFRICA

Another kind of problem is illustrated by the United States' dealings with South Africa. This republic of 19,000,000 people is composed of about 3,500,000 whites, 13,000,000 blacks, and 2,500,000 Indians and other Asians. Although South Africa is the wealthiest African country, the per capita income of its black citizens is only $162 a year — roughly one eighth that of the whites. American investments are considerable there in spite of the official governmental policy of apartheid, a rigorous form of segregation and discrimination. This policy became especially restrictive after 1960, when 67 unarmed blacks were killed and 200 wounded at the town of Sharpeville. The provocation was slight; the Anglican bishop reported that over 70 percent of the victims had been shot in the back. Since then, apartheid measures directed against blacks and Asians have further restricted housing, freedom of movement and work, and the right to vote.

The United States, along with the United Nations, has attempted to ameliorate the problem without sacrificing good relations with the South African government. In 1967, when the American carrier *Independence* called at Capetown, South African officials tried to restrict shore leave to whites. The visit was thereupon canceled, as was that of the *Enterprise*, also due to call. Repeated incidents in which visas were denied to black athletes led the Olympic Games commission to ban the 1968 South African team. Regardless of this and of the hostility of some nearby African states, prospects for a change in South African policy during the 1970's seem remote.

THE UNITED STATES' ASIAN ALLY: JAPAN

Since regaining its sovereignty in the early 1950's, Japan has successfully and democratically used its technology and skilled labor potential to raise the standard of living and well-being of its citizens. The United States still plays a major role in Japan's economy even though military assistance has sharply decreased. More important, the United States acts as Japan's best customer, buying over 25 percent of its total exports. The Japanese also capitalized on their insignificant defense expenditures during the 1950's to develop their heavy industry, which has been a major factor in their prosperity. By 1970 Japan was exceeded only by the United States, the USSR, and West Germany as an industrial producer. Symbolic of the development of all facets of Japanese life was Japan's successful sponsorship in 1970 of the first world's fair ever to be held in Asia.

Although the United States and Japan maintain excellent relations, there have been differences. A series of conservative older leaders in Japan have generally been unsympathetic toward Japanese youth, many of whom are militantly pacifist. This pacifist attitude has caused large-scale protests and riots whenever American nuclear submarines have visited Japan. Another and more serious problem was the debate over the Ryukyu Islands. At the end of the 1960's the Japanese government insisted that the United States return the islands, which had long been considered part of the Japanese homeland. After a series of conferences, Premier Eisaku Sato conferred with President Nixon in Washington and in November 1969 signed a pact providing for the restoration of the Ryukyus to Japan by 1972.

With one exception, there is every reason to believe that Japan, while pursuing its own interests, will remain a staunch friend of the United States. The exception is the increasing Japanese disapproval of the continued American presence in Indochina.

COMMUNIST CHINA, TAIWAN, AND NORTH KOREA

The years since 1955 have witnessed the awesome rise of Communist China, first as a nuclear power, then as a possessor of intercontinental missile capability. China's rise has been matched by an intransigence in foreign affairs that has, among other things, transformed the USSR from an ally into an occasional enemy. The same rigidity has prevented those Western countries that have recognized the Communist regime from doing more than a minimal amount of trading with it. After Geneva, the United States held periodic informal talks with China, first in Geneva and later, between 1965 and 1968, in Warsaw. As far as the United States was concerned, such talks constituted an attempt to soften its own rather inflexible position. In 1961 a high State Department official, with President Kennedy's blessing, gave a conciliatory speech in which he stated that the State Department realized that Communist China existed! However, Communist China's aid to neighboring countries that have been at war with the United States, combined with the problem of what to do about Chiang — still considered the official representative of China in the eyes of the State Department — have merely reinforced the situation that has existed since Mao came to power in 1949.

Chiang Kai-shek's control of Taiwan has resulted in economic gains and prosperity for this Asian country second only to Japan's. But it has also meant a continued large American investment in military assistance and the maintenance of a major fleet in the area. The Nationalists have played little part in the struggle for Asia, but, most surprisingly, they have achieved moderate success in giving technical assistance to certain new African nations, where they have effectively countered the much larger programs undertaken by the Communist Chinese.

KOREA AND THE RESULT OF NON-VICTORY

When the Korean War ended in 1953 with an uneasy truce, South Korea was in ruins. For the remainder of the decade the United States poured economic aid and military assistance into the country — $1.9 billion worth by 1960. In 1960 the autocratic Rhee was ousted. He was succeeded by a military junta led by General Chung Hee Park who, adopting some trappings of democracy, was elected president in 1963 and reelected in 1967 and 1971. The South Korean army developed the capacity to defend itself and eventually sent about 50,000 troops to fight in South Vietnam.

North Korea, with less than half the population and fewer resources than the south, received large amounts of aid from both the USSR and Communist China but still lagged far behind South Korea. Nevertheless, it kept up unceasing propaganda and continued trying to infiltrate agents across the truce line. The armistice talks continued at Panmunjom but they became ritualized and accomplished nothing. Suddenly, on January 23, 1968, the North Koreans captured a United States intelligence ship, the U.S.S. *Pueblo,* which had entered North Korean territorial waters. The American public reacted with indignation, demanding that the crew and the ship be recovered, forciby if necessary. The Johnson administration, surfeited with difficulties in Vietnam, chose instead to negotiate for their release. After eleven months the men were freed but the ship was not. The North Koreans had mistreated the *Pueblo* captives, obtaining confessions which they then used for propaganda purposes. Nevertheless, the tone of the official American reaction contributed to the men's release and offered the slight possibility that some day meaningful negotiations might take place with the North Korean government.

INDONESIA AND THE PHILIPPINES

Both Indonesia and the Philippines reflected some of the problems of the new Asian states. The Philippines' dynamic President Ramón Magsaysay died in 1957, and his leadership has not so far been equaled. Nationalism grew comparatively slowly among the 35,000,000 Filipinos, but by the mid-1960's was expressing itself in demands for the end of American extraterritoriality and influence. In 1966 President Ferdinand E. Marcos visited the United States and negotiated a pact which reduced the United States lease on Philippine bases from 99 to 25 years. It also called for an increase in economic aid and military assistance. The Philippine government sent a contingent of engineering troops to Vietnam, but they became the source of so much internal political bickering that they were withdrawn in the late 1960's. In any case, the Philippines have remained a close ally and a firm supporter of SEATO.

In the years following the Bandung Conference, Indonesia experienced major economic difficulties. President Sukarno was at first successful in playing off the Cold War belligerents against each other, but by 1964 he had committed his government to the overthrow of Malaysia and was sending raiding parties into Borneo and putting the country on a war footing. Inflation had become rampant by the time Indonesia withdrew from the United Nations in January 1965. During that year anti-American demonstrations reached a crescendo. On September 30, 1965, the large, well-organized Communist party attempted a coup. The army reacted, in one of the bloodiest episodes in recent history, by killing over 250,000 Communists and their sympathizers. The army eventually deposed Sukarno, ended the war with Malaysia, and brought Indonesia back into the United Nations. The United States again tendered economic aid and military assistance. Although the government has thus far kept the internal peace, this nation of about 120,000,000 people is so divided by geography, culture, language, and religion that its future as a nation-state, at least in its present form, is still subject to reasonable doubt.

INDIA, PAKISTAN, AND THE UNITED STATES

The relationship of India and Pakistan with each other and with the United States changed little between 1955 and October 1962. Then, during the Cuban missile crisis, the Communist Chinese suddenly launched an invasion through India's northern outposts, overwhelming the Indian army. In response to an urgent request for assistance, American war material was airlifted to India. Unaccountably, the Chinese ceased fire and withdrew a month later, leaving almost as rapidly as they had come. They left India more friendly to the United States, but Pakistan vigorously protested the American aid and threatened to withdraw from CENTO. In September 1965 India and Pakistan once more began to fight over Kashmir, this time using American weapons. The United Nations Security Council imposed a cease-fire several weeks later, but it remained for the Soviet Premier,

Aleksei Kosygin, in January 1966, to work out a mutual withdrawal from the disputed territory. Since then both countries have been too preoccupied with internal political problems to renew the struggle; both have continued to receive American economic and military aid.

In the late 1960's Pakistan began suffering social upheavals, especially in East Pakistan, which led in March 1969 to the fall of the government of General Ayub Khan, who had been in office since October 1958. He was succeeded by another military leader.

In India, Nehru had died in 1964, but his successor governed less than two years. He in turn was succeeded by Nehru's daughter, Mrs. Indira Gandhi (no relation to Mahatma Gandhi). After an internal party struggle and one election, Mrs. Gandhi by 1970 emerged as undisputed leader of the country.

VIETNAM, LOAS, AND CAMBODIA: THE BEGINNING OF AMERICAN INVOLVEMENT

In 1955 the United States seemed to have little choice but to continue its economic and military assistance to Ngo Dinh Diem, the ruler of South Vietnam. Diem announced that the elections scheduled to take place in 1956, as provided by the Geneva Accords, would not be held because of the unlikelihood of a fair election in Vietnam. At the time, Secretary Dulles supported this position. In Laos and Cambodia there were also nationalist movements that were anti-French and pro-Communist. Most important was the Pathet Lao in Laos, which in the late 1950's seemed capable of overrunning the country. American aid bolstered a local anti-Communist army, which nevertheless was able to hold only the major centers of population. The Viet Minh in North Vietnam and also the Viet Cong, the South Vietnamese antigovernment forces, both used Laos and Cambodia as supply routes and staging areas.

By 1961 America's increased involvement in the area with the use of military advisers was a factor that served to shatter the shaky truce in Laos, and again the Pathet Lao seemed poised to take over the whole country. The Thais made an urgent request to President Kennedy, fearing an invasion by the Pathet Lao into Thailand. Kennedy ordered the Seventh Fleet into the area and began landing American combat troops in Thailand in May 1962.

At the same time, the signatories to the Geneva Accords had reassembled in Geneva in mid-1961 to debate the possibility of neutralizing Laos. This was finally accomplished in June 1962 and the Laotian crisis receded. But the future of Laos, with its internal divisions and vulnerable geographical location, did not appear bright.

A similar picture obtained in Cambodia, which was also receiving American aid. In 1963 it espoused neutrality — without benefit of a Geneva

AMERICA AND SOUTHEAST ASIA

President John F. Kennedy and Secretary of State Dean Rusk discuss the situation in Laos, April 1961.

conference — and its colorful ruler, Prince Norodom Sihanouk, proceeded to play first one side and then the other. Caught in the middle of the ideological Cold War, Sihanouk's nation was also flanked by the Vietnamese on one side and by the Thais on the other, both historical antagonists. In May 1965 he broke off diplomatic relations with the United States because of its increasing involvement in Vietnam, but reversed his position four years later.

When Kennedy became President in 1961, he began to accelerate military assistance to Diem. Diem had by then become so unpopular with his people that he was a liability to the American military advisers, whose advice he disregarded. For the most part, Diem represented a small Catholic land-owning upper class and not the bulk of the people, who were farmers owning or renting small plots of land. Adding to Diem's difficulties were the conglomerate peoples and languages in the country. Although most of the South Vietnamese were not pro-Communist, neither were they pro-Diem. To cite one example of the incredible complexity of the situation, the Montagnards, culturally less advanced people who live in the mountains,

Map 14. Vietnam and Southeast Asia

represent no more than 500,000 in a total population of nearly 17,000,000. Yet the Montagnards themselves are divided into more than two dozen tribal nations, each with its own language, not to mention a variety of dialects. This heterogeneity is common in Indochina and historically has made for divisiveness rather than unity. In addition, both the Laotians and the Cambodians have long resented the Vietnamese, who in the past have often conquered them or controlled them economically.

In this complicated and unstable situation, President Kennedy's military advisers reported that for Diem to survive, massive American technical and military aid would have to be committed. Therefore, by the summer of 1962 there were 8,000 American servicemen in Vietnam acting as advisers to or as helicopter pilots for the South Vietnamese army (ARVN). By the end of 1963 the total had more than doubled, and Americans were now suffering battle casualties as well as the loss of planes. In November 1963, the same month President Kennedy was assassinated, Diem was overthrown, a victim of Buddhist uprisings that had come in retaliation for his hostility toward them. Diem was murdered and a military junta took over. The government was unstable for the next two years while the members of the junta jockeyed for position. Eventually, Nguyen Van Thieu became President, since which time he has governed autocratically while simultaneously maintaining a facade of democratic institutions.

President Johnson, Kennedy's successor, had earlier made a fact-finding trip to Vietnam, after which he had urged increased American participation. However, upon becoming President he did not significantly alter the American contribution until after the 1964 election. He was opposed by the conservative Republican Senator Barry J. Goldwater, who demanded a United States victory in Vietnam.

In early August 1964 an American destroyer was attacked by North Vietnamese torpedo boats in the Gulf of Tonkin, off the coast of North Vietnam. President Johnson thereupon asked Congress for authority to repulse an armed attack in the area. Congress overwhelmingly passed the Gulf of Tonkin Resolution on August 7, 1964; the circumstances were reminiscent of those in which the Formosa Straits Resolution had been passed in 1955 at the request of President Eisenhower.

VIETNAM AND THE AMERICAN PUBLIC

President Johnson easily won the election. By the beginning of 1965 he stepped up air raids against the North, describing them as retaliatory. American bombing also killed civilians and destroyed nonmilitary targets, causing world opinion even among NATO members to become hostile. Beginning in March, American troops were committed for the purpose of gaining a clear-cut military victory over the elusive Viet Cong. The addition of thousands, then of tens of thousands, and finally of a half-million troops still did not produce the victory that the President had promised was close at hand. The news media talked of a "credibility gap" between what was said about Vietnam and what was actually happening. Dissension within the United States, vocal by 1965, now divided the American people as no other issue within memory had done. Those supporting the war were termed "hawks," those opposing it, "doves." Worse still was the angry rhetoric and increasing tempo of demonstrations, particularly by young people, that personified the growing American frustration at the inability to end the war.

For over three years the Johnson administration escalated the war, until by August 1968 the United States had sent 541,000 men to Vietnam. The tonnage of American bombs dropped on North Vietnam exceeded the total for World War II. On two occasions, President Johnson halted the bombing briefly, hoping that the Viet Cong and the North Vietnamese would negotiate, but to no avail. On the contrary, after a series of optimistic reports in early 1968, the United States forces in Vietnam were struck by the enemy during Tet, the lunar New Year holiday. The North Vietnamese and the Viet Cong captured and temporarily held several major Vietnamese cities before the Americans successfully counterattacked. The psychological impact on the American public was devastating.

First, a little-known Democratic senator from Minnesota, Eugene McCarthy, who was opposing Johnson in the primaries as a peace candidate, saw his popularity burgeon. Using little money, but with the support of enthusiastic college students, McCarthy soon became a serious candidate. Next, Senator Robert Kennedy, brother of the late President, also entered the primaries as an antiwar candidate. Finally, on March 31,1968, President Johnson announced to the nation that he would not seek reelection but would devote his energies to ending the Vietnam struggle.

In May the North Vietnamese agreed to hold preliminary peace talks in Paris, after which Johnson ended the bombing of the North in November 1968. The talks soon turned into routine propaganda exercises, however, and after more than two years there was still little progress.

By the time Richard M. Nixon was elected President in November 1968 the number of American dead in Vietnam had risen to over 29,000 and the financial cost to more than $25 billion. By July 1970 the personnel figures had passed 430,000. Unable to win the war decisively and realizing the increasing division of opinion among Americans, President Nixon announced a policy of "Vietnamization," that is, of gradually turning the fighting over to the ARVN. He coupled this with an announcement of troop withdrawals, which by May 1970 amounted to about 110,000 men.

On the other hand, the President may well have escalated the war by authorizing an invasion of Cambodia in April 1970 to strike at the Viet Cong sanctuaries. Nixon's decision alienated a much larger segment of American youth, who reacted with large demonstrations. His decision also caused consternation within the State Department and among America's NATO allies. The military action was thereupon quickly brought to a close and by the end of June 1970 all American troops, though not the Vietnamese, had left Cambodia. A pro-American military junta had already overthrown Prince Sihanouk in March 1970 and was immediately recognized by the United States.

The final word on Vietnam has yet to be written. The American goal of military victory has long since faded; the prospect of a complete Vietnamization of the conflict seems equally remote. The United States military operation will probably be slowly phased out of Vietnam after a long and painful struggle. In any event, the American presence in Asia, whether in Taiwan, the Philippines, or Thailand, certainly will last long beyond the present decade, with the ever present possibility — perhaps "threat" is a better word — of another Korea or another Vietnam.

Further Reading

Refer to Paul Y. Hammond as well as Robert Engler, *The Politics of Oil,* noted at the end of Chapter 19.

Few books exist on American diplomacy in Africa. Two by diplomats who served there are William Attwood, *The Reds and the Blacks* (New York, 1967) and G. Mennen Williams, *Africa for the Africans* (Grand Rapids, Mich., 1969), although they leave much of that vast continent uncovered.

In contrast, the literature relating to American involvement in Asia is large and continues to grow rapidly. Unfortunately most of the books are dated within a short time. Three pertinent titles are Robert Shaplen, *Road from War: Vietnam 1965-1970* (New York, 1970) and *Time Out of Hand: Revolution and Reaction in Southeast Asia* (New York, 1969), also by Robert Shaplen; and Robert Thompson, *No Exit from Vietnam* (New York, 1970). For reflections on American policy by a noted senator see *J. William Fulbright, *The Arrogance of Power* (New York, 1967). Again, resort to *The New York Times* for the best available coverage of both Africa and Asia.

Asterisk denotes paperback edition.

Epilogue: Today and Tomorrow

In preference to pronouncements or prognostications regarding United States foreign policy, it might be more instructive to review recent relations with one of America's closest neighbors and best friends, Canada. Such a survey would indicate some of the problems and one or two of the pitfalls that American foreign policy and diplomacy have had since 1945. One must add the disclaimer that obviously a whole range of ideological, military, and economic problems are excluded; also, that relations with a nation having only one tenth the population of the United States, a geography slightly larger, but other factors which are comparable have resulted in unique circumstances.

World War II fundamentally altered relations between the two countries. In 1940 a Permanent Joint Board on Defense was established by FDR and Canadian Prime Minister William Lyon Mackenzie King. Throughout the war the two countries worked together closely, developing several joint boards committed to the defense of the hemisphere. While American-Canadian cooperation continued at the war's end, the hope that Canada would become a member of the OAS did not materialize.

Insofar as the United States was concerned, the problem of defense was the overriding consideration in its postwar relations. By 1950 the two countries had developed a joint radar system entirely in Canada, just north of the border, and in 1953 they added a second system 500 miles to the north. A third network, established in 1955, was the Distant Early Warning System (DEW), located near Canada's northern boundary. DEW was financed, built, and at first operated by the United States. Thus, for the first fifteen years after the war the Joint Chiefs of Staff had far more to say about relations with Canada than did the State Department.

While Canada generally supported American foreign policy, it began to take an independent line during the 1960's. Canada has acted as a leading middle-power country in helping to make the United Nations General Assembly more effective. At the same time, on such issues as the recognition of Communist China and American involvement in Indochina, Canada has pursued its own course. As the most powerful and wealthiest of Britain's dominions, Canada has become, if not a senior trading partner with the mother country, at least an equal.

But Canada's domestic economy is in large part a captive of the United States. American capital began replacing British capital in Canada as early as 1930 and reached $5 billion by the end of the war. Since then this figure has more than quadrupled, causing Canadians to say that Americans own 95 percent of the auto industry, 92 percent of the rubber industry, 80 percent of the chemical industry, 70 percent of the oil, gas and electrical industries, as well as 52 percent of the mining and 43 percent of the pulp and paper industries. Such domination, taken with the sharp rise in Canadian nationalism — fostered partly by the centennial celebration of Canada's nationhood in 1967 — has caused a flurry of anti-Americanism and the beginning of discriminatory legislation to lessen economic ties. In 1970, when the United States sent an oil tanker through the Arctic Sea north of Canada to test the feasibility of shipping oil from Alaska, the official Canadian reaction was to put the route within Canadian territorial waters by declaring a hundred-mile water limit as Canada's northern boundary. All these problems must be dealt with by the State Department in the years to come.

Nevertheless, none of these issues will lead to adverse changes in the Canadian-American relationship. What could make a difference is the United States' continued lack of understanding of its northern neighbor and its particular problems. For instance, if Americans were really aware of the difficulties besetting the Canadian government and social structure, including bilingualism and federalism, then they would come to realize that there is and always has been a significant difference between the countries. This, in turn, could lead to a more diplomatic approach to a nation that the United States has long taken for granted.

President Harry S. Truman characterized the American attitude when he said that "we no longer think of each other as 'foreign countries' " but that "we think of each other as friends." The question is: What have the Canadians said about this lately?

Further Reading

The paucity of books and other information about Canada available in the United States makes reading about relations between the two countries difficult. Two books which are somewhat outdated but which have excellent background material make an excellent beginning: Hugh G. T. Aitken et al., *American Economic Impact on Canada* (Durham, N.C., 1959) and William R. Willoughby, *The St. Lawrence Waterway: A Study in Politics and Diplomacy* (Madison, Wisc., 1961).

Two more recent and recommended works are Gerald Clark, *Canada: Uneasy Neighbor* (New York, 1965) and Gerald M. Craig, *The United States and Canada* (Cambridge, Mass., 1968).

Index

Acheson, Dean, 273-74, 276, 282, 313
Adams, Brooks, 138
Adams, Charles Francis, 108-109, 111, 112, 116, 132
Adams, John, 4, 5, 12-13, 17, 25, 27, 36-37 and peace with England, 19-20, 23
Adams, John Quincy, 16, 53, 57, 59, 60-61, 65, 79
    Monroe Doctrine and, 62-63
Adee, Alvey A., 122, 199
Africa, 318-23
Agency for International Development (AID), 292
Aguinaldo, General Emilio, 147-48
Aix-la-Chapelle, Treaty of (1748), 2
Alabama (commerce raider), 111, 116-17, 132
Alaska, 62, 117-19, 177
Algeciras Conference (1906), 176
Alien and Sedition Acts (1798), 37
Allen, Horace N., 167
Alliance for Progress (1961), 311-12
Alliance of 1778, 14, 36, 37
Alsace-Lorraine, 191, 193
American Revolution, 9-23
Amiens, Peace of (1802), 42
Anglo-Japanese Alliance, 202, 203
Anti-Communism, 198, 273-74
Anti-imperialism; U.S. in Word War II and, 243-45
ANZUS Pact (1951), 279
Arbenz Guzmán, Colonel Jacobo, 307
Argentina, 64, 216-17, 234-35
Arms limitation, 201-206
Aroostook War (1839), 73-74
Arthur, Chester A., 136
Asia, 99-101, 130-31, 207, 323-32
Aswan Dam, 293-94
Atlantic Charter (1941), 233, 236-37
Attlee, Clement, 252, 266, 281

Atomic bomb, 245-46, 252, 257-58
Atomic Energy Commission, 258
Austria, 1, 13, 92, 223, 262-63
Austro-Hungarian Empire, 187, 191, 192
Ayub Khan, Mohammed, 327

Baghdad Pact (1955), 279, 288
Bagot, Charles, 58
Balaguer, Joaquín, 316
Balfour Declaration (1917), 244-45
Balkans, 180, 229, 251
Bancroft, Edward, 13-14
Bandung Conference (1955), 285-86
Barbary States, 39-40, 56-57
Baring, Alexander (Lord Ashburton), 44, 74-76
Barron, Commodore James, 47
Batista, Fulgencio, 309
Bay of Pigs invasion (1961), 310-11
Bayard, James A., 53
Beaumarchais, Pierre Augustin Caron de, 11-12
Beckwith, George, 31-32
Belgium, 190, 226
Bemis, Samuel F., 23
Beneš, Eduard, 223
Berlin Blockade (1948), 276
Berlin Wall (1961), 299-300
Bernstorff, Count Johann von, 184, 186
Beveridge, Albert J., 166
Biafra, 322-23
Bidlack's Treaty (1848), 94
Blaine, James G., 139
Blount, James H., 143
Bogotá, Act of (1959), 309
Bolívar, Simón, 65
Bolivia, 139, 316
Bonvouloir, Achard de, 11
Borah, William E., 195, 201-202, 206, 224
Bosch, Juan, 315

Boxer Rebellion (1900), 170-72
Brazil, 64, 210-11, 234-35
Brest-Litovsk, Treaty of (1918), 191
Brezhnev, Leonid, 303
Briand, Aristide, 205
Bricker, John W., 284
    Bricker Amendment (1953), 274
"Brinksmanship," 284
British Guiana, 141-42, 316
British North America Act (1867), 116
British West Indies, 69-70
Brussels, Pact (1948), 290
Bryan, William Jennings, 149, 174, 175,
    178, 180-81, 183, 190
Bryan-Chamorro Treaty (1914), 159, 161
Bucareli Agreements (1923), 211-12
Buchanan, James, 96, 101, 106
Bulgaria, 262-63
Bulloch, Captain James D., 111
Bunau-Varilla, Philippe, 155-56
Burke-Wadsworth Act (1940), 226
Burlingame, Anson, 103, 169
Burlingame Treaty of 1868 (China), 103,
    118
Burr, Aaron, 45
Burritt, Elihu, 78
Butler, Anthony, 71, 72
Byrnes, James F., 257, 262

Calhoun, John C., 49
California, 72, 87, 94, 130-31, 174, 207
Calles, Plutarco Elias, 211-12
Callières, François de, 2
Camacho, Manuel, 219
Cambodia, 266, 286, 327-32
Canada, 9-10, 19-20, 58, 98-99, 115-16,
    177, 333-34
    insurrection in (1837), 72-73
    fisheries accords with, 132-33
    pelagic sealing, 133
Canning, George, 48, 62, 64
Cárdenas, Lázaro, 218
Caribbean, 117, 159-61
Carleton, Guy (Lord Dorchester), 27, 31, 32
Carlisle Commission, 18
Carnegie, Andrew, 149
Caroline (steamboat), 72-73
Carranza, General Venustiano, 162-64, 187
Carroll, Charles, 9
Casablanca Conference (1943), 239
Castillo Armas, Colonel Carlos, 307-308
Castro, Cipriano, 158
Castro, Fidel, 309-11, 313-14
Cavell, Edith, 181
Central Intelligence Agency (CIA), 275,
    293, 307
Central Treaty Organization (CENTO), 279
Chamberlain, Neville, 223

Chambers, Whitaker, 273
Chapultepec, Act of (1945), 235, 305
Chase, Samuel, 9
Chesapeake affair, 46-47
Cheves, Langdon, 49
Chiang Kai-shek, General, 208, 223, 242-43,
    248, 264-65, 324-25
Chile, 64, 140, 234
China, 25, 77, 102-103, 130-31, 207, 259,
    284-85
    between the wars, 208-10
    Boxer Rebellion, 170-72
    Communists win control of, 264-65,
        324-25
    Japanese invasion of, 221-22
    Korean War and, 279-83
    Open Door policy, 169-70, 174-75
    Sino-Russian split, 303
    World War I and, 189-90
    World War II and, 242-43, 248
Chinese Exclusion Law (1882), 131
Choiseul, Étienne François, Duc de, 10-12
Chou En-lai, 280-81
Churchill, Winston, 227-28, 236-37, 239-40,
    248-51
Civil War; events leading up to, 94-104
Civil War diplomacy, 106-119
Clark, George Rogers, 35
Clay, Cassius, 108
Clay, Henry, 49, 53, 56, 57, 62, 64, 65
    as Presidential candidate, 81-82
Clayton, William L., 269
Clayton-Bulwer Treaty (1850), 94-95,
    126-27, 176
Clemenceau, Georges, 192
Cleveland, Grover, 122, 141, 143, 145
Cold War, 260-63
Colombia, 64, 94, 125, 155-57, 210
Comintern (1947), 271-72
Common Market, 298-99
Congo, 131, 320-22
Congress of Panama (1824), 65
Connolly, Tom, 247
Containment policies, 271-72
Convention of 1800 (Mortefontaine), 37
Convention of 1818, 58-59
Coolidge, Calvin, 200, 204, 211, 212
Costa Rica, 161
Coughlin, Father Charles E., 207
Cox, James, 196
Crampton, John, 98
Crawford, William, 49
Crittenden, W. L., 92
Cromwell, William Nelson, 155
Cuba, 91-92, 95-96, 124-25, 144-47,
    153-54, 216
    Castro and, 309-11, 313-14
Cushing, Caleb, 77, 102

Czechoslovakia, 193, 223, 224, 271, 303

Dana, Francis, 16
Danish West Indies, 186
Darlan, Jean, 238-39
Davis, Jefferson, 85, 95
Dawes Plan, 201
de Gaulle, Charles, 226, 239, 244, 298,
    301-302
Deane, Silas, 10, 11-12, 13, 15
Decatur, Commodore Stephen, 40, 56
Declaration of Independence, 12
Denmark, 70, 117, 226
Destroyer deal (1940), 227
Dewey, Admiral George, 147, 158
Dewey, Thomas E., 247, 276
Díaz, Porfirio, 161-62
Dickinson, John, 9
Diem, Ngo Dinh, 286, 327-30
Dien Bien Phu, 286
Dole, Sanford B., 143
"Dollar Diplomacy," 167-68, 175
Dominican Republic, 114, 117, 158,
    315-16
Drago Doctrine (1907), 158
Dubourg, Barbeu, 11
Dulles, John Foster, 283-84, 289-90,
    307-308
Dumbarton Oaks Conference (1944), 233,
    248
Dunkirk, 226
Dutch East Indies, 223, 236, 266

East Germany, 290
Eaton, William, 40
Eden, Sir Anthony, 294
Egan, Patrick, 140
Egypt, 175, 229, 244, 287, 293-94, 302
1812, War of, 48-54
Eisenhower, Dwight D., 238, 274, 282-83,
    289-91, 297, 308
Eisenhower, Milton, 307, 308
Eisenhower Doctrine (1957), 295-96
El Salvador, 161
Elgin, Lord (James Bruce), 98
Embargo Act (1807), 47-48
England, 2-3, 25-27, 30-32, 45-47, 98, 175
    American Revolution and, 9-23
    Anglo-American entente, 133-35, 176-77
    arms limitation and, 202-206
    China and, 169-70, 175
    Civil War and, 109-13, 115-17
    Egypt and, 175, 293-94
    Germany and, 262
    Japan and, 172, 202, 203
    Palestine and, 267
    Samoan Islands and, 128-30
    settlements with, 131-32

Seward and, 108-109
U.S. anti-imperialism and, 243-45
Van Buren and, 72-73
Venezuelan border dispute and, 141-42
West Indies trade settlement and, 69-70
World War I and, 180-97
World War II and, 225, 229
Erskine Agreement (1809), 48
Estonia, 226
Ethiopia, 220
European Coal and Steel Community,
    288-89
European Economic Community (EEC),
    298
European revolutions (1848), 92

Fillmore, Millard, 92
Finland, 226, 237, 262, 263
Fish, Hamilton, 123-24, 127, 132
Fisheries Accords (1877), 133
Fiske, John D., 137
Five-Power Treaty (1922), 202, 206
Florida, 41, 45, 49-51, 59-61
Floridablanca, Conde de, 16
Foreign Ministers Councils, 262-63
Foreign Service Act (1946), 268
Formosa Resolution (1955), 285
Foster, Augustus John, 49
Four-Power Treaty (1922), 203
Fourteen Points, 190-91
France, 1-3, 10-15, 23, 27, 191, 218
    Alliance of 1778, 14, 36, 37
    arms limitation and, 202-206
    French Revolution (1789), 5, 34-36
    Germany and, 260-63
    in Indonesia, 266, 286
    intervention in Mexico by (1864),
        114-15
    Jackson and, 70-71
    Latin America and, 62, 64
    Napoleon; Louisiana Purchase and, 41-43
    pre-World War I, 175-76
    recognition of the Confederacy and,
        110-13
    Suez crisis and, 293-94
    Treaty of Paris (1783), 20
    undeclared war (1798), 36-37
    World War II and, 225, 226
Franco, General Francisco, 220, 292
Franco-Prussian War (1870-1871), 132
Franklin, Benjamin, 4, 5, 9-12, 13-14, 17-20,
    23
Frémont, John C., 87
Fuchs, Klaus, 273
Fulbright, J. William, 246

Gadsden Purchase (1853), 97
Gallatin, Albert, 39, 44, 53, 56

Gandhi, Indira, 327
Gandhi, Mohandas, 244
Gardoqui, Don Diego de, 28
Garfield, James A., 139
Genêt, Edmond C., 35-36
Geneva Accords (1954), 286
Geneva Protocol (1924), 204
Gentlemen's Agreement (1908), 174, 207
Gérard, Count Conrad Alexandre, 14-15
Germany, 128-30, 141, 175-76, 223-24,
    260-63, 276
  fate of, at Yalta, 248-50
  Hitler, World War II, and, 220, 223,
    224-25, 235, 251
  reunification of, 290-91
  World War I and, 181-87, 189, 191-92,
    193
Gerry, Elbridge, 36
Ghent, Treaty of (1814), 52-54, 58
Giddings, Joshua R., 79
Giraud, General Henri H., 239
Gladstone, William E., 116, 132
Goering, Hermann, 263
Goldwater, Barry J., 330
Gompers, Samuel, 149
Gomulka, Wladyslaw, 293
Gowon, Yakubu, 322
Grant, Ulysses S., 117, 121, 124-25
Greece, 64, 229, 251, 268-69, 302
Greenland, 229
Grew, Joseph C., 230
Grey, Sir Edward, 182
Grotius, Hugo, 1-2
Grundy, Felix, 49
Guadalupe Hidalgo, Treaty of (1848),
    90-91, 97
Guam, 148, 189, 224, 235
Guano Act (1856), 99
Guatemala, 139, 161, 307-308
Guevara, Ernesto "Che," 309, 316

Hague Conferences (1899; 1907), 177-78
Haiti, 117, 124, 158-59, 211, 216
Hamilton, Alexander, 24, 29, 31-32, 36-37
Hammond, George, 31-32
Harding, Warren G., 196, 198-99, 202
Hare-Hawes-Cutting bill (1932), 222
Harriman, Edward H., 167, 175
Harris, Townsend, 101
Harris Treaty of 1858, 101
Harrison, Benjamin, 139, 140, 143
Harrison, William Henry, 49
Hartford Convention (1814), 52
Hartley, David, 20
Hatta, Mohammed, 285
Havana, Declaration of (1940), 218
Hawaiian Islands, 99, 117-18, 127, 142-43
Hawaiian Sugar Treaty (1875), 127

Hawley-Smoot Tariff (1930), 211, 215
Hay, John, 139, 169-70, 178
Hay-Bunau-Varilla Treaty (1904), 156
Hay-Pauncefote Treaty (1901), 154, 163
Hayes, Rutherford B., 125-26
Haymarket Riot (1886), 168
Hearn, Lafcadio, 130
Hearst, William Randolph, 144
Henry, Patrick, 26
Herter, Christian, 297
Hippisley, Alfred E., 170
Hirohito (Emperor of Japan), 231, 264
Hiroshima, 252
Hiss, Alger, 273
Hitler, Adolph, 220, 223, 224-25, 251
Ho Chi Minh, 286
Hoar, George F., 149
Honduras, 161, 211, 307
Hoover, Herbert, 204, 209, 211, 224
Hoover-Stimson Doctrine (1932), 209-10
Hopkins, Harry, 251
Hotze, Harry, 109
House, Edward M., 181-82, 190
Houston, Sam, 72, 82
Howe, Lord William, 18
Hotze, Harry, 109
Huerta, Victoriano, 162-63
Hughes, Charles Evans, 186, 196, 199, 202,
    203, 206
Hukbalahaps, 285
Hull, Cordell, 214, 215, 216-18, 223,
    230-31, 234, 245
Hungary, 92, 262-63, 292-93
Hunter, William, 107, 122
Hurley, Patrick J., 243, 265
Hussein (King of Jordan), 216

Iceland, 229
Ickes, Harold, 224
Immigration, 81, 122-23, 168-69, 198-99
Inchon, 280
India, 242-43, 266, 287, 326-27
Indochina, 230, 266, 286
Indonesia, 285-86, 326
Inter-American Conference (1889), 139-40
Iran, 244, 266, 288
Iraq, 244, 294-96
Iriye, Akira, 222
Ishii, Viscount Kikujiro, 190
Isolationism, 219-22, 224, 225-27
Israel, 267, 287, 294, 302
Isthmian Canal Act (1902), 155
Italy, 202, 204, 220, 239, 262-63
Izard, Ralph, 15-16

Jackson, Andrew, 52, 60-61, 65
Jackson, Francis J., 48
Jamaica, 316

Japan, 77, 99-101, 130-31, 133, 207, 225, 259
  California and, 174
  Far Eastern power politics and, 172-73
  Hawaii and, 143
  invasion of China by, 221-22
  MacArthur and, 264
  Manchuria and, 174-75, 208-10
  Philippines and, 223
  prosperity of, 323-24
  Samoan Islands and, 128-30
  School crisis and, 173-74
  Washington Naval Conference and, 201-204
  World War I and, 189-90
  World War II and, 230-32, 235-36, 240-42, 252
Japanese-American Treaty of Commerce and Navigation (1911), 223, 230
Japanese Peace Treaty (1951), 283
Jay, John, 5, 9, 16, 17, 19-20, 23-25, 29
Jay's Treaty (1794), 32-34
Jefferson, Thomas, 12, 19-20, 26, 27, 29, 31-32, 35
  Cuba and, 91
Jews, 223-24, 244-45
Johnson, Andrew, 118
Johnson, Hiram, 195
Johnson, Lyndon B., 300, 315, 330-31
Johnson, Reverdy, 116
Johnson, Richard M., 49, 57
Johnson-Clarendon Convention (1869), 116-17
Johnson Doctrine (1965), 315
Jones, Samuel Milton, 166
Jones, Thomas, 87
Jones Act (1916), 222
Jordan, 287-88, 296
Jordan, David Starr, 149
Juarez, Benito, 114-15

Kanagawa, Treaty of (1854), 101
Kansas-Nebraska Bill (1854), 95-96
Katsura, Count Taro, 173
Kearny, Stephen W., 87, 90
Kellogg, Frank B., 178, 194, 206, 212
Kellogg-Briand Pact (1928), 205-206
Kennan, George F., 268, 269, 271
Kennedy, John F., 297-99, 310-31, 327-30
Khrushchev, Nikita S., 296-97, 303, 313-14
Knowland, William F., 284
Knox, Philander, 167, 175
Konoye, Prince Fumimaro, 230-31
Korea, 118, 130, 173, 263-64, 325
Korean Treaty (1882), 130
Korean War, 279-83
Kosygin, Aleksei, 303, 327

Kubitschek, Juscelino, 308
Kurusu, Saburo, 231

Ladd, William, 78, 193
LaFollette, Robert, 166, 195
Lansing, Robert, 183, 184, 186
Lansing-Ishii Agreement (1917), 190
Laos, 266, 286, 327-32
Latin America, 61-62, 139-42, 153-65, 305-316
  American Navy in Caribbean and, 159-61
  between the wars, 210-11
  Central America, 161
  Congress of Panama, 65
  good neighbor policy, 215-18
  World War II and, 234-35
Lattimore, Owen, 274
Laurens, Henry, 17, 19-20
Lebanon, 244, 294-96
Ledyard, John, 41
Lee, Arthur, 10, 11, 13, 15
Lend-Lease (1941), 227-30, 260
Lenin, Vladimir Ilyich, 188-89
Lesseps, Ferdinand de, 125-27
Liliuokalani (Queen of Hawaii), 142-43
Lima, Declaration of (1938), 217
Lincoln, Abraham, 88, 101, 106, 108
Lincoln Brigade, 221
Livingston, Robert R., 42-43
Lloyd George, David, 192, 202
Locarno, 204-205
Lodge, Henry Cabot, 138, 149, 157, 193-97
Logan Act (1799), 37
Lôme, Dupuy de, 145
Long, Huey P., 207
López, Narciso, 91-92
Louisiana Purchase (1803), 42-43, 44-45
Ludlow, Louis, 221
Lumumba, Patrice, 321
Lusitania; sinking, 184

MacArthur, Douglas, 240, 264, 280-83
McCarran Internal Security Act (1950), 274
McCarthy, Joseph, 273, 283-84
Machiavelli, Niccolò, 1
McKinley, William J., 143, 144, 145-49
McKinley Tariff Act (1890), 139, 142
McLeod, Alexander, 73-74
Madero, Francisco, 162
Madison, James, 29, 32, 42, 48, 51, 52-53
Magsaysay, Ramón, 285, 325
Mahan, Alfred T., 137-38, 149
Maine (steamship), 145-47
Maine Boundary Settlement (1842), 74-75
Manchuria, 172-73, 174-75, 190, 208-210, 230, 264-65
Mao Tse-tung, 264-65
Marcy, William L., 95-96, 98, 102, 110

Marcy-Elgin Treaty (1854), 98-99, 115
Marshall, George C., 265, 268, 276
Marshall Plan (1947), 269-71
Matsuoka, Yosuke, 230
Maximilian (Emperor of Mexico), 114-15
Mexico, 64, 139, 211-12, 218-19, 234-35,
    314
    California and, 87
    French intervention (1864), 114-15
    internal problems of, 85-86
    Mexican War (1846-1847), 87-91
    revolutions in, 161-64
    Texas and, 71-72, 82-83
Missionaries, 79-80, 102-103, 169
Mobutu, Joseph, 322
Monroe, James, 35-36, 42-43, 56, 57, 60
Monroe Doctrine, 51, 62-65, 113-14, 141,
    150, 218, 235
    Roosevelt Corollary to, 158-59, 211
Montagnards, 328-29
Moore, John Bassett, 122, 206
Morgenthau, Henry M., Jr., 247-48
Morocco, 24, 175-76, 318, 319
Morris, Gouverneur, 31, 35
Morris, Robert, 11
Morrow, Dwight W., 212
Mortefontaine, Treaty of (1800), 37
Moscow, Declaration of (1943), 247
Motley, John Lathrop, 124, 132
Munich Conference (1939), 223
Murphy, Robert D., 249
Mussolini, Benito, 220, 225, 239

Nagy, Imre, 293
Napoleon Bonaparte, 37, 41-43
Napoleon III, 112, 114-15
Nasser, Gamal Abdel, 287, 293-96, 302
National Origins Act (1924), 199
National Security Council, 275
Nehru, Jawaharlal, 287, 327
Netherlands, 16-17, 27, 218, 226, 266
New Orleans affair (1891), 168-69
Nicaragua, 94, 97-98, 117, 126-27, 159,
    211
Nicholas II (Czar of Russia), 177-78
Nigeria, 322-23
Nine-Power Treaty (1922), 203-204
Nixon, Richard M., 297, 308, 310, 331-32
Nonaggression Pact (Germany-Russia), 225
Non-Importation Act (1806), 46-47
Nootka Sound incident (1789), 30-31
North Atlantic Treaty Organization (NATO),
    276-78, 289-90, 301-302
Norway, 226
Nuclear Nonproliferation Treaty (1968),
    300
Nuclear Test Ban Treaty (1963), 300-301

Nye Munitions Investigating Committee,
    220

Obregón, Alvaro, 164, 211
Ojukwu, Olumegwu, 322-23
Olney, Richard, 141
Onís, Luis de, 59-61
Open Door policy, 169-70, 174-75, 203-204,
    210
Oregon, 61, 83-85
Organization of American States (OAS),
    279, 306-308
Orlando, Vittorio, 192
Ostend Manifesto (1854), 96

Page, Walter Hines, 182
Paine, Thomas, 4, 13, 15, 35
Pakistan, 266, 287, 326-27
Palestine, 244-45, 267
Panama, 210-11, 216, 314-15
Panama, Declaration of (1939), 217-18
Panama Canal, 92, 94-95, 117, 125-27, 154,
    155-57
Panay incident (1937), 221
Panmunjom, 325
Paris, Declaration of (1856), 110
Paris, Treaty of (1763), 2
Paris, Treaty of (1783), 17-23
Paris, Treaty of (1898), 148-49
Park, Chung Hee, 325
Parker, Peter, 102-103
Pathet Lao, 327
Pauncefote, Sir Julian, 134, 154
Peace Corps, 312, 320
Pearl Harbor, 331-32
Perón, Juan, 235, 306, 308
Perry, Commodore Matthew C., 100
Pershing, General John J., 164
Peru, 64, 139
Pétain, Marshal Henri Philippe, 226
Petroleum Code (1927), 212
Philippine Trade Act (1946), 265
Philippines, 193, 174, 203, 207, 222-23,
    325-26
    annexation of, 147, 148-49
    independence of, 265-66, 285
    in World War II, 240-42
Pierce, Franklin, 92, 95-96, 99, 101
Pinckney, Thomas, 31-32
Pinckney's Treaty (San Lorenzo, 1795),
    34, 41
Plan of 1776 (maritime code), 13, 16, 17,
    24, 33, 53
Platt Amendment (1901), 153-54, 211, 216
Point Four program (1949), 278
Poland, 112-13, 191, 193, 225, 226, 237,
    250-51

1956 rioting, 293
  postwar, 263
Polignac Memorandum, 64
Polk, James K., 81-82, 87-91
Porter, Peter B., 49
Portsmouth, Treaty of (1905), 173
Portugal, 16, 70
Potsdam Conference (1945), 252
Powers, Francis Gary, 297
Prussia, 13, 15
  treaty with (1785), 24
Pruyn, Robert H., 101
Pueblo (U.S. intelligence ship), 325
Puerto Rico, 147

Quadruple Alliance (1815), 62, 64
Quebec Act (1774), 19
Quebec Conferences (1944), 247
Quitman, John A., 95
Quota Act (1921), 207

Randolph, Edmund, 26
Rawlins, General John H., 124
Reciprocal Trade Agreement Act (1934),
  215, 299
Reciprocity Treaty (1830), 70
Reed, Thomas, 149
Rhee, Syngman, 279, 283, 325
Richelieu, Cardinal, 2
Ridgway, General Matthew B., 282
Riga, Treaty of (1921), 250
Rio de Janeiro Conference (1942), 234
Rio Pact (1947), 306
Rockhill, William W., 167, 170
Rogers Act (1924), 199, 268
Rome, Treaty of (1957), 298
Roosevelt, Franklin D., 196, 206, 214-15,
  218-20, 221, 224
  World War II and, 226, 234, 237, 239-40
  at Yalta, 248-51
Roosevelt, Theodore, 139, 162, 166-67,
  173-74, 176, 178
  Panama Canal, 155-57
  Roosevelt Corollary to Monroe Doctrine,
    158-59
Root, Elihu, 153, 165, 167, 178, 206
Root-Takahira Agreement (1908), 174
Rosenberg, Julius and Ethel, 273
Rule of 1756, 3, 32, 45-46, 53, 110
Rumania, 262-63
Rush-Bagot Agreement (1818), 58
Rusk, Dean, 298, 311
Russell, Jonathan, 53
Russia, 13, 16, 18, 62, 70, 133, 210
  atomic weapons and, 257-58
  Civil War and, 112-13
  Cold War and, 260-61, 268-69

Cuban Missile Crisis and, 313-14
  nonaggression pact (1939), 225
  postwar, 260, 276
  recognition of, by FDR, 215
  Revolution (1917), 187, 188-89
  Russo-Japanese War (1904-1905),
    172-73
  Sino-Soviet split, 303
  Sputnik, 296
  Treaty of Brest-Litovsk (1918), 191
  Turkey, Iran, and, 266
  U.S. purchase of Alaska and, 118
  in World War II, 226, 230, 235
Ryswick, Treaty of (1697), 2

San Ildefonso, Treaty of (1800), 41
Sanford, Henry S., 131
Santa Anna, Antonio López de, 89
Santo Domingo, 42, 96, 114, 117, 124
Sato, Eisaku, 324
Schuman, Robert, 288-89
Schurz, Carl, 149
Scott, Winfield, 73-74, 89-90
Sealing, pelagic, 133
Seward, William H., 57, 73-74, 103,
  106-109, 110, 113-19
Siam, 77
Sihanouk, Norodom, 328, 332
Slidell, John, 87-88, 109
Soulé, Pierre, 95-96
South Africa, 320, 323
Southeast Asia Treaty Organization
  (SEATO), 279
Spain, 1, 3, 18, 41, 114, 292
  Civil War in, 220-21
  Cuba and, 91-92, 95-96, 124-25
  Federalists and, 28-29, 34
  Florida and, 45, 49-51, 59-61
  Independence and, 15-16, 20, 23
  Nookta Sound incident and, 30-31
Stalin, Josef, 225, 237, 239-40, 248-52,
  262
Stalingrad, 237, 239-40
State Department, 121-22, 187-88, 199,
  233-234, 268, 274-75
  anti-Semitism of, 224
  atomic bombs and, 245-46
  reorganization of, 78, 167
  Seward and, 107-108
  in World War I, 188
Steinberger, Colonel Albert B., 128-29
Stettinius, Edward R., Jr., 246
Stevens, John L., 142-43
Stilwell, General Joseph W., 242-43
Stimson, Henry L., 209
Strategic Arms Limitation Talks (SALT),
  301

Sweden; treaty with (1783), 24
Sudan, 318, 322
Sudetenland, 223
Suez crisis (1956), 288, 293-94
Sukarno, 285, 326
Sumner, Charles, 116-17, 118, 124, 132
Sun Yat-sen, 208
Syria, 244, 288, 295

Taft, William Howard, 157, 158, 159, 162,
    167-68, 175
Taft-Katsura Agreement (1905), 173
Taiwan, 265, 284, 324-25
Takahira, Baron Kogoro, 174
Talleyrand, Charles Maurice de, 43
Tangiers, 175
Taylor, Zachary, 87-88, 89-90, 91
Teheran Conference (1943), 247
Texas, 61, 71-72, 82-83
Thailand, 327
Thieu, Nguyen Van, 330
Tientsin, Treaty of (1858), 102
Tojo, General Hideki, 230-31
Tonkin Gulf Resolution (1964), 330
Trade Expansion Act (1962), 299
Transcontinental railroad, 96-97
Transcontinental Treaty (1819), 61, 64
Trent affair, 109
Trinidad, 316
Tripoli; War with (1803-1805), 39-40
Trotsky, Leon, 188-89
Trujillo, Rafael, 315
Truman, Harry S., 245, 246, 252, 257-58,
    260, 267
    MacArthur and, in Korean War, 279-83
    NATO and, 276-78
Truman Doctrine (1947), 268-69
Tshombe, Moise, 321-22
Turkey, 64, 245, 266
Twenty-One Demands (1915), 189-90
Tydings-McDuffie Act (1933), 222
Tyler, John, 73-74, 77, 82

U-2 incident, 297
United Arab Republic, 295-96
United Nations, 236, 246-48, 251-52, 258
Utrecht, Treaty of (1713), 2-3, 16

Van Buren, Martin, 72-74
Vandenberg, Arthur H., 247, 276
Venezuela, 141-42, 158
Vergennes, Charles, Comte de, 10-12, 13-14,
    18-19, 20, 27
Vermont, 27
Versailles, Treaty of (1919), 193-97
Vichy, 226, 230, 238-39
Vietnam, 266, 286, 327-32

Villa, Pancho, 164
Vinson Naval Expansion Act (1938), 224
Virgin Islands, 117
Virginius (gunboat), 124-25

Walker, Admiral J. G., 155
Walker, William, 97
Wanghia, Treaty of (1844), 77, 102
Warsaw Pact (1955), 290
Washington, George, 9, 26, 31-32
Washington, Treaty of (1871), 132
Washington Naval Conference, 201-204
Wayne, General "Mad Anthony," 32
Webb, William H., 128
Webster, Daniel, 73-76, 80, 92
Webster-Ashburton Treaty (1842), 76, 83
Wedemeyer, General Albert C., 243
Welles, Sumner, 233, 234, 245
West Indies, 69-70
Western European Union (1954), 290
Weyler, General Valeriano, 144
White, William Allen, 227
Wilkes, Lt. Charles, 72, 77, 83, 109-110,
    128
Wilkinson, General James, 28-29, 34, 45, 52,
    59
Wilkie, Wendell, 227
Wilmot Proviso (1846), 91
Wilson, Woodrow, 157, 158-59, 162-64,
    174, 175
Wilson-Gorman Act (1894), 144
Wood, General Leonard, 153
Wood, Robert E., 227
World Court, 204, 206-207
World Disarmament Conference (1932), 206
World Economic Conference (1933), 215
World Peace Foundation, 219
World War I; events leading up to, 166-79
World War I diplomacy, 180-97
World War II, 224, 233-52
    first year of, 235-39
    Pacific theater, 240-42

XYZ Affair, 36

Yalta Conference (1945), 243, 248-51
Ydígoras Fuentes, Miguel, 308
"Yellow journalism," 144-45
Yemen, 295
Young Plan (1928), 201
Ypirango (steamer), 163

Zapata, Emiliano, 164
Zelaya, José, 159
Zimmerman telegram (1917), 187

Picture Sources

Page

15   Brown Brothers.
18   Culver Pictures.
33   Culver Pictures.
40   Library of Congress.
44   Culver Pictures.
50   John C. Calhoun: Culver Pictures.
           Felix Grundy: Culver Pictures.
           William H. Crawford: Culver Pictures.
           Richard M. Johnson: Culver Pictures.
54   Courtesy of National Collection of Fine Arts, Smithsonian Institution.
57   Library of Congress.
70   Courtesy of the New-York Historical Society, New York City.
73   Culver Pictures.
84   Culver Pictures.
89   Library of Congress.
100   Library of Congress.
107   Culver Pictures.
112   Culver Pictures.
119   Culver Pictures.
123   Courtesy of The New-York Historical Society, New York City.
129   Culver Pictures.
142   New York Public Library.
146   *New York Journal,* February 17, 1898: The Granger Collection.
           Destruction of the U.S. Battleship *Maine:* Library of Congress.
157   Theodore Roosevelt Association.
170   Culver Pictures.
176   Culver Pictures.
185   Brown Brothers.
191   Culver Pictures.
203   Culver Pictures.
209   The Granger Collection.
216   Brown Brothers.
249   United Press International Photo.
269   United Press International Photo.
289   United Press International Photo.
310   Morse in the Los Angeles *Mirror-News.*
319   United Press International Photo.
328   United Press International Photo.

A B C D E F G H I J   9 8 7 6 5 4 3 2